Reese M. Carleton

PEL

VICT

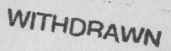

Professor Asa B
and Vice-Chanc
Sussex. From 195
Modern History at Leeds University. Born in 1921, he took a double first in history at Cambridge. Among his publications are *The Age of Improvement* (1959), *Chartist Studies* (1959), which he edited, *The Birth of Broadcasting* (1961), *The Golden Age of Wireless* (1965) and *The War of Words* (1970), and *Victorian People* (1954), a companion volume to this book. Asa Briggs, who is married and has four children, lives at Lewes in Sussex.

Victorian Cities

ASA BRIGGS

Penguin Books

Penguin Books Ltd, Harmondsworth, Middlesex, England
Penguin Books Australia Ltd, Ringwood, Victoria, Australia
Penguin Books Canada Ltd, 41 Steelcase Road West, Markham, Ontario, Canada
Penguin Books (N.Z.) Ltd, 182-190 Wairau Road, Auckland 10, New Zealand

—

First published by Odhams Press 1963
Published in Pelican Books 1968
Reprinted 1971, 1975

—

Made and printed in Great Britain
by C. Nicholls & Company Ltd
Set in Monotype Garamond

TO ROSE AND BERNARD

Contents

There are many revisions and additions in this new edition of *Victorian Cities*. Since the first edition appeared in 1963 there has been a 'boom' both in Victorian studies and in urban studies. I have done nothing, however, to change either the shape of the book or its main lines of argument. It is a companion to *Victorian People* and I am planning to complete a trilogy with a book called *Victorian Things*.

A.B.

The English are town-birds through and through, today, as the inevitable result of their complete industrialization. Yet they don't know how to build a city, how to think of one, or how to live in one.

D. H. LAWRENCE

CHAPTER ONE

Introduction

I

THIS book is the product of many years of research. The literature of cities is prodigious both in its volume and its variety, and many of the most illuminating sources are buried away in the most unlikely places. Monographs on particular cities are invaluable, but they seldom exist in the form that the general historian needs. Moreover a collection of monographs, however scholarly or enlightening, does not constitute a synthesis. I have tried in this book to achieve a synthesis, as I did in *Victorian People* (1954), not by assembling all the material I could find on the subject – this would be more than a lifetime's work – but by selecting examples from nineteenth-century history and relating them to each other.

In *Victorian People* I was concerned with a brief period, the middle years of the nineteenth century from the late forties to the early seventies, years of orderly progress, continued economic development and social peace. I tried to account for the 'unity' of these years by choosing a number of people whose attitudes and careers reflected or directed the tendencies of the period and by examining the way in which their ideas and achievements converged. In *Victorian Cities*, which is a companion volume, I have chosen a number of cities and concentrated on particular facets of their history. These facets, singly or together, reveal and explain essential elements in Victorian society. The task of selection has been more difficult and must be considered more arbitrary than it was in my earlier venture. Not all urban problems or achievements find a place in this book. There is far more about the new than the old. Other cities might well have been included: some of the cities included might have been left out. There is a natural bias towards the cities I know. This is legitimate enough in so far as Victorian cities are still alive, whereas the Victorian people I described in 1954 were all long since dead. There is no substitute for knowing a city: reading about it is second-best.

The period covered in this volume is longer than the period covered in *Victorian People*. It corresponds closely to the reign of Queen Victoria as a whole. I am not seeking in this study to account for the 'unity' or balance of one central part of that long reign but to assess one aspect (a changing aspect) of Victorian experience.

The Victorians began to interest themselves in cities in the late 1830s and early 1840s when it was impossible to avoid investigation of urgent urban problems. They were horrified and fascinated by the large industrial cities which seemed to stand for what a writer in 1840 called 'a system of life constructed on a wholly new principle'.[1] Both Blue Books and novels demonstrated the horror and the fascination. So did the reports of religious and charitable agencies and the surveys of provincial statistical societies. Newspapers and periodicals also provide an indispensable record of contemporary opinions. By the last years of Victorian England, attention had shifted back from the provinces to London. Again it was what was thought of as the unprecedented character of many of the problems which gripped people's imagination. Patrick Geddes's early twentieth-century account of London was typical and remains well known. He saw London as a 'polypus', 'a vast irregular growth without previous parallel in the world of life – perhaps likest to the spreading of a great coral reef'.[2]

A different way of describing the period covered in this book would be to say that it falls between the coming of the

1. *Bentley's Miscellany*, Vol. VII (1840).

2. P. Geddes, *Cities in Evolution* (1949 edn), p. 9. The language was not without previous parallel. The word 'polypus' was applied to London at least as early as 1776 when Horace Walpole stated that 'rows of houses shoot out every way like a polypus'. Quoted by H. J. Dyos in 'The Growth of a Pre-Victorian Suburb: South London, 1580–1836' in *Town Planning Review*, Vol. XXV (1954). For the image of the coral reef, see the *Quarterly Review*, Vol. 167 (October 1888), p. 542, where the life of London is said to be 'as disintegrated as that of a coral reef in which every individual polyp has its own separate existence'.

railway and the coming of the automobile. The railway linked the new cities together and made their growth possible: like the cities themselves, it was a symbol of 'improvement'. As Emerson put it, 'railroad iron is a magician's rod in its power to evoke the sleeping energies of land and water'. Railways were also often believed, like cities, to be symbols of 'democracy', in Dr Arnold's words 'destroying feudality for ever'. The first impetus to build them came largely from groups of active businessmen in the great cities, like the 'Liverpool Party', for example, who were responsible for the building of Crewe.[1] The first railways encouraged the concentration of urban population. Some new towns, like Barrow-in-Furness, owed their dynamism to railway interests and to men like James Ramsden, appointed Locomotive Superintendent of the Furness Railway in 1846.[2] Some older towns without railways withered away, like Courcy in Trollope's *Doctor Thorne* (1858). Some of the best pictures of cities are to be found in George Measom's Official Illustrated Railway Guide Books, and Bradshaw's, the great manual of the railways, was not the least impressive product of industrial Manchester.

The automobile by contrast scattered the cities, pushing them farther and farther away from their mid-Victorian centres to new suburbs. At the same time it narrowed the gulf between urban and rural life, transformed the outlook and prospects of the village and of many market towns, and in the process caused large tracts of countryside to become neither truly urban nor truly rural, what American sociologists have called 'rurban' territory.[3]

After the urban came the 'sub-urban', the 'con-urban' and,

1. The story of the struggle of the 'Liverpool Party' with groups based on Manchester and Birmingham is told in W. H. Chaloner, *The Social and Economic Development of Crewe* (1950), Ch. 1.

2. Ramsden's career is discussed in J. D. Marshall, *Furness and the Industrial Revolution* (1958).

3. Yet Dickens in *Dombey and Son* (1846) noted in North London the development of an area which was 'neither of the town nor of the country. The former, like the giant in his travelling boots, has made a stride and passed it and has set his brick and mortar heel a long way in advance; but the intermediate space between the giant's feet, as yet, is only blighted country, and not town'.

to use the last of the cluster of ugly adjectives, the 'ex-urban'. Sociologists have talked of a 'rural-urban continuum'. In this process the automobile became a symbol not of democracy but of status. Against the massive investment in Victorian railways, a great collective achievement which is now being frittered away, we have to set the hire-purchase nexus of private property, the faltering public programme for road development, and the traffic 'crisis' in old and new cities alike.

This story lies outside the range of this book. Indeed, the automobile age separates our own urban experience from the Victorian urban experience just as surely as the coming of the railway separated the Victorian age from earlier ages. The Victorians themselves were well aware of the significance of their great change. 'It was only yesterday,' one of Thackeray's characters remarked of the pre-railway age, 'but what a gulf between now and then. *Then* was the old world. Stage-coaches, more or less swift riding horses, pack horses, highwaymen, Druids, Ancient Britons . . . all these belong to the old period. I will concede a halt in the midst of it and allow that gunpowder and printing tended to modernize the world. But your railroad starts a new era. . . . We who lived before railways and survive out of the ancient world, are like Father Noah and his family out of the Ark'.[1]

Transport was also important in determining the chronology of Victorian urban development. Railway building led to drastic changes, usually in the poorer parts of the cities. Slums might be pulled down without much care being given to the rehousing of the slum dwellers. 'We occasionally sweep away the wretched dens, hidden in back courts and alleys, where the poor are smothered: but far too rarely do we make provision for them,' Charles Knight complained in his study of London.[2] More specifically Manby Smith in his *Curiosities of London Life*

1. The passage is quoted in K. Tillotson, *Novels of the Eighteen-Forties* (1954), pp. 105–6.

2. C. Knight, *London* (1841–4), Vol. IV, p. 254. See also H. J. Dyos, 'Some Social Costs of Railway Building in London' in the *Journal of Transport History*, Vol. III (1957). It was not only railways which created such problems. When the St Katherine's Dock was built in the late 1820s, eight hundred houses were destroyed and eleven thousand people turned out into the streets. See R. Sinclair, *East London* (1950), p. 245.

(1853) wrote of 'the deep gorge of a railway cutting, which has ploughed its way right through the centre of the market-gardens, and burrowing beneath the carriage-road, and knocking a thousand houses out of its path, pursues its circuitous course to the city'.[1]

If railways were symbols of progress, all too often the railway embankment became a symbol of the ruthless terror of the mid-Victorian city: it reappeared in Charles Booth's massive survey of London life as a frontier hemming in secluded groups of suspicious neighbours who hated intruders from outside. The building of local and suburban railway lines helped to determine the main lines of suburban growth. The first local passenger service to be authorized in London was started between Tooley Street, Southend and Deptford in 1836: the first workman's fare was introduced in London by the Metropolitan Railway Company in 1864 and on a section of the Stockton and Darlington Railway in the north of England as early as 1852. The Cheap Trains Act of 1883, which compelled the railway companies to offer workman's fares as and when required by the Board of Trade, was deliberately designed for 'further encouraging the migration of the working classes into the suburbs' in order to relieve housing congestion in the central areas.[2]

Trams served the same purpose. First introduced in Birkenhead in 1860 by the American engineer, George Francis Train, they were of enormous importance, particularly in the provincial cities. After the Tramways Act of 1870 gave local authorities the option to buy out private tramways by compulsory purchase after twenty-one years of operation, Birmingham, Glasgow, Portsmouth, Plymouth and London were quick to take advantage of the new facilities. By the end of Queen Victoria's reign sixty-one local authorities owned tramways and eighty-nine undertakings were managed by private enterprise.[3] Richard Hoggart has described trams as 'the gondolas of the people'.[4] They certainly brought new

1. C. Manby Smith, *Curiosities of London Life* (1853), p. 361.
2. S. A. Pope, *The Cheap Trains Act* (1906), p. 15.
3. Cmd 305 (1900), *Joint Select Committee on Municipal Trading.*
4. R. Hoggart, *The Uses of Literacy* (1957), p. 120.

areas of the city within access of working men by reducing the time taken to get to work. They also made it possible to get to the football grounds and to the holiday firework displays and galas in the public parks. Their introduction was a local landmark in all the provincial cities: battles between the protagonists of different systems of operation and of different structures of ownership enlivened late-Victorian local government.

In London, where the advent of trams was fiercely resisted, the first electric railway, the City and South London, was opened in 1890 and the first section of underground railway, the Metropolitan, from Paddington to Farringdon Street, built on a system of 'open cutting', began operating as early as 1863. The Inner Circle was complete by 1884. The City and Southwark Subway Company followed in 1890 and a number of other lines were in operation by the end of the reign. There was always a direct relationship between urbanization and transport. Perhaps the best area from which to illustrate it is 'Metroland', the district covered by the North Metropolitan Railway. In 1868 an independent railway company had opened a line from Baker Street to Swiss Cottage, and in 1880 the North Metropolitan extended this to Harrow. Other lines followed and, as the railway arrived, places like Willesden, which had been quiet and detached, were drawn into the vortex of London: North Harrow and West Harrow were new names, centred on the local station. The slogan of the Metropolitan Railway – 'Live in Metroland' – showed that it was not so much satisfying existing needs as creating new residential districts.

2

The cities of this book are the cities of the railway and tramway age, of the age of steam and of gas, of a society sometimes restless, sometimes complacent, moving, often fumblingly and falteringly, towards greater democracy. The building of the cities was a characteristic Victorian achievement, impressive in scale but limited in vision, creating new opportunities but also providing massive new problems. Perhaps their outstanding feature was hidden from public view – their hidden network of pipes and drains and sewers, one of the biggest technical and social achievements of the age, a sanitary 'system' more comprehensive than the transport system. Yet their surface world was fragmented, intricate, cluttered, eclectic and noisy, the unplanned product of a private enterprise economy developing within an older traditional society.

To the early twentieth-century critic of Victorianism the cities seemed as unsatisfactory as Victorian people: to a later generation they have acquired a charm and romance of their own. It is fascinating to compare H. G. Wells with John Betjeman. To Wells the cities were even more grim when they were considered as wholes than when they were judged by their component parts. 'It is only because the thing was spread over a hundred years and not concentrated into a few weeks', he wrote in his *Autobiography*, 'that history fails to realize what sustained disaster, how much massacre, degeneration and disablement of lives was due to the housing of people in the nineteenth century.' Betjeman has found interest and excitement, above all enjoyment, in at least some of the houses and in many of the public buildings which Wells would have condemned. 'Many a happy hour have I spent when ill in bed, turning over the pages of [Victorian] scrap-books, looking now at a new bank, now at a new town hall, warehouse, or block of artisans' dwellings, but chiefly at churches.'[1]

Quite apart from changes in taste or differing individual capacities for enjoyment, we are by now far enough away from Victorianism to understand its various expressions more sympathetically while at the same time retaining our freedom to criticize. We can and should criticize the appalling living conditions in Victorian cities, the absence of amenities, the brutal degradation of natural environment and the inability to plan and often even to conceive of the city as a whole. There is truth in Lewis Mumford's remark that 'the new industrial city had many lessons to teach; but for the urbanist its chief lesson was in what to avoid'. At the same time we realize also

1. H. G. Wells, *Experiment in Autobiography*, Vol. I (1934), p. 277. cf. *Victorian People*, p. 14 (Pelican edition); John Betjeman, 'The English Town in the Last Hundred Years', *Rede Lecture* (1956), and *English Cities and Small Towns* (1943).

that in a very different twentieth-century society we are often just as hard pressed as the Victorians were to make cities attractive and inspiring. The story of twentieth-century local government has not been a story of 'ever-onward progress', as the Victorians hoped it would be. The appearance of cities has been spoilt by 'subtopian' horrors which the Victorians could not have foreseen. Year by year we are pulling down the older parts of our cities – Victorian and pre-Victorian – with a savage and undiscriminating abandon which will not earn us the gratitude of posterity. If the detailed study of Victorian cities is not pursued at this perilous moment of time, when we are still poised between the nineteenth and twentieth centuries, it may be difficult to pursue it at all.

The worst aspects of nineteenth-century urban growth are reasonably well known. The great industrial cities came into existence on the new economic foundations laid in the eighteenth century with the growth in population and the expansion of industry. The pressure of rapidly increasing numbers of people and the social consequences of the introduction of new industrial techniques and new ways of organizing work involved a sharp break with the past. The fact that the new techniques were introduced by private enterprise and that the work was organized for other people not by them largely determined the reaction to the break.

The industrial city was bound to be a place of problems. Economic individualism and common civic purpose were difficult to reconcile. The priority of industrial discipline in shaping all human relations was bound to make other aspects of life seem secondary. A high rate of industrial investment might mean not only a low rate of consumption and a paucity of social investment but a total indifference to social costs. Overcrowding was one problem: displacement was another. There were parts of Liverpool with a density of 1,200 persons to the acre in 1884: rebuilding might entail the kind of difficulties which were set out in a verse in *The Builder* of 1851:

> Who builds? Who builds? Alas, ye poor!
> If London day by day 'improves',
> Where shall ye find a friendly door,
> When every day a home removes?

We know relatively little of how Victorian cities were actually built except that in the early and middle years of the reign building was often left to small speculators of limited resources.[1] E. Dobson's *Rudiments of the Art of Building* (1849) went through thirteen editions in forty years. There were some examples, however, of working-class self-help through freehold land societies (the initiative came from Birmingham), many examples of capitalist philanthropy, with mill-owners and railway companies building and letting houses, and a marked growth of building societies and housing associations, the earliest of which were the Metropolitan Association for Improving the Dwellings of the Industrious Classes, founded in 1841, and the Society for Improving the Condition of the Labouring Classes, founded in 1844. The Peabody Trust, set up in 1862, was active in London, and its work, limited in conception by considerations both of economy and of taste, can still be seen. There were also a few big builders like Thomas Cubitt, a characteristic Victorian self-made man, whose work, huge in scale, can be seen as a contribution to a long tradition in speculative building going back to the seventeenth century. By the end of the century the share of the bigger builders in London was increasing. So too was the pressure to re-examine the special housing problems of the working classes, the subject of a Royal Commission in 1884.[2]

It was not until after the 1870s that health conditions in the poorer parts of the cities began to improve. From an average of 22.4 in the decade from 1841 to 1851 the national death rate fell slightly to 22.2 during the next decade, rose again to 22.5 during the 1860s and still remained at 22 over the five years from 1871 to 1876. Infant mortality remained more or less constant around 150 per 1,000 live births until the twentieth century. The crude national rates need to be broken down into the figures for particular places, particular social groups

1. For examples of local studies see H. Richards and P. Lewis, 'House Building in the South Wales Coalfield 1851–1913' in the *Manchester School*, Vol. XXIV (1956), and J. Parry Lewis, 'Indices of House Building in the Manchester Conurbation, South Wales and Great Britain' in the *Scottish Journal of Political Economy*, Vol. VIII (1961).

2. H. J. Dyos is exploring the details of this story. See also D. J. Olsen, *Town Planning in London in the Eighteenth and Nineteenth Centuries* (1964).

and particular diseases, but they remained alarmingly high in the worst urban districts. The inquiries of the late 1860s and 1870s, backed by advances in medical science, were more productive of results than the noisier inquiries and the better publicized legislation of the 1840s, when the 'Sanitary Idea' was inspiring poets, moralists and artists as well as philanthropists and administrators. If only for this reason, there is need to devote adequate attention in all studies of Victorian cities both to the relationship between qualitative and quantitative evidence and to the administrative significance of the late-Victorian reforms which identified differences between the best and the worst and pointed to the need for more active national policies of social control. The Sanitary Commission of 1869 to 1871, which collected ample evidence concerning the ignorance, petty jealousies and unwillingness to spend money of the mid-Victorian Local Boards of Health, was the prelude to the setting up of the Local Government Board in 1871, the Public Health Act of 1872, the comprehensive Public Health Act of 1875, which divided the country into urban and rural sanitary districts with clearly defined duties, and the Artisans' and Labourers' Dwellings Improvement Act of the same year.

Belated public interest in housing and constant interest – fluctuating in intensity and range of appeal – in the 'Sanitary Idea' characterized the Victorian city, which was the locus and focus of all theories and policies of environmental control. The theories and the policies had to be backed by statistics and to be fought for by dedicated men. As late as 1869, when professional and administrative skills were greatly superior to those of 1848, the language of some of the pioneers of the Sanitary Commission echoed that of the pioneers of the Public Health Act of 1848. 'Our present machinery', Dr John Snow told the Social Science Congress in Bristol, 'must be greatly enlarged, radically altered, and endowed with new powers', above all with the power of 'doing away with that form of liberty to which some communities cling, the sacred power to poison to death not only themselves but their neighbours.'[1]

1. *The Times*, 5 October 1869. *The Times*, which had asked in 1848 for a 'bettish and personal opposition [to the Public Health Bill] just enough to

Lack of general concern for social costs was related to the pressures not only of urbanization but of industrialization. The city offered external economies to the businessman: it was all too easy to forget that the economies entailed social costs as well. In a new industrial society belief in private property survived as the foundation of the whole social system. The belief was sustained by the law. It had also shaped eighteenth- and early nineteenth-century schemes of improvement. When Victorian legislation was passed which tampered with the rights of private property, it was always contentious and difficult to implement. A Nuisance Removal Act, for instance, had been passed as early as 1846 and there was further legislation in 1855, 1860, 1863 and 1866, yet nuisances remained unchecked and prominent in all the cities. Sir John Simon, the great sanitary reformer who took over where Chadwick left off, claimed in 1868 that disease resulting from non-application or sluggish application of the nuisance laws accounted for a quarter of the entire mortality of the country.[1]

Throughout the Victorian age the most effective argument for sanitary reform was that it would actually save money in the long run, not squander it. 'Civic economy' was a branch of political economy. As the *British and Foreign Medico-Chirurgical Review* put it in the 1840s, 'one broad principle may be safely enunciated in respect of sanitary economics – that it costs more money to create disease than to prevent it; and there is not a single structural arrangement chargeable with the production of disease which is not also in itself an extravagance'.[2] The broad principle was more easy to accept as a principle than as a precept. There were protracted local

quicken Lord Morpeth's energies', noted in 1849 that while apathy was still the main problem, 'the stage of universal consent has never been reached'.

1. See the important article by E. P. Hennock, 'Urban Sanitary Reform a Generation before Chadwick' in the *Economic History Review*, Vol. X (1957), and *Eleventh Annual Report of the Medical Officer to the Privy Council* (1868). For Simon's work, which points forward to the twentieth century, see R. Lambert, *Sir John Simon and English Social Administration* (1963).

2. For the attitudes of the 1840s, see my lecture 'Public Opinion and Public Health in the Age of Chadwick', *Chadwick Lecture*, 1946.

arguments before it could be shown to the satisfaction of ratepayers, first that the equations were correct, and second that the long run was worth bothering about. Those branches of civic reform which could not be justified in terms of the principle were generally neglected until late in the century. It was largely for this reason that the public provision of working-class housing was neglected throughout the century.

The early advocates of the 'Sanitary Idea' were usually amateurs, men like Chadwick himself, who 'seized on an abuse with the tenacity of a bulldog' and believed that he was battling against Fate itself, or Charles Kingsley, who identified sanitary reform with the will of God. The moral strength of Victorianism often lay in its reliance on amateurs rather than on professionals to get things done. At the same time, delay in implementing legislation was made worse by the tardiness of the Victorians to develop the necessary skills for managing growing cities – civil engineering skills, for example, and medical skills. The noisy opposition to Chadwick made the most of his self-confident dogmatism, his eagerness to provide non-expert answers to highly complex technical problems. Simon, by contrast, was distinguished not only for his moderation of temperament but for his greater willingness to accept expert advice when it could be made available. Yet he too reached an impasse. It is difficult to avoid the conclusion that if half the technical skill applied to industry had been applied to the Victorian cities, their record would have been very different. As it was, Victorian cities were places where problems often overwhelmed people.

Even when a labour movement developed (and as it developed it was very slow to develop the demand for improved health and housing), even when working hours were cut, even when social investment increased, even when attempts at planning were made, and even when engineering and medical skills improved, as they did in the last phases of Queen Victoria's reign, the city remained a centre of problems. Far more remained to be done than had been done. Some of the changes within cities were the product of conscious municipal policy. Most changes, however, were the result of a multitude of single decisions, public and private: inevitably there had to be bargains and compromises. The general plan of the Victorian city continued to express all this. At the end of the reign the cities remained confused and complicated, a patchwork of private properties, developed separately with little sense of common plan, a jumble of sites and buildings with few formal frontiers, a bewildering variety of heights and eye-levels, a social disorder with districts of deprivation and ostentation, and every architectural style, past and present, to add to the confusion. It is not surprising that George Bernard Shaw suggested that all British cities, like all Indian villages, would have to be pulled down and built again if people were to live in an environment worthy of them.

This, however, is only one side of the picture, the side which impressed the young H. G. Wells. The sheer magnitude of Victorian urban problems directed attention to issues about which people had hitherto been silent. The growth of the new industrial city meant that people took a closer look at the problems both of the old market town and of the village. It was true, as one of the great Blue Books of the 1840s put it, that 'more filth, worse physical suffering and moral disorder than Howard describes as affecting the prisoners, are to be found among the cellar population of the working people of Liverpool, Manchester, or Leeds and in large portions of the Metropolis',[1] but factual knowledge of these conditions and the conscience and drive to do something about them influenced pre-Victorian towns like Exeter and Norwich which had hitherto pushed their urban problems into the background. 'The discovery of the laws of public health,' the Registrar-General noted in 1871, 'the determination of the conditions of cleanliness, manners, water supply, food, exercise, isolation, medicine, most favourable to life in one city, in one country, is a boon to every city, to every country, for all can profit by the experience.'[2]

Social conditions in the new communities encouraged both the amassing of facts and the airing of viewpoints. However great the resistance, there was persistent pressure to control

1. *Report on the Sanitary Condition of the Labouring Population* (1842), p. 60.

2. Quoted in H. Jephson, *The Sanitary Evolution of London* (1907), p. 100.

social change. Victorian cities were not the 'insensate' ant-heaps which find a place in Mumford's pages. At their worst they were always more than 'mere man-heaps, machine warrens, not organs of human association'.[1] They were never mere collections of individuals, some weak, some strong. They had large numbers of voluntary organizations, covering a far wider range of specialized interests than was possible either in the village or the small town. They were more free of aristocratic 'influence'. They allowed room for middle-class initiative and for greater independence and greater organization of the 'lower ranks of society' than did smaller places: by the end of the century, both independence and organization were being reflected in new policies and in genuine transfers of power. Moreover, the cities possessed in their newspapers what were often extremely effective propaganda agencies focusing attention on local issues and through competitive rivalry stimulating the development of articulate opinions. 'In the forums of the public press,' one nineteenth-century writer put it, 'we see the forms of all the greater and lesser associations into which society at large has wrought itself.'[2] At their best, the cities created genuine municipal pride and followed new and bold courses of action.

The two sides of the picture must be taken together in assessing Victorian experience. There was alarming waste and confusion before there were signs of effective control, but the speed of urban development and the energy which lay behind it impress posterity even more than they impressed contemporaries. The visitor to Birmingham could 'expect to find a street of houses in the autumn where he saw his horse at grass in the spring'. In late-Victorian South London, according to Sir Walter Besant, the houses 'sprang up as if in a single

1. L. Mumford, *The Culture of Cities* (1938 edn), p. 148. The remark is repeated in *The City in History* (1961), p. 450. The same view is expressed in G. M. Trevelyan, *Illustrated English Social History*, Vol. IV (1952), p. 118. 'The modern city, in the unplanned swamp of its increase, lacks form and feature; it is a deadening cage for the human spirit.' See also J. L. and B. Hammond, *The Town Labourer* (1917), especially Chapter III, and *The Age of the Chartists* (1930).

2. R. Vaughan, *The Age of Great Cities, or Modern Society Viewed in its Relation to Intelligence, Morals and Religion* (1843), p. 278.

night: streets in a month, churches and chapels in a quarter'.[1] 'Alexander's armies', wrote Wilkie Collins in *Hide and Seek* (1861), 'were great makers of conquests; but the modern guerrilla regiments of the hod, the trowel, and the brick-kiln, are the greatest conquerors of all; for they hold the longest the soil that they have once possessed ... with the conqueror's device inscribed on it – *This ground to be let on building leases.*'

The people of the twentieth century, able to draw more easily on expert skills, have had to wrestle with complex urban problems bequeathed by the Victorians – health, housing, education and traffic, for example: at the same time they are still relying (and this in itself is a part of 'the plight of the contemporary city') on the vast accumulation of social capital which the Victorians raised, usually by voluntary or by municipal effort. Much of the effort went into church building – this reflected Victorian concern for the future of religion in an urban environment[2] – but particularly in the last twenty-five years of Queen Victoria's reign there was a huge development of public offices, hospitals, schools, sewage farms and water works. The Victorian phase in city development cannot be ignored even as a visible factor in the present. It obtrudes in every provincial city and in London itself, although it is now being destroyed in the name of 'progress', a cause which was used by the Victorians themselves to sanctify much of their own destruction.

It is this side of the Victorian city that Betjeman has understood and appreciated. He recognizes that the right approach to a Victorian city is from the railway station, that 'the best guide books are the old ones published in the last century', that the 'restorations' of the Victorians reveal their mood and purposes as plainly as their new buildings, that the symbolism outside and within the Victorian public buildings is in its way as interesting (and as dated) as medieval symbolism, that both the variety and the individuality of private middle-class houses

1. J. A. Langford, *A Century of Birmingham Life* (1870), p. 100; Sir Walter Besant, *South London* (1899), p. 318.

2. See M. H. Port, *Six Hundred New Churches* (1961), for early Victorian development; and G. Kitson Clark, *The Making of Victorian England* (1962). See also below, p. 63.

merit sensitive and discriminating attention, that to understand the detail of the cities is more important than seeking to generalize about the general effect of the whole.

Your sense of the whole depended, of course, on your own place in it. G. M. Young emphasized that this was true of Victorian people. 'Suppose you fall asleep tonight and wake up in 1860. What is the first thing you would notice?' There is no single answer. It would depend on where you woke up.[1] Suppose you arrived at a Victorian railway station, key building of the age, your impressions of the city world beyond the waiting room and the new station hotel would be determined not only by your mood or your company, but as likely as not by the direction in which you first decided to go. Very quickly, within a few yards of the station, you might find yourself among the workshops and warehouses 'on the wrong side of the track'. For miles beyond there might stretch more workshops and more warehouses, gas works and breweries, long rows of ugly working-class houses in brick or stone, with occasional churches and chapels, institutes and clubs, dingy public houses and small corner shops, cemeteries and rubbish-heaps. You would pass through what Engels called those 'separate territories, assigned to poverty', where, 'removed from the sight of the happier classes, poverty may struggle along as it can'. If you were more fortunate, you might move instead towards the crowded 'city centre' with its covered market, its busy exchanges, its restored (?) parish church, its massive 'city chapels', its imposing town hall, its cluster of banks, its theatres and its public houses, the newest of them gleaming with rich mahogany, engraved glass and polished brass. It says much for the Victorians that despite these varieties of urban condition, they were occasionally able to create a general shared enthusiasm for the city as such, an enthusiasm which transcended the facts and consciousness of social class. Yet it was an enthusiasm which the collective achievement of the city often did far too little to justify.

1. See *Victorian People*, p. 13 (Pelican edition).

3

There were, of course, great changes within the cities during the Victorian period, particularly as they grew in size. Sprawling expansion at the outskirts was accompanied by a decline in the population of the central parts of the city and by a redrawing of social boundaries in the huge areas between the centre and the periphery. The City of London, for instance, first lost in population in the decade from 1801 to 1811. In Liverpool, the census of 1851 recorded the population peak of the crowded wards of the city centre: every ward of central Liverpool was decreasing in population by 1871, and the 'blanket of terrace housing, wrapped around the Georgian and early Victorian town' was mid- and late-Victorian.[1] In Birmingham, four of the central wards lost population between 1851 and 1871: in Leeds, Kirkgate Ward was declining in population from 1841: in Bradford, which had developed later, the population of the West End Ward fell from 23,138 in 1871 to 18,143 in 1881 and 15,999 ten years later.

As the houses were pulled down, shops, factories, warehouses, banks and offices took their place. Railway building itself led to much large-scale clearance. The process went further during the 1880s and 1890s, when the great provincial cities acquired central 'lay-outs' which in many cases did not alter substantially until the 1950s. There were marked changes, however, in possession. Family shops gave way to chain shops and large department stores. W. H. Smith & Sons, directly dependent on the railway, began to build their network in the 1850s, and department stores, which also had their origins in this decade, began to flourish both in London and the provinces in the 1880s and 1890s; thirty years later the music halls gave way to cinemas and the trams to buses. Formerly 'desirable residences' near the city centre, in the 'middle ring' and at the city end of the radial routes leading out to the suburbs often passed into the hands of people from lower

1. See the useful study by R. Lawton, 'The Population of Liverpool in the Mid-Nineteenth Century' in the *Transactions of the Historical Society of Lancashire and Cheshire*, Vol. 107 (1955); E. Cannan, 'The Growth of Manchester and Liverpool' in the *Economic Journal*, Vol. IV (1896).

income groups. The houses might remain, but whole districts of what has been called 'the blighted belt' could change in social character.

The most dramatic long-term contrast was to be seen in areas of former elegance, like the Saltmarket in Glasgow, which in the process of time became slums. These 'new slums' must be distinguished from the cellar dwellings of Liverpool or the back-to-back streets of the West Riding which were designed from their beginnings as low-cost housing. Over far shorter periods of time than it took to convert elegance into squalor, once isolated villages were drawn into the unbroken territory of near-by cities. Burmantofts, near Leeds, once 'a place of pleasantness', was absorbed into Leeds by 1851 and 'associated with Quarry Hill, one of the most insalubrious districts of the town'. Yet Quarry Hill itself had once been a spa. Horton, near Bradford, the local historian Cudworth had to remind his readers in 1886, was once 'a distinct place divided from the town by a long stretch of green fields'. In London large quantities of strawberries were grown in Deptford and Camberwell in the 1830s, and twenty years later there were market gardens in Bermondsey and Rotherhithe. A resident of Bow in the 1850s described how it was once 'all fields around' and how he had been able to see from his bedroom window twenty-nine church spires. At Leyton people had walked over cornfields to the church.

On the outskirts of every city undeveloped land was turned into suburbia. In the early part of Queen Victoria's reign this term did not necessarily suggest 'superior' properties. The 'industrial suburbs' of Hunslet and Holbeck near Leeds had much the same kind of reputation as the *faubourgs* of medieval cities where artisans, who could not find or could not afford accommodation within the city, lived and worked. They were often more unhealthy than the 'city centres': this was as true of the suburbs of nineteenth-century Sydney as of those of Elizabethan London. As the nineteenth century went by, however, the term 'suburbia' became increasingly associated with flight from the worst parts of the city. It had been used in this sense in the Manchester and Birmingham of the 1790s. Stress was laid on the superior amenities, including 'the pure breath of Heaven', which could be found outside the smoke and noise of the city. Builders were natural propagandists, selling without too much difficulty when times were good the 'detached villas of pleasing and picturesque appearance' which they said would become 'the seats of families of distinction'.

Between these favoured areas and the city centre there would be not only inferior housing districts but patches of unused land, 'desolate gaps so familiar to all dwellers in great towns at a period of expansion'. Frequently the housing pattern followed the rural field pattern which had existed previously. 'The units of purchase by builders were fields, and houses and streets had to be fitted into them.' This was true of parts of Leeds and Nottingham:[1] it was also true of Brighton, where the demand for building land was so great that individual agricultural strips were sold to builders without the usual kind of enclosure award.

Not all cities, of course, followed the same process of growth. Some grew from the nucleus of a smaller and older town. They retained some of their old buildings and their old institutions. Manchester and Salford were twin towns separated by the River Irwell, a tranquil stream in the Middle Ages when the manorial boundaries were drawn, but a 'flood of liquid manure' in early Victorian England. Other cities were amalgamations of towns, fused into a new urban area. Newcastle, Gateshead, North Shields, South Shields, Wallsend and Jarrow made up a great new urban complex. No stranger could tell, for example, where Newcastle ended and Wallsend began. A few Victorian towns, like Middlesbrough, Barrow-in Furness[2] or Crewe were new – as new as the cities of the British Empire, many of which had a genuine Victorian character.

The diversity of patterns of growth makes detailed statistical

1. Some interesting evidence is given in Professor M. W. Beresford's lecture 'Time and Place' (Leeds, 1961). Nottingham's borough fields were not enclosed for building until 1845. The lateness of urban development on the borough fields led to overcrowding and squalor in other parts of the town. See below, p. 367.

2. The newly incorporated Barrow Corporation (1867) met at first – before the Town Hall was built – in the railway offices.

comparison difficult. Boundary changes alone need to be examined carefully when the data from successive censuses are compared. The exact unit of measurement needs to be defined carefully, also, if precise comparisons are being made. Is the municipal borough to be the unit or the parliamentary constituency, the township or the collection of townships? The municipal borough of Wolverhampton had a population of 49,985 in 1851, the parliamentary constituency a population of 119,748. Leeds was incorporated as a township in the seventeenth century, but the municipal borough during the nineteenth century included ten townships. The Tyneside 'conurbation' consisted and consists of a large number of separate administrative units. In 1851 Newcastle, with a population of 87,784 people within the limits of the municipal borough, was still a compact town, the centre of which had been rebuilt with taste by Robert Grainger in the ten years before Queen Victoria came to the throne, but during the last decade of the reign it expanded in size at the same time as the whole region was expanding under the control of a tangle of authorities.

In London different sets of statistics refer to different units. The square mile of the City of London had its own government and its own connexions with the outside world rather than with London itself. In 1829 the Metropolitan Police District was created to cover all the parishes of which any part was within twelve miles of Charing Cross or of which the whole was within fifteen miles of Charing Cross. Nine other parishes were thrown into the area. When in 1855 a Metropolitan Board of Works was created, its boundaries were drawn on the basis of mortality statistics and drainage facilities. The Board covered an area of about 117 square miles. The expanding city had already pushed far outside these boundaries, and the term 'Greater London', covering roughly the same area as the Metropolitan Police Districts, had to be used by the Registrar-General in the statistics of the 1870s and the census statistics of 1881. The Registrar-General divided the area into 'inner' and 'outer' rings, and the area within the inner ring became with modifications the administrative County of London in 1888.

The area of 'Greater London' was still increasing rapidly at the end of the nineteenth century, and the progress seemed relentless. 'I have tried to keep Hornsey [in North London] a village,' the Rector of the parish complained, 'but circumstances have beaten me.' Places as far away from London as Brighton, a town which had grown more rapidly than any other place in Britain between 1821 and 1831, became metropolitan rather than provincial in character. As early as 1841 Brighton had been described as 'the greatest sanitarium of the largest and wealthiest city in the world': fifty years later G. A. Sala wrote of how 'rich merchants and stockbrokers' went up to town in the morning from Brighton, 'exceptionally eligible as a place of residence', and returned in time for dinner. Eastbourne and Hastings were also described at this time as 'isolated suburbs of London'.[1]

It is not necessary in this particular study of Victorian cities to depend upon precise sets of statistics or to standardize evidence in terms of comparable boundaries.[2] There is, however, another difficulty which must be mentioned. The word 'city' itself has been used in so many different senses, legal, administrative, geographical and demographic, that a 'common-sense view' of what it means has been taken for granted in this book. It was maintained by Coke and Blackstone that a city in England is an incorporated town which is or has been the see of a bishop. The great exception was Westminster, although Thetford, Sherborne and Dorchester, which by this definition might have been called cities, never were. In the nineteenth century a number of boroughs were given the status of cities, some of them places which had been incorporated as boroughs during the early years of the reign.

1. A. L. Wigan, *Brighton and its Three Climates* (1845); G. A. Sala, *Brighton as I have Known It* (1895), p. 13; S. J. Low, 'The Rise of the Suburbs' in the *Contemporary Review*, Vol. LX (1891).

2. For the statistics, see A. F. Weber, *The Growth of Cities in the Nineteenth Century* (1899); T. W. Freeman, *The Conurbations of Great Britain* (1959), and H.M.S.O., *Guides to Official Sources*, No. 2, *Census Reports* (1951). Among the outstanding contemporary articles in the *Journal of the Royal Statistical Society* are those by R. Price Williams, 'On the Increase of Population in England and Wales' (1880), and by E. G. Ravenstein on 'The Laws of Migration' (1885).

Manchester, for example, incorporated in 1838, was made the centre of a bishopric in 1847, and became a city in 1853. Birmingham, which was also incorporated in 1838, did not become a city until 1896. Liverpool was transformed into a city by Royal Charter when the new diocese of Liverpool was created in 1880. Leeds, which had no Anglican cathedral, became a city in 1893, and the title of its chief magistrate was changed to that of Lord Mayor four years later. In Australia, Sydney became a city in 1842.

The title of 'city' was a coveted badge of status, and most of the places described in this book either were or became cities in Queen Victoria's reign. The most notable exception is Middlesbrough, an interesting and significant product of the reign, which has remained a borough from the time of its incorporation in 1851. To include it requires no particular justification. It would have been called a city in many other countries, including the United States, and the problems of rapid urbanization which it posed may be usefully compared with those in places which, technically speaking, were cities. To have used throughout this book the term 'large towns and populous districts', a term favoured by the mid-Victorians themselves, would have been cumbrous and pretentious.

The idea of a city, moreover, whatever its legal and administrative definition in this country, had deeper and more universal undertones. It was enriched by the knowledge that there had been great cities in the past and the belief that there could be even greater cities in the future. The sense of the city, never as strong in England as in certain other parts of the world, was nonetheless strong enough to qualify and extend simpler notions of the autonomy of private enterprise and the priority of individual interest. It carried with it a sense of 'dignity', if only a latent sense. In active form, it could stir voluntary bodies, influence the programme of political parties, and inspire mayors, aldermen and councillors.

Religion and history came into the picture at many points. The King James Bible spoke usually of cities not of towns. It could be used to point to the need both for civic obligation and social reform. The experience of both the Greek *polis* and the Renaissance city-state was held up for study and emulation. Sometimes the need was stated in other terms. James Hole, the Leeds housing reformer, believed that mere contemplation of the 'horde who dwell in the most wretched houses and streets of our large town' should lead people to redress civic shortcomings: W. R. Lethaby, designer, writer and architect, born in 1857, wrote that 'every town is a Zion and has had its prophets'. 'A civilized life cannot be lived in undisciplined towns. . . . The civic arts are the arts of civilization, and the arts of civilization are civilization itself.'[1]

4

Lewis Mumford misleads in suggesting that Victorian cities, with all their problems, were 'insensate'. He misleads also in saying that they were all alike, the same place with different alibis, Dickens's Coketown, alias Smokeover, Mechanicsville, Manchester, Leeds, Birmingham, Elberfeld, Essen, Lyons, Pittsburgh, and Youngstown. The first effect of early industrialization was to differentiate English communities rather than to standardize them. However much the historian talks of common urban problems, he will find that one of his most interesting tasks is to show in what respects cities differed from each other. Lord Bryce once wrote that the only difference between American cities was that some were constructed in brick and others in stone. The remark was insensitive, although common difficulties of municipal government in the United States and monotony in patterns of land use gave it superficial meaning. Horace Cleveland, the pioneer landscape architect, noted 'the endless repetition of the dreary uniformity of rectangles' in most American cities of 'the West'.[2] Below the surface, however, in the United States, as in England, nineteenth-century cities not only had markedly different topography, different economic and social structures, and quite different degrees of interest in their surrounding regions, but they responded differently to the urban problems which

1. J. Hole, *The Houses of the Working Classes* (1866), pp. 20–21; W. R. Lethaby, *Form in Civilization* (1900), p. 100.

2. See H. W. S. Cleveland, *Landscape in Architecture as Applied to the Wants of the West* (Chicago, 1873).

they shared in common. A study of English Victorian cities, in particular, must necessarily be concerned with individual cases.

The differences are brought out in this book at every point. The classic example of such differences is that between Manchester and Birmingham. For Mumford they were both 'insensate industrial towns' created by the development of cotton, iron and steel. In fact, they diverged very strongly in their economic life, their social structure and their politics. It is their points of divergence which are of formative influence in English history. The two great cities of Scotland, growing within a different legislative and administrative framework from those of England, were very different, too, in texture and in policy. Both might figure in the Blue Books of the 1840s and both might have a City Improvement Trust, demolishing old property and widening streets in the late 1860s and 1870s, but it was where they differed which was historically interesting.

Patrick Geddes brought out the particular richness of Edinburgh's past in the exhibition which he planned for the Royal Academy in 1910. He included material relating to its geology, economic life, architecture, housing and history, not least the history of its 'golden age'. In his *Cities in Evolution* he wrote also of a 'greater Glasgow' comparable with 'Greater London' and including the Clyde ports and watering places, parts of Ayrshire, Falkirk and Grangemouth, and merchant villas at Stirling and even as far away as Dunblane. It was Glasgow which was the real Victorian city in Scotland, with a rapidly growing proportion of Scotland's inhabitants living inside its boundaries. Victorian Scotland, indeed, concentrated population in Glasgow more dramatically than Victorian England concentrated population in London. From being a commercial centre, Glasgow became an industrial centre also, responding with remarkable adaptability to the collapse of old opportunities and the rise of new ones, generating immense civic enterprise. Vitality and squalor went together, so that by the end of the nineteenth century Edinburgh stood out 'all edge, style and gesture' while Glasgow, for all its pioneering slum-clearance schemes, seemed at first sight 'a huge amorphousness'.[1] To Geddes, Glasgow and Edinburgh were far remoter in type and spirit than the small railway distance between them suggested: they were really the respective regional capitals of East and West Scotland, far apart in many ways – 'geographical, meteorological, racial and spiritual'. 'To Glasgow, indeed, the contrast with Edinburgh may seem as great as that between Liverpool and York; while a still larger contrast may be made from the Edinburgh point of view, as that between the main cities of Sweden and Norway, of both of which Scotland in many ways is a condensed miniature; say – Stockholm with Uppsala for Edinburgh, and for Glasgow – Greater Bergen and Christiana'.[2]

Geddes talked in terms of 'life forces'. Starting with the facts of economics, the differences between cities admit of more precise analysis. At least five elements in economic life must be taken into account in any comparative study of cities – first, the range of occupations in the city; second, the size of industrial undertakings; third, the character of local industrial relations; fourth, the extent of economic mobility; and fifth, the vulnerability of the community to economic fluctuations. Obvious differences between Manchester and Birmingham or between Glasgow and Edinburgh can be noted in each of these five basic elements of economic life.[3] Yet they are clearly not the only elements to be taken into account in comparing local social structures. Sheffield had much in common with Birmingham in its economic system, but the shape of its society and the chronology and trend of the municipal history were quite different.[4]

A full study of social structure must take account of property

1. See J. M. Reid, *Glasgow* (1957), and A. McArthur and H. K. Long, *No Mean City* (1957).

2. Geddes, op. cit., p. 18. He went on to say that in the future they might well be linked together: they were 'poles of a vast and growing conurbation', caught up in a 'growth process' which would 'submerge the differences beneath its rising tide'.

3. See below, pp. 184–6.

4. See my article 'Thomas Attwood and the Economic Background of the Birmingham Political Union' in the *Cambridge Historical Journal*, Vol. 1 (1948); A. Gatty, *Sheffield Past and Present* (1873); S. P. Pollard, *A History of Labour in Sheffield* (1959).

relations as well as of income, of religion as well as economics, and not least of demography, which provides a quantitative basis for much subsequent generalization. The transition from workman to master was as common in Sheffield as in Birmingham. Sheffield was as vulnerable to economic fluctuations. For long it was a city of small workshops. Yet it lacked the social and political leadership which gave Birmingham a civic gospel. It was essentially a working-class city, for long not one single city but a number of relatively distinct working-class communities: when Birmingham had established its claim to be considered 'the best governed city in the world', Sheffield was described in an official report as quite unlike a city at all. 'The population of Sheffield is, for so large a town, unique in its character, in fact it more closely resembles that of a village than a town, for over wide areas each person appears to be acquainted with every other, and to be interested with [*sic*] that other's concern.'[1]

Local leadership in Birmingham, slow though it was to develop in the 1850s, was responsive to local challenges during the 1870s and 1880s. In Sheffield, by contrast, local industrialists left a far less effective mark on the life of their city. It was not that they did not give money away but that 'the range of their gifts was narrow'. 'The town has little to boast in the cultivation of science or in the encouragement given to the fine arts', G. C. Holland, an eccentric physician who conducted social investigations among the poorer inhabitants of the city, complained in 1843. 'We fear that to exhibit a taste for either rather deteriorates than improves the position of an individual in the estimation of the public. The acquisition of wealth is accompanied with little solicitude to exalt the intellectual character.' More simply he concluded that 'one of the evils inherent in the accumulation of wealth is that it is not necessarily associated with intelligence'.

There was certainly no place like Edgbaston in Sheffield: the rich Victorian suburbs at Endcliffe, Ranmoor and Tapton, a hillside dotted with mansions and miniature parks, were stately, but scarcely centres of initiative or taste. Radicalism was strong in Sheffield, but it was relatively uninfluential in

1. M. Walton, *Sheffield, Its Story and Its Achievements* (1952), p. 187.

local life. Nor was there an invasion, as in Birmingham, of energetic people from outside. In the meantime working-class pressure was not quick to assert itself in Sheffield politics. The relative high earnings and standard of comfort of the Sheffield artisans, except in periods of bad trade, kept them uninterested in large schemes of municipal reform for most of the Victorian age. Their trade societies were often societies complete in themselves, and it was not until the twentieth century that they became an active force in municipal government. If they had been able or willing to apply pressure earlier, even the demographic history of Sheffield might have been different.

All demographic comparisons between cities must take account not only of different sizes of community but of different spatial densities – Melbourne, one of the Victorian cities described in this book, covered a far bigger area than London or Chicago and is particularly interesting in this connexion – and of the surrounding population pattern in the near-by region. Birmingham, for example, depended on the Black Country, but it had a quite different social and political structure from its region. Manchester was the business capital of a whole constellation of textile towns and villages. Leeds, by contrast, was in no sense the capital of the West Riding: its relationship to Bradford was quite different from that between either Birmingham or Manchester and any of their neighbours. Within the cities, demographic factors of great importance include the proportion of 'newcomers' to native inhabitants, the place of origin of the newcomers, the age-structure of the whole population, the sex ratios, and the differential birth and death statistics in different districts. These factors were interdependent, as was clearly shown by E. G. Ravenstein in his paper on 'the laws of migration' read to the Royal Statistical Society in 1885. A whole Victorian urban typology could be constructed on the basis of these and other urban statistics along the lines of a recent study of twentieth-century British towns:[1] indeed, it could go further than that study in providing a comparative chronology of landmark dates in different urban centres.

1. C. A. Moser and W. Scott, *British Towns, A Study of their Social and Economic Differences* (1961).

In the fundamental study of comparative property relations obvious points to note are the pattern of ownership of urban land, the extent of aristocratic interest (including absentee interest), the volume of industrial investment, the amount of corporate wealth, and the total rateable value. The statistics of each of these elements in urban life are difficult both to measure and to interpret. Some of them are difficult to discover. Many of the crucial facts of nineteenth-century urban life are buried away neither in factories nor in town halls but in solicitors' offices. Much, however, is clear. The history of the West End of London was determined by the building plans and leasing arrangements of great aristocratic estates either entailed in a family or held in trust by a corporation. The achievement of the estates in the great age of Georgian architecture has been described in detail and is still visible in many of the most beautiful parts of London. In Victorian England the process of building on estate land continued, however, in an age of declining taste and of confusion of tastes when there was no generally accepted traditional authority.[1]

In the provincial cities the existence of protected estates like the Calthorpe Estate, which owned and managed Edgbaston in Birmingham, had a strategic influence on the whole development of the city. The owners of such estates, served by solicitors and themselves serving as patrons of urban parishes, governors of grammar schools and presidents of charitable associations, often provided the backbone of a 'conservative' interest in cities whose flavour was essentially radical. Absentee ownership was as real in many English cities as it was in Irish farms. The history of Barrow-in-Furness, for example, would have been very different had the Duke of Devonshire not been one of the chief landowners. The process was reciprocal. Many men who made their money in the cities chose to own land in the country, and even in distant Australia members of an incipient 'colonial gentry', who held land in Sydney, chose to live abroad as rich *rentiers* 'at a time when their influence might have helped promote more civic con-

1. See J. Summerson, *Georgian London* (1945), especially Chapter XXI, 'The Ends of the Threads'.

sciousness and a higher standard of local administration'.[1]

The corporate wealth of cities like Bristol and Liverpool permitted their corporations to do many things which less wealthy bodies could not have afforded to do. Lord Palmerston once said that the first word in Liverpool's motto 'Deus nobis haec otia fecit' ought to read not 'Deus' but 'Dues'.[2] Even in such favoured cities, however, there was an annual battle about the rates 'burden', perhaps the keener since rate assessments were related then as now not to the distribution of incomes but to the distribution of real property. Taxes, it has been said, are paid in sorrow, rates in anger, and there are innumerable Victorian instances of this response. In Liverpool, for example, there was fierce resistance to the attempt to levy an improvement rate in 1853. The Corporation had spent £62,947 on improvement during the previous year, an amount equal to the product of a tenpenny rate. Such expenditure, the protagonists of improvement argued, should be covered in part at least by income derived from rates. 'We have been too long idly hoping that improvements would drop from the clouds without any effort on our part – too long looking up to the corporate purse in order to save our own.'[3] Leeds was already levying an improvement rate of fourpence in the pound in 1853, and Manchester's borough rate, which included 'improvement' expenditure, was at the high figure for the time of 1s. 8½d. in the pound.

It is extremely difficult to compare the value of local property in different nineteenth-century cities because of different methods of rating assessment, even in adjacent cities like Leeds and Bradford, and different degrees of local efficiency. It is difficult also to compare local rates in the pound because of the extraordinarily varied pattern of specific rates which different authorities levied under different headings and often at different times – improvement, highways, water, drainage, watch, poor law and so on. In most cities the town council was merely one of the authorities levying rates

1. See A. Birch, *The Sydney Scene* (1962), pp. 94–5.

2. Quoted in Sir John Lubbock, 'A Few Words on the Government of London' in the *Fortnightly Review*, Vol. LI (1892).

3. *Liverpool Mercury*, 6 May 1853.

for a large part of the Victorian period. It was not until 1871, for example, that the Manchester Overseers of the Poor collected the Township and Highway Rates (there were still six separate rates for each township) as well as the Poor Rate, and it was not until five years later that one city rate was levied which included the School Board precept in the total.[1] The Town Clerk of Bristol reported in 1886 that he could not inform Whitehall of the city's rate in the pound 'as there are six different rating authorities', each with its own system.[2] Poundage was nothing more, of course, than total civic expenditure financed from rates divided by the rateable value, and if the assessment of rateable value was low the poundage seemed correspondingly high. It is difficult even to make comparisons between different years in the same city because assessments changed.[3]

Given all the difficulties, however, three general conclusions may be drawn. First, although the total rate expenditure of England and Wales increased from £10 million to £16½ million in 1868, £28 million in 1890 and, very substantially indeed, to £56 million in the middle of the first decade of the twentieth century, the average rate poundage changed little until the 'explosion' of the 1890s. Rateable value rose more rapidly than population, and corporations could spend more without increasing the rate. In the last years of Victorian Britain, rates were rising largely as a result of educational developments and of increased activity on the part of county councils. Second, despite this general picture, the willingness of cities to spend money was conditioned not only by their 'civic drive' or by their capacity to harness business flair but by the facts of their financial strength. Capital expenditure, in particular, on 'improvement', for example, or on parks and

1. S. Simon, *A Century of City Government* (1938), pp. 132–3.

2. House of Commons Paper, No. 138 (1886). Compare the similar return for 1865 (House of Commons Paper, No. 80).

3. See below, p. 214. Similar difficulties arise in the interpretation of American urban history during this period. Investigations made in Chicago in 1895, for example, revealed that the average assessment of real estate was not more than 10 per cent of its market value. See R. H. Whitten, 'The Assessment of Taxes in Chicago' in the *Journal of Political Economy* (1897).

hospitals, was restricted if cities felt themselves poor. Third, most cities had brief spells of relatively lavish civic spending followed by long spells of 'economy', when ratepayers' pressures were strong enough to prevent the start of large-scale building projects. When Leeds levied a borough rate of one penny in the pound in 1850 and this was stated to be the lowest rate ever levied in the town, the *Leeds Mercury* described the fact as 'honourable to the economical spirit of the Town Council, who have faithfully watched over their constituents'.[1] When Middlesbrough planned a local health act in 1859, 'a property holder' wrote to the local newspaper objecting to the expense. 'Darlington has spent £10,000, Middlesbrough has expended £4,000, and yet we are told that the mortality of the two towns is not lessened thereby.'[2] In distant Swansea there were the same kind of struggles a few years earlier.[3] In Newcastle-under-Lyme two ratepayers' candidates were elected in 1853 after they had described the first sanitary improvements as an 'injudicious and uncalled-for expense', and the theme persisted there throughout the century.[4] However eloquent the arguments for civic improvement, it was a 'fact of life' that if owners made improvements to their own property the rateable value of their property increased and their rate burden rose.

Corporate wealth and rates, specific or general, were not the only means of financing the rise in local government expenditure in the Victorian period. Grants-in-aid from central government, though small in volume, increased somewhat, thereby relieving the local ratepayers at the expense of increases in national taxation, and there was a substantial increase in sums raised from loans. Grants-in-aid involved far more than financial issues. The allocation of costs between local and national government depended upon current conceptions of which governmental functions should be properly

1. *Leeds Mercury*, 6 April 1850.

2. *Middlesbrough Weekly News and Cleveland Advertiser*, 12 March 1859.

3. G. Roberts, *The Municipal Development of the Borough of Swansea* (1960), p. 47.

4. See F. W. Bealey, 'Municipal Politics in Newcastle-under-Lyme', Part I, 1835–72, in the *North Staffordshire Journal of Field Studies*, Vol. III (1963); Part II, 1872–1914, op. cit., Vol. V (1965).

administered by central and which by local authorities. The price of increasing central control, through compulsory legislation and universal inspection, was more generous financial assistance. Such assistance entailed discussion both of proper local standards and of the most effective means of control. During the early 1870s the annual total paid to local authorities in the shape of exchequer grants amounted to about £1 million. By the end of the 1870s it had increased (largely as a result of educational expenditure) almost three times. By 1890 the figure was nearly £5 million, and at the end of the reign, after much the biggest burst of expansion, over £12 million. In the meantime, the total expenditure of local authorities increased from nearly £29 million to over £76 million, and outstanding loans reached a figure of over £300 million.[1] Liverpool led the way in floating a consolidated municipal stock in September 1880. Other cities followed. These sums were of greater significance than those raised from grants-in-aid, yet it is even more difficult for historians to gauge the influence of one city on another than it is to disentangle the complicated set of relationships between the centre and the localities.

The financial figures reflect a gradual transformation of civic policies and administration. The Municipal Reform Act of 1835, which had reorganized the forms of local government in 263 places which enjoyed chartered or prescriptive municipal privileges, paid relatively little attention to functions. Scope was left for great diversity both in the reformed corporations and the newly incorporated towns, and this inevitably implied that the early- and mid-Victorian cities would confront urban problems with differing degrees of imagination and efficiency. 'Centralization' remained a bogy word. The development in late-Victorian England of grants-in-aid and of systems of inspection and the increase in national legislation requiring positive action on the part of local

1. These figures are derived from the Annual Reports of the Local Government Board. For convenient summaries, see H. Finer, *English Local Government* (1945 edn), p. 381; A. K. Cairncross, *Home and Foreign Investment* (1953), pp. 142–4. Professor Cairncross gives a useful breakdown of the different purposes for which the debt of local authorities was contracted.

authorities smoothed out many of the basic differences. What differences remained were frequently differences of conscious policy. Some Victorian cities quite deliberately embarked upon large-scale programmes: others lagged behind. In considering this story both economic and social factors on the one hand and political factors on the other must be taken fully into account.[1] Some of the studies in this book have a direct bearing on this theme.

Beginning, therefore, with economic differences between Victorian cities, a much more complex set of differences unfold. Some are concerned with leadership. What was the social composition of Victorian town and city councils? How were social prestige and economic power reflected in political action? How far did changes in social structure and fluctuations in income and employment determine the main lines of civic policy? What were the relationships between 'established' groups and new groups in local life? How far did the creation of continuing machinery for civic administration change the character of local leadership? All these questions can be answered only in the context of the life of particular cities.

Other and more complex local differences relate to local 'culture'. Provincial cities might be united against London, but they were divided amongst themselves. 'Londoners', wrote G. J. Holyoake, 'are the lapidaries of the nation. They polish the diamond from the counties, and sometimes if no one challenges them they take credit for the jewel.'[2] In fact, there were many different jewels. The story of Victorian cities in the nineteenth century is the story of the development of separate provincial cultures which during the last ten years of Queen Victoria's reign were increasingly 'nationalized'. Some of the cultures had their origins in eighteenth-century loca life: others grew out of the vigorous energies of new mer chants and industrialists. After money had been mad 'culture' interpreted in a different sense, the favourite middl class sense of a veneer or polish, was expected to follow. 'T

1. See E. P. Hennock, 'Finance and Politics in Urban Local Gove ment in England' in the *Historical Journal*, Vol. VI (1963).

2. G. J. Holyoake, *Sixty Years of an Agitator's Life*, Vol. I (1892), p.

first effects of newly acquired wealth are always seen in the buildings of a town', wrote John Marshall, the great Leeds flaxmaster. 'Refinement of taste and manners are of slower growth. It is the next generation which must spend what their fathers have learnt to accumulate.'[1]

It was unfortunate that the spending took place in an age when assured standards of taste had lapsed and when neither the architecture of houses and public buildings nor the design of what went into them was as beautiful (although as Betjeman shows, it was often as interesting) as in the Georgian period. The Victorians were reacting quite deliberately and with no regrets against what they considered to be the dull, monotonous, uniform architecture of Georgian England. They had no desire to reproduce the styles of Bath or Brighton. J. S. Morritt, a gentleman of taste, born in 1768, could already criticize 'long rows of shops and houses . . . tortured into strict uniformity, exactly of the same height, with the same thin slices of pilasters, the same little flourishes of ornament'.[2] A. W. Pugin's 'contrasts' of ancient and modern architecture – in the second edition of his book he included contrasting pictures of ancient and modern cities, the former dominated by cathedral towers and spires, the latter by factory chimneys – pushed the theme to ideological conclusions. Later Victorians revelled in the ransacking of old styles. They identified Georgian architecture not only with formal dullness but with lack of imaginative inventiveness, and once they had fought out inconclusively their own famous 'battle of styles' between the Greek and the Gothic, they allowed for a limited amount of specialization (Gothic for churches, classical or Renaissance motifs on public buildings) or settled down to a comfortable eclecticism.

The eclecticism was displayed, often ostentatiously, not only in individual Victorian buildings but in Victorian city streets. Disraeli, a good as well as an eminent Victorian, admired both

1. Quoted by W. G. Rimmer, *Marshall's of Leeds* (1960), p. 103.

2. Quoted in J. Stegman's excellent study, *Consort of Taste, 1830–1870* (1950), p. 80. The motto of this book is a quotation from the Rev. H. Wellesley in the *Quarterly Review* of 1844: 'The century we live in is not more remarkable for its railways and marvels of science, than for a reaction from preceding barbarism in matters of taste.'

forms of expression.[1] In *Coningsby* (1844), a novel which will be examined in a different context, the context of early industrial Manchester, he described Millbank's house, Hellingsby, with evident relish. It was 'one of those true old English halls built in the time of the Tudors ... it stood a huge and strange blending of Grecian, Gothic and Italian architecture with a wild dash of the fantastic in addition. The lantern watch-towers of a baronial castle were placed in juxtaposition with Doric columns employed for chimneys, while under Oriel windows might be observed Italian doorways with Grecian pediments.' It is interesting to note that much of *Coningsby* was written in Deepdene, the home of a connoisseur of eighteenth-century architecture. Disraeli was not being ironical. He said also that London became interesting only east of Charing Cross. Belgravia and Marylebone were dull and dreary – speculators' architecture dictated by act of Parliament. He might have said, 'Whig architecture'. 'Looking towards Northumberland House and turning your back on Trafalgar Square,' he went on, 'the Strand is perhaps the first street in Europe, blending the architecture of many periods.'[2]

This seemed to be a great virtue. There were some Victorians, a minority, who wanted a style of their own, with a sensible and imaginative use of new materials, just as there were Victorians who wanted to plan towns on formal eighteenth-century lines. The majority, however, liked a diversity or a blending of styles. Just because they lived in an age which had abandoned the rule of taste, they took immense pains to educate people in taste or to use one of their favourite verbs, to 'elevate' taste. They liked 'imposing' buildings with 'pretensions'. They loved symbolism. They were seldom afraid of exuberance. Individuality and status-seeking were both expressed in their villas: their banks and shops became more and more ornate and decorated as the century went by. Even mills, warehouses and docks, which retained a dignified and still handsome functionalism throughout the early years of the industrial revolution, became places to decorate as well

1. See below, p. 93. See also the account of Disraeli in *Victorian People*, Chapter X.

2. Quoted in Stegman, op. cit., p. 107.

as to use. Their churches might be in many styles, for they ceased to be dominated by rules as to which style was appropriate for which kinds of building. Their town halls were the subjects of lively and sometimes exciting debate. It is quite misleading to suggest, as G. M. Trevelyan has done, that 'civic pride and civic rivalry among the industrial towns of the north was almost entirely materialistic and not aesthetic. The pall of smoke and smuts in itself was enough to discourage any effort after beauty or joy in the visible aspect of life'.[1]

There was an effort, whatever may be thought of its results. Many Victorian buildings were appalling: others have withstood the test of time. Mid-twentieth-century reaction against 'bare' functionalism has encouraged a revision of judgement concerning a number of Victorian buildings. The detail of the buildings deserves a closer examination than it has often received, and greater imaginative power is needed than is usually applied to envisage the colours and even the general appearance of buildings now begrimed in industrial soot. Victorian architecture in Australia – and even in India – has suffered less in this last respect, and it is far easier to appreciate the appearance of a Victorian town in twentieth-century Ballarat, where there is some superb Victorian architecture, than in twentieth-century Middlesbrough. Yet at the end of the century in what Lewis Mumford has called 'the Brown Decades' most of the interesting new adventures in architecture, those with genuine creative power, were to be found in the United States, not in Britain.

The willingness to express hopes and fears in buildings and not to pay too much attention to what experts said ought to be admired or condemned was a general feature of the Victorian approach to 'culture'. The culture of the mind also remained less specialized and more open to amateur influences than the culture of the twentieth century. There was scope for genuine amateur contributions to the natural sciences. A Sheffield man, Henry Clifton Sorby, who was archaeologist, chemist, metallurgist, biologist, Egyptologist and painter as well as geologist, made one to geology. There was scope also for argument and controversy in the new and unestablished social

1. G. M. Trevelyan, op. cit., p. 118.

sciences. Provincial culture had a vitality of its own in places far smaller than the great provincial cities, in George Eliot's Coventry, for example, or in Samuel Smiles's Leeds. 'I gave a course of four lectures to the Mechanics Institute at Leeds', Gideon Mantell wrote to a friend in 1882. 'I was never in the town before and never wish to visit it again.... Yet there is a good local museum in the town; and the Philosophical Institution and the Mechanics must draw large audiences.'[1]

The Mechanics Institutes were nineteenth-century inventions, products of the age of improvement, and were subsequently transported round the English-speaking world. The Literary and Philosophical Societies almost all had pre-Victorian foundations. The Mechanics Institutes stood for the diffusion of knowledge among all classes, particularly among the skilled artisans: the Literary and Philosophical Societies were proud of their role as the local cultural élite. Their presence or absence in the nineteenth-century cities (or the date when they came into existence) was of considerable cultural and civic importance. Manchester's Society came into existence in 1781, Newcastle's in 1793, Liverpool's in 1812. Leeds founded its Society in 1819, Sheffield three years later. It was to the Sheffield Society that Sorby, who was also a patron of university extension, gave much devoted service. There was no such society in nineteenth-century Birmingham – the famous Lunar Society founded in 1766 had passed out of existence – and this may account in part at least for the intensely political flavour of the 'civic gospel' as it was preached in Birmingham.[2]

Library facilities, the existence of clubs and reading rooms, the growth of musical societies and of statistical societies, the blossoming and withering of local periodicals, some of the first of them concerned specifically with local theatres, the local pull of national cultural bodies like the National Society for the Promotion of Social Science, must all be taken into account in examining the cultural life of a Victorian city, whether in England or in Australia. It would not be difficult

1. J. Stokes, *Life of Gideon Mantell* (1893), p. 400.
2. See below, p. 222.

to assemble an imposing anthology of statements by distinguished men of letters and scientists about the warm reception they received in the provincial cities. Pilgrimages to the annual meetings of the British Association led from one great provincial centre to another – Newcastle in 1863, for instance, Birmingham in 1865 (with Bath in between), Nottingham in 1866, Dundee in 1867, Norwich in 1868, Exeter in 1869, Leicester and Liverpool in 1870. Smaller and older provincial cities, including those in decline, were visited also. York, for example, was the scene of the first meeting of the British Association in 1831, and subsequent meetings were held there in 1844 and 1881.

Londoners were often unaware of what the quality of provincial life at its best could be. They knew, however, that during the early and middle years of Victoria's reign the national capital, while gaining absolutely in population at an enormous rate, had been losing comparatively 'by the rule of a new order of towns which have come into being as the result of a ... vast revolution'. A writer in 1881 set out to show how London, once 'the very focus of national thought and industry, surrounded on every side by the most flourishing parts of the country', had become 'isolated in the midst of the agricultural south'. 'The existence of a Manchester School or a Birmingham School has only been possible in the last fifty years, and has been rendered possible by this comparative isolation.... The position has largely divorced the feelings of London from the feelings of the industrial centres.'[1]

During the 1890s the pull of London tightened. Local newspapers began to lose ground to national newspapers. National advertising began to increase greatly in scope and scale. The same branded goods began to be offered in shops in all parts of the country. Neither the aesthete nor the expert was as much at home in the provinces as he was in the huge metropolis. Political and economic trends began to depend less on local social and market forces and more on national pressures from the centre. It was then, as the same kind of working-class houses were being built in the same kind of suburbs under the

1. G. A., 'The Origin of London' in *The Cornhill Magazine*, Vol. XLIII (1881).

building by-laws of the 1875 Public Health Act, that cities began to be more alike – and not in the early years of the industrial revolution.

The First World War and the rise of the mass communications system of the twentieth century completed the process. Whereas the word 'masses' was first used in the nineteenth century to describe the mysterious working-class population of the great new industrial cities, it began to be used increasingly during the twentieth century in a national context. It came to mean first the London crowd and then the faceless millions who could be manipulated from a single cultural centre. There is room for intensive research on the 1890s, one of the least studied decades of recent British history. It is clear from what has already been written, however, that it was not merely the coming of the automobile nor even the death of Queen Victoria which brought the age described in this book to an end.

5

The method of study in this book is similar to that in *Victorian People*, but it is somewhat extended. Just because cities, like people, are of various ages and are alike in some respects and different in others, their proper understanding requires a partnership between historians and sociologists. But historians and sociologists cannot be the sole partners. The study of the sites and situations of cities is a matter for geographers, their livelihood and shifts of fortune are the concern of economists, their government and administration have always interested political scientists, their effect upon personality and social behaviour (there has been much talk of an 'urban personality' and of an 'urban way of life') has fascinated one school of psychologists and sociologists. Many different academic specialisms converge on the city, and each specialism has produced its own theories and concepts.

The role of the historian in this company is not merely to supply detail. He must relate 'community building', what George Unwin called 'the most important aspect of history',[1]

1. G. Unwin, *Samuel Oldknow and the Arkwrights* (1924), p. 159. He seems to have meant small communities, however. He contrasted Saltaire

to other aspects of history. He must evaluate the changing place of the city in different sets of social environments, bearing in mind the serious danger of personifying places instead of examining the people and the forces which were at work in them. He must consider both the contribution of particular cities and the role of urbanization in social change. He must compare urban experience in one country with that in another or in two periods of time. He must disentangle the value judgements which have shaped the attitudes of people towards both city and country. He must study the theories and concepts of academic specialists in this context and relate them to the practical knowledge of engineers, architects and technologists, people who have tried not so much to understand the city as to control aspects of its development. He must draw on the comments not only of reformers but of journalists – they have always understood one level of city life far better than anyone else – and he must seek to understand and perhaps to influence the attitudes of town planners. Patrick Geddes in his plan for Colombo in 1921 wrote that 'neither the most practical of engineers nor the most exquisite of aesthetes, neither the best of physicians nor of pedagogues, neither the most spiritual nor the most matter-of-fact of its governing classes can plan for the city alone.' The historian must be concerned in the inquiry which would be the prelude to the kind of plan Geddes envisaged.

In practice, until recent years, the historian has hardly tried to live up to these high expectations. There have been three main types of city historians – the antiquarians, the boosters, and the academics. The types, of course, are not mutually exclusive. Many academics have been antiquarians at heart: others, even consciously, have been boosters.

The antiquarians have produced many useful studies of particular facets of cities, and they were well entrenched in Victorian England when it was considered to be as praiseworthy to give cities long pedigrees as it was to trace family trees. The faster things grew, the more necessary it seemed

and Port Sunlight with 'the more extensive and attenuated communities, such as the nation, the city and the joint stock company'.

that they should be rooted in the past. It had to be shown even in an account of a completely new community like Middlesbrough that there had once existed on the spot where the town was built a medieval priory dedicated to St Hilda. Glasgow, too, it was necessary to insist, had been founded by a saint, and had been an ecclesiastical before it became a commercial or industrial centre. Only in some American cities or in Australia and New Zealand could it be admitted that there was no past.

> Here are no storied tombs, nor sculptured shrines,
> On which we read a Saint's or Hero's praise,
> The ancient Harper never poured his rhynes,
> Nor Troubadour e'er sang melodious lays.[1]

The work of the antiquarians, even when purged of its excesses, had three main weaknesses. First, it was of strictly limited interest, appealing necessarily to a local public in the know. Second, it was insufficiently selective: it gave equal value to every fact, even the dullest fact. Third, it stopped short frequently just at that moment in the history of cities which is of particular interest to students of the Victorian Age. Nineteenth-century historians of Leeds dwelt on the Middle Ages and ignored the huge changes of their own time. Sir Walter Besant in his studies of Westminster and London ended long before his own birth: his study of nineteenth-century London was far less detailed in scope. It could be argued that the preoccupation of most Victorian historians of cities with the period before their own and their failure to examine the present robbed even their study of the distant past of much of its insight and vitality.

The boosters had opposite weaknesses. They might spend time proclaiming the glories of their city's past, but they were concerned above all else with guaranteeing its future. Their emphasis necessarily shifted from the parish chest and the muniment room to the trade directory and the chamber of commerce. A number of Victorian histories of English cities, many of them somewhat sketchy introductions to pages of

1. *Headlong Lines by a Policeman* (Launceston, 1843). Quoted by G. Nadel, *Australia's Colonial Culture* (Melbourne, 1957), p. 59.

contemporary information, were produced by writers, often anonymous, who were dominated by the same sense of civic pride which inspired the building of the imposing and often expensive Victorian town halls. The boosting tradition did not disappear with the end of Victorian optimism. It has continued to inspire much twentieth-century writing about cities both in Britain and overseas. A classic example of such literature is the monthly periodical *Philadelphia* started in 1909 after a stormy and controversial decade of city history. It advanced a whole series of proud propositions ranging from 'Philadelphia is the home of our Flag and the Liberty Bell' to 'Philadelphia manufactures each year 12,000,000 dozen hose and half-hose, enough to allow two pairs for every man, woman and child in the United States'.[1]

Buried in the writings of the boosters there is an enormous mass of invaluable material for the historian, and the civic pride which they demonstrated is just as interesting an urban phenomenon to study as the social problems of the city which have captured most attention from general historians. The main difficulty of the literature is that it is totally uncritical. And in England it was never counterbalanced by the kind of 'muck-raking' literature about 'the shame of the cities' which was produced in such quantities in the United States in the late nineteenth and early twentieth centuries. The nearest approach to 'muck-raking' is to be found in the writings of men like Henry Mayhew, the eloquent and perceptive journalist of mid-century, whose *London Labour and the London Poor* (1861) remains a twentieth-century best-seller. Mayhew was one of a group of journalists who contributed a number of articles to the *Morning Chronicle* in 1849, 1850 and 1851 describing 'the real conditions' of life both in the metropolis and the provinces. Yet these articles, designed for a new and critical reading public, lack the political 'bite' of American muck-raking, which was anticipated in the 1870s by a literature of exposure which reached its climax in the 1890s before the beginning of 'muck-raking' more narrowly defined. The English journalist W. T. Stead's *If Christ*

1. See D. F. Wilcox, *Great Cities in America, Their Problems and their Government* (1910), pp. 247–9.

Came to Chicago (1893) links the two national histories.[1]

Academic city histories until very recently have been few in number, particularly in England, and they also have suffered from at least two dangers. The first has been for the historian to start with a known account of national history and to go on by seeking to illustrate this account from local material. The second has been to ignore or pay inadequate attention to the writings of other specialists on the city. The first danger makes for the corroboration of accepted views rather than for their reappraisal. Instead of looking, for example, at the local history of health and mortality *de novo*, the historian is content to pick out the same variety of extracts about sanitary conditions as were picked out in the national Blue Books of the 1840s and in all subsequent studies. Instead of peering as through a microscope at the local forces in politics – individuals, clubs, parties and pressure groups – he describes local politics as following the known national trend. The second danger makes for planlessness; satisfaction with chronicle rather than with analysis. It is only when the historian is familiar with some of the concepts used by urban sociologists about urban growth and change, concepts borrowed, for example, from biology and ecology, that he can look at the growth of his particular city and ask useful leading questions. He will be able to make far more of the place of cities as regional capitals if he understands some of the techniques for measuring regional influence which have been developed by urban geographers – through a study of newspaper circulations, for example, or journeys to work.

Fortunately, recent trends in historical studies have provided new insights from history itself. New life has been given to detailed slices of Census evidence and to evidence derived from scattered election pollbooks. The study of urban landscape, townscape – what can be seen in a city – has become far more exciting since Betjeman has told people to see as well as to read, since industrial archaeologists stimulated curiosity

1. See R. Hofstadter, *The Age of Reform* (1955); C. C. Regier, *The Era of the Muckrakers* (1932); L. Filler, *Crusaders for American Liberalism* (1939); and, above all, the work, including the autobiographies, of the muckrakers themselves.

about buildings and machines, since town planners concentrated on the visual element in planning, and since W. G. Hoskins and his colleagues of the 'Leicester School' began to approach the past in a deliberately 'visual' way.[1] Sometimes there has been great vividness of impact. Of South Wigston, a characteristic late-Victorian township of Leicester, where the first streets began to go up in 1883 and where within seven years there were six hundred identical brick cottages, several 'handsome engine sheds' and factories and a cast-iron church, Dr Hoskins writes – 'the sight of South Wigston on a wet and foggy Sunday afternoon in November is an experience one is glad to have had. It reaches the rock bottom of English provincial life; and there is something profoundly moving about it.'[2] Visual social history may recover something of the mood of the past. At the same time the introduction of greater discipline into social history as a whole is making for a deeper knowledge of the causes of the main changes of the nineteenth century. Disciplines derived from demography are of particular value.

Against this background, this study of Victorian cities has been written with a double purpose in mind. As a companion volume to *Victorian People*, it is designed to illuminate the attitudes, achievements and limitations of the Victorians. As a study of Victorian *cities*, it is designed to illuminate some of the themes which are of interest to the many different kinds of specialists who approach '*the* city' from quite different angles. My interest in the second object goes back before the writing of *Victorian People* to the writing of the second volume of the *History of Birmingham* which was published in 1953. I realized then that the fascination of a great industrial city like Birmingham lay partly at least in trying to decide what was unique about it. This could only be decided when it was compared with other places. The vigour of its civic gospel in the age of Joseph Chamberlain, which appeared at first to be a sign of Birmingham's leadership in the concerns of local government,

1. See W. G. Hoskins, *The Making of the English Landscape* (1956); G. Martin, *The Town* (1961). For a different approach, see K. Lynch, *The Image of the City* (1960).

2. W. G. Hoskins, *Leicestershire* (1957), p. 84.

proved on closer examination to depend on a determined attempt to catch up. Glasgow, for instance, was far ahead of Birmingham in its civic policies before the rise of Chamberlain.

It was not only British cities with which it seemed wise to make comparisons. The literature of Chicago in the 1890s was as relevant to this work as the literature of the English Victorian cities, and the work of the Chicago School of urban sociologists, when studied in its historical context, seemed as relevant as the writings of any school of historians. It is through the work of that school and through the tradition of empirical social inquiry in British cities that the perspectives of urban sociology are best appreciated. They are perspectives which alter the whole approach to history. As history itself becomes more comparative, we will find it easier to range more freely over both space and time, asking more searching questions and seeking more comprehensive answers. Essentially, however, this book is about English history, with relevant cross-references to European and, above all, American experience.

The urban sociology of the Chicago School was associated in the first instance with the battle to wipe out the slum. Commitment and curiosity were its motive forces. As it developed, its professors evolved theories, some of them sophisticated, all of them needing careful criticism. The real driving force behind it, however, was the life of a great city, collecting its inhabitants from every part of the world. It seemed to be a city without precedent, 'an ideal laboratory for the study of human behavior and social organization'.[1] Julian Ralph, who described Birmingham as 'the best-governed city in the world', wrote of Chicago: 'Those who go clear-minded, expecting to see a great city, will find one different from that which any precedent has led them to look for.'[2] It was thought of as a new phenomenon, a portent, a place which the 'clear-minded' had to visit if they wished to understand the world.

1. T. V. Smith and L. D. White (eds.), *Chicago, an Experiment in Social Science Research* (1929).

2. J. Ralph, *Our Great West* (1893), p. 1. See also below, p. 232.

At the same time it was a shock city. It was a centre of problems, particularly ethnic and social problems, and it provoked sharply differing reactions from visitors. Rudyard Kipling said that having seen Chicago he 'urgently desired never to see it again'. Yet W. T. Stead wrote in 1894 that while it was for the future to say whether or not Chicago would become 'the ideal city of the world', she already had 'the opportunity at her feet'. 'She is not laden down by any *damnosa hereditas* of the blunders and crimes of the past; her citizens are full of faith in the destiny of their city.'[1] The phrase 'city of destiny' recurs time and time again. 'From a struggling village sunk in the mud of a prairie creek, Chicago rose within the memory of living men to a great metropolis, ranking fifth in the roll of the world's greatest cities. It was inevitable that Chicago should assume this rank, for Chicago is a city of destiny.'[2]

If Chicago was the 'shock city' of the 1890s, one of the British nineteenth-century cities – Manchester – was the shock city of the 1840s, attracting visitors from all countries, forcing to the surface what seemed to be intractable problems of society and government, and generating as great a variety of opinions as Chicago did later or Los Angeles did in the 1930s and 1940s. Every age has its shock city. The study of individual Victorian cities in this book begins with Manchester in the 1840s. It was the *Manchester Guardian* itself which stated as early as 1832 that 'the manufacturing system as it exists in Great Britain, and the inconceivably rapid increase of immense towns under it, are without previous parallel in the history of the world'.[3] By the end of Queen Victoria's reign it was London, as we have seen, which seemed most interesting to Englishmen and to foreigners alike. Henry Mayhew had referred in 1861 to labels like 'this vast capital – this marvellous centre of the commerce of the world'[4] as 'stereotype phrases of civic elegance': the stereotypes acquired new life and

1. This and other fascinating comments on Chicago can be found in B. L. Pierce, *As Others see Chicago* (1933).

2. J. Paul Goode, *Report to the Chicago Harbor Commission*, 10 November 1908.

3. *Manchester Guardian*, 17 November 1832.

4. Mayhew, *London Labour and the London Poor* (1851–62), Vol. I, p. 3.

meaning in the last years of the nineteenth century. London comes last in this volume, therefore, because its problems dominated all British discussions of the city in the late-Victorian period. The evidence relating to it, like the evidence relating to early-Victorian Manchester, is not simply material from Blue Books, royal commissions or newspaper and review articles. From Gissing to Wells London fascinated or horrified successive generations of writers. They could not leave it alone. Booth thought of it not as a laboratory but as a stage.

In between early-Victorian Manchester and late-Victorian London, both of which have a symbolic significance, there is room for Leeds, where the detailed story of the building of a new town hall in the 1850s illuminates almost every facet of the Victorian approach to cities; for Birmingham, where the new civic gospel was recognized even at the time to mark the start of a new phase in British civic history; for Middlesbrough, where a new community was brought into existence which the Victorians thought of as 'the epitome of modern times'; and for Melbourne, whose absorbing history shows how Victorianism spread far beyond the frontiers of this island. The older cities, which were not Victorian at all but which had a Victorian element in their development, are discussed very briefly in the epilogue. Many of them have come into their own again in the twentieth century. American cities also are given their place in this final reckoning, on the grounds that their history illuminates the nineteenth-century story at every point.

The different cities described in this book are treated quite differently and at different levels. In some cases weight is attached to chronology, in others to the intrinsic interest of particular events or images. Yet in this chapter and the next and in the book as a whole there is a basic unity. It is possible to synthesize, provided that account is taken of symbols as much as of facts. Harriet Martineau, deservedly one of the most eminent of the early Victorians, said that whenever she went to a strange city she went at once to the highest point in the neighbourhood from which she could see the city as a 'living map' below her. 'It is scarcely credible', she wrote with the air of having made a great discovery, 'how much time is saved and confusion of vision obviated by these means.'[1]

Perhaps for the same reason, more than one generation of Victorians was fascinated by what they called 'balloon views'. These were very far removed from the meticulous social surveys of the city, factual in character and exploratory in approach, which appealed to the voluntary societies of the 1840s and – after a mid-Victorian break – to the new social investigators of the 1880s and 1890s. Climbing high above the streets, the travellers by balloon were concerned neither to find out 'the truth about cities' nor to save time. They were seeking a new and more ordered vision. 'It was a wonderful sight', two of them wrote after seeing London from the air in 1862, 'to behold that vast bricken mass of churches and hospitals, banks and prisons, palaces and workhouses, docks and refuges for the destitute, parks and squares, and courts and alleys, which made up London – all blent into one immense black spot – to look down upon the whole as the birds of the air look down upon it, and see it dwindled into a mere rubbish heap – to contemplate from afar that strange conglomeration of vice and avarice and low cunning, of noble aspirations and human heroism, and to grasp it in the eye, in all its incongruous integrity, at a single glance – to take, as it were, an angel's view of that huge town where, perhaps, there is more virtue and more iniquity, more wealth and more want, brought together into one dense focus than in any other part of the earth.'[2]

The historian cannot take an angel's view either of London or of the busy provincial cities which were far more Victorian than the capital. He will find it useful, however, before losing himself in the complexities of particular cities, to seek some vantage point from which to gain an initial sense of unity and order.

1. H. Martineau, *Retrospect of Western Travel* (1838), Vol. 1, p. 228.

2. H. Mayhew and J. Binny, *The Criminal Prisons of London* (1862), p. 143. See also J. Glaister, *Travels in the Air* (1871).

CHAPTER TWO

City and Society: Victorian Attitudes

If any nation is to be lost or saved by the character of its great cities, our own is that nation.

ROBERT VAUGHAN, *The Age of Great Cities* (1843)

The tendency of people in the later stages of civilization to gather into towns is an old story. Horace had seen in Rome what we are now witnessing in England – the fields deserted, the people crowding into cities. He noted the growing degeneracy. He foretold the inevitable consequences.

J. A. FROUDE, *Oceana* (1886)

I

MOST Victorian writers on society thought of their age as 'an age of great cities'. To some of them this was a matter of pride – cities were symbols of growth and progress: to others the spread of cities and the increase in their numbers were matters of concern, even of alarm.

About the facts themselves there could, of course, be no dispute. The population of England, in Ruskin's words, was being 'thrown back in continually closer crowds upon the city gates'. When Queen Victoria came to the throne in 1837 there were only five places in England and Wales outside London with a population of 100,000 or more. In 1800 there had been none. By 1891 there were 23. Between 1841 and 1891 the population of London increased from 1,873,676 (11.75 per cent of the total population of England and Wales) to 4,232,118 (14.52 per cent of the total population). In 1841 only 17.27 per cent of the population lived in London and cities of 100,000 inhabitants or more: by 1891 the proportion had risen to 31.82 per cent. In Scotland, Glasgow, as has been shown, exerted an even greater pull than London did in England. It ontained 5.1 per cent of the population of Scotland in 1801, 8.6 per cent in 1831, 11.5 per cent in 1851 and 19.4 per cent in 1891. The Victorians liked facts: they also liked laws. There seemed to be abundant factual evidence, as a French writer put it, that 'the force of attraction in human groups, like that of matter, is in general proportionate to the mass'.

Yet if this was held to be a law, there was no unanimous belief that it was a beneficent one. The word 'mass' itself was one of the perpetual sources of difficulty when it was applied to people. If you concentrated on the mass and forgot the individuals and families who constituted it, you might well be alarmed, particularly in under-policed early-Victorian England, by the anonymity and brute force of numbers in the cities: you might be tempted, as hundreds of writers, including poets and novelists, were tempted, to contrast the 'natural order' of the peaceful countryside with the restlessness and disturbance of the turbulent city. You might dwell on the urban threat both to property and to tradition, and end by arguing that 'the speedy disappearance of the city crowds, either by dispersion or by almost any other means, so far from being a matter to be deplored, should be an object of solicitude'.

The growth of great provincial concentrations of population and the increasing complexity of industrial society strengthened a fear of numbers which had previously exposed itself forcibly in relation to London. 'Is there not a Tumour in that place, and too much matter for mutiny and Terror to the Government if it should burst?', Robert Southwold had asked Sir William Petty in 1686. William Cobbett, who hated 'the great Wen' and tried to escape from it whenever he could, generalized his argument to cover not only London but all cities, and to cover not only all cities but also schools, factories, barracks and jails. 'If after all a school must be resorted to,' was his advice to young men, 'let it, if it be in your power, be as little populous as possible.... Jails, barracks, factories, do not corrupt by their walls, but by their condensed numbers. Populous cities corrupt for the same cause.' Rousseau made the same point in *Émile*. 'Men are not made to be crowded together in ant-hills, but scattered over the earth to till it. The more they are massed together, the more corrupt they become.'

Even if, as an enlightened Victorian, you had little sympathy either with old-fashioned beliefs in the moral virtues of small numbers or with the barely concealed value judgements which shaped pastoral myths, you might be afraid of the new industrial cities. If you were quite unmoved by the anxieties Wordsworth expressed about 'the dissolute city' in his poem *Michael* (and with increasing concern throughout the later years of his life), you might still be disturbed at the emergence of the 'masses'. The old fear of the mob was given a new dimension in an industrial context. William Cooke Taylor, an apologist of the new industrial system, not one of the critics, a man who liked large factories and schools, though not barracks and jails, held that one day the 'masses' must 'like the slow-rising and gradual swelling of an ocean ... bear all the elements of society aloft upon their bosom'. The mob could be dispersed: the masses were part of history.

Cooke Taylor was as frightened of the movements of the ocean as some twentieth-century politicians have been frightened of 'winds of change'. Resort to metaphors of this kind, derived from nature, reveals a certain lack of confidence about humanity. Cooke Taylor accepted the facts of change, but admitted the uneasiness. He noted that 'as a stranger passes through the masses of human beings which [*sic*] have been accumulated round the mills [in the populous northern industrial areas] he cannot contemplate these crowded hives without feelings of anxiety and apprehension amounting almost to dismay. The population is hourly increasing in breadth and strength. It is an aggregate of masses, our conception of which clothe themselves in terms which express something portentous and fearful.'

This was one reaction; it became a stock one. If, however, you penetrated the dark recesses of the city behind the busy roads leading in and out of the centre you might, of course, be more alive to the dangers implicit in the use of the word 'masses' than in the existence of the masses themselves. Doctors and clergymen, who often, though not always, knew far more about cities than most of their contemporaries, were necessarily concerned about individuals and families within the mass: they provided some of the richest social documentation of the century. It was a Leeds clergyman of the 1840s who with great percipience warned his readers of the dangerous lure of the word 'masses'. 'Our judgements', he stated, 'are distorted by the phrase. We unconsciously glide into a prejudice. We have gained a total without thinking of the parts. It is a heap, but it has strangely become indivisible.'

Social segregation necessarily induced and still induces strange ways of thinking about other human beings. The fear of the city, like other kinds of fear, was often a fear of the unknown. It was because the 'crowded hives' were mysterious as well as crowded that cities provoked alarm even on the part of some of the people who lived in them. Because of their contrasts of experience, they also titillated the romantic imagination of popular writers like G. W. M. Reynolds who wrote luridly of 'the lazar house, the prison, the brothel, and the dark alley ... rife with all kinds of enormity'. Readers were always panting for writing of this kind. Reynolds's *Mysteries of London*, running to four series, was the metropolitan prototype (itself based on Eugène Sue's *Mysteries of Paris*) of a thriving national literature. Such exploitation of romantic fear must be distinguished from the 'rational fears' of the consequences of specific urban problems – overcrowding, high mortality, disorder, and political discontent. Yet there was a romantic vein in the style of writing about both, and for most kinds of writers on cities there was a dominating emphasis on 'exploration'. The 'dark city' and the 'dark continent' were alike mysterious, and it is remarkable how often the exploration of the unknown city was compared with the exploration of Africa and Asia. Richard Oastler set the fashion early in the century when he compared conditions in the worsted mills of Bradford with those in 'hellish' colonial plantations. Nobody had bothered to note, he added in highly romantic language, that 'the very streets which receive the droppings of an "Anti-Slavery Society" are every morning wet by the tears of innocent victims at the accursed shrine of avarice'.

There were two particular concerns which sharpened

'rational' fear of the unknown. The first, as in Oastler's case, was religion. In the village, the power of religion rested upon personal contact and influence, on the strength of a social system where people knew their place and other people knew what that place was. Religion reflected and reinforced such notions of hierarchy. In the city, personal contact was more difficult and the idea of social place was jeopardized. There were no 'roots'. Lord Shaftesbury, evangelical in religion and conservative in politics, a common combination, considered that the masses of the cities were cut off from hope of salvation: nothing restrained them but 'force of habit'. They were 'uninfluenced by because untouched by any moral or religious discipline'.

The comments collected during the religious census of 1851, the one national religious census of the Victorian age, seemed to underline this opinion. In the words of Horace Mann, the chief statistician, the 'labouring myriads, the masses of our working population ... are never or but seldom seen in our religious congregations'. In rural areas and small towns a far greater proportion of the population attended church than in the cities. The places in which church-going was lowest included every large town described in the census report as a cotton town, the two greatest woollen towns, Leeds and Bradford, every large coal town except Wolverhampton, and the two great metal centres of Birmingham and Sheffield. Everywhere clergymen in towns and cities spoke of the difficulties of attracting mass support. According to Mann's calculations, fewer than one person in ten attended church or chapel on census day in Birmingham, Liverpool, Manchester, Sheffield and Newcastle. The metropolis, particularly in its crowded areas like Lambeth and Tower Hamlets, was equally indifferent to the call for regular worship. 'What is St Paul's?' Henry Mayhew asked one of his London costermongers. 'A church, sir, so I've heard,' was the reply. 'I never was in church.'

The existence in the cities of a small minority of militant secularist working men, imbued 'with an inveterately hostile sentiment' towards religion, and of a large 'floating population' added to the sense of moral danger. The very big cities provided ample evidence to alert Christian critics. The Liverpool Domestic Mission noted in 1859, for instance, that probably not more than a quarter of its neighbours stayed in the same house or even in the same street over two consecutive years. In large areas of London people seemed to be completely 'anonymous'. 'In a neighbourhood where every man is known,' wrote a Unitarian minister, Robert Vaughan, who preferred life in the cities to life in the countryside, 'where all his movements are liable to observation, and the slightest irregularity becomes a matter of local notoriety, a strong check is constantly laid upon the tendencies of the ill-disposed. In such connexions it is felt that should the law fail to punish, society will not. The crowded capital is to such men as some large and intricate forest, into which they plunge, and find, for a season at least, the places of darkness and concealment convenient for them.'

Even where the forest seemed less intricate and when the people described were 'settled inhabitants', not people on the move, cities were thought to be 'dangerous to religion' because of their social segregation. As the cities grew, the separation of middle-class and working-class areas became more and more marked. Consequently, it was felt, the religious influence of one class was not brought to bear upon another. Disraeli talked of 'two nations' inhabiting the same small island: before he coined the phrase it was employed in 1841 by the famous Dr William Channing of Boston, one of the greatest Unitarian ministers of America, who set out to understand and to explain the 'moral significance' of the growth of cities. 'In most large cities,' he wrote, 'there may be said to be two nations, understanding as little of one another, having as little intercourse as if they lived in different lands.' Once again, a parallel was drawn with exploration in distant and primitive societies. 'A hovel in one of the suburbs which they know least' would be as strange to most Londoners as a village in the African forests. In Liverpool it seemed a 'crying evil' that 'two communities whose members dwell within the sound of the same bells and under the same chief magistrate should in many respects be practically as wide apart as if they resided in two quarters of the globe.'

If the threat to religion was the first source of 'rational' fear, the threat to deferential politics, the politics of personal influence, was the second. In the village or the small market town, 'influence' was direct and measurable: in the 'large towns and populous districts' 'opinion' could be manufactured. However necessary manufactured goods might be to the well-being of the economy, manufactured opinion for a long time was felt to be a challenge to the constitution. Disraeli compared Thomas Attwood of Birmingham with Tamberlaine. He suggested that all 'agitation' had its origin in the life of the city: there was one single historical process in which the *Birmingham* Political Union, the *Manchester* Anti-Corn Law League and the ubiquitous and amorphous movement of urban protest called Chartism were all phases.

When the social conflicts of the 1840s gave way to the balances and compromises of the 1850s and 1860s, cities were still viewed with suspicion as natural centres of extreme views inculcated by irresponsible demagogues, who would have been thrown out of the village or the small town. 'The Tories hate big Borough and Municipal Corporations,' wrote A. J. Mundella, the Liberal Member of Parliament, in 1872. 'The former return Radical M.P.s, the latter petition for Ballot and other obnoxious Bills and are always wanting sewage farms or interfering with the fishing by polluting the streams, or doing some other disagreeable thing. The number of landlords who have some grudge against, or litigation pending with Boroughs is really surprising, and *they hate them.*'

During the late 1870s and 1880s the hatred was mixed with fear of the 'caucus', the most advanced form of urban party organization, which, according to *The Times*, 'manufactured' opinion more efficiently than any previous political apparatus, 'mechanically' setting local and national agitation in motion. Once again Birmingham was identified with the 'caucus' as it had been with 'union' forms of organization earlier in the century, and the candid language of its leaders did little to restore the confidence of traditionalists. 'It is no longer possible', Joseph Chamberlain told his opponents bluntly, 'to attempt to secure the representation of a great constituency for the nominee of a few gentlemen sitting in private committee, and basing their claims to dictate their choice of election on the fact that they had been willing to subscribe something to the expenses.'

Chamberlain himself was a rich man, if not quite a gentleman, and there was an even deeper layer of fear which influenced assessments of the political role of 'masses' in the cities. Would they always remain under the control of men of property, landed or industrial? Might they not seek to take advantage of the fact that they were 'masses', that the strength of numbers could be used to secure not radical but socialist objectives. 'Already we have a revolution, slumbering but gathering power in all our cities,' wrote E. P. Hood, the man who first used the adjective 'Victorian' in 1851, 'and still we pursue our way with intrepid stupidity, dreaming of Eden in the very midst of a reign of terror.'

At moments of tension in the middle years of Queen Victoria's reign, like the Hyde Park disturbances of 1867, when the railings of the park were torn down, the old eighteenth-century fear of the mob was always revived. During the late 1880s it was given a new twist with the development of socialism, particularly in the metropolis. The turbulent demonstrations in Trafalgar Square in 1886, in 'flagrant defiance of constituted authority', were considered to be 'monstrous riots' by men of property. *The Times* recalled the Chartist danger of 1848, and Queen Victoria expressed her indignation at what she considered 'a momentary triumph of socialism and a disgrace to the capital'. It was at a later meeting in Trafalgar Square that H. M. Hyndman, the socialist in the top hat, told a huge crowd that if all the 'political factions' were against the socialists, it would be 'so much the worse for them'. 'We flourish: they decay.' The message, true or false, had local point in the provincial cities where the distinction between capitalist and worker was the social basis of the new industrial structure and where sometimes the communities were little more than adjuncts to the factories.

Socialism, however, had only strictly limited strength in the provincial cities. At most it was a phantom of the future rather than a danger in the present. Far from being afraid, many of the new businessmen of the nineteenth century, men like Joseph Chamberlain himself, sought not so much to exorcize the fear of the city as to hurl it back with contempt. The critics of the city, the people who were shocked either by the fact of the existence of the 'masses' or by the new ways of thinking about them, were always challenged, even at the time, by vigorous defenders of 'numbers' and of 'urban progress'. 'Men only feel their consequences and they can only act in a collective capacity and with vigour and effect,' a writer in the *Edinburgh Review* had argued in 1824, 'after they have been condensed into masses and collected into cities.'

The defenders of the city were for the most part eloquent men, who were at home in the pages of their local newspapers or on the public platform. Joseph Chamberlain was one. Joseph Cowen, politician and newspaper proprietor in Newcastle, who disagreed with Chamberlain on many issues, was another. 'The gathering of men into crowds', Cowen wrote in 1877, 'has some drawbacks, yet the concentration of citizens, like the concentration of soldiers, is a source of strength. The ancient boroughs were the arks and shrines of freedom. Today, behind the dull roar of our machinery, the bellowing of our blast furnaces, the panting of the locomotives and the gentle ticking of the electric telegraph . . . we can hear the songs of children who are fed and clad, and the acclaim of a world made free by these agencies. When people declaim in doleful numbers against the noise and dirt of the busy centres of population, they should remember the liberty we enjoy as a consequence of the mental activity and enterprise which have been generated by the contact of mind with mind brought together in great towns.'

What was said by Chamberlain in Birmingham and by Cowen in Newcastle was said by Edward Baines, the owner of the *Mercury* in Leeds, by J. A. Roebuck, Member of Parliament for Sheffield, and by Mundella, his successor, and by almost every proud Mancunian. These men did not argue on the defensive. They persistently carried the attack into the countryside, comparing contemptuously the passive with the active, the idlers with the workers, the landlords with the businessmen, the voluntary initiative of the city with the 'torpor' and 'monotony' of the village, and urban freedom with rustic 'feudalism'. Engels, who wrote incisively about Manchester without being a proud Mancunian, agreed with other Mancunians in this particular indictment.

The two particular 'rational fears' of the city became matters of pride for many of these supporters of urban progress. They included a substantial number of Nonconformists, men who were content to watch the Church of England wrestling with the difficulties of urban conditions. They or their fathers had often fought bitter battles against compulsory Church rates earlier in the century – there were struggles about Church rates even in the middle years of the century until national legislation was passed in 1868 – and they saw little reason for commiserating with a Church on the defensive. 'The inhabitants of Liverpool appeared to me to be divided between Church and Dissent by a wall harder than the wall of Balbus to leap over,' wrote Augustine Birrell. A militant Churchman's view was well expressed by the Rev. Dr Clark in his *The Church as Established in its Relations with Dissent* (1866). Dissent was '*mercantile* in spirit': it preached the gospel 'only to those who can pay for it': 'the lower strata of society' were left 'to rot in their vice and squalor'.

Nonconformists knew that they had considerable strength in the great provincial cities, although they might not be able to claim the allegiance of large masses of the population. Gloomy though the statistics of the religious census might appear, Nonconformist attendances made up more than 50 per cent of total attendances in Bradford, Leeds, Oldham, Wolverhampton and Sheffield, and between 40 and 50 per cent in Birmingham, Manchester, Salford and Newcastle. When the Roman Catholic group was taken into the reckoning – it accounted for over 30 per cent of attendances in Liverpool and over 20 per cent in Manchester – Anglicans were in a minority in all the large cities which lay within the 'chief manufacturing districts'. The Nonconformists themselves were divided both in social composition and in outlook, and in most cities included a large Methodist element, not always completely assimilated into Nonconformist ways of life until the last years of Queen Victoria's reign. They were far more important, however, than even their numbers suggested in leading the local politics of cities and in presenting the 'urban case' to their contemporaries. Small sects, particularly the Unitarians, often had a strategic part to play in civic life, providing mayors and officials, and encouraging interest in reform. The Methodists were much more passive.[1]

The political 'vitality' of the city was also a matter of pride rather than of fear to the spokesmen of urban progress. 'The great towns as they now are,' the *Radical Programme* of 1885 boasted, 'constitute the source and centre of English political opinion. It is from them that Liberal legislation receives its initiative; it is the steady pressure exercised by them that guarantees the political progress of the country.' The extent of participation in local politics and the freedom from patronage were taken to be virtues. So also was 'municipal freedom', an all too vague concept, which might mean the liberty to do nothing or the mandate to implement a civic gospel. The variety of functions exercised by municipal corporations after the Municipal Reform Act of 1835 – for that matter, the variety of the types of corporations themselves – was perhaps less of a matter of pride than the example set by the most enlightened authorities. G. C. Broderick, writing in 1875, advocated 'imperial intervention' in local government to redress the 'bitter experience of the abuses and disorders incident to an excessive subdivision of local powers', yet he sang the praises of some of the big Town Councils. Their members, he said, were 'men thoroughly conversant with every detail of local affairs, stimulated to industry and fortified against jobbery by the vigilance of their colleagues, raised above personal jealousies by a sense of corporate dignity, and made to feel the full weight of individual responsibility by a careful division of labour'. Their management was 'certainly not surpassed by the conduct of public business in the House of Commons, or in most of the public offices'.

Behind the vigour of the urban reaction was the force of the industrial revolution which gave a new twist to the older rivalries between town and country. In the eighteenth

1. For the religious kaleidoscope, see below, pp. 195–204.

century and earlier, towns had been distinguished from countryside less because of the presence of industry in them than because they were market centres, focal points of distribution for their neighbouring districts. Some of them were drawn into far wider trade connexions and some, like Manchester and Birmingham, into industry, but the general tendency to identify urban life with industrial life came late. London was distinguished quite sharply from the great provincial 'hives of industry' which fascinated foreigners and Englishmen alike. 'France, Germany and the Netherlands do not exhibit provincial towns to be compared to Manchester, Glasgow, Birmingham, Sheffield or Leeds,' a traveller noted in 1822. The manufacturing system as it existed in Great Britain, along with 'the inconceivably immense towns under it' was felt, as we have seen, to be 'without parallel in the history of the world'.

De Tocqueville described Birmingham as 'an immense workshop, a huge forge, a vast shop': from the 'filthy sewer' of Manchester 'pure gold' flowed. Taine concluded when he went to the North of England that man was an insect and that it was the army of machines which held the attention. The industrial community was the place where, in de Tocqueville's phrase, 'humanity attained its most complete development'. Ironically also, it attained what he believed to be its 'most brutish development'. 'Civilization works its miracles, and civilized man is turned back almost into a savage.'

Something far more than traditional rivalry between town and country, rivalry going back to the ancient and medieval world, was expressed in comments of this kind. What de Tocqueville and Taine found 'brutish', manufacturers might find 'invigorating'. The 'savagery' of the mill hand – the term is difficult to defend – would be esteemed nobler than the obsequious deference of the Dorsetshire labourer. Manchester working men were not expected to touch their caps to their masters. Even the smoke might be defended. Every trade directory focused attention on the energy of the city rather than on the problems it had to face. And as far as the problems themselves were concerned – for example, the problem of public health – it could be argued, rightly as has been suggested,[1] that the concentration of people in cities directed attention to social failings and abuses which had been accepted without question in previous generations. The 'clean party' in the cities were making possible improvements in rural health conditions which few people had cared about until the cities began to grow. Inside the city, as Vaughan put it, 'manufactures, commerce, religion, all become subjects of discussion. All these are looked upon from more points of view, talked about more variously, and judged of more correctly as being matters in which many minds are interested ... not only to form conclusions, but to form them with a view to utterance and action'.

The debate about the Victorian city, therefore, was a debate with different voices making themselves heard inside the city itself, and with the struggle between the defenders of the city, those who in various ways were proud of it, and its critics, particularly those who were afraid of it, ranging widely and probing deep. The facts of the city forced people to become articulate about their values and their aspirations, to speculate about riches and poverty, success and failure, 'improvement' and 'waste', private property and public interest, fate and social control. They were driven to concern themselves not only with the contrast between city and countryside but with contrasts within the city. During the 1840s and later in the century during the 1880s and 1890s the detailed study of the poorer parts of the cities became highly systematic and organized, and in the conclusions of social surveys, founded on statistical investigation, the reading public was familiarized with the facts of poverty and deprivation. The fears lingered, however, and as late as 1904 the brilliant journalist C. F. G. Masterman observed that to some people 'the change [from rural to urban] was charged with a menace to the future. They dread the fermenting, in the populous cities, of some new all-powerful explosive, destined one day to shatter into ruins all their desirable social order. In these massed millions of an obscure life, but dimly understood and ever increasing in magnitude, they behold a danger to security and to all pleasant things'.

1. See above, p. 21.

There was a peculiarly English complication behind the debate. Vigorous though the defenders of the city were, they faced a persistent diversion. Throughout the nineteenth century, as in earlier centuries, large numbers of English businessmen who had made money in the city wanted nothing better than to establish themselves in appropriate style in the country. The exodus of the successful from the city was as important socially as the pull of the aspiring into the city was economically. From furnace to field, from ledger-book to coat of arms, from Sunday School for yourself to Public School for your children – all these were favourite Victorian modes of advancement. Towns were places where men made a livelihood: country houses were places where people lived. Man made the town: God made the country.

Anti-urban biases, it has been suggested, go back in England to Roman times. Whereas the Romans, like the Greeks before them, had believed that membership of an actual physical city was a condition of true civilization, for the English public life needed no town: 'its elements already existed in every man's household'. Taine, as a European, took up the point, quoting a sixteenth-century traveller who had noted that 'among the English the nobles think it shameful to live in the towns; they reside in the country, withdrawn among woods and pastures'. In the nineteenth century there was a contrast in this respect not only between England and Europe but between England and America. 'The best society of Philadelphia was trying to improve and glorify Philadelphia,' G. M. Young has written. 'The best society of Manchester was trying to get out of it.' Not only were industrial cities shunned: York, an ancient city, was inhabited almost entirely by shopkeepers. Nor was it only the 'best society' which was attracted to dreams of rural contentment: the appeal of a country cottage or, if that failed, of a house and a garden on the edge of the town attracted even the shopkeepers.

Men argued so strongly about cities because they knew all this. Vaughan, who coined the phrase 'our age is pre-eminently the age of great cities', knew it profoundly. For him great cities 'in all ages and in all lands' had been centres of 'vast experiments in the history of society'. His generalizations about the tendencies of his own age were presented with all the ringing assurance common to the defenders of the Victorian city. 'We are both stronger and weaker than our neighbours,' he wrote. 'We possess greater force than they in favour of the new, but we are more beset with impediments deriving their strength from affinity with the old. The elements of social life which tend necessarily to collision, are nowhere so powerful, nowhere so nearly balanced; and as the natural consequence of such a relation of parties we are, perhaps, at this moment, the most contentious people upon earth. But this deep and ever-active struggle must not be regarded as so much pure evil. On the contrary, it should be viewed, in great part, as the sign of life and health. When there is no life, there will be no movement.'

There was plenty of movement in the Victorian city – it was founded upon it – and those who preferred order to movement started with an initial aversion that they did not find it easy to overcome. Others sought to impose a new order on what they saw in the cities. The ugliness of living conditions in the worst parts of the cities and the failure of builders and politicians to see the needs of the city as a whole drove them to construct models of ideal cities in their imagination. The first of these – the plans of Minter Morgan and James Silk Buckingham – derived part of their inspiration from the writings of Robert Owen. Morgan's belief, for example, that if a man lived in a village or an open part of a large town he would be a much better man than if he lived in a crowded and crooked lane had a characteristic Owenite ring about it.

Buckingham's model of an ideal city, called 'Victoria' after the Queen, was published in 1849: it was a most ingenious plan, a genuine model, for, as Buckingham pointed out, the 1840s was an age of models; model villages, model apartments, model lodging-houses and even model beds. Buckingham sought what he could not find in the actual cities of early Victorian England – 'the greatest degree of order, symmetry, space and healthfulness'. He argued that the city should ensure 'the comfort and convenience of all classes'. Some of his ideas can be traced in later schemes of town planning –

emphasis on low densities, zoning, ample space for gardens, and 'social balance': in the community as a whole he accepted the principle of zoning house accommodation by income, and had a strongly authoritarian note in his emphasis on 'codes of conduct'. His city was to have a spectacular centre – an inner square flanked by the mansions of 'the members of the government and the more opulent capitalists'. In the centre of the great open square, thought of as a kind of Roman forum or Greek agora, was to be an octagonal tower crowned with a spire three hundred feet high. It was to contain 'an electric light for lighting the whole town, with apartments at each stage and galleries leading from them around the tower for the enjoyment of the air and the view'.

No actual Victorian city incorporated the detail of Buckingham's plan, although people in most cities dreamed of great squares, like the squares of Renaissance Italy, and actually built towers to command the skyline. The 'opulent capitalists' chose to live, as we have seen, not in the centre but outside or at the periphery, and many of the buildings which Buckingham banished from the city area altogether – cattle markets, factories and cemeteries – occupied strategic positions determining the main lines of urban development. The ugliness of cities continued to shock. When George Eliot saw the Hunslet and Holbeck suburbs of Leeds from the train, she lamented that it was 'difficult to keep one's faith in a millennium within sight of this modern civilization'. Charles Dickens in his picture of Coketown provided his own kind of model of what a city should *not* be, 'a town of unnatural red and black, like the painted face of a savage'.

This was the usual imaginative response, expressed in Dickens's language with powerful individuality. 'It had a black canal in it and a river that ran purple with evil-smelling dye, and vast piles of buildings full of windows where there was a rattling and a trumbling all day long, and where the pistons of the steam engine worked monotonously up and down, like the head of an elephant in a state of melancholy madness.' Turning from Coketown to London, Dickens could write in *Nicholas Nickleby* of 'streams of people apparently without end' pouring 'on and on, jostling each other in the crowd and hurrying forward' oblivious of their environment, while John Ruskin, who attacked provincial, industrial cities as 'mere crowded masses of store, and warehouse and counter ... drains for the discharge of a tormented mob', described the 'great foul city of London' in 1865 as 'rattling, growling, smoking, stinking – a ghastly heap of fermenting brickwork, pouring out poison at every pore – a cricket ground without the turf, a huge billiard table without the cloth, and with pockets deep as the bottomless pit'. William Morris in his prologue to *The Earthly Paradise* contrasted 'a nameless city in a distant sea' with 'hideous' London: he reverted to the same contrast in advancing the social arguments of *News from Nowhere*.

Such reactions heightened the fear of the city. It was a dangerous place not only for the man of property but for the artist. It poisoned at the source. Most artists ignored it or tried their best to ignore it, describing it in their letters but leaving it out of their novels and poems. Others believed that it could be redeemed only if country and town could be 'married', as Ebenezer Howard, the town planner, was to put it. 'There are in reality not only, as is so constantly assumed, two alternatives – town life and country life – but a third alternative, in which all the advantages of the most energetic and active town life, with all the beauty and delight of the country, may be secured in perfect combination.' Charles Kingsley anticipated this vision in the same way as he anticipated in *The Water Babies* Morris's vision of a transformed River Thames. England would not rise to its opportunities unless there was 'a complete interpenetration of city and country, a complete fusion of their different modes of life and a combination of the advantages of both, such as no country in the world has ever seen'.

Only a minority of artists – and then only late in the century – followed the example of earlier French writers in expressing the same kind of enchantment with the light and shade of London as had been freely expressed concerning Paris. Against the judgements of Ruskin and Morris must be set the judgements of Henry James. As early as 1881, he wrote that while London was 'not a pleasant place ... not agreeable, or cheerful, or easy, or exempt from reproach' it was 'only magnificent ... the biggest aggregation of human life, the most complete compendium of the world'. When a 'tremendous list' had been drawn up of the reasons why it should be insupportable, the list quickly became irrelevant. This approach was shared by other writers of the 1880s and 1890s, when 'the quickened, multiplied consciousness' of the artist, as Walter Pater described it, could transform London into a Babylon. The very old and the very new overlapped. Indeed, for Arthur Symons in 1892 the test of 'poetry which professes to be modern' was 'its capacity for dealing with London, with what one sees or might see there, indoors and out'.

2

The debate about cities in Victorian England was part of an international debate in which different points of view were expressed in every country – France, Germany, Australia, the United States. In Australia, which is described in this volume, the debate had many points in common with the English debate: it was fed, indeed, on the same sources of inspiration until a new nationalist interest in what has been called the 'Australian legend' developed during the 1890s and gave added meaning to the rural values of the Australian outback. Australia was the most urbanized of all the new countries, yet it put its faith in the bush. 'Just when the results of public education acts, improved communications, and innumerable other factors were administering the *coup de grâce* to the actual bushman of the nineteenth century,' Russel Ward has written, 'his idealized shade became the national culture-hero of the twentieth.'

In the United States also there was what Richard Wohl has called 'a country-boy myth'. It had its origins deep in the past. The local rural genius of the prairies of the middle west was contrasted with the slick sophistication of the cities, the country-bred men of integrity with the city sharks and paupers. 'Plain old country boys' always had an advantage in American politics even when they were born in the cities. The 'muck-rakers', who relentlessly exposed the inefficiency and corruption of the late nineteenth-century American cities, were proud of their country origins and turned from wicked cities to peaceful farms with relief and satisfaction. As the American cities grew in size and number, the muck-rakers criticized them singly and together. Their 'social realism' often had its origins in rural nostalgia. The fact that most of the new immigrants, American or foreign, approached the city through the slum and were very quickly brought into contact with 'corruption' tended to confirm rural values. It was much more popular to 'expose' the city than to transform it.

There were many apparent paradoxes in all this. In America, as in Australia, the communication of rural values depended on urban instruments. In Australia the main instrument was the *Bulletin*, a weekly periodical published in Sydney, which did more than any other agency to turn the 'bushman' into a hero. In America muck-raking depended directly on the development of popular newspapers and mass-circulation magazines. The publishers of magazines such as *McClure's*, which touched off the whole muck-raking movement by printing articles by Lincoln Steffens and Ida Tarbell, came to realize that muck-raking provided a successful formula for increasing circulation. Many of the muck-rakers themselves were journalists, who knew intimately about the life of the city through their reporting. In such muck-raking the facts of poverty as well as the details of municipal corruption were exposed. Jacob Riis, for example, whose first book, *How the Other Half Lives*, appeared in 1890, was a reporter for the New York *Sun*. Robert Park in Chicago was to link journalistic knowledge with the developing study of urban sociology, devoting special attention to what he called the 'natural history' of the newspaper.

'Natural history', indeed, provided many ideas for early students of the American city, more often than human history or conventional political science. Their interest in ecology went much further than that of most writers in Britain, with the outstanding exception of Patrick Geddes. Different kinds of slums were classified ecologically: the sequence of social events which made them was described. Land economics and geography were studied also in ecological terms. Less attention was paid to the conscious and purposive re-making of the urban environment than to 'natural areas', 'natural forces', 'invasion', 'succession' and 'assimilation' and the agencies of regulation brought to bear upon them. Riis's autobiographical *The Battle With the Slum* (1902) with its commitment to social reform anticipates this tradition, which was ultimately articulated in Park's seminal essay of 1915 'The City, Suggestions for the Investigation of Human Behavior in the Urban Environment'.

Studies of this kind came relatively late in the urban history of the United States. In the age which Englishmen call 'Victorian' there was much in common between British and American writings about cities, with significant and revealing differences. The fear of the city in the 1830s and 1840s was nourished from similar sources both in England and in the United States. Writers like Thoreau or Emerson employed stock romantic arguments, contrasting Nature with man-made Civilization and lamenting the equation of Civilization with 'New York streets, built by the confluence and wealth of all nations ... stretching out toward Philadelphia until they touch it, and northward until they touch Boston'. Wordsworth's Michael had his American counterpart in Daniel Wise's Arthur, the country boy of 1852 who was totally unprepared to resist the wiles of the city. Wise's *The Young Man's Counsellor* was typical of a whole genre of writing about manners and morals in which the city figured as a centre of infection and contagion. *The Spider and the Fly or Tricks, Traps and Pitfalls of City life by One who Knows* (1873, New York) can be set alongside J. W. Buel's *Metropolitan Life Unveiled, or the Mysteries and Miseries of America's Great Cities* (1882, St Louis).

Very similar arguments about the effects of city life on religion were advanced both in England and the United States. 'Adam and Eve were created and placed in a garden', wrote J. H. Ingraham, a popular religious novelist. 'Cities are the result of the fall'. To deal with some of the effects of the fall the settlement movement swept through both countries, with Toynbee Hall, founded in 1884, serving as a source of inspiration for Chicago's Hull House (1889). Jane Addams, the founder of Hull House, was only one of a band of Americans who visited East London's Toynbee Hall during the 1880s and 1890s. The others included Stanton Coit, the founder of New York's Neighborhood Guild, and Charles Zueblin, the pioneer of Chicago urban sociology. The fact that as many as eighteen nations were represented in the area around Hull House distinguished Chicago from London. Ethnic problems were as dominating as class problems were in Manchester. There were other differences also. The fear of city crime in the United States, particularly of highly organized crime, was greater than that in Britain. There was no English book quite like C. L. Brace's *The Dangerous Classes of New York*. As for the fear of city politics, there was no English counterpart of the American agrarian radical movements. The English countryside still belonged to the landlord and the squire.

One interesting mid-century American writer, A. D. Mayo, stressed the special fears of Americans in his fascinating book *The Symbols of the Capital; or Civilisation in New York* (1859). European cities, he argued, forgetting the existence of places like Manchester, had enjoyed long periods of slow, organic growth. They had historic roots and guiding traditions, yet, as Vaughan had pointed out, they also were serving the cause of human progress in the nineteenth century by wrestling political liberty from feudal overlords. In America the overlords were the city bosses. The cities themselves were transit camps. The slums were not excrescences but collecting points for new arrivals. The saloons were more wicked than inns or public houses. 'An American city is only a convenient hotel, where a free country people come up to tarry and do business. ... It is not the deep, firm root out of which rises the trunk and foliage of a great nationality; rather a boat tossed on the billows of American enterprise and emigration.' Brace came to similar conclusions when he started to survey living conditions in New York City in 1852.

The decade from 1840 to 1850 had seen a sharp rise in the city population of the United States, yet the sharpest rise of the century did not take place until after Mayo had written.

During the decade from 1880 to 1890 there was a dramatic leap ahead, associated with large-scale immigration. The United States went through its great 'urban revolution' in the late nineteenth and early twentieth centuries. Between 1860 and 1910 places with more than 50,000 inhabitants increased in number from 16 to 109. Chicago more than doubled its size in the single decade from 1880 to 1890; the Twin Cities of Minneapolis-St Paul actually trebled in size. Detroit, Milwaukee, Columbus and Cleveland increased by 60 to 80 per cent. Los Angeles, which was to be a 'shock city' in the twentieth century, increased in number from 5,000 in 1860 to more than 100,000 in 1900. By 1890 New York (including Brooklyn) had almost caught up with Paris. 'We are now a nation of cities,' wrote W. H. Tolman in 1895.

The response to this 'urban revolution' showed the same ambivalence as the British response. 'Where the carcase is, the vultures gather together,' wrote Francis Parkman. On the other side Josiah Strong, with equal eloquence, called cities 'the mighty heart of the body politic sending out whole streams of light pulsating to the very finger-tips of the whole land.' Walt Whitman on returning to New York in 1870 had praised 'the splendour, picturesqueness, and oceanic amplitude' of the great American cities. Another American, Oliver Wendell Holmes, tired of hearing Cowper's line, 'God made the country and man made the town', offered his own version – 'God made the cavern and man made the house'.

The American 'urban revolution' made contemporaries ask exactly the same questions as Englishmen had asked in the explosive years of the 1840s – 'What shall we do with our great cities? What will our great cities do with us?' The answers drew upon the same variety of sources of inspiration as the English answers. Clearly cities in the ancient world had been thought of as 'fireplaces of civilization', yet America was not the ancient world. The 'degradation' was more often apparent. Clearly cities could be extremely well managed and sometimes were, but then American cities had no traditions of government, no ingrained sense of order, and they were inhabited by large numbers of new immigrants who at best thought of them as welcome places of refuge rather than as potential utopias. James Bryce considered municipal government 'the one conspicuous failure of the United States'. Andrew D. White asserted in 1890 that 'with very few exceptions, the city governments of the United States are the worst in Christendom – the most expensive, the most inefficient, and the most corrupt.' Words like 'shame' and 'redemption' were freely applied to the destiny of cities, not only by the muck-rakers. Josiah Strong coupled his eloquent defence of the social influence of the city with an equally eloquent demand that the problems of the city should be attacked energetically and courageously. The alliance of politicians with vested economic interests should be broken, as should the debasing alliance between party bosses and new immigrants dealing in municipal franchises. Jefferson had called cities 'ulcers on the body politic': the favourite late nineteenth-century word was 'cancer'.

To these local expressions of a wide-ranging international literature the Americans added an increasing knowledge (through reading or travel) of the cities of other parts of the world. They recognized that their great burst of urban growth was not simply an American phenomenon. Henry Fletcher, for instance, Professor at the University of Minnesota, in his study of *The Drift of Population to Cities* (1891) described the suburban movement as 'universal', compared America with Australia, and quoted Sir Charles Dilke. The urban movement, he complained, 'swells the number of the classes most exposed to agitation and discontent, intensifies the dangers to be apprehended from social upheavals and widens the growing chasm between classes'. He ended with the somewhat forlorn hope that 'the accumulated miseries of over-grown cities' would eventually 'drive the people back to the land'. 'A pure sky amid the quietness of nature' represented his ideal of healthy living.

Fletcher's 'back to the land' ideas were not acceptable to A. F. Weber, America's first statistician of cities, to Delos F. Wilcox, whose *Great Cities in America* brings out the individuality of each of the American cities, or to the outstanding city reformer, Frederick C. Howe, whose writings provide a kind of epilogue to the nineteenth-century American story. *The City, the Hope of Democracy* (1905) was a manifesto, particularly relevant in a decade of exceptional interest in schemes for city reform. Howe accepted the city as the greatest social innovation of modern times. 'Through it, a new society has been created. Life in all its relations has been altered. A new civilization has been born, a civilization whose identity with the past is one of historical continuity.' It is significant that Howe followed this manifesto with a book on *The British City* (1907). It is even more significant, however, that the Report of the Commission on Country Life presented to President Theodore Roosevelt in 1909 acknowledged the diminishing esteem in which country life was held in the United States and indirectly endorsed the primacy of urban life. While emphasizing that 'the great recent progress made in city life is not a full measure of our civilization', it noted the failure of country life, 'as it exists at present', to satisfy 'the higher social and intellectual aspirations of country people'. In the background of an authoritative statement of this kind was a long-term change in popular valuations. As Professor A. M. Schlesinger has put it in his pioneer study, *The Rise of the City, 1878–98* (1933), 'It was the city rather than the unpeopled wilderness that was beginning to dazzle the imagination of the nation. The farmer, once the pride of America, was descending from his lofty estate, too readily accepting the city's scornful estimate of him as a "rube" and a "hayseed"'. 'We must face the inevitable,' Josiah Strong exclaimed; 'the new civilization is certain to be urban, and the problem of the twentieth century will be in the city.'

American urban experience – and American attitudes towards it – was of great interest to Englishmen or at least to those Englishmen who were interested in the relationship between cities and society. Conservative writers, in particular, argued that it was in America and in Australia that the 'dangers' of the city were most apparent, just as it was there too that the worst excesses of democracy were most apparent. Even liberals were often shocked by the government of almost all American cities. On a visit to New York in 1867–8 Charles Dickens wrote that 'the general corruption in respect of local funds appears to be stupendous'.[1] 'The light of Mammon gleams on nearly every face in Broadway and Wall Street,' an Englishwoman remarked in the 1870s. Another feature of New York that was often commented upon was its 'high pressure' living. The 'nervous, spasmodic, excitable' aspect of life in a city seemed to have been magnified in New York: Oscar Wilde, arriving in 1882 to lecture on the English Renaissance, said that all the inhabitants seemed to be 'in a hurry to catch a train'. A year earlier Dr George Beard in his *American Nervousness* had coined the word 'neurasthenia' to describe the malady of the noisy and crowded streets.

Chicago, as we have seen, fascinated many English visitors. An excellent article in the *Fortnightly Review* by Henry Trueman Wood, the Secretary to the Royal Commission for the British Section of the Chicago Exhibition of 1893, sharply criticized his fellow compatriots who had called it a 'purposeless hell'. He extolled the 'wonderful city' which was more interesting than any English provincial city and even London itself. 'London, or Manchester, or Leeds today is practically identical with London or Manchester or Leeds of twenty years ago. [This was quite untrue.] A description of the Chicago of five years back is now obsolete and inapplicable.' At the same time he had reservations. 'The soft coal burnt in Chicago produces a grimy smoke that would do credit to Manchester or Leeds.... The nominal boundaries of the city are miles away out on the prairie. They were made as Napoleon made streets in Paris, by ruling lines on maps with a big pencil, and even at its present rate of growth Chicago will take a generation or two before she fills out to them.... If the citizens could only know the drawbacks of greatness, could realize the hideous inconveniences, they would not be in such a hurry to extend their boundaries.'

The reference to Napoleon III was duplicated in many

1. He also wrote, however, that 'The Irish element is acquiring such enormous influence in New York city, that when I think of it, and see the large Roman Catholic cathedral rising there, it seems unfair to stigmatize as "American" other monstrous things that one also sees.' For these and other comments on New York, see Professor Bayrd Still's volume *Mirror for Gotham, New York as seen by Contemporaries from Dutch Days to the Present* (New York, 1956).

articles on cities both in the United States and in Britain, at least as often as late nineteenth-century writers referred back to Baudelaire. The planning and rebuilding of Paris, in particular, was a favourite theme of civic reformers. Napoleon's interest in sanitary reform won the approval of Chadwick: the sponsors of the Birmingham improvement scheme of the 1870s dreamed of creating Parisian boulevards as the citizens of Brussels and Barcelona were creating them. In the United States, Daniel Burnham's plans for Washington and Chicago owed much to Napoleon and his great planner, Baron Haussmann. In the last year of the century, when reform of London's government was in the air, there were frequent cross-references to Paris in the English debate. The opponents of strong and unified London government on an elected basis were at pains to point out that although there was a Municipal Council in Paris, the city was effectively governed by the Prefect of the Seine and his colleague the Prefect of Police, both of whom were appointed by the government and were responsible directly to the Minister of the Interior. Strong executive power in Paris was admired by a minority of Englishmen throughout the whole Victorian age – just as a bigger and more influential minority admired the efficient bureaucratic government of some of the German cities. 'Oh! for a temporary but sharp despotism,' Lord Shaftesbury once exclaimed in a fit of exasperation, 'which would pass beneficent laws and compel men even against their wills to do wisely.'

English religious attitudes, Evangelical or Nonconformist, prohibited real admiration of the way of life of European cities, their Continental Sundays, open-air cafés, promenades in the twilight, and even some of their ancient traditions. Yet another minority took up the challenge. Taine described a society to secularize Sundays which demanded that museums be opened on Sundays, concerts allowed and also public lectures. During the 1890s there was an Anti-Puritan League in London which won the support of some of the ablest men of the age. Among them was G. K. Chesterton.

During the last years of the century, in what was called at the time 'fin-de-siècle London', there was increasing recognition that all cities, Continental and English, were posing similar problems and providing similar opportunities. There had been great urban growth throughout Western Europe during the previous forty years. Paris, like London, had doubled its population between 1851 and 1891: its demographic and social history, for all the differences of mood, was dominated by what were often similar trends. Berlin had more than quadrupled its size during the period as Germany was industrialized and the political structure was unified. There had been 21 cities in Europe with a population of more than 100,000 in 1801; in 1901 there were 147, accounting for at least a tenth of Europe's population. In all the countries of Europe during this period urban gains were associated with rural losses: the debate about rural and urban values was often fought out not with myths about cowboys and bushmen but with hard statistics concerning movements of the population and the balance of economic interests.

3

It is necessary to turn from the debate, British and foreign, to the detailed experience of particular cities in order to understand both cities and 'Victorianism'. What the Victorians said about cities illuminates what they thought and felt about much else. Yet it was the fact that they lived in the cities – or chose not to live in them – which dominates Victorian social history.

For all their problems, the cities were often focal points of affection and loyalty. The provincial cities nurtured the sense of loyalty through rivalry with each other and solidarity against the metropolis. They used their status as regional capitals to challenge the claims of the national capital, both culturally and politically. The affection which they inspired could not be manufactured. People felt that they belonged to particular cities, and each with its own identity. And sometimes even those who manifestly did not belong might feel affection. Alexander Herzen, the romantic exile, writing of London not very long before Ruskin condemned it so scathingly, admitted that he came 'to love this dreadful ant-heap, where every night thousand men know not where they will lay their heads and the police often find women and children dead of a hunger beside hotels where one cannot dine for less than two pounds'.

London was *sui generis*, vast, seemingly limitless, equivalent, according to Taine, to twelve cities the size of Marseilles, ten as big as Lyons, two the size of Paris in a 'single mass'. 'Words on paper are no substitute for the effect on the eyes. You have to spend several days in succession in a cab, driving out north, south, east and west, for a whole morning, as far as those vague limits where houses grow scarcer and the country has no room to begin.' By the end of the century it was beginning to be difficult to tell where London ended. It is interesting to note that between 1881 and 1891 the four communities with the highest rates of population growth in England were all suburbs of London – Leyton, Tottenham, West Ham and Willesden. In the next ten years the story was the same, with Croydon, East Ham, Hornsey and Walthamstow added to the previous four in the top group.

The facts of demography as much as the facts of politics forced London into increasing prominence during the 1880s and 1890s. That is one reason why this book ends with the metropolis. It begins, however, with the English provincial cities, which grew at what seemed fantastic rates just before and just after Queen Victoria came to the throne. Between 1821 and 1831 the population of Manchester increased by 44.9 per cent, that of Leeds by 47.3 per cent, that of Bradford by 65.5 per cent, that of Birmingham by 41.5 per cent, that of Liverpool by 45.8 per cent, that of Sheffield by 40.5 per cent. The increase continued during the following two decades at a somewhat diminished rate. Leeds, for instance, grew from 152,054 in 1841 to 172,270 in 1851, Bradford from 34,560 to 103,778, Manchester from 217,056 to 250,409, Liverpool from 286,487 to 375,955, Birmingham from 182,922 to 232,841.

The facts by themselves are not enough, not only because of the debate about their general significance but because each city was itself the subject of debate. There were often the same differences of opinion about particular places as there were about urbanization as a whole. Mrs Siddons thought

Leeds 'the most disagreeable town in His Majesty's dominions' and Dickens called it (in its early-Victorian phase) 'a beastly place, one of the nastiest places I know', yet G. S. Phillips, a local writer strongly influenced by Emerson, called it 'one of the grandest poems which has ever been offered to the world'. 'I find in it passages of such wondrous terror and beauty,' he went on, 'revelations so profound and thoughts so awful and tremendous that in the utter impotence of man to have conjured up the magnificently suggestive creation I can believe in it only as an effusion of the Eternal Mind.' Yet a further response to Leeds, this time purely rhetorical, was the heading given to one of Macaulay's early electoral speeches by his first biographer – 'Loveliness and Intelligence of Leeds'.

What may be called the 'image' of the particular city depended, therefore, not only upon the facts but upon the imaginative power with which people arranged the facts in a pattern. It was through its image as much as through the facts relating to it that Manchester, the first city in this book, established itself as the 'shock city' of the age.

CHAPTER THREE

Manchester, Symbol of a New Age

Manchester streets may be irregular, and its trading inscriptions pretentious, its smoke may be dense, and its mud ultra-muddy, but not any or all of these things can prevent the image of a great city rising before us as the very symbol of civilization, foremost in the march of improvement, a grand incarnation of progress.

Chambers' Edinburgh Journal (1858)

I

WHEN William Cobbett visited Frome in Somerset in 1826, he described it, simply but contemptuously, as 'a sort of little Manchester'. 'A very small Manchester indeed,' he added, 'but it has all the *flash* of a Manchester, and the innkeepers and their people look and behave like Manchester fellows.'

Manchester, like Birmingham, already had its reputation. It was not a new community, but during the last quarter of the eighteenth century it had 'extended on every side'. In early Tudor England Leland had described it as 'the fairest, best buildid, quikkest and most populous tounne of all Lancashire', and that was long before the local economy was transformed by the development of the cotton industry during the boom years of the 1770s and 1780s. Cotton made modern Manchester. It created a small class of wealthy men – they were perhaps the first men to think of themselves as a 'class' – and a large class of 'working men' who were often doomed to severe suffering. Cotton also transformed the whole appearance and prospects of the neighbourhood.

A French visitor in 1784 called Manchester a 'large and superb town ... built almost entirely in the past twenty to twenty-five years'. Between the late 1780s and the first census of 1801 the population of the township rose from over 40,000 to over 70,000. By 1831, when it had a population of 142,000, it was still a small place by later standards, yet it was felt to be one of the 'phenomena of the age'. It was already associated far outside its tangled administrative boundaries with size, with industry, with newness, with squalor, and, above all else, with unfamiliar and, on occasion, alarming social relationships.

The population of Manchester in 1831 had increased nearly six times in sixty years, and by nearly 45 per cent in the previous decade, its greatest decennial rate of growth in the nineteenth century. No one doubted that the cotton industry explained the increasing size and wealth of the town: the 'din of machinery' was the music of economic progress. There was no local government either to encourage or to restrain. All depended on individual enterprise. Manchester became 'one of the commercial capitals of Europe' long before it became an incorporated town in 1838. Its 'progress' was reflected both in the newness of the buildings and in the squalor. Few of the buildings were distinguished, and many of them were already blackened with smoke by the beginning of the nineteenth century. They were buildings which the nostalgic Southey, a prejudiced observer, noted were 'as large as convents without their antiquity, without their beauty, without their holiness'. The squalor was the by-product, thought to be a necessary by-product, of increasing wealth. 'The town is abominably filthy,' a visitor from Rotherham (of all places) declared as early as 1808, 'the Steam Engine is pestiferous, the Dyehouses noisesome and offensive, and the water of the river as black as ink or the Stygian lake.'

The social relations of Manchester were frequently discussed in general terms both inside and outside the town, by inhabitants and by strangers. As early as the 1780s, writers were describing a 'growing gulf' between rich and poor. By 1820 it was a commonplace to attribute basic social and political differences to economic divisions of interest between mill owners and workers, factory hands and handloom weavers. In a bad year, like 1817, the Blanketeers could talk of 'making a Moscow of Manchester'. In 1819, the year of 'the massacre of Peterloo', with which Manchester was afterwards irrevocably associated, the handloom weavers, hitherto politically conservative, could themselves be drawn into social disturbances d to threaten not only local peace but national pital of an industry became the capital of dis- ... Here there seems no sympathy between the upper and lower classes of society,' a local newspaper complained in August 1819, 'there is no mutual confidence, no bond of attachment.' 'Their wretchedness', *The Times* reported of the discontented Manchester working classes a few days after Peterloo, 'seems to madden them against the rich, who they dangerously imagine engross the fruits of their labour without having any sympathy for their wants.'

Samuel Bamford, a working-class Radical who was involved in the bitter disturbances at the end of the Napoleonic Wars and ended his life as a respectable and respected mid-Victorian Liberal, called the bridge across the 'turbid and black' River Irwell, which linked Manchester and Salford, 'the Bridge of Tears'. 'Venice hath her "Bridge of Sighs"; Manchester its "Bridge of Tears".'

Although the tears were wiped away during boom years of the early 1820s, after the boom came slump. The year 1829 saw renewed outbreaks of popular discontent. There was no opportunity of canalizing this discontent along constitutional channels as was possible in the popular parliamentary constituency of near-by Preston. The result was that in the course of the Reform Bill struggles of the years 1831 and 1832 Manchester enhanced its national reputation as a centre of social disturbances, even as a possible cradle of revolution. The handloom weavers remained restive. Some of them, Francis Place suggested, hoped for revolution rather than for reform; for 'a revolution in which they might gain but could not lose'. The relatively sophisticated cotton spinners, the aristocracy of the new labour force, admitted 'the misrepresentation of the people' under the existing political system, but were sceptical of parliamentary reform unless it involved social readjustment based on the right of workmen to the 'whole fruits of their labour'.

So powerful were working-class interests in Manchester that it proved impossible there to unite middle classes and working classes in one single reform movement as Thomas Attwood was able to do in Birmingham. Extremists were too active to allow the moderates room to manoeuvre. Archib. Prentice, the Manchester radical journalist, who wanted t lead a common agitation, complained unhappily that 'two classes were ranged against each other in a hostility, which daily grew more bitter, each taking that antagonistic position to the other that they should have taken against that which occasioned the distress of both.' The successful candidates at the general election of 1832, Mark Philips and Poulett Thompson, were regarded as doctrinaire opponents of factory legislation and of further extension of the suffrage and bitter enemies of the working classes.

The language of the struggle was rich and colourful. A parody on the Litany, the Reformers' Prayer, was circulating freely in Manchester in 1831 – 'From all those damnable bishops, lords and peers, from all those bloody murdering Peterloo butchers, from all those idle drones that live on the earnings of the people, good Lord deliver us.' There was fear rather than hope behind a plea of the *Manchester Guardian* in June 1832 that there never was a time when it was more incumbent on the middle and higher classes to show 'their poorer brethren' that 'the bond between them' was not yet broken. The *Manchester Guardian* was itself described a little later by its rival the *Manchester Advertiser* as 'the common heap in which every purse-proud booby shoots his basket of dirt and falsehood . . . foul prostitute and dirty parasite of the worst portion of the mill owners'.

These social relations, already determining the pattern of local politics, were directly related to the other four features of Manchester which Cobbett and others discovered. The size of the city seemed to diminish the power of traditional social influence and of accepted local leadership. The industry determined not only who had wealth and who had no wealth but who was listened to and who had to listen. The newness implied the tearing up of roots and the absence from Manchester, both for good and ill, of those ties, links and bonds of attachment which were taken for granted in older places. The squalor went with the increasing social segregation, particularly in those districts which were concealed from the view of the richer inhabitants or were inhabited by poor Irish

The most notorious area was 'little Ireland', ived near the River Medlock a community unity. 'This unhealthy district lies so low', J. P. Kay, a local doctor, in 1832, 'that the chimneys of its houses, some of them three stories high, are little above the level of the ground.' The district was 'surrounded on every side by some of the largest factories of the town, whose chimneys vaunt forth dense clouds of smoke, which hang heavily over this insalubrious region.' Inside the houses several families might be living under one roof or even in 'the pestilential atmosphere' of one room.

It is hardly surprising that in such circumstances Manchester enjoyed 'an unenviable notoriety on account of its rioting propensities'. 'The civic force of the town' was recognized to be 'totally inadequate to defend property from the attacks of lawless depredators'. With no adequate police, no effective machinery of modern local government, a disturbed social system which lacked the 'benevolent influence' of 'natural gradations', and an economy subject to fluctuations and developing on the basis of obvious conflicts of interest, Manchester was felt to provide a persistent threat to that 'good order' on which statesmen and moralists loved to dwell. In the eighteenth century and even in the late Napoleonic Wars there had been a strong residual conservatism in Manchester, which made the town a centre of 'loyalism' and 'patriotism'. The contrast between then and now was even more real to Cobbett's political enemies than to Cobbett himself. The town could no longer be 'controlled'. Ten years after Peterloo, in the riots of May 1829, it was reported that while troops moved up and down the streets to disperse rioters, 'the crowds ran down the narrow lanes and passages by which the principal streets are intersected; and no sooner had the troops passed than they issued from their retreat and crowded the streets as densely as before'.

Ten years later, Manchester was still associated with the same basic features which contemporaries had seized upon after the Napoleonic Wars and during the Reform Bill crisis. In the meantime, however, outside interest in Manchester had increased. The town was felt increasingly to be a kind of

symbol, a centre of 'modern life' which all students of so
were required to understand, what a writer in the *Peop..*
Journal in 1847 called 'the type of a new power in the earth'.

The often quoted comments in Disraeli's *Coningsby* (1844) about Manchester are not as exceptional as they are sometimes taken to be. They were representative, indeed, of most contemporary social comment. 'The age of ruins is past,' Sidonia told Coningsby when they met at the forest inn. 'Have you seen Manchester?' he asked. Coningsby's social education really started only when he left the forest and devoted several days to 'the comprehension of Manchester'. 'Certainly Manchester is the most wonderful city of modern times,' he concluded. 'It is the philosopher alone who can conceive the grandeur of Manchester and the immensity of its future.'

These statements followed Disraeli's visit to Manchester in October 1843 when he addressed a literary meeting at the Free Trade Hall with Charles Dickens in the chair and Richard Cobden on the platform. Two years earlier George Smythe and Lord John Manners, the leaders of 'Young England', the movement of the 'new generation', for whom and about whom *Coningsby* was written, had also visited Manchester. They were fascinated by its 'vitality' and alarmed by its problems: there never was a more complete feudal system, so they thought, than that in the mills, and they believed that to control exploitation there should be government regulation of working conditions. Carlyle, who influenced Disraeli through his writings, particularly his *Past and Present* (1843), had visited Manchester too. For him Manchester was 'every whit as wonderful, as fearful, as unimaginable, as the oldest Salem or prophetic city'. He considered also, however, that 'sooty Manchester' was built 'upon the infinite abysses'. There was wonder in the prospect, but there was also alarm.

Interest in Manchester was greater during the late 1830s and 1840s than in 1832 or even in 1819. It was also, as these extracts suggest, more profound and searching than the earlier interest. There were two images of Manchester in the late 1830s and 1840s, not one. The first was the older image of the city as a cradle of economic wealth and of social disorder.

s a newer image of the city as a cradle both of ew and formative social values.

xcitement of Manchester was that behind its qualor it seemed to be creating a new order of nessmen, energetic, tough, proud, contemptuous of the old aristocracy and yet in some sense constituting an aristocracy themselves – an urban aristocracy – men who were beginning to seek political as well as economic power, power not only in Manchester but in the country as a whole. Disraeli's Millbank, although his factory was outside Manchester, was a symbolic figure of this world, 'a new world pregnant with new ideas and suggestive of new trains of thought and of feeling'. He was the kind of man who built 'illumined factories with more windows than Italian palaces and smoking chimneys taller than Italian obelisks'. He made money, but he was interested in something more than making money. His great factory, the scene of 'the last and the most refined inventions of mechanical genius' had been 'fitted up by a capitalist as anxious to raise a monument of the skill and power of his order, as to obtain a return for the great investment'.

Other 'critics' of Manchester took a different line and discerned the outline of a new order not in the aspirations of businessmen but in the discontent of the Manchester working classes. Friedrich Engels, who drew on Carlyle at least as heavily as Disraeli did, agreed with Manners and Smythe that the influence of the factory owner 'went further than that of the Norman baron'. Engels reached a radically different conclusion about the future, however, and set out to demonstrate that this new 'feudalism' could only end – in an industrial city – in successful 'proletarian revolution'. Urban life helped 'to weld the proletariat into a compact group with its own ways of life and thought and its own outlook on society'. Manchester, which he claimed that he knew as well as his own native Rhineland, was 'the classic type of modern industrial town'. It was a grim place to live in, but its growth was a necessary and exciting stage in the unfolding of modern history. What would become of its 'populous millions' who 'owned nothing and consumed today what they earned yesterday'? What was to be the future of 'those who are daily becoming more and more aware of their power and pressing more and more strongly for their share of the social advantages of the new era'? Engels was confident. The snapping of 'the bond of personal devotion', which undoubtedly entailed distress and disorder, was a necessary act if the 'proletariat' was to become conscious of its own destiny. It was this change 'which forced the workers to think for themselves and to demand a fuller life in human society'.

Disraeli deplored the existence of 'two nations' and the new division of England into classes which he noted in Manchester. 'How are manners to influence men if they are divided into classes – if the population of a country becomes a body of sections, a group of hostile garrisons?' Dickens also welcomed the fact that in the Athenaeum building, where he once took the chair for Disraeli, they were upon 'neutral ground, where we have no more knowledge of party differences, or public animosities between side and side, or between man and man, than if we were at a public meeting in the commonwealth of Utopia'. Engels sharply disagreed. Despite his economic and social position, he welcomed the conflict. He believed that workers in Manchester had made their first steps along the road towards 'liberation' when they had escaped from 'the happy vegetation' of the countryside to live in the growing city. They were equipping themselves with effective new armour when they exchanged their older feelings of personal obligation for a new sense of class. In exposing the slums, Engels did not thereby attack the existence of the city. He would never have coined a phrase like Lewis Mumford's 'insensate industrial town'.

Neither Disraeli nor Engels was exceptional in his line of argument. Throughout the 1840s, contemporary observers, British and foreign, came to the conclusion that the social divisions of Manchester were creative rather than destructive, that they generated something more than riots and disturbances, and that they deserved prophets rather than policemen to understand them. There was no shortage of social prophecy in the 1840s – Engels predicted revolution 'with the certainty of the laws of mathematics or mechanics' – and it is remarkable that however much the prophets disagreed in the remedies they advocated, they presented very similar diagnoses. Economic historians writing in the twentieth century may refuse to draw sharp distinctions between 'the hungry forties' and the decades of the twenties or thirties, but the social prophets of the day did. They showed a preference for figures of speech to statistics, pointed unanimously to what Carlyle called the grip of the 'cash nexus', soundly admonished parliament for failing to provide leadership, 'explained' why discontent led to agitation, and sought to 'read' the 'true character' of their age both by comparing it with other ages in the past and by relating it to new ages in the future. In all these activities they felt that they had to go to Manchester to help them to find out 'the truth'.

All roads led to Manchester in the 1840s. Since it was the shock city of the age, it was just as difficult to be neutral about it as it was to be neutral about Chicago in the 1890s or Los Angeles in the 1930s. Chicago forced to the surface ethnic problems, the relations between one linguistic group and another in a national 'melting pot': Manchester forced to the surface problems of 'class', of the relations between rich and poor.

There were three main reasons why interest in Manchester increased in the late 1830s and 1840s. The first was the inevitable lag in imaginative response to the most interesting new phenomena of the age. Writing about English society as a whole was more vivid and more influential during the 1840s than it had been in the 1820s or the early 1830s. This was partly, of course, because of actual changes in society and the feeling that new generations demanded new insights as well as new information. It was also because 'pure politics', the politics of the Reform Bill, had proved so unsatisfactory. There was a demand for social rather than for purely political explanations and for social rather than purely political remedies. The enormous growth of the cities between 1831 and 1841 provided writers with almost limitless material: it was all concerned, as George Saintsbury wrote later in the century, with 'strange and to a certain extent unnatural conditions of life, not paralleled in any former state of history'. The local defenders of Manchester might argue, as did the Rev. R. Parkinson, Canon of the Collegiate Church, in 1839, that there was nothing 'unnatural' or 'opposed to the will of God' in the growth of manufacturing industry, but they failed to convince everyone that the 'civic economy' was healthy and beneficial.

The second reason, the economic depression in Manchester and the industrial districts which followed the financial crisis of 1836, was related to the first. The depression was the first great prolonged depression since the industrial revolution, much more severe in the cotton districts than the slump which followed the boom of the early 1820s. It entailed a fall in businessmen's profits and large-scale unemployment for the workers. Both these consequences gave a powerful impetus to 'agitation', middle-class and working-class. Manchester was a centre of disturbance again, but it was disturbance of a cyclical kind within the framework of a new system rather than the structural change of an old system. What would happen to social relations in such a setting? Manchester seemed to hold the key to 'the condition of England' question on the national stage.

The third reason was linked with the second. Two political movements emerged, Chartism and the Anti-Corn Law League, which attracted national attention. The former, although it began with a London manifesto, was shaped by North of England experience and objectives: the latter was clearly stamped from the start with the designation 'made in Manchester'. To understand the two main movements in contemporary politics – in both cases the politics were social – it was necessary above all else to understand Manchester.

2

The first of these three reasons for intensified interest is reflected in the great vogue of Thomas Carlyle as 'the interpreter of the age'. 'There was the utmost avidity for his books ... especially among the young men' and 'phrases from them were in all young men's mouths and were affecting the public speech'. Carlyle emphasized that the answers to ultimate as well as to contemporary questions lay in imagination rather than in logic. 'To know, to get into the truth of anything, is ever a mystic act.' Reacting as Disraeli and, in a different sense, Engels, did against the 'fallacies' of utilitarianism, he held that imagination could point in two directions – 'Priest and Prophet to lead us heavenward; or Magician and Wizard to lead us hellward.' He revelled in contrasts of mood as well as of direction, and the new industrial cities were theatres of contrast: indeed, absolute contrasts always fascinated him, as they fascinated so many writers who examined the consequences of industrialization. The phenomena of his own time had eternal as well as transitory significance. 'Mere political arrangements' provided no answer to social ills, nor did the accumulation of 'mere statistics' about economic progress. In saying this, Carlyle was often close both to Disraeli and to Engels. It was his approach as much as the content of his work which gave it its appeal.

At the same time during the 1840s there was increasing scope for developing these themes not only through tracts and pamphlets but through fiction. The phenomena of the age could be 'considered by any one in an absolutely historical spirit' because of 'changes of economic and political opinion', Saintsbury wrote, and novels had special interpretative value because they would take account of many opinions. 'There exist not a few pictures, avowedly or slightly disguised,' he added, 'of the state of affairs . . . which the rise of the modern cotton trade in what is called Cottonopolis has brought about.' There were other reasons why fiction became the medium of interpretation. Disraeli gave it as his reason for writing his trilogy of political novels, *Coningsby* (1844), *Sybil* (1845) and *Tancred* (1847), that fiction 'in the temper of the times offered the best chance of influencing opinion'. Kathleen Tillotson has shown how general this reasoning was in her fascinating monograph, *Novels of the Eighteen-Forties* (1954). Society novels were giving way to novels about society during the 1840s, and books about fashion, particularly the old silver-fork novels of the 1820s and early 1830s, were becoming increasingly unfashionable. Carlyle's attack in *Sartor Resartus* on one of the older style of novels, *Pelham*, was important in this connexion. So too was Dickens's offer in his introduction to *Oliver Twist* (1841) to render a 'service to society' by painting pictures not of 'moonlit heaths' but of 'cold, wet, shelterless midnight streets of London'. Where are now all the novels patronizing fashionable life with which the shops of publishers teemed, and the shelves of circulating libraries groaned, not ten years ago?' *Blackwood's* asked in 1845. 'Buried,' it answered, 'in the Vault of the Capulets.'

Manchester was exciting enough to attract writers as the older themes lost their point, for a time much more exciting than London. Equally important, it was exciting – and mysterious enough – to attract readers. The resistance of the more conservative readers doubtless had to be overcome with friendly advice from reviewers that they 'need not be alarmed at the prospect of penetrating the recesses of Manchester', but the more adventurous turned to novels about Manchester precisely because they were both novels and social documents. Englishmen have always preferred to take doses of sociology in the form of fiction. If 'people on Turkey carpets with their three meals a day' were anxious to know 'why working men turn Chartists and Communists', they meditated on Mrs Gaskell's *Mary Barton* (1848), sub-titled 'A Tale of Manchester Life', with its detailed eye-witness account of the contemporary town. *Fraser's Magazine* explicitly recommended the novel because it answered questions of the kind Carlyle asked. 'Do they want to know why poor men ... learn to hate law and order, Queen, Lords and Commons, country-party and corn-law league alike – to hate the rich, in short? Then let them read *Mary Barton*. Do they want to know what can madden brave, honest, industrious north-country hearts, into self-imposed suicidal strikes, into conspiracy, vitriol-throwing and midnight murder? Then let them read *Mary Barton*.... Do they want to get a detailed insight into the whole science of starving? ... Let them read *Mary Barton*.'

The language of this passage makes it abundantly plain that novels about Manchester were felt to have their own 'romance'. The social novel marked not so much an anti-romantic reaction as a shift in romantic interest from high society to urban society, and, for many writers, to low society. Mrs Gaskell tried deliberately to discover 'romance in the lives of some of those who elbowed me daily in the busy streets of the town Manchester where I resided'. Disraeli, more conventionally, had Sidonia introduce the theme of Manchester to Coningsby in an adventure in a genuinely romantic Forest.

Manchester mill owners themselves, who were thought by one of their most enlightened spokesmen, W. R. Greg, to have been treated very unfairly indeed by Mrs Gaskell, were not above emphasizing the romance of their own calling. Had Providence not planted the cotton shrubs, they maintained, 'those majestic masses of men which stretch, like a living zone, through our central districts, would have had no existence; and the magic impulse which has been felt during that period in every department of national energy, which has affected more or less our literature, our laws, our social condition, our political institutions, making us almost a new people, would never have been communicated'. There was more romance in the achievements of the cotton merchants and mill owners, they implied, than in the improvidence of the cotton operatives. 'What a satisfaction it is to every man going from the West to the East, when he clambers up Mount Lebanon, to find one of the ancient Druses clothed in garments with which our industrious countrymen provided him.' Henry Dunckley, who won an Anti-Corn Law League prize for an essay called *The Charter of the Nations* (1854) and later became editor of the *Manchester Examiner*, wrote proudly, 'trade has now a chivalry of its own; a chivalry whose stars are radiant with the more benignant lustre of justice, happiness, and religion, and whose titles will outlive the barbarous nomenclature of Charlemagne'.

Readers of novels about Manchester appreciated them, however, because they were exciting, not because cotton shirts were agents of civilization. The novels revealed much which it was difficult to find out from other sources, precisely because class dividing lines (and dividing lines between North and South) were sharply defined and people's knowledge of 'the other nation' was usually strictly limited. The novelists were recognized to be social explorers. Disraeli advertised *Sybil* as a study of the unknown. 'So little do we know of the state of our own country, that the air of improbability which the whole truth would inevitably throw over these pages, might deter some from their perusal.' One of his reviewers saluted him as 'a traveller into new regions of humanity ... who setting out from the salons of the luxurious, penetrates into the dark and unknown regions of the populace'. Charles Dickens, who dedicated *Hard Times* (1854) to Carlyle, was praised for the same reason. Mrs Gaskell, who wrote of Manchester from direct personal experience, her novel growing in her mind 'as imperceptibly as a seed germinates in the earth', set out to 'give utterance to the agony ... of dumb people'. Concerned as she was with particular individuals, she was conscious of one great 'prevailing thought', 'the seeming injustice of the inequalities of fortune'. It is said that *Mary Barton* was read by the cotton operatives also – they clubbed up to buy it – because it helped them to realize 'the heights as well as the depths' of their nature.

The accounts by novelists of their social explorations helped to put Manchester on the map. So too did the Blue Books and official and unofficial statistical reports of the 1840s, which demonstrated that Manchester, although one of the most thriving cities in the country, was also one of the most unhealthy. Differences in mortality rates were directly related to differences in economic livelihood. In the famous *Report on the Sanitary Condition of the Labouring Population of Great Britain* (1842) Manchester statistics were put beside those of Rutland. This was hardly intended as a compliment.

CLASSIFICATION	AVERAGE AGE OF DEATH (*years*)	
	In Manchester	*In Rutlandshire*
Professional persons and gentry, and their families	38	52
Tradesmen and their families (in Rutlandshire, farmers and graziers are included with shopkeepers)	20	41
Mechanics, labourers, and their families	17	38

The 'inequalities of fortune' were reflected not only in the pattern of industrial relations within the factories but in the embryonic public services of the town. 'The expense of cleaning the streets of Manchester', the report noted, 'is £5,000 per annum. For this sum the first class of streets, namely the most opulent and the large thoroughfares, are cleansed once a week, the second class once a fortnight, and the third class once a month. But this provision leaves untouched, or leaves in the condition described in Dr Baron Howard's report, the courts, alleys and places where the poorest classes live, and where the cleansing should be daily.'

The Blue Books were freely used by the novelists. So also were the local reports on Manchester which had been prepared often years before, by men like J. P. Kay and Peter Gaskell. Kay's famous pamphlet, *The Physical and Moral Condition of the Working Classes employed in the Cotton Manufacture in Manchester*, which ran into two editions in 1832, and Gaskell's *The Manufacturing Population of England* (1833) were fascinating studies of a new society in the making. Kay went on to play an active part in the setting up of the Manchester Statistical Society in 1833, the first of a network of provincial societies concerned with the collection of statistics for social purposes. One of his closest colleagues in the Society was W. R. Greg, who was later to be one of Mrs Gaskell's sharpest critics. The Gregs represented Manchester business at its most conscientious. They accused Mrs Gaskell of portraying caricatures rather than real people.

A number of similar charges were made and have been made recently against most of the other social critics of Manchester in the 1840s. Their 'bill of indictment' against what Messrs Love and Barton called 'the metropolis of manufacturers' in the sub-title of their invaluable local guide book has been followed by the framing of a bill of indictment against them. First, it is said, their pictures of the businessman were oversimplified, particularly Dickens's picture of Mr Gradgrind in *Hard Times*. The complexity of his motives, the benevolence of his intentions (at least if he was a 'good' businessman), the scale of his achievement and the breadth of his interests were all minimized or ignored. Second, they oversimplified Manchester itself, turning it into a kind of abstraction. They ignored the existence of those elements in the city which they knew would rob the abstraction of its plausibility.

The first complaint dwells too much on Mr Gradgrind. In her novel *North and South*, the first parts of which appeared in 1854, the same year as *Hard Times* (which Dickens thought of calling 'Two and Two are Four', 'Simple Arithmetic' or 'A Mere Question of Figures'), Mrs Gaskell qualified the picture of the Manchester businessman she had painted in *Mary Barton*. The *Manchester Guardian* had accused her of 'sinning generally against matters of fact' and displaying a 'morbid sensibility to the condition of the operatives'. Her picture of the businessman softened just when that of Dickens hardened. Disraeli, moreover, could never be accused of underestimating the role of the businessman in the North of England whether in *Coningsby* or *Sybil*, which were written in the 1840s themselves. He admired Cobden, and later in his life was to pay a tribute to him as 'close, coherent, sometimes even subtle'.

Cobden for his part had great reserves about Manchester businessmen: he vividly portrayed 'the sturdy veterans of the late 1820s with £100,000 in each pocket, who might be seen in the evenings smoking clay pipes and calling for brandy and water, in the bar parlours of homely taverns'. He considered that their successors were a heterogeneous group who deserved censure not for their rough-and-ready manners and their unqualified belief in self-help or *laissez-faire* but for their 'toadyism'. 'Our countrymen, if they were possessed of a little of the *mind* of the merchants and manufacturers of Frankfort, Chemnitz, Elberfeld, etc., would become the De Medicis, and Fuggers, and De Witts of England, instead of glorying in being the toadies of a clodpole aristocracy, only less enlightened than themselves.' One of Mrs Gaskell's critics had accused her of bearing a grudge against 'the gentry and landed aristocracy': perhaps this is why Cobden himself greatly admired *Mary Barton*.

There is enough literature about Manchester businessmen in the Victorian age to attempt profiles of the different sections of the business community. The literature ranges from Mrs

Linnaeus Banks's successful novel *The Manchester Man* (1876) to Beatrice Webb's account in *My Apprenticeship* (1926) of the values which had sustained her father's generation, from the sensitive study by Katharine Chorley, *Manchester Made Them* (1950), to A. J. P. Taylor's brilliant portrait of twentieth-century Manchester in *Encounter* (March 1957). A number of points stand out. Manchester businessmen did not conform to type, but they accepted the economic system which produced Manchester and its outworks, including the comfortable residential area of Alderley Edge. Katharine Chorley writes that a socialist was 'unthinkable' at Alderley Edge and would have been treated with 'a mixture of distrust, contempt and fear': Mrs Gaskell anticipated her by making one of her characters say that anybody who wished to have the opportunity of cultivating genuine social relations 'beyond the mere cash nexus' was always faced with shaking of heads and grave expressions. 'It might be the point Archimedes sought from which to move the earth.' The Manchester businessmen did not believe, in Mr Taylor's words, in 'putting the needs of the majority first'. 'They had succeeded by their own energy; and they supposed that the duty of society was discharged if it gave others the chance to do the same.' There was a premium on achievement, which was neatly expressed in a speech before the Manchester Mechanics Institution in 1827 when John Davies told his audience that 'Man must be the architect of his own fame'.

Not surprisingly, Manchester businessmen disliked prestige without achievement: they resented fundamental criticism and frustrating external control. 'Each man for himself. Your bad weather, and your bad times, are my good ones.' They suspected, even if they were not always completely impervious to, the values and virtues of the gentry, which were taken for granted in most parts of England when Cobden first decided to go to Manchester in 1828. They were suspicious too of the values and virtues of working-class 'union' or 'solidarity', which were being preached in different forms and at different dates in Manchester by 'Blanketeers', working-class radicals, co-operators and trade unionists. It seemed just as dangerous to bury individual character and effort in collective organization as to overlook character and effort altogether. They were shocked by the views expressed by Higgins in Mrs Gaskell's *North and South* – 'our only chance is binding men together in one common interest; and if some are cowards and some are fools, they must come along and join the great march whose only strength is numbers.' Some of them were shocked too by the demand to 'protect labour' which seemed as dangerous as the demand to protect land or corn. Manchester businessmen, therefore, always had to defend – at first it seemed like attack – on two fronts. Judgements about them depend upon the angle of vision and upon the generation of the judge. That they could be stereotyped was a tribute to their acknowledged importance.

The second and more substantial indictment against the social critics of the 1840s is that they presented not a profile but a simplified model of a whole society. Manchester was far more than a 'metropolis of manufacturers': it was above all a centre of trade of a whole region, linked with a whole world. The mill-owner type was at its most characteristic not in Manchester itself, but in the smaller Lancashire towns which depended upon Manchester. Coketown was really Oldham: as Disraeli saw, the most up-to-date factories of the early 1840s were not in Manchester but in Staleybridge. The Manchester merchant (as distinct from the mill owner) demanded more attention than he received from the first writers of fiction and social comment. His horizons were far wider than the long rows of working-class streets and the chimneys of factories. 'His attention is drawn as naturally to questions of Custom and Excise,' it was said of him in 1854, 'as that of the farm labourer to the state of the weather in time of harvest.' His plea was, 'I must have the world for my workshop and the world for my customer.' Because of the dimensions of the foreign trade of Manchester and the very large share it took of Britain's foreign trade as a whole, Manchester men were bound to be interested in all major national questions of fiscal policy. These questions often loomed more important than the kind of questions Engels discussed in his *Condition of the Working Class*. They certainly altered perspectives. Engels himself describes a conversation with a 'middle class gentleman' about the 'disgraceful unhealthy slums' of Manchester and 'the disgusting condition of that part of the town in which the factory workers lived'. 'I declared that I had never seen so badly built a town in my life. He listened patiently and at the corner of the street as we parted company he remarked: "And yet there is a great deal of money made here. Good morning, sir."'

Engels drew no clear distinction between manufacturers and merchants, although he himself was a representative of the second group. It was a very mixed group. Manchester always had a more cosmopolitan flavour than Birmingham, partly because its merchants were interested in foreign trade, partly because foreigners, like Engels, settled there. The German term *Manchesterthum* would never have been coined if Manchester's 'way of life' had not had international bearings. Given his theme, Engels rightly concentrated on the large proportion of Irish workers in the local labour force – one fifth of the population of Manchester in 1840: he had no particular reason to dwell on the numbers of foreign merchants in the middle classes of Manchester, and referred to his German compatriots only once when he described how they 'wasted their time' becoming special constables in 1842, 'smoking cigars and carrying staves'. John Scholes, however, had started a manuscript register of Manchester's foreign merchants in 1784 and as early as 1799 a German, Karl Friedrich Brandt, had been nominated as borough reeve of the town. Dr Aikin, who was one of the first observers to note the middle-class flight to the suburbs in 1795, also noted how 'the vast increase of foreign trade ... caused ... foreigners to reside in Manchester'.

By the 1830s the warehouses of Manchester were more impressive than the mills; massive, simple, austere, they were later to be praised for their 'real beauty'. They were held to represent 'the essentials of Manchester's trade, the very reason for her existence'. It is interesting to compare the 1839 and 1842 editions of Love and Barton's handbook to the town. In 1839 the mills and warehouses were treated together in one chapter: in 1842 there was a separate chapter on 'commercial buildings'. 'Within the last few years Mosley Street', we read, 'contained only private dwelling houses: it is now a street of warehouses. The increasing business of the town is rapidly converting all the principal dwelling-houses, centrally situated, into mercantile establishments, and is driving most of the respectable inhabitants into the suburbs. So great, about the year 1836, was the demand for such conversions, that some of the land in Mosley Street, intended for warehouse erections, sold for a rental of fourteen shillings per square yard per annum!'

The Manchester Exchange, first opened to the public in 1809, was greatly extended in 1838, so that it became 'the largest Exchange room in Europe'. This was not the only claim made for it. 'Architects consider the dome of the Exchange, which is composed of carpentry, resting on Ionic columns, one of the finest pieces of workmanship in the kingdom.' It was thought of 'as the parliament house of the lords of cotton'. Bustling with activity one hour, it would be 'as silent and deserted as one of the catacombs of Egypt' the next. The cotton lords themselves were held to be 'thoughtful' and 'intelligent' as well as confident and enterprising. 'A phrenologist will nowhere meet such a collection of decidedly clever heads; and the physiognomist who declared that he could find traces of stupidity in the faces of the wisest philosophers would be at a loss to find any indication of its presence in the countenances assembled on the Exchange in Manchester.'

The Exchange, like so much else in Manchester, was itself a symbol: the real details of the life and work of the Manchester merchants have been carefully described by Professor Redford in his volumes on *Manchester Merchants and Foreign Trade*. Yet in looking at Manchester as a new kind of city in Britain, the details are less relevant than the broad consequences. Foreign merchants had to come to Manchester in the first instance as suppliants. Because there was usually no difficulty in selling Lancashire's cottons outside Europe, dealers in the smaller European markets had 'virtually to beg for every yard of cloth they wanted'. In their wake came other foreign settlers in other industries or in other occupations. Charles Hallé, for example, although he was far more than an example, arrived from Paris in 1848 after the French Revolution had caused a slump in music. The texture of Manchester's cultural life was permanently influenced by this early immigration.

The other broad consequence of Manchester's growth as a trading and service centre was directly related to its local environment. It was a great regional capital, drawing upon the productive energy of one of Britain's leading industrial areas. When Queen Victoria came to the throne well over a third of the members of the Manchester Exchange were 'country manufacturers', and it was partly to meet their demands that the premises were extended in 1838. When Manchester men complained of the dominance of London in national life, they were speaking, therefore, in the name of more than a city. They represented a different version of life.

Something of this can be discerned in the literature, but the literature is deficient also in delineating the part played by other groups in Manchester, the 'shopocracy', for instance, which in Cobden's opinion 'carried the day' in the struggle for the incorporation of Manchester as a borough in 1837 and 1838. Shopkeepers are a neglected group in existing studies of Victorian cities, despite the cliché that England is a nation consisting entirely of them, although recently Dr Vincent has pointed to the political roles of butchers and innkeepers. In general, their relations with their customers have received far less attention than the relations between mill owners and their 'hands'. Shopkeepers were a very mixed group of people, some of them extremely close to the working classes, going into the retail trade with the minimum of capital and leaving it when times were bad, some of them growing rich enough to marry into prominent mercantile and industrial families. Their role in local government was always considerable and often decisive, and they were able both to exert 'influence' and to benefit from it. Of the sixty-four members of Manchester's first town council, thirty-four were merchants and manufacturers, and ten were shopkeepers. The proportion of shopkeepers greatly increased in the middle and late years of Victorian England, so that when Beatrice Webb visited Manchester in 1899 she found them dominant. 'The abler administrators', she concluded, 'have no pretension to ideas, hardly any to grammar – they are merely [*sic*] hard-headed shopkeepers divided in their mind between their desire to keep the rates down and their ambition to magnify the importance of Manchester as against other cities.'

Shopkeepers are not the only missing group in the novels and articles. Solicitors are another. So too are bankers and doctors, yet, as Professor Ashton has shown, both bankers and doctors played a particularly prominent part in the Manchester Statistical Society. Its first president and first secretary were drawn from Heywood's Bank. Its first treasurer, J. P. Kay, represented both occupations, for he had served his apprenticeship at a bank in Rochdale. Manchester's bankers influenced the demand the city made for a new fiscal policy – they had no sympathy with the bankers of the Midlands whom they thought to be quite 'unsound' – and many of them had a genuine interest both in thorough social investigation and in public education. They had serious 'pretensions' to culture. The warehouses were simple and austere: the banks had gables and turrets.

The doctors were genuinely interested in the darker side of the city's life. Engels paid tribute to Kay for his 'excellent book', adding (with a good eye for basic distinctions in the 'lower ranks of society') that 'the author compares the factory workers with the working classes in general'. It was difficult not to talk in terms of large groups in Manchester – of 'middle' and 'working class' arrayed in hostility to each other – but the town springs to life when the interplay of the groups and the relations within them are studied in something of their intricate detail.

Another omission in the general literature is the 'family nexus' which is almost as important to a proper understanding of early Manchester as the 'cash nexus' itself. Manchester was not a collection of separate individuals, but a network of families, each with its own history. Benjamin Heywood, in whose house the plan for the setting up of a Statistical Society was finally agreed upon, inherited from the Heywood side of his family not only a bank but a tradition of critical inquiry. His mother was the daughter of Dr Thomas Percival, who had founded the Literary and Philosophical Society in 1781 and the Board of Health fifteen years later – the latter a local pioneer organization genuinely interested in sanitary reform, although unable to achieve its main objectives. Two of Heywood's sons married daughters of his banking colleague, William Langton, to whom pride of place must be given, according to Professor Ashton, in the creation of the Statistical Society. Langton was also a founder of the Manchester Athenaeum and of the Manchester and Salford District Provident Society (1833) 'for the encouragement of frugality and forethought ... and the occasional relief of sickness and unavoidable misfortune amongst the poor'. He was a close friend of Kay and of W. R. Greg. Greg married one of the daughters of James Wilson, the editor of the *Economist*. Walter Bagehot married another. James Wilson was the elder brother of George Wilson, who was a leading figure in the history of the Anti-Corn Law League.

All things connect. These sociologists who talk of the 'anonymity' of the city should look again at the close personal relationship, through friendship and marriage, without which a city like Manchester could never have developed either its own culture or its links with the outside world.[1] Those historians who are content to repeat in different terms the well-worn contrast between 'Manchester men' and 'Liverpool gentlemen' should look again at what was implied in the Manchester side of the comparison. There was certainly a 'network' in Liverpool, and an extremely interesting one, but a proper comparison of the two cities should begin with a recognition that Manchester had its 'depth' in the 1840s as well as its riches and poverty. It was by no means as raw as some of its shocked visitors thought.

A final complaint against the writings of the social critics of the 1840s relates to their reliance in their contemporary analysis on data which related to the Manchester of an earlier phase. The imaginative lag which made them express great interest in Manchester only during the late 1830s and 1840s thereby, it is said, occasioned serious historical confusion. Conditions before the late 1830s were not distinguished from

1. For the significance of a similar network in Birmingham, see below p. 204.

conditions during the late 1830s and the 1840s. The conditions in the 1840s were still bad, but both Engels and Disraeli were guilty of the telescoping of facts relating to different dates. In particular they both underestimated the significance of the changes in local government which gave Manchester its first borough council in 1838. They ignored many of the manifestations of increasing interest in local reform which led the Manchester Improvement Committee in 1844, the very year of Engels's study, to describe 'the health and comfort of the working classes' in the worst areas of Manchester as 'a subject of vital importance . . . engrossing much of the attention, not only of scientific men, but also of the legislature of the country, and indeed of all classes of society'. By means of such measures as the Borough Police Act of 1844 and the Sanitary Improvement Act of 1845, Manchester was drafting, however inadequately, a local sanitary code 'and was thereby giving a lead to most of the other large towns of the country'. The radical *Manchester Times* hoped in 1844 that the town 'would become an inspiriting example to every city and town in the kingdom in this great work of civic reform'.

The social critics of the 1840s ignored the significance of this local legislation as they ignored (or even distorted) the significance of Peel's reforms in national government during the same period. The reason for both these inadequacies of analysis was a simple one. The writers were concerned with the short-run rather than with the long-run. They saw catastrophe ahead, not adaptation. They underestimated the forces which ultimately checked riot and revolution in Britain, and magnified the revolutionary potentialities of the situation. So long as their perspectives were widely accepted, Manchester retained its imaginative power as a symbol, even when local conditions were changing: it was only after 1848 when there was no revolution and particularly after 1850, when 'prosperity' came to Manchester (along with increasing 'respectability') that contemporaries tended to lose interest.

Paradoxically it was after Manchester officially became a city in 1853 that interest in it slackened. Writers might occasionally continue to focus attention on the city, but they were no longer 'excited' or 'shocked' by what they saw. The

Manchester Guardian might write on the occasion of the visit of the Social Science Association in 1866 that 'nowhere are the social changes which are now in progress ... more manifest than among the teeming population of which this city is the centre and the metropolis', but this was by now a local not a national comment. When nineteen years after its publication as a novel Mrs Gaskell's *Mary Barton* was dramatized, with the title *The Long Strike*, it had a very short run. The failure, it has been claimed, was because the book had been written 'for a stated time, and for a fixed purpose, and also because it was so very sad'. There was a deeper reason also. It was also because Manchester was beginning to be taken increasingly for granted, a fact rather than a symbol, just as Chicago began to be taken for granted after 1900 and Los Angeles after the Second World War. Cities usually have only a relatively short 'shock' phase. The problems which they seem to 'incarnate' may persist – 'class' in Manchester, 'ethnic division' in the 'melting pot' of Chicago – but the issues became increasingly abstract and generalized, less attached to particular and specific local situations.

A symbolic turning-point in nineteenth-century Manchester was Queen Victoria's visit in 1851, the year of the Great Exhibition. 'The streets were immensely full,' the Queen wrote, 'and the cheering and enthusiasm most gratifying. The order and good behaviour of the people, who were not placed behind any barriers, were the most complete we have seen in our many progressions through capitals and cities – London, Glasgow, Dublin, Edinburgh, etc. – for there never was a running crowd. Nobody moved, and therefore everybody saw well, and there was no squeezing.... Everyone says that in no other town could one depend so entirely upon the quiet and orderly behaviour of the people as in Manchester. You had only to tell them what ought to be done, and it was sure to be carried out.' It is true that the Queen noted what 'a painfully unhealthy-looking population' she saw, 'men as well as women', but the white rosettes were as evident as the white faces.

Just because Manchester ceased to excite the emotions after 1851, the year when the adjective 'Victorian' was first coined.

it is necessary to make an imaginative leap back in order to understand the 1840s when it did. We have to use our imagination even more than the imaginative writers of the period did. They were not merely swallowing whole ill-digested pieces of local and national evidence: they were seeking to interpret just as Carlyle was seeking to interpret. Disraeli, through Sidonia, offered the suggestion that those 'commercial causes of which we hear so much' had little to do with the deep causes of that social disturbance which Manchester represented: Engels made economic causation the foundation of a theory of history and an explanation of politics. Neither saw Manchester 'objectively'. Who could? Their own attitudes and aspirations were caught up in their assessments.

This is why what they wrote must be judged sensitively as well as critically. Engels, in particular, can be dismissed as biased, inaccurate, brash, at best a myth-maker, at worst an unsavoury agitator. In fact, his book is a valuable product of the Manchester which he claimed he knew so well. It explains much about the age and thereby how that age provided the background of Marxist theories which have subsequently gained world-wide significance. In his historical introduction Engels drew heavily on Peter Gaskell's idealized picture of eighteenth-century English village life, but he used key phrases like 'industrial revolution' – at that time virtually a new phrase – which Gaskell did not use and he drew a completely different conclusion from Gaskell at all the crucial points in his analysis. Gaskell believed that the domestic worker was 'more advantageously placed' than the factory worker, that 'combinations of workmen' necessarily entailed the 'arbitrary and tyrannical assumption of power', that 'the improvement which has taken place in the great body of masters within the last few years is perhaps the best guarantee for improvement among the men'. Engels rejected all this as much as he rejected the 'boosting' of Manchester which can be found in the guide books and directories of the period.

He might have incorporated into his account without difficulty, however, several passages at least from the Love and Barton handbook of 1842. It is this local handbook which begins a chapter on 'Habits and Social Conditions of the

Operatives of Manchester' with the sentence – 'The heading of this chapter suggests a great subject for inquiry. The condition of the working population of Manchester – that portion which form the myriads – is one of immense interest.' Much of the chapter is concerned with the merits of providence and temperance, but Canon Parkinson is quoted several times in this chapter and in other parts of the book. Engels himself quoted Parkinson's remark, also taken up in the handbook and printed in italics, that 'the poor give more to each other than the rich give to the poor'. He did not quote another long and interesting passage:

> There is no town in the world where the distance between the rich and the poor is so great, or the barrier between them so difficult to be crossed. I once ventured to designate the town of Manchester the most *aristocratic* town in England; and, in the sense in which the term was used, the expression is not hyperbolical. The separation between the different classes, and the consequent ignorance of each other's habits and condition, are far more complete in this place than in any country of the older nations of Europe, or the agricultural parts of our own kingdom. There is far less *personal* communication between the master cotton spinner and his workmen, between the calico printer and his blue-handed boys, between the master tailor and his apprentices, than there is between the Duke of Wellington and the humblest labourer on his estate, or than there *was* between good old George the Third and the meanest errand-boy about his palace. I mention this not as a matter of blame, but I state it simply as a *fact*.

It is interesting and revealing to compare what social critics like Engels had to say with the comments not only of local people but of foreign travellers, who saw Manchester more briefly. Among them were Eugène Buret, who wrote a volume not dissimilar to that of Engels called *De la Misère des Classes laborieuses en Angleterre et France* (2 vols., 1840), Léon Faucher, whose essay on Manchester in *Études sur l'Angleterre* (2 vols., 1845) was thought worthy of being printed separately in English translation, Friedrich von Raumer with his *England im Jahre 1835* (2 vols., 1836; second enlarged edition, 1842) and the Americans C. E. Lester, who wrote *The Glory and Shame of England* (2 vols., 1841), and *The Condition and Fate of England*

(2 vols., 1843), and Henry Colman, who described a visit to Manchester in the late 1830s in his *European Life and Manners* (1845).

The greatest of all travel commentators, Alexis de Tocqueville, had visited Manchester in 1835. He thought that it compared very unfavourably with Birmingham. The people looked less healthy, less well-off, 'more preoccupied', and 'less moral', the police were less efficient, and there was a terrible contrast between the signs of 'civilization' and the scenes of 'barbarism'. 'Fine stone buildings' with Corinthian columns suggested that Manchester 'might be a medieval town with the marvels of the nineteenth century in it'. 'But who could describe the interiors of these quarters set apart, homes of vice and poverty, which surround the huge palaces of industry and clasp them in their hideous folds?' In Manchester 'humanity attains its most complete development and its most brutish; here civilization works its miracles, and civilized man is turned back almost into a savage'.

These lines alone would be sufficient to demonstrate why Manchester was a symbol. The 'savage' theme runs also, as we have seen, through Dickens's deservedly famous account of Coketown in *Hard Times*. De Tocqueville, like Dickens, saw how little of Manchester had been really planned. Local improvement acts or not, 'everything in the exterior appearance of the city attests the individual powers of man; nothing the directing power of society. At every turn human liberty shows its capricious creative force. There is no trace of the slow continuous action of government'.

There was no more moving writing than this in the 1840s, and although de Tocqueville did not anticipate Engels in his account of working-class organization he noted the salient points of what might have been a fuller analysis: 'evident lack of government'; 'inability of the poor to act in isolation' (this was the driving force behind all attempts at 'union'); 'separation of classes, much greater at Manchester than at Birmingham'. 'Why!' he exclaimed, 'three weeks stoppage of work would bring society down in ruins.' With no love of revolution, de Tocqueville could nonetheless write that 'the respect paid to wealth in England is enough to make one despair.'

Emerson said the same. So too did his fellow-American visitor Henry Colman, much less acute in his judgement, but in some ways the more interesting since he was associated with no philosophical stance. 'Wretched, defrauded, oppressed, crushed human nature, lying in bleeding fragments all over the face of society,' Colman wrote. 'Every day I live I thank Heaven that I am not a poor man with a family in England.' He went on a tour of the black spots of Manchester with Dr Lyon Playfair and two police officers and saw 'exhibitions of the most disgusting and loathsome forms of destitution, and utter vice and profligacy'. He told a friend that he could not describe the visits in detail, for 'the paper would, I fear, be absolutely offensive to the touch'. The visits had left such a mark on him that 'it will make my life hereafter an incessant thanksgiving that my children have not in the inscrutable dispensation of Heaven been cast destitute, helpless, and orphans in such a country as this'.

Colman thought the worst in Manchester much worse than the worst in an old city like Edinburgh: he had recently found Chesterfield 'dismal' and Sheffield 'exceedingly dirty'. The contrasts de Tocqueville so frequently drew between Manchester and Birmingham suggested deeper differences. His conclusions confirm the view that the industrial cities of Britain were by no means all alike, as Mumford argued. Manchester was the shock city of the industrial revolution, but it was not typical. Its real interest lies in its individuality. The comparative history of the economic and social structures and political movements of Manchester and Birmingham shows just how different two individual cities could be.[1] If Engels had lived not in Manchester but in Birmingham, his conception of 'class' and his theories of the role of class in history might have been very different. In this case Marx might have been not a communist but a currency reformer. The fact that Manchester was taken to be the symbol of the age in the 1840s and not Birmingham, which had fascinated Dr Johnson and Edmund Burke in the late eighteenth century, was of central political importance in modern world history.

Another of the foreign writers on the Manchester of the

1. See above, p. 35, and below, pp. 185 ff.

1840s had extremely interesting points to make in this connexion. Léon Faucher saw Manchester as the cradle of universal industrialism. The other states of Europe which had later acquired factory industries should never, he said, forget this. The growth of population followed the growth of industry and the problems of Manchester would recur in other places. Need all countries undergoing industrialization experience such sufferings as this? Need all countries create new towns without squares and fountains, promenades and trees? Need all countries provide such grim means of escape from overwork – overcrowded inns and, what in his view were even grimmer, Protestant chapels?

Faucher said no to many of these questions (Lyons and Mulhouse, he noted, were quite different from Manchester as industrial cities) and he admitted that there had been 'improvements', that the Gregs were 'good employers', that the Manchester Statistical Society was evidence of local middle-class interest in reform, and that there was greater 'order' than there had been ten or twelve years before when special constables had to patrol the streets to keep order after Sunday morning service. He may be said to have taken a more long-term view of what had happened and what was happening. In one sense, indeed, he took an even longer view than the critics of the critics have done. He ended his account of Manchester with a warning that indefinite industrial progress was not to be taken for granted even in Manchester. 'The day when industry reached its peak and there was no further prospect of increased work, then England would begin to decline and would cede its place to another nation.' Manchester should remember its 'horoscope of ambition':

> 'Et monté sur le faîte, il aspire à descendre.'

3

This fear may have been present in Manchester itself. It may have darkened the already gloomy mood created by the economic depression of the late 1830s and early 1840s. The depression created a 'crisis' in English society and politics, and out of that crisis Manchester spoke with the voice of the Anti-Corn Law League. A fall in businessmen's profits and a sharp increase in working-class unemployment coincided with bad harvests which raised the price of bread. The Anti-Corn Law League, founded in March 1839, claimed that repeal of the corn laws would at the same time assist businessmen and relieve working men. It would dispose both of economic depression and of the 'condition of England question'. Before the depression the demand for repeal had come from isolated politicians, economists and writers, a few operative anti-corn law societies in the growing towns, like the Mechanics' Anti-Bread Tax Society in Sheffield, and (in 1836) an ineffective Anti-Corn Law Association in London. The depression pushed Manchester to the centre of the stage. 'Wisehead, at last,' wrote Ebenezer Elliott, the Sheffield 'Bard of Free Trade', who had published his famous *Corn Law Rhymes* in 1830, 'was born of Empty-Pockets in a respectable neighbourhood; and from that moment Monopoly began to tremble.'

Whatever the extent of Manchester's contribution to the change in national fiscal policy in 1846, when Sir Robert Peel, a Lancashire man, repealed the corn laws, the existence of the Anti-Corn Law League and the leadership of Richard Cobden further added substantially to the outside interest in Manchester during the 1840s. The Leaguers talked of identifying Manchester with their cause 'just as Jerusalem was the centre of our faith'. Sometimes they confused the allusion and talked of Mecca instead. Such comments were not mere rhetoric. The League was founded in Manchester, and the initiative came from the Manchester Anti-Corn Law Association, which had been created in September 1838 in the York Hotel, the same hotel where Manchester's Town Council first met.

Seven men meeting behind a faded red curtain were the founding fathers; like the seven men of Preston, who created the temperance movement, they made the most of their mythology. When repeal had been won and the League was about to dissolve itself, Cobden said how he had once told Prentice in the early days at the York Hotel, before the *éclat*, the applause and the power – 'What a lucky thing the monopolists cannot draw aside that curtain, and see how many of us there are; for if they could, they wouldn't be much frightened.' During the first years of its existence, the League drew almost nine tenths of its funds from the Manchester district. The head office of the League was for long in Newall's Buildings in Manchester, and it was from this office that a great torrent of propaganda flowed throughout the whole country, as much as a hundred tons of paper (the League loved statistics) in a year.

'The League is Manchester,' Cobden once wrote, and both his Tory opponents and his Radical rivals agreed with his judgement. Manchester spoke, of course, in the name of the provinces, and the provinces spoke in the name of England. John Bright, addressing a crowded meeting of the League in Drury Lane, London, in March 1843, did not hesitate to tell Londoners that 'the provinces had spoken out and acted as well as spoken.... They [the people of London] were the centre of a great empire, the fate of which was trembling in the balance.... The provinces without which they could not exist, and from which they drew all their wealth – all their sustenance – had done that which was the duty of the people of London.'

In the course of the struggle there was a hidden tension between Manchester and London which can be studied in the private papers of the Leaguers. 'My hopes of agitation are anchored on Manchester,' J. B. Smith, a veteran opponent of the Corn Laws, nicknamed 'Corn Law Smith', or 'Mad Smith', remarked at the start of the national agitation. 'We can do more there with a sovereign than a mixed committee in London would do with two.' On his first visit to London in connexion with the work of the League, he complained that the change of feeling was 'something like descending into an ice-box compared with Manchester'. The Londoners reciprocated the suspicion. It is fascinating to read the comments of inveterate London wire-pullers who had never been in a factory in their lives, men like Francis Place, who grumbled that Manchester politicians needed 'none but mere servants to carry out their propaganda', and philosophical Unitarian clergymen like W. J. Fox, who wrote in 1842 after the League headquarters had been transferred to London, purely on tactical grounds, that 'the League office is become perfectly horrible since the main body of the Goths and Vandals came down from Manchester; it is worse than living in a factory'.

This kind of far from polite backchat was doubtless alluded to by John Morley in his definitive *Life of Cobden* when he notes that London was a far less suitable centre than Manchester from which to launch the repeal agitation. 'In London there is no effective unity; interests are too varied and discursive; zeal loses its direction and edge amid the distracting play of so many miscellaneous social and intellectual elements. It was not until a body of men in Manchester were moved to take the matter in hand that any serious attempt was made to inform and assure the country.'

There were three aspects of Manchester's leadership which are directly related to the 'image' of the city. First, it was extremely well-organized business leadership, which relied on methods which had already been perfected in industrial organization. The economic enterprise of Manchester was thus advertised in a political agitation. 'At the Council Board of the League Cobden has around him other rich men who make little figure in public,' a correspondent to the *Morning Chronicle* wrote, 'but whose wealth and mercantile operations are known for their vastness throughout the whole civilized world. Several of them who are there every day employ each from 500 to 2,000 work-people. . . . All the members being habituated to business they go to their work of agitation with the same precision in the minutest details as they do in their work of cotton spinning.'

For those who did not like Manchester businessmen, the League was a dangerous political innovation. It introduced the townsfolk of quiet market towns and the villagers even of remote southern villages to the 'methods' of Manchester. Tory newspapers and periodicals treated it in consequence as an agent of urban sedition. 'Lecturers are paid to perambulate the country, and to declaim against the atrocities of landed monopoly. What though these men are empty, conceited blockheads . . . their uncontradicted falsehoods come at length to be regarded as truths.' The 'city' was identified with 'agitation', with the creation of discontent in towns like

Bedford or Winchester or Lewes, where there had been no agitation before. The same complaint against the city was to be made later in the century when Joseph Chamberlain and Jesse Collings, planning their land campaign from Birmingham ('three acres and a cow'), deliberately set out to woo the rural labourer in the early 1880s.

The language and the tactics of the League may be said to have justified the complaint. It attacked aristocracy and deference with single-minded dedication even in aristocratic strongholds. It attempted to separate the interests of tenant farmers from those of landlords, and sometimes of village labourers from both. It spotlighted the social problems of the countryside. 'The further people were removed from the manufacturing districts, the worse was their condition.' While Lord Shaftesbury condemned living and working conditions in the towns, Cobden and Bright were relentless in their exposure of conditions in the village, where, they claimed (using the kind of parallel from overseas which had previously been the monopoly of the anti-urbanites), labourers often lived in 'dwellings worse than the wigwams of the American Indian'. A pair of trousers belonging to a Dorsetshire peasant was exhibited at the Free Trade Hall in Manchester: they stood upright with grease and patches. Sometimes in their own urban strongholds the leaders of the League spoke like merchant princes in the Middle Ages. 'They had heard of the Union of the Hanse towns. Why did they unite? To put down aristocratic plunderers; and they would say to the aristocracy of England, Why do you plunder the beehives of Lancashire and Yorkshire?'

With an engaging capacity to see himself in perspective – this was perhaps the reason why Disraeli called him subtle – Cobden admitted in private that much of the language the League used was harsh and intemperate. 'Do not judge me by what I say at these tumultuous public meetings. I constantly regret the necessity of violating good taste and kind feeling in my public harangues.' He also admitted that Manchester's leadership of the anti-corn law struggle was not to the liking even of some repealers or of some possible converts to the cause. Manchester 'cotton lords' shared some of the contempt expressed, at least intermittently, for other kinds of lord.

Much more important than these admissions, however, was an uncompromising detestation of the 'feudal system' which amounted to hatred. Cobden feared that other people might compromise, that Manchester would compromise: he had no intention of ever yielding himself. He was not a successful businessman – he lost money both in industry and in urban land speculation in Manchester – but he was determined to harness the full resources of Manchester's business system to achieve his objectives. He lost money in the cause, although he was given a generous subscription when repeal was won. Born in Sussex, he did more than any other single man to make Manchester count in national politics. He gave and received many of the hardest blows of the struggle. 'Melancholy was it to witness', the *Morning Chronicle* reported in 1843 after he had spoken in Parliament, 'the landowners of England, the representatives by blood of the Norman chivalry, the representatives, by election, of the industrial interests of the empire, shrinking under the blows aimed at them by a Manchester money-grubber.'

Manchester's leadership of the repeal struggle affected the image of Manchester in a second way. Opposition to the corn law of 1815 had started in Manchester on the basis of self interest. Class interest, Cobden said, was at stake. In the eighteenth century, when Manchester's costs had been higher than those of foreign competitors, the industrialists were protectionist: in the nineteenth century they came to see that they could do best from free trade. The moral arguments which were used with such force by the League during the 1840s were developed only as the organization became vocal and effective. One of the leading Manchester radicals, Archibald Prentice, who later wrote a history of the League, stated flatly that the manufacturers of Manchester, when they first opposed the corn law of 1815, 'took the untenable and unpopular ground that it was necessary to have cheap bread in order to reduce the English rate of wages to the continental level; and so long as they persisted in this blunder, the cause of free trade made but little progress'.

Many of them persisted in this 'blunder' to the end, but

while the League spoke inconsistently about the effects of free trade on wages, it complained forcefully and persuasively about the 'moral injustice' of 'class legislation' in the interests only of a small and privileged landed oligarchy. The chief Leaguers paid particular attention throughout the agitation to the sufferings of the working classes under the 'bread tax' and the 'selfishness' of their opponents. As Morley again writes, smoothly covering over extremely controversial issues of tactics and outlook, the 'strictly commercial aspects would not suffice. Moral ideas of the relations of class to class in the country, and of the relations of country to country in the civilized world lay behind the contentions of the hour, and in the course of that contention came into new light. The promptings of a commercial shrewdness were gradually enlarged into enthusiasm for a far-reaching principle, and the hard-headed man of business gradually felt himself touched with the generous glow of the patriot and deliverer.'

The natural language of Manchester, when it turned from interest to principle and from manufacturers and merchants to 'patriots' and 'deliverers', was the language of the Bible, and this gave a particular cast to the propaganda of the League. The Nonconformist element in Manchester, strong there, as it was in the other great cities of the north, was particularly responsive to the religious appeal, the consideration of the iniquities of the bread tax in the light of 'the revealed law of God'. Although Wesleyan Methodists stood aloof, Congregationalists, Baptists and Unitarians were often enthusiastic Leaguers who enjoyed the struggle as well as believed in the object for which the League was fighting. 'As a nation of Bible Christians,' Heywood exclaimed, 'we ought to realize that trade should be as free as the winds of Heaven.' Ministers from smaller distant towns, like Trowbridge or Banbury, were sometimes drawn into the city orbit through their connexions with the League. In the widened campaign, both a distinctive sense of history and a dislike of the Church of England and of the Establishment generally undoubtedly played their part. Anglican parsons could be accused of having their own sectional commitment to protect. In 1842 Cobden suggested to Knight that he should include this point in an article on distress. 'The Church clergy are almost to a man guilty of causing the great distress by upholding the Corn Law – *they having themselves an interest* through tithes in the high price of bread.'

The religious element in the struggle between town and country was obvious enough at a great conference of Nonconformist ministers summoned by the League at Manchester in 1841. It was powerful enough throughout to unite at least some sections of the working classes with the middle classes in a common agitation. Cobden, who was a member of the Church of England himself (while expressing great interest in phrenology), yielded neither to the Church of England nor to George Combe, the phrenologist, in their efforts to draw him away from Nonconformist connexions. He trusted more in the Nonconformists, he told Combe, than in 'any other party in the State'. When the rector of St John's, Deansgate, the church which he attended, asked him to contribute to a fund for building ten new churches in Manchester in 1842 – the most active expression of Anglican concern and initiative in the cities – Cobden refused. 'The feeding of the hungry', he said, should have priority over all other 'public undertakings'.

Manchester became thought of as the centre of Nonconformity as well as of League politics so that when churchmen were appointed to important positions there, they were conscious of the fact that they had an especially difficult and challenging task to perform. James Prince Lee, the first Bishop to be appointed when the new diocese was created in 1847, was a scholar who concentrated on church building: he had run into difficulties with radicals in Birmingham when he was headmaster of King Edward's Grammar School and the *Edinburgh Review* described him as 'imperious, easily irritated, and not easily appeased'. In the last years of his episcopate he retired from the turmoil of the city to Mauldeth Hall on the rural borders of Cheshire. His successor, James Fraser, appointed in 1870, was told by Gladstone that Manchester was 'the centre of the modern life of the country'. Gladstone added that he could not 'exaggerate the importance of the area, or the weight and force of the demands it will make on the energies of a Bishop, and on his spirit of self-sacrifice'.

Nonconformity was a powerful force behind both the League and its successors. The tactical skill of the League rested on its skilful concentration on one single practical objective – repeal of the corn laws: its emotional strength, however, depended on a combination of discontents and ambitions. The leaders of the League were interested in other political and social objectives which they thought repeal could make easier to achieve. They wanted a genuine 'transfer of power from one class to another'. Although the League was dissolved in July 1846, in a mood of 'exultation', many of its leaders believed in what Bright called 'a new order of things'. The settling of the greatest radical issue left the way open for a number of other possible radical priorities – education, financial reform, extension of the suffrage, or a reshaping of the civil service, domestic and foreign. These and other objectives were canvassed with different degrees of enthusiasm by different Leaguers – there was even a difference of opinion about priorities between Cobden and Bright. Within a few years of 1846, however, they all found a place in what was described at the time and afterwards as the platform of the 'Manchester School'.

The term was first used by Disraeli in February 1846. It became popular during the late 1840s and early 1850s. It had been a familiar maxim twenty years before that 'the schoolmaster now walks abroad in the land'. By the end of the 1840s it was clear that the men of Manchester had designed the main outlines of the syllabuses.[1] An article in Littell's *Living Age* for 1853 saluted Manchester for its political vision. 'The whole kingdom has seen that district which it condemned as a region of grinding capitalists, without a thought save of cotton and stunted serfs . . . suddenly dart into magnificent political energy and power, found a new economic and social system; and by the peculiar clearheadedness of its views, and the still more peculiar working energy of its people, triumphantly direct the policy of the land.'

The phrase 'Manchester School' was acknowledged to be

1. See *Victorian People*, Chapter VIII, for the 'Manchester School' in its national and international setting. The argument of that chapter and the argument of this chapter meet.

an apposite one by the leaders of the free trade movement themselves. They were quite prepared, Cobden said, to be thought of as 'professors' if not as schoolmasters. 'We are called the Manchester party', declared John Bright in the Free Trade Hall in Manchester in 1851, 'and our policy is the Manchester policy, and this building, I suppose, is the schoolroom of the Manchester School.' The Free Trade Hall was a most appropriate setting in which to make this acknowledgement. No public hall in Manchester had been big enough to hold the meetings of the League, and in January 1840 a temporary wooden building (built by a hundred men in eleven days) was opened. This was replaced in 1843 by a larger brick building, big enough to hold between seven thousand and eight thousand people. A gigantic Anti-Corn Law banquet celebrated the event.

This building was in its turn demolished, and an 'imposing' Free Trade Hall 'in the Lombard Venetian style of architecture' was opened in 1856, ten years after the repeal of the corn laws. It cost £40,000 to build and was thought of as a monument not only to Cobden and Bright or Peel but to the seven hundred ministers of religion who had protested against the iniquity of the law. It is interesting to note, as A. J. P. Taylor has pointed out, that whereas other cities might have halls named after a public personality or a saint, Manchester's chief hall was dedicated to a proposition. Above all, it was a monument, and the site on which it stood was the site not only of the triumphs of the League but of the Massacre of Peterloo. The double element in Manchester's tradition was visually commemorated until the hall was destroyed by enemy action in 1940.

By then the 'Manchester School' was a memory. In its heyday, however, it was a genuine if strictly limited influence in national life, long outlasting the League which was its first political instrument and which was briefly revived in 1852. It was a school rather than a party (it never agreed on priorities), and the teachers were not academic economists or students of politics but men of business. They trusted in the virtues and the mission of the new industrial middle classes, and did much to formulate middle-class consciousness. At the same time they believed that the strength of the middle class depended upon active economic competition between the members of the class. They held also that both middle-class and economic competition, in the long run at least, were in the interests of the working classes. No class could gain by leaning on the State for protection. Nor could any nation. The third main article in their faith was 'internationalism', the peace of the nations, 'the unity of mankind'. What was good for Manchester was good also for the world.

In the advocacy of the wider programme of the School there was the same logical inconsistency, which can be noted in the arguments of the Anti-Corn Law League, and the same blend of interest and principle which made Cobden speak at times like a kind of middle-class Marxist. 'Manchester's political theory', A. V. Dicey maintained, 'was shaped by the practical inferences that it drew from commercial experience.' The continuing interest of the Manchester School is that it cannot be described entirely in these simple terms. It was prompted by emotion as much as by pragmatism: it always felt after what economists call welfare arguments rather than talked simply in terms of costs. By pressing for a great extension of the suffrage, as Bright did, its leaders knew that they might be digging their own graves. Goldwin Smith, indeed, who was a real professor not a businessman in disguise, thought later that it might have been a mistake to have been 'somewhat too trustful of the masses, and too ready to concur in the sweeping extension of the suffrage. For this, perhaps, more than for anything else, we may have to fear the verdict of posterity.'

A detailed examination of the speeches, pamphlets and articles of the School, like a detailed examination of those of the League, shows that its different spokesmen spoke with different voices in support of somewhat different conclusions. Some supported trade-union organization: others, like Greg, bitterly resented it, preferring to live 'under a Dey of Algiers than a Trades Committee'. Some opposed all factory legislation: others temporized or changed their minds. Some thought that 'adulteration of food was only a form of competition': others wanted inspection and control. Some wanted a substantial extension of the suffrage, others a 'moderate' or gradual extension. All wanted 'land reform', but they were not agreed on what land reform entailed or on the best way of achieving it. All liked cheap government, but they were not agreed on what should be the functions of government. Cobden, for example, would have had a ministry of education with what would have been bound to be a costly establishment.

Nonconformity continued to speak after 1846 in the name of 'conscience' and 'independence'. Cotton, itself an intensely moral commodity, spoke in the name of new markets and a greater volume of mutually beneficial international trade. The differences of emphasis can be noted in the speeches of each prominent member of the School. They reflected not so much philosophical divergences as the pluralism of allegiances which made Manchester men what they were – commitment to industry, to religion, to Manchester itself, the burning desire to influence national politics, 'to square the policy of the country', as John Bright put it, 'with the maxims of common sense and plain morality.'

The doctrines of the School and the extent of its influence on national life are not the specific concern of this chapter. The main reason why the influence was intermittent rather than general was that the traditional social system was tougher than it had seemed to be at the height of the corn-law controversy: a subsidiary reason was that after the corn laws had been repealed no single cause was left with as much power to unify or to direct. The old diffusion of radical energies was once more apparent. What is of basic relevance to this study, however, is the strictly limited appeal of the School in Manchester itself, the place with which it was identified. There was a growing contrast in the 1850s between the image of Manchester, as it had established itself or had been established nationally during the 1840s, and the facts of Manchester itself. During the Crimean War Bright's effigy was burned in Manchester, and in 1857 he was defeated at the general election. Cobden wrote gloomily of 'the sudden break-up of the school of which we have been the professors.... We have brought what is true into our school, but the discipline was a little too much for the scholars'.

A closer examination of Manchester's social and political history makes Cobden's judgement somewhat superficial. There was nothing sudden about 1857. The facts of Manchester's social and political life had always been different, as Cobden had often acknowledged, from what the League had wished them to be. The League itself had its origins in Manchester's history long before 1838 or 1839: it stirred up animosities which can be traced on the eve of the Reform Bill of 1832 and during the fight for the incorporation of the borough. It came into existence with the very grudging approval of some at least of Manchester's merchants and manufacturers and with the active dislike of others. There was a split in the Manchester Chamber of Commerce when the total and immediate repealers won the day in December 1838, and the President, G. W. Wood, resigned. At the general election of 1841 Cobden was not chosen as candidate for Manchester but for nearby Stockport. A year earlier when Milner Gibson, a Suffolk landowner and an ex-Conservative, had been chosen as prospective candidate for Manchester, Cobden had expressed disgust: 'What wonder that we are scoured by the landed aristocracy, when we take such pains to show contempt for ourselves.'

Throughout the whole existence of the League the *Manchester Guardian*, the newspaper which later in the century was to tell the world what Manchester was and what it was thinking and feeling, was highly critical. The *Manchester Times*, under the editorship and control of Prentice, supported the League, but it had far less influence in Manchester than its rival. In 1841 the *Guardian* attacked 'the presence and labours' in the town of 'a number of gentlemen who call themselves philosophical reformers [they seldom did] and who propose to regulate all their political conduct by a strict adherence to certain dogmas which they call principles without paying the slightest regard to expediency'. A year later it argued 'that the *ultra members* of the Anti-Corn Law League now represent their *own* opinions but not those of the community at large.' In 1845 when the periodical *The League* condemned the opinions of the *Guardian* as 'unstable', the *Guardian* retorted that it was '*not* an organ of the Anti-Corn Law League, or in any way connected with that body'. Its hero in 1846 was not Cobden but Peel. In 1845 also the Manchester Commercial Association had split off from the Manchester Chamber of Commerce, in opposition to what it called 'free trade fanaticism'. It took with it the leading members of the 'moderate' group.

During the next ten years there was increasing criticism in Manchester of the continued power of the local 'machine' which was still controlled by the same people who had brought the League into existence and led it to victory. George Wilson's attempts to retain leadership of local liberalism were stoutly resisted by 'the old Reform party' which had the support of Jeremiah Garnett, the printer and publisher of the *Guardian*, and John Potter, the son of Sir Thomas Potter, a leading Manchester merchant and Manchester's first mayor. Thomas Potter's father had been a yeoman farmer at Tadcaster. Thomas became rich and influential, and strongly supported Milner Gibson's candidature (against Cobden) in 1841. He was a Unitarian, like Garnett and J. E. Taylor, the proprietor and editor of the *Guardian*, with whom he was closely associated. The Cross Street Unitarian Chapel, indeed, provided many of the leaders who were to defeat the 'Leaguers' in 1857. Both John Potter (by then Sir John Potter) and James Aspinall Turner, the Manchester cotton spinning manufacturer, who beat Bright and Gibson, in 1857, were regular worshippers at Cross Street. Mrs Gaskell's husband was junior (and after twenty-six years senior) minister there: his predecessor had been Thomas Worthington, who was once engaged to Harriet Martineau.

Many accounts of the defeat of 1857, when Bright was in a minority in every ward in Manchester (he had headed all but one in 1852), dismiss Potter and Turner as complete non-entities. C. A. Vince, for example, the Birmingham Baptist minister who wrote an excellent brief life of Bright in 1898, referred to them anonymously as 'two local Liberals of Palmerston's school, whose undistinguished names may be found in the poll books': another well-known comment is that Potter was 'a vain man who ate and dined his way to a knighthood through the Mayoralty of Manchester'.

Potter was, in fact, three times mayor of Manchester from 1848 to 1851, and was knighted on the Queen's visit in 1851: the family from which he came not only played a conspicuous part in Manchester but was active in politics in Lancashire. His uncle was Member of Parliament for Wigan and his brother succeeded Cobden as Member for Rochdale on Cobden's death in 1865. The Potter and Norris warehouse was one of the biggest warehouses in Manchester. Perhaps the most that could be said against Potter was that he lived not in Manchester but in Salford.

Turner was chairman of the Manchester Commercial Association, which still remained separate from the Chamber of Commerce, and gave warm support to Palmerston not only during the Crimean War but when both Radicals and Conservatives were attacking his government's policies in India, China, and the Near East.

The *Manchester Guardian* backed Potter and Turner with enthusiasm at the 1857 election. It criticized Wilson and his friends for 'maintaining for factious purposes a great organization originally instituted by a great party for a grand national purpose' and went on to condemn 'a narrow, bigoted and unpatriotic section which has palmed itself off upon this country and upon the world as the representatives of the vast industrial communities of Lancashire.' Potter was praised as a local hero rescuing the city from 'the thraldom of the Anti-Corn Law League'.

The victory of Potter and Turner was followed by a reconciliation in 1858 of the Commercial Association and the Chamber of Commerce. Turner was first president of the new united body, and Thomas Bazley, another cotton spinner and merchant who had been a founder member of the League, the Chairman of the Manchester Chamber of Commerce (after the split), and a Commissioner for the Great Exhibition of 1851, became vice-president. Soon after the reconciliation Bazley was returned unopposed to Parliament as Member for Manchester on Potter's death. A year later there were signs of a further political reconciliation when the Lancashire Reformers' Union was founded with George Wilson as chairman. The Union offices were at Newall's buildings where the League had had its headquarters and which the *Guardian* had attacked two years before as the centre of a 'clique'. A new Manchester Reform Association was founded soon afterwards which was to be the precursor of the Manchester Liberal Association of 1874, the instrument of a party not the voice of a 'school'.

In the meantime more radical elements in local liberalism were unhappy about the new rapprochements. In 1859 Alderman Abel Heywood, a bookseller and publisher of Radical literature, stood at the general election against Bazley and Turner. He won 5,420 votes: this was felt to be a Radical triumph, although he did not win the seat.

The changes in Manchester were social as well as political. Heywood could rely on a large number of working-class votes: it was estimated that there were 5,822 working-class voters in Manchester in 1866. Bazley had increasing social prestige. He became a landowner and controlled over five thousand acres in Lancashire and Gloucestershire. The Potters had been made knights: Bazley became a baronet in 1889. In 1868 Bazley was joined as Member of Parliament for the city by a Conservative, Hugh Birley, a descendant of the Birley who had commanded the troop of Manchester Yeomanry which charged into the crowd at Peterloo. In 1872 Disraeli visited Manchester for the third time in his life. In 1843 he had talked to the Athenaeum, in 1859 he had distributed prizes; in 1872 he spoke as a politician in, of all places, the Free Trade Hall. In 1874 two out of the three successful candidates for Manchester were Conservatives.

Cobden did not live to see this final denouement, but in 1857, when Bright was defeated, he called the defeat a mark not only of ingratitude but of 'snobbishness'. The 'great prosperity' which Manchester enjoyed and 'for which it is mainly indebted to Bright' had increased the number of Conservatives, 'cooled down to a genteel tone the politics of the Whigs' and taken the sting out of Radicalism. Cobden anticipated that the process would go on for so long as Manchester remained prosperous. It was an unfortunate by-product of an 'affluent society'. What he did not see was that depression would lead not to the re-emergence of a militant League but to the revival of protectionism, that Manchester would never again be what it had been during the 1840s.

With the demise of the League, Manchester Liberalism ceased to be a ruling force in the life of the nation, and influence switched back to Birmingham where it had been dominant in the days of the struggle for the first Reform Bill.[1] The defeat of Bright robbed Manchester of its great national political personality, and the next great personality who was to represent it was A. J. Balfour, an aristocratic Conservative with the blood of the Cecils in his veins.

4

The League had been merely one of the two great expressions of Manchester's political life during and after the depression of the 1830s. Chartism was the second, and the local Chartists, augmented by Chartists from the neighbouring towns, challenged both the philosophy of the League and its political tactics. Competition was a curse not a blessing; 'cheapness' meant cheap labour as well as cheap goods, what a local writer called 'the cheap labour trap'; individualism meant long working hours and opposition to all government intervention as 'doctrinaire'; and unemployment was a sign not of economic adaptation but of social disorder. The League, which came into existence only after the Chartists had organized first, was the expression of the middle-class desire to prevent the workers claiming their social and political rights: in fact, a parliament of cotton magnates would be worse than a parliament of squires. The same selfishness which the manufacturers discovered in the landlord the militant Chartists condemned in their own employers.

Manchester had a huge working-class population; Faucher thought that 64 per cent of Manchester's population were wage-earners in 1836 (as against Salford's 74 per cent and Staleybridge's 90 per cent). In 1851 over 80,000 people were engaged in the cotton industry alone. The population included not only the large colony of Irish families (34,000 in 1841) but a large number of 'floaters'. Through their suffering

1. See below, p. 185.

one section of the working population, the handloom weavers, expressed the whole philosophy of failure as vividly as the new manufacturers expressed the philosophy of success. Yet distress was not confined to them. In 1837 50,000 workpeople in Manchester were unemployed or on short time. There were fears of 'wholesale plunder and confiscation', and old-fashioned Radicals, like Bamford, warned the new generation of the danger of 'unbridled violence'. General Napier, who was sent to the north of England to command the troops in the period of emergency, described Manchester in 1839 as 'the chimney of the world. Rich rascals, poor rogues, drunken ragamuffins and prostitutes form the moral, soot made into paste by rain the physique, and the only view is a long chimney: what a place! The entrance to hell realized!'

Manchester remained an important working-class centre throughout the mid-Victorian period, and conferences of Chartists, co-operators, socialists and trade unionists continued to assemble there. The National Charter Association was founded in the city in 1840, and it was in the headlines two years later during the Plug Plot disturbances. Manchester ceased, however, to capture that same public attention as a new kind of working-class city which it had received in its years of greatest disturbance. This was partly because the League dominated the scene until 1846, partly because Manchester working-class movements after 1842 were often less boisterous than those in other parts of the country, partly because the language of conflict turned more and more into the language of conciliation during the late 1840s and 1850s, and partly because many of the working classes were Conservative or 'Tory' in outlook as they had been in 1832. It is perhaps significant that Hugh Birley, the first Conservative to be returned for Manchester, was returned on the wider suffrage which followed the second Reform Act of 1867.

More important than any of these factors, however, was that industrialism itself ceased to be thought of as exciting when it became more and more a matter of routine. The complaints against its social consequences were not stilled, but they merged into more general complaints. Almost the last great assault on Manchester was that of Ruskin in *Fors Clavigera*

(1877). 'Taken as a whole, I perceive that Manchester can produce no good art and no good culture; it is falling off even in the quantity of its cotton; it has reversed and vilified in loud lies, every essential principle of Political Economy; it is cowardly in war, predatory in peace.'

Such a general indictment of Manchester is as misleading as general indictments of cities as a whole. As Manchester ceased to be a symbol, efforts were made, quite inadequately and much too slowly, to develop necessary civic policies and to create necessary public administration. Nor was Manchester completely lacking in interest in art, literature or music. Its record in many of these pursuits may be favourably compared with that of most English cities.

First it got parks, not the first public parks in the country (Birkenhead led the way) but the first in a large provincial city. There had been complaints just before Queen Victoria came to the throne that it was scarcely 'in the power of the factory workmen to taste the breath of nature or to look upon its verdure': indeed, it was Mark Philips, regarded as the arch-enemy of the working classes in 1832, who pressed in May 1843 for the provision of 'some public walks or places of recreation for our over-worked and under-fed population'. A year later a number of private donors, including Sir Robert Peel, augmented ten times over a sum of £3,000 provided by the Government, and two years later still, in the same month that the Queen gave her assent to the repeal of the corn laws, three parks were formally opened in Manchester with great ceremony. The *Manchester Guardian* hoped that the provision of parks would be followed quickly by 'the utmost possible extinction of the smoke nuisance', but despite smoke clauses in local legislation and prosecutions for 'nuisances' more than a century was needed to achieve this.

What came second was a College, Owens College, from which Manchester University, the greatest of the early civic universities, was to grow. John Owens died in 1846, leaving the bulk of his fortune to found a university where, like London, there would be no test of religious opinions. A house formerly occupied by Cobden was chosen by his trustees as the first house of the university, and in 1851 five professors and two teachers set to work as pioneers. They were genuine pioneers in that they refused slavishly to copy the curriculum of Oxford and Cambridge and put their trust not only in an extension but in a remodelling of university education. When in 1880 the college was given its independence as the chief constituent college of a new Northern university named after Queen Victoria, it had already made a genuine cultural impact on the life of Manchester.

A year after the college came a Free Library. Manchester was the first large town to take advantage of the Free Libraries Act of 1850, and John Potter as mayor was the initiator of the proposal. Somewhat surprisingly the Chartist *Northern Star* claimed that thereby 'the essential principle of Socialism had been admitted'. 'The New Library is the first fruits of the struggle to introduce higher and more unselfish principles into social action.' Salford had already established a public library under an earlier and more restricted act of 1845 and Manchester was proud in this case to follow. The old Owenite 'Hall of Science' was bought by the town to hold the first collection of books, and Sir Oswald Mosley, the absentee Lord of the Manor, proved very generous in the terms he required for the acquisition of the freehold. According to Ewart's act, a poll of ratepayers was necessary before municipal authorities could spend up to a halfpenny rate on library services, and two thirds of the ratepayers had to be in favour: Manchester's ratepayers responded with a tremendous vote of support – four thousand in favour and only forty against.

Five years later, in 1857, Manchester held a great exhibition of art treasures, the first exhibition in the country of pictures gathered together from private collections. The Exhibition was a natural sequel to the Great Exhibition of 1851. The Prince Consort, who took a great interest in it, believed that the stimulus to industry provided by the Great Exhibition should be followed up by the provision of a new stimulus to art. There was no better stimulus, he believed, than an exhibition which would 'elevate taste' and offer 'educational direction'. He persuaded a deputation of Manchester men who visited him in the summer of 1856 to forgo the idea of a large general exhibition on the lines of 1851 for the idea of a smaller and specific exhibition of art. He doubtless felt that such an exhibition would not only 'elevate taste' but would raise the standard of design in manufacture. The Exhibition certainly gave an 'educational direction' to the appreciation of art: in particular, it brought to public attention the work of the early Italian masters. Over 1,300,000 people visited the Exhibition, including the Prince Consort himself, the Queen, the Prince of Wales, and the Princess Royal. Ruskin was one of the visiting lecturers, speaking on 'The Political Economy of Art'. Manchester is now known for its pre-Raphaelite paintings and the Ford Madox Brown frescoes in the Town Hall. Its Albert Memorial has rightly been described as a 'shabby version of the resplendent London structure'. In 1857, however, thanks largely to Albert, Manchester staged what a historian of taste has described as one of the 'epoch-making' exhibitions of the Victorian age.

A cultural by-product of the Exhibition of 1857 was to be far more influential in the twentieth century. Music was needed to make the Exhibition a success, and the conductor of music was Charles Hallé who had arrived in Manchester some time before. The orchestra and chorus he conducted were not disbanded when the Exhibition ended, and in 1858 the first of the Hallé concerts was held in Manchester. Until his death in 1895 Hallé was indefatigable and imaginative in developing a local musical tradition which, it is fair to say, began before his arrival. The tradition has long survived the Victorian mode of thinking about 'the diffusion of a taste for music' as a part of 'increasing elevation of character'. The Free Trade Hall, which was built as a theatre of political argument, became a great centre of music. Manchester's first knights and baronets had been cotton magnates: the knighthood conferred on Hallé in 1888 was the first royal recognition of the city's achievement in culture.

There were to be other achievements before the century was finished. They gave a lustre to the image of Manchester. The *Manchester Guardian*, the Hallé Orchestra, the University and Rylands Library (1899) are invariably mentioned when the particular heritage of Manchester as a great city is being assessed and interpreted. Public administration was a slower growth, and Manchester's story lacked the excitement and public appeal of the story of Chamberlain's Birmingham. It has been told by Professor Redford in his invaluable *History of Local Government in Manchester* and by Shena Simon in her knowledgeable and instructive *Century of City Government.* H. L. Beales in a review which deserves to be disinterred from the dusty pages of an old periodical described Lady Simon's book as 'an historical essay upon the slow and continuous action of government in a community in which flourished the most tenacious and acquisitive economic individualism'. Starting with de Tocqueville's picture of Manchester – 'evident lack of government', 'disorder, dirtiness, improvidence' – and ending with Lady Simon's picture of complex city government – Beales concluded that the hero of Manchester's development as a city was anonymous, 'public administration' itself, cumulative, largely irreversible, and ultimately creative.

The Exchange and the Free Trade Hall were Manchester's greatest public buildings until the 1860s. Then in 1868, in what has been called 'the Victorian dark ages', Manchester started to build a new Town Hall, huge, Gothic, a creation of Alfred Waterhouse, which cost a million pounds and was not completed until 1877. The building was too late to be symbolic, and the decision to choose Waterhouse's plan was taken primarily on utilitarian grounds. It could hardly be called a crowning glory of Manchester, but it was the kind of building which showed that Manchester wanted to tell the world that it took local government seriously. It shocked no one except the anti-Victorian rebels of the twentieth century. Manchester had long outgrown the days when it could be described as 'a system of society constructed according to entirely new principles'.

CHAPTER FOUR

Leeds, a Study in Civic Pride

The AIRE below is doubly dyed and damned;
The AIR above, with lurid smoke is crammed;
The ONE flows steaming foul as Charon's Styx,
Its poisonous vapours in the other mix.
These sable twins the murky town invest –
By them the skin's begrimed, the lungs oppressed.
How dear the penalty thus paid for wealth;
Obtained through wasted life and broken health.
The joyful Sabbath comes! that blessed day,
When all seem happy, and when all seem gay!
Then toil has ceased, and then both rich and poor
Fly off to Harrogate, or Woodhouse Moor.
The one his villa and a carriage keeps;
His squalid brother in a garret sleeps,
HIGH flaunting forest trees, LOW crouching weeds,
Can this be Manchester? or is it Leeds?

WILLIAM OSBURN, *A Poem read before Members of the Leeds Philosophical and Literary Society* (1857)

I

ON the other side of the Pennines, where the woollen and worsted industries developed later than the cotton industry, two cities shared in the substantial Victorian increase in population and wealth. Leeds, with a borough charter of 1626, was the seventh largest town in England at the beginning of the nineteenth century: it was already 'the home of over 1,400 merchants and traders, whose genteel residences lined Hunslet Lane, Boar Lane, Meadow Lane and Albion Street'. It was said to be a clean and handsome town in course of rapid development. 'Houses, nay whole streets, are building every year. The streets in the old part of the town are narrow; but those occupied by the merchants, manufacturers, and superior tradesmen, are broad and spacious; the houses are uniform, elegant, and so clean, even externally, that scarcely a speck is to be seen on the broad foot pavement.' As late as 1850 one of the writers on provincial life in the *Morning Chronicle* began his account of Leeds by noting that it had 'none of that hot-house appearance' which distinguished Manchester: 'it seems in its physical peculiarities a more substantial and slower growing town than its high-pressure cotton neighbour, and it possesses none of the metropolitan attributes of the latter'.

Bradford, a smaller and rougher town, was in some ways more of a world centre: 'Worstedopolis', indeed, was the name given it both by boosters and by critics. In 1800 it was 'inhabited chiefly by manufacturers, many of whom are opulent'. It grew at a startling rate after 1815, however, and was proudly described as 'one of the most striking phenomena in the history of the British Empire'. In no decade between 1811 and 1851 did the growth of its population fall below 50 per cent. In 1851 less than half the inhabitants of Bradford had been born within the borough. Its total population was then 103,778: that of Leeds 172,258.

The two cities shared many of Manchester's problems and opportunities. In both places industry reigned supreme, although the mercantile side of the textiles industry – the side represented by markets and warehouses – was of particular importance as the cities grew. 'The colossal greatness' of Bradford, wrote its first historian James in 1857, was dependent on the invention of the steam engine. There had been one mill in Bradford in 1801 and in 1841 there were sixty-seven. 'The manufacturers are removing to Bradford as fast as they can get accommodated with looms,' the *Bradford Observer* noted in 1836. A decline in the number of mills during the decade after 1851 was a sign that Bradford's role as a mercantile centre was being strengthened. In 1815 there were only two stuff merchants in Bradford; by 1830 there were twelve or fourteen, and in 1893 there were 252.

In Leeds, which was an old market centre, there were said to be over a hundred woollen mills employing nearly ten thousand people in 1838. 'The town', wrote G. Dodd in 1851, 'presents marked evidence by the numerous tall chimneys visible on every side, of the extensive manufactures carried out'. John Marshall's flax mill, opened in 1840, was one of the wonders of the age, with its conical glass skylights, its slender iron columns, its tall chimney disguised as Cleopatra's Needle and its temple-like Egyptian façade.

There were thirty firms spinning flax in Leeds in 1841, and they employed five thousand workers. As in Bradford, there was a decline in the number of mills – and a marked shrinkage in the number of textile workers – during the decade from 1841 to 1851, but new engineering enterprises were being started, which proved as important to mid-Victorian Leeds as the steam engine had been to early Victorian Bradford. 'In the rapid advancement, which of late years the town of Leeds has made in its manufactures,' a local writer noted in 1858, 'that of self-acting engineers' and machine tools has increased to a most important extent, so much so that we believe in this particular the town is second to none.'

Both communities sang hymns to 'progress', but in both there was the same grim contrast between the fortunes of rich and poor which Engels and his fellow-critics had described in Manchester. 'Class stands opposed to class,' wrote James Hole, an influential member of the Leeds Redemption Society, which was set up in 1845, 'and so accustomed have men become to pursue their own isolated interests apart from and regardless of that of others, that it has become an acknowledged maxim, that when a man pursues his own interest alone he is most benefitting society – a maxim, by the way, which would justify every crime and folly.'

'Mr Hole of Leeds' was an Owenite. He had lived for a time in Manchester and had been a member of the Mechanics' Institute there during the early 1830s; he was a vigorous critic of contemporary social conditions, particularly housing conditions, and a pioneer of adult education. Starting with the experience of Manchester and Leeds in mind, he picked out the two great social facts of his time, first that 'the masses of society are depending on capital not their own' and second that 'they are increasing faster than the capital which employs them'. He foresaw catastrophe, but he worked for peaceful change, and ended his life not as a Labour leader but as agent or organizing secretary of the Associated Chambers of Commerce in London.

The most vigorous critic of working conditions in Bradford, Richard Oastler, was of different stamp. He saw industry and commerce as the causes of working-class misery. He dreamed not so much of the making of a new social order as the restoration of an old one. He was a 'Tory Radical', a type which was not uncommon in the West Riding of Yorkshire in early Victorian England, and he was employed for many years not in a city but as a land agent. He detested Nonconformist 'cant' and the 'march of improvement', and had more followers in Bradford than in any other city.

A number of small squires in what Faucher described as a 'county of contrasts' – men like Ferrand who introduced Disraeli to the West Riding – sympathized with the mill workers against the mill owners. They focused attention on the problems of the poor in Bradford and Leeds with something of the zeal that the Anti-Corn Law League displayed in its concern for the plight of the village labourer. They were nearer to the towns, however, than the Leaguers were to the country, and they could see directly for themselves. Inside the towns there were flourishing Tory operative clubs. Large sections of the Leeds working classes had supported Michael Sadler, a Tory factory reformer, against Marshall and Macaulay, at the first general election of 1832, and the first Tory operative club in the country was founded in Leeds three years later.

Macaulay might compare Sadler with a hyena decoying the unwary into its den by 'imitating the cries of little children', but Sadler was appealing to a working-class population which was conscious of genuine grievances. Pamphlets circulated in Leeds in 1832 attacking Marshall as a selfish capitalist employing mechanical power to 'crush operatives, men, women and children into the earth', and when Macaulay resigned his seat a year later Edward Baines defeated Sir John Beckett, the Tory candidate, by only thirty-one votes in a high poll. Beckett was at the head of the poll at the general election contest of 1834. He said that he supported 'union' among the operatives to prevent cuts in wages and to defend social rights.

Leeds was the first industrial city to return a Tory candidate, and there was strong working-class resistance to Liberalism both in Leeds and Bradford throughout the whole Victorian age. In Bradford Tory-Chartism was quickly converted into radicalism, and later in the century, indeed, it was in Bradford that the Independent Labour Party was founded in 1893.

The merchants and manufacturers of Leeds and Bradford were a proud group, however, and in men like Edward Baines they found eloquent spokesmen. It was their 'energetic and persevering industry' allied to 'the highest mechanical skill, large capital and mercantile intelligence and enterprise', Baines proclaimed, that constituted 'the mainspring' of Britain's wealth, population and power. Before Queen Victoria came to the throne the merchants and manufacturers were being flattered by ambitious Whig politicians. 'We don't now live in the days of Barons, thank God,' Brougham exclaimed in the Cloth Hall Yard in Leeds in 1830, 'we live in the days of Leeds, of Bradford, of Halifax and of Huddersfield.' At a Reform Dinner held later he described Leeds as 'one of the finest towns of the Empire, the seat of the greatest commercial community in Yorkshire. Whether we regard its population, its wealth, its intelligence or the ingenuity, the skill or the industry of its inhabitants, [it] is among the most important of all the towns which stud the British Empire'.

During the 1840s and 1850s the new rich of Bradford and Leeds, 'the families of distinction', fortified by a diet of compliments and a surfeit of self-praise, were beginning to live in greater style. Domestic comforts were accompanied by the extension of local amenities, and the ways of life of those neighbourhoods where individual choice could express itself in displays of 'taste' diverged from those where the pattern of life was dictated by necessity. The contrasts in ways of life were heightened as new ideas about 'progress' spread. In the working-class districts of Leeds, those described at a later date by Richard Hoggart in his *Uses of Literacy*, a working-class way of life developed in the most difficult conditions of privation and segregation. Hunslet, a working-class district of Leeds, was 'meanly built, consisting of narrow and dirty lanes': Holbeck, with fewer good houses, as 'one of the most crowded, one of the most filthy and one of the most unhealthy villages in the county of York'. Yet on the other side of the railway line Headingley revealed the effects of 'prosperity and opulence' and Roundhay, developing later, had numbers of 'elegant villas surrounded with paddocks and pleasure grounds'.

In 1858 five omnibuses left the centre of Leeds each day for the Three Horse Shoes Inn at Headingley, and two for Roundhay. The first Leeds tram of 1871 had Headingley as its destination. Until Roundhay Park was acquired by the city in 1872 for £139,000 and the inhabitants of Leeds were provided with the finest provincial park in England, they had to make do with Woodhouse Moor, which as late as 1858 was known as 'the lungs of Leeds'. 'Here,' it was said, with some exaggeration, 'the invalid may breathe pure and invigorating air and at the same time enjoy the charming scenery which lies before him.'

In Bradford there were just as sharp contrasts, then and later in the century, between the prosperous villas of Manningham Lane and the slums of the Irish colony in Silsbridge Lane and what James Burnley called its 'dirty tributaries'.

Burnley, who wrote for the *Bradford Observer* and later in life was the author of a novel, *Looking for the Dawn* (1874), about 'Woolborough', said that he had visited many parts of Bradford which were 'regarded by dwellers in spacious streets and commodious habitations as forbidden regions' but he had never seen anything as 'dingy, dilapidated and depressing' as the area around Silsbridge Lane. 'I wonder how many of the well-dressed, well-fed people, who daily pass up and down Westgate, have really any experience of, or seriously consider, the wretchedness, the misery, and the disease, of which the entrance to Silsbridge Lane is the threshold.'

One of the well-dressed, well-fed men who had noticed was W. E. Forster, who was to pass into the history books as the framer of Britain's first national Education Act in 1870. Forster arrived in Bradford in 1841, a young Quaker business-man who later married the daughter of Thomas Arnold of Rugby. Within a year of arriving he had reached a conclusion about 'England's plight' which was not very different from that of Engels – 'the increasing disproportion of property, growing value and power of capital, and difficulty to get it except by means of capital – the weight preventing the poor man from rising becoming more and more heavy – all tending to widen the distance between the labourers and the property men and making the poor man more and more provoked with the rich man *because he is rich*.' Forster read Carlyle 'vehemently', attacked *laissez-faire*, sympathized with the Chartists, visited Paris in 1848 and prophesied cataclysm in England. 'Demand for labour decreasing, at any rate not keeping pace with production of labour, and consequent growth of poverty amongst the masses, even to the extent of wide-spreading hunger, and this same hunger is apt to beget convulsion.'

In both Bradford and Leeds there was a serious problem of public health. In addition to the ill-health caused by bad sanitary conditions and inadequate civic administration, there were recognized occupational diseases, to which a Leeds doctor, C. T. Thackrah, still in his thirties, devoted a pioneer study in 1831. Thackrah contrasted the 'wonders which science and art have effected' with the horrors which manufacturing industry brought with it, the increase of wealth with the decline in health. 'Take indifferently twenty well fed husbandmen, and compare them with twenty manufacturers [industrial workers] who have equal means of support, and the superiority of the agricultural peasants in health, vigour and size will be obvious.' Thackrah was as forceful as Oastler in condemning child-labour, particularly for its effects on physical health. 'The employment of young children in *any* labour is wrong. The term of physical growth ought not to be a term of physical exertion.'

Leeds was fortunate in its doctors. Thackrah's strictures on working conditions were followed by Baker's strictures on housing conditions. His detailed evidence about overcrowding, inadequate drainage and offensive nuisances stands out in the 1842 Blue Book on the *Sanitary Condition of the Labouring Population of Great Britain*. Along with thirty-five other Leeds medical men, Baker took part in an indignant meeting in 1833, after Leeds had been scourged by the cholera, to demand drainage, proper sewage disposal and street paving. He was influential in the setting up of the Leeds Statistical Society in 1838 and gave great assistance to the Health of Towns Association. 'In the manufacturing towns of England,' he wrote, 'most of which have enlarged with great rapidity, the additions have been made without regard to either the personal comfort of the inhabitants or the necessities which congregation requires. To build the largest number of cottages in the smallest available space seems to have been the original view of the speculators, and having the houses up and tenanted, the *ne plus ultra* of their desires!' The property which paid the best annual interest of any cottage property in Leeds was a *cul de sac* known as the Boot and Shoe Yard in Kirkgate, where seventy-five cartloads of manure were removed in the days of the cholera.

Baker was sceptical about the willingness of the Leeds Town Council to remedy matters. He began his reply to a question put by the Health of Towns Association in one of its questionnaires – had the local authority done anything to guarantee a good supply of water? – with the ironical comment that after the municipal reform of 1835 one of the new town councillors in Leeds, 'supposing that the new Council was for the good of the people', tried in vain to do something about it. James Hole was even less hopeful about the Leeds Council. 'Where local self-government means merely *mis*-government we are apt to wish for a little wholesale despotism to curb such vagaries.'

There were fewer doctors in Bradford of the quality of Baker, but there were the same expressions of urban disorder. The Board of Surveyors, appointed in Bradford in 1843, following a procedure laid down in the Highway Act of 1835, themselves described the Bradford Canal in lurid terms. 'The drains of the town are emptied into this water-course, and principally above the floodgates. Besides, on both sides of the stream there are a great many factories of various kinds of manufacture, etc., the soil, refuse and filth of which fall into the beck. In summer-time the water is low, and all this filth accumulates for weeks, or months, above the floodgates, and emits a most offensive smell. This noxious compound is conveyed through the sluice into the canal, when it undergoes a process which renders it still more offensive. For the mill owners below the floodgates, having a deficiency of water, contract with the proprietors of the canal, for a supply of water for their boilers. The water is conveyed for this purpose in pipes to the boilers, and, after being used for the generation of steam, is conveyed back again into the canal, so that the waters of the canal are scarcely ever cool in summer, and constantly emit the most offensive gases.' The canal occasionally 'took fire': even when it was quiescent there were complaints of 'noisome effluvia'. With urban features of this kind, it is scarcely surprising that one of the Health of Towns Commissioners described Bradford as 'the dirtiest, filthiest and worst regulated town in the Kingdom'.

The smoke nuisance was bad both in Leeds and Bradford. Leeds was described by Faucher as dark and disagreeable: 'Sheffield is the only city in England which presents as gloomy an appearance as Leeds.' Dickens, who knew that it was a 'great town' – he spoke with feeling in 1847 at a Mechanics' Institution soirée with George Stephenson as a fellow-guest – had described it also, as we saw, as 'beastly and nasty'. Bradford men either liked their own smoke or made fun of it. Just as one of its councillors defended the canal, which had acquired the nickname 'River Stink', so Councillor Baxendale called smoke a 'good thing'. A local satirist took up the theme:

How beautiful is the smoke
The Bradford smoke:
Pouring from numberless chimney-stacks,
Condensing and falling in showers of 'blacks',
All around
Upon the ground,
In lane, and yard, and street;
Or adding a grace
To the thankless face
Of yourself or the man you meet:
Now in the eye and now on the nose,
How beautiful is the smoke?

One of the reasons why public health problems created so much interest in the Victorian age is that they were problems which were posed in visual terms – or, even if the eye could not see them, the nose could smell them out.

Opinion battered against interest, all too often in vain. The problems of local government seemed more complex, and the answers to them (where there were answers) reflected the variety of local interests. Leeds, unlike Manchester or Bradford, was an old borough, but its council was refashioned after the Municipal Corporations Act of 1835. The first mayor under the new constitution was George (later Sir George) Goodman, a bachelor, a Baptist and a wool merchant. The second mayor, Dr Williamson, also a Nonconformist, objected to marching in procession to the Leeds Parish Church for a civic service as all his predecessors had done.

In Bradford there was a long struggle about incorporation. A pro-incorporation party met in the Mechanics' Institute in 1843 and drafted a petition which was signed by 56 merchants, 98 woolstaplers, 220 worsted manufacturers, 60 innkeepers, 16 ministers of religion, 13 solicitors, 13 surgeons, 13 dyers, 2 bankers, 2,100 shopkeepers and 8,187 operatives: it also had the support of 32 of the Lighting and Watching Commissioners, elected under the act of 1803, and of 12 out of the 13 surveyors. Despite the strength of this support for incorporation, particularly amongst Dissenters, a counter-petition attracted even greater support. The Vicar and 8 clergymen were opposed to Bradford becoming a borough, as were the ladies of the Manor, 11 West Riding magistrates, 21 solicitors, 3 bankers, 2 physicians, 18 surgeons, the Low Moor and Bowling Iron Companies, and 235 ladies and gentlemen.

Many of these interests were Conservative, but it was clear that professional people were almost as divided as industry itself. Fifty-two merchants, 105 worsted spinners and woolstaplers, 90 manufacturers, 98 innkeepers, 1,003 shopkeepers, and 10,535 operatives were against it. There were signs in Bradford, therefore, of exactly the same 'Tory-Radical' alliance against incorporation about which Cobden had complained in Manchester. Twenty-six Commissioners also opposed incorporation. Their opponents accused them of 'notorious inattention to the duties of office' and said that they had rendered themselves ineligible to give an opinion on the question.

The Privy Council sent Major Jebb to Bradford in May 1845 to assess both the strength of local feeling and the state of local government. He discovered that although many people had signed both petitions, there was a majority against incorporation – 8,715 ratepayers for (with assessed property of £78,512) and 10,716 against (with assessed property of £96,432). This conclusion roused the pro-incorporation party to new efforts in 1846. The same people who were active locally in the Anti-Corn Law League were prominent in the incorporation agitation, and in January 1847 they presented a new petition to the Privy Council. This time it was successful, and a charter was granted in April of that year. The new corporate body consisted of a mayor, fourteen aldermen, and forty-two councillors: the motto of the town was '*Labor omnia vincit*'.

Bradford's difficulties did not end when it became a borough. The 'propensity to riot', which had given Manchester its first unsavoury reputation, was more marked in Bradford than in Leeds. There had been serious anti-Poor Law riots in 1837, when there was fighting between the operatives and the 15th Hussars; Chartist riots in 1839 after the Chartists had drilled in the open on Fairweather Green; plug-drawing riots in August 1842, when a troop of rioters moved on from Bradford to Leeds; and Orange disturbances in 1844, after which five people were charged with manslaughter. In the spring of 1848, with the new Council in charge of law and order, the Mayor had to issue a proclamation and to order the employment of dragoons as well as policemen and special constables to quell Chartist disturbances. Many people were wounded in the serious clash on 29 May, a demonstration that northern Chartism not only survived the so-called 'fiasco of Kennington Common' but provided a more serious threat to law and order than ever before. Bradford at this time was in 'a state of siege', when, as Burnley put it, 'workmen with hollow cheeks and threatening eyes . . . congregated at street corners, talked wildly of justice and tyranny, and turned with an angry scowl whenever any of the local mill owners happened to pass them'. Serious disturbances continued until August.

Leeds was quieter than Bradford largely because it had more troops stationed in it, but the troops themselves were a cause of riot on at least two occasions during the 1840s. In January

1844 a number of soldiers armed with bayonets made an indiscriminate attack on every person they met in the centre of the city: they were roused, it was said, by a notice on a public house table 'No swaddy Irishmen or soldiers wanted here'. A few months later in June there was fierce fighting in Leeds between soldiers and police. Seven privates of the 70th Regiment of Foot were arrested after skirmishes on a Sunday evening. In an effort to gain revenge, forty or fifty soldiers assembled in a body the following night and beat up all the policemen they could find. 'The populace generally' sympathized with the soldiers, cheered them through the streets, and were sometimes drawn into the fighting. Although the ringleaders of the soldiers were arrested by a piquet and marched back to barracks, there were further disturbances the following night.

2

Leeds and Bradford had much in common, therefore, in early-Victorian England, but there were marked differences between them which were perpetuated in late-Victorian England and remain sharp today. Sometimes the differences were deliberately accentuated in intense urban rivalry. Close to each other, yet never part of one great whole as were Manchester and Salford, Leeds and Bradford prided themselves on their individuality. Their pride was echoed in all the smaller communities of the West Riding. Huddersfield, which was not incorporated until 1868, had its own local culture and traditions; Wakefield and Halifax not only looked forward to the age of progress but looked back to a rich and colourful past. Dewsbury and Batley had a vitality – and argument – of their own. Keighley and Bingley were rivals not only in sport but in education and politics. The West Riding may be called a 'conurbation', but the sturdy civic pride of its constituent parts, 'a self-assertive attitude of independence', dominated its nineteenth-century history. The pride loomed larger than the problems, and it has survived in the new setting of the twentieth century. Pudsey, for instance, which became a municipal borough in 1899, staunchly preserves its 8.3 square miles between the 59 square miles of Leeds and the 40 square miles of Bradford. Morley, which became a borough in 1885, controls 15 square miles within easy reach of Leeds Town Hall.

All the lesser local rivalries are mirrored, as it were, in the rivalry between Leeds and Bradford. Leeds was at the edge of both the textiles district and the coalfield. These industrial areas each carried with them a quite different way of life. To the north the neighbourhood of Leeds was and is non-industrial, and the town had many links with a landed society which stood for older values than the new cities. Its newspapers were read in this district as much as in Leeds itself. If Manchester was a frontier town, with a mountain frontier with Yorkshire and an economic frontier with Cheshire, Leeds was a place where frontiers met within a county. Indeed, it drew on quite different social areas within its own borders. Bradford, by contrast, belonged to its area. It was the representative city of the textile belt which depended upon it but struggled against its dominance. Built in dark West Riding stone, much of its building touching the rock, it was a Pennine town, and, as Lady Chorley has written, all the Pennine towns are alike in their unity with the country from which they spring. 'The Pennine towns are not *at one* with their surrounding country, they are one with it.' Leeds by contrast was a community where many of the houses were brick, like the houses of the mining area to the south-east. Only a number of public buildings and the villas of the well-to-do were in stone.

There were economic differences between Leeds and Bradford too.

Leeds after 1850 was a town with many trades. By 1861 the engineering industry, which had grown extremely rapidly between 1840 and 1860, provided more jobs for men than textiles; the ready-made clothing industry, which grew fastest after 1870, was carried on in three hundred small workshops at the end of Queen Victoria's reign. The basic industrial structure of Leeds has scarcely changed since. Bradford was pre-eminently a textiles town both in early- and late-Victorian England, although it lost its handloom weavers after the 1850s. Unlike Leeds, it had an early foreign community engaged in merchanting and industry, which was not very different from the foreign community in Manchester.

In 1827 there were no foreign worsted merchants in either Leeds or Bradford; 10 years later there were 7 in Leeds and 8 in Bradford; 10 years later still there were 7 in Leeds and 34 in Bradford. By 1861 there were only 3 in Leeds and 65 in Bradford. The warehouse district of Bradford became known, indeed, as 'little Germany'. Names like Behrens, Flersheim, Furst, Gumpel, Hertz, Mayer, Schlesinger and Sichel can be found in Ibbetson's *Directory* of 1845 jostling with the Bradleys, Briggses, Brooks, Whitakers, Wilkinsons, and Wilsons. In 1864 Bradford had its first foreign-born mayor, Charles Seman, from Dantzig.

Many of the German warehouses were of greater architectural interest than any of the other buildings of Bradford: their owners were prominent in the founding not only of the Bradford Chamber of Commerce but of cultural institutions like the Liedertafel (1856) and the Schiller Verein (1859). Jacob Behrens, who settled in Bradford in 1838, played an important part in the reconstitution and rebuilding of Bradford Grammar School and the inauguration of regular subscription concerts. The musical tradition in Bradford owed much to the members of its German colony, who welcomed Charles Hallé from Manchester with unflagging enthusiasm and provided many of the amateur members of local orchestras. Burnley describes 'young Belltinkler, a foreign correspondent in one of the German houses. He can play any instrument from a piccolo to a double bass, sing anything you like to name, from "Sally, come up" with banjo accompaniment, to a vocal setting of the dance music from *Dinorah*.' Bradford had its regular subscription concerts from 1864 onwards; the concerts of Leeds were overshadowed by its great festivals. The foreign colony which settled in Leeds after the Continental anti-Jewish pogroms of the 1880s was less interested in music than the early German colony of Bradford, which by then had a recognized place in the life of the city. The growing numbers of Jews in Leeds – there were fifteen thousand by the end of Queen Victoria's reign – had to make life for themselves, often in conditions of great difficulty.

There were other differences between Leeds and Bradford. Leeds, for example, attracted far more Londoners than Bradford: it had three times as many as Bradford in 1851. Bradford had relatively more Irishmen and migrants from the more distant parts of rural England. Bradford had the reputation for many years of being a far more Radical city than Leeds. After W. E. Forster had failed to win a nomination for Leeds in 1857 and had lost the election of 1859, he turned to Bradford where the electors were 'on the whole more inclined towards Radicalism'. It was only later in the century, in the light of the economic difficulties of the woollen and worsted industries, that Bradford's reputation for radicalism was lost, and by then its association with the Independent Labour Party, founded in 1893, was ensuring it a greater share of public attention.

The rivalry between Bradford and Leeds gained in intensity not only from the differences between the geographical, economic and political bases of the two communities but from their competition to do the same kind of thing. Building was one form of competition. Neither town was renowned for its public buildings during the 1840s. 'Bradford is not famous for the number or beauty of its public buildings', Ibbetson's *Directory* confessed in 1845. All it could point to was the Court House (1834), designed for utility, not ornament, the Grecian Exchange Buildings (1828), the Mechanics' Institute (1839), 'large and commodious', and the New Infirmary, 'the best specimen of architecture in Bradford, built in the Tudor style' and 'combining lightness with substantial elegance and symmetrical beauty'. Leeds had some good eighteenth- and early-nineteenth-century buildings, but they were little appreciated by the mid-Victorians. When the old infirmary building, built in 1767 by Carr, the architect of Harewood House, was replaced by a large Gothic structure designed by Sir Gilbert Scott in 1866, there were few laments for the 'spacious but plain building' which disappeared. The new building with its elaborate bright stained glass was heralded as 'a fine adaptation of medieval architecture'.

Bradford was the first of the two communities to sponsor a handsome new public building which was designed to 'elevate' taste and to meet the 'cultural needs of a business metropolis'. Samuel Smith, Mayor of Bradford from 1851 to 1854 – he was a stuff dyer and finisher and the first citizen to be elected mayor for three years in succession – called a public meeting in 1849 to consider the erection of a 'great building' in Bradford. A committee of thirty was appointed 'to inquire as to the mode of construction and the cost of similar buildings in other towns and to view any site that may be considered eligible for the purpose'. The committee recommended the formation of a joint stock company with a capital of £16,000 in £10 shares, and went ahead collecting subscriptions.

The foundation stone of the building was laid (with Masonic honours) by the Earl of Zetland in 1851, and the local architects, Lockwood and Mawson, produced a massive building complete with Corinthian pillars, large arched windows and interior decorations which were 'highly ornamental and executed in the best style'. The building had a restaurant 'for the accommodation of mercantile men', a large hall and gallery to accommodate over 3,100 people, and an organ, 'a magnificent instrument, possessing a firm tone and a great power'. The gas lighting was a special feature: a continuous line of 1,750 gas jets was served by pipes carried round the upper surface of the cornice.

In opening the building, Smith, who was by then in the first year of his mayoralty, boasted that it would be 'the best-known specimen' of concert hall building in England. 'We are eleven feet wider than the hall at Birmingham, and about as much longer. We are exactly the same width as Exeter Hall, London, with greater length, a loftier ceiling and a much better arrangement of the audience.' He claimed that the hall would meet the needs not only of the 'mercantile men' of Bradford but of the operatives, who after attending concerts would go back to their homes 'elevated and refreshed, rising in the morning to their daily toil without headache and without regret'. There were loud 'Hear, hears' at this point. Smith did not need to remind his audience that Bradford, a stronghold of Puritan Nonconformity, had been the first town in England to erect a Temperance Hall in 1837.

The *Bradford Observer*, a Liberal newspaper edited by William

Byles, a friend of Forster, dwelt on the cultural significance of St George's Hall 'frankly and with pleasure'. Bradford no longer produced only factories, warehouses and cottages: it had schools, churches, and now a hall to go with a new park, Peel Park, which was not finally handed over to the Corporation until 1863. 'Commercial enterprise had laid the foundations and superstructure of our material life', but provision was also being made for 'the intellectual, moral and spiritual parts of our nature'. The *Observer* felt that it was necessary to comment on its use of the word 'spiritual'. Six new churches had been built in Bradford since Queen Victoria came to the throne, but this was obviously not what the *Observer* meant by 'spiritual' progress. It hinted, indeed, that there had been opposition to the idea of the hall from the Church of England, some of whose representatives asked, 'What had laymen to do with the moral and religious life of the people? Had not the ecclesiastical councils and assemblies provided for that?' Much Victorian social history is implied in the *Observer*'s answers to its own questions. 'Something more attractive than dogmatic theology is needed to draw away the votaries of the beer shops and the public houses. Cheap music was suggested; and now the suggestion stands substantially before us in the New Music Hall, an experiment conceived in the best spirit, and to the development of which we look forward with mingled hope and fear.'

It was not merely that St George's Hall in Bradford was to improve the architectural appearance of Bradford. What happened inside it was to raise the tone of society also. Smith's project was a private one, yet he was Mayor of Bradford when it came to fruition and in the civic life of Bradford he was just as anxious both to improve appearances and to raise tone. Bradford did not build a new Town Hall until 1873, but Smith, 'a man of sterling character, distinguished by strong commonsense and enthusiastic in every good work to which he put his hand', received from a number of his fellow-citizens in 1854 a massive gold mayoral chain, weighing, as we are told with pride, twenty-nine and a half ounces and costing £250. Bradford, with Smith as mayor, was to be a city with civic pride, and the letters on the medallion of the chain, 'V R', perpetuate the Victorianism of this particular manifestation of status and prestige.

Smith concerned himself also with many substantial issues of civic policy. There had been a 'fight like Kilkenny cats' with the Bradford Waterworks Company in 1852 and 1853 after the Corporation had proposed a new waterworks and the municipal acquisition of the company: it ended in 1854 with the transfer of the waterworks to the Corporation.

'Improvement' of streets and buildings had been carried out with vigour since the passing of an Improvement Act in 1850. This important progress, which provided for substantial municipal initiative, had been opposed by what was called 'The Minority of Muck', a far more vivid phrase than 'the dirty party'. Once it was passed, however, the minority ceased talking of 'the greatest swindle ever practised upon a Committee of the House of Commons' and tolerated, if they did not always welcome, the cleaning-up of the centre of the town. Streets were widened, old buildings were destroyed, and in 1854 the first building regulations in Bradford were introduced. Before this date, there had been no restriction on the operations of speculative builders, and houses had almost always been crowded into the smallest possible space; this was the same pattern as that described by Baker in Leeds. The regulations of 1854 at least marked a recognition of the case for social control, but they did not forbid back-to-back housing, one of the special features of West Riding working-class living accommodation, as distinctive as the tenements of Glasgow or the cellars of Liverpool. Out of 1,601 plans sanctioned in 1854 in Bradford, 1,079 were back-to-back houses. A serious attempt to get rid of them was defeated in 1860, and they continued to be built in large numbers both in Bradford and Leeds throughout the Victorian age: the last back-to-back house in Leeds, indeed, was built as late as 1937.

Limited though the reforms of the 1850s were, they displayed a vigour of direction which makes Smith deserve to be remembered along with greater nineteenth-century civic reformers like Joseph Chamberlain. It is interesting to note that his mayoralty coincided with the completion of Titus Salt's model factory 'in the boldest style of Italian architecture' and the beginning in 1853 of the new town of Saltaire with its 'wide streets, spacious squares, with gardens attached, grounds for recreation, a large dining hall and kitchens, baths, and wash-houses, a covered market, schools and a church'.

Salt, a Bradford manufacturer of alpaca and mohair and by religion a Congregationalist, was a hero of self-help. It was said that he made a thousand pounds each day before other people were out of bed. He had been mayor of Bradford from 1848 to 1849 and an early advocate of incorporation. He wished Saltaire to combine 'every improvement that modern art and science had brought to light', a town free of smoke, thereby 'in this respect as in many others, teaching an important practical lesson to the mother town of Bradford'. Saltaire grew and attracted immense interest, but it never rivalled Bradford, and it was for Bradford that Salt was returned as Member of Parliament in 1859. Ten years later he became a baronet, a tribute more to his benevolence and vision than to his wealth. There were few Saltaires in the Victorian age, but there could have been no Saltaire had there not been first a Bradford. The work of a far from rich town council under Smith deserves to be set alongside the work of one of England's richest manufacturers. 'It used to be a reproach against us', the *Observer* wrote in 1859, 'that Bradford was a *settlement* rather than a community ... of late years we have been proud to see an *esprit de corps* unknown before diffusing itself among us, with a justifiable pride on the part of the inhabitants in their fellow-townsmen and their town.'

3

Leeds was interested in all these near-by developments outside its boundaries, and among the special trains that carried visitors to Bradford for the opening concert in the new St George's Hall there were trains from both Leeds and Manchester. Many new buildings were going up in Leeds during the late 1840s and early 1850s – the Leeds Club, for example, in 1846; Mill Hill Unitarian Chapel in 1847 ('in the pointed or perpendicular style of the fifteenth century enriched with a variety of ornament'); the Leeds Stock Exchange in 1848; and the Church of St John the Evangelist at Holbeck, built and endowed by the Marshalls, and completed in 1850.

It was in July 1850 that the first public meeting 'to ascertain the feelings of the inhabitants as to the erection of a large public hall' was held in Leeds in connexion with plans to commemorate the work of Sir Robert Peel. The meeting recommended that a public hall should be built in Leeds, the money to be raised by shares, as it had been for the building of St George's Hall in Bradford. A sum of not less than £15,000 was to be raised in £10 shares. For some reason Leeds proved less enterprising than Bradford, and although adequate subscriptions to build a statue of Peel were collected – Leeds was quicker than Bradford in achieving this – little interest was shown in the shares for a public hall.

The result was a switch of plans. Instead of building a public hall by a joint stock company, the suggestion was made that a Town Hall should be built by the Town Council out of the rates. Councillor Edwin Eddison, formerly the Town Clerk of Leeds, moved a resolution to this effect at a meeting of the Town Council in October 1850. Although a decision was deferred until after the ratepayers had been given a chance to express their views at the municipal elections of November; it was taken up again in January 1851 when the Town Council carried by twenty-four votes to twelve a motion to build a town hall. 'As the attempt to raise funds by public subscription has failed,' the resolution read, 'it is in the opinion of this Council desirable to erect a Town Hall, including suitable corporate buildings.'

A committee of the Town Council was appointed to make inquiries. It consulted Joseph Paxton, the designer of the Crystal Palace, and sent deputations to Manchester, Liverpool, and other large towns to see what plans they had for building public halls before presenting its report in July 1851. It eventually recommended that a new Town Hall should be built in Park Lane on a site belonging to John Blayds. A house inhabited by Dr Richard Hobson existed on the site, and the committee recommended that a sum not exceeding £45,000 should be set aside for the site and the new building. There was a delay, caused by disagreements concerning the exact amount of money necessary to provide accommodation for judicial purposes in the new hall, but in September 1851 the Town Council accepted the Committee's report by twenty-one votes to seventeen. A sum of £22,000 was allotted for a Town Hall and corporate buildings. Soon afterwards Park House and its garden were bought from John Blayds, the owner, for £9,500. The matter was not yet finally settled, for in February 1852 a resolution was proposed that it was 'unwise and inexpedient to proceed with the Hall'. This motion was defeated by twenty-eight votes to fourteen, as were other motions to limit the cost of the venture.

The building of Leeds Town Hall provides a magnificent case-study of Victorian civic pride and its place in the life of provincial communities. It is most illuminating when it is studied in its detail, and it is with the detail that this study is concerned. The story of Manchester is fascinating in its bold outline: it is the intricate pattern of problem, personality, and performance which fascinates the historian of Leeds, the pavement view rather than the vista from the balloon.

'It may seem a small matter to those who have not studied these questions of local politics,' T. Wemyss Reid, the nineteenth-century biographer of Dr J. D. Heaton, a prominent Leeds doctor, wrote, 'whether a Town Hall in a provincial city shall be of one style of architecture or another, whether it shall be large or small, handsome or the reverse. As a matter of fact, a great deal may depend upon the decision which is arrived at in such a matter by the authorities upon whose judgment the final decision depends.' 'A Town Hall', Sir Charles Barry was to write in 1859, when discussing plans with Halifax Corporation, 'should, in my opinion, be the most dominant and important of the Municipal Buildings of the City in which it is placed. It should be the means of giving due expression to public feeling upon all national and municipal events of importance'. It should serve, 'as it were, as the exponent of the life and soul of the City'.

Such a high-minded statement needs to be fitted into the context of local interests. Pride and prejudice went together. It was provincial pride, fortified by distrust of the claims of London, which inspired Leeds, along with jealousy of what was happening in Bradford. 'No one would wish to underestimate the importance of the metropolis,' wrote Wemyss Reid, who was also the biographer of W. E. Forster, 'but, after all, it is not in London that we find the best specimens of our English architecture. . . . It is in what were once provincial cities or hamlets that we discover the most venerable and the most striking memorials of the taste and self-consecration of our forefathers. And the time may come when the archaeologist of a future age will look for the best specimens of the buildings of the present reign, not to the Law Courts or in the Houses of Parliament, but to some provincial towns, where possibly the hurry and rush of life have not been as great as in the capital.'

The size of the minority opposed to the building of a new Town Hall in Leeds reveals the precarious balance of forces in nineteenth-century local life. The desire for 'economy' was a dominating motive in mid-Victorian local government, and it influenced Radicals as much as Conservatives. It could only be over-ridden if very genuine advantages could be proven. At the same time the members of the majority on the Leeds Town Council were clearly prepared, like the majority in Bradford, for a more vigorous local policy at this time. In April 1852, for example, the Council decided to purchase the Leeds Waterworks – the voting was twenty-two to sixteen – and in the same year work began on a long delayed project of constructing sewers for the main streets.

The majority on the Council was backed by a number of public-spirited individuals outside it. A Leeds Improvement Society had been founded in January 1851 'to suggest and promote architectural and other public improvements in the town'. Its secretary was Dr Heaton and its treasurer Thomas Wilson. It often collided with the Council, but it strongly supported – with some misgivings as to the Council's capacity to manage the project – the building of the Town Hall. So too did the Leeds Philosophical and Literary Society, which had been founded in 1818, and included among its members some of the most enlightened citizens of Leeds. After 'languishing' during the 1840s, it revived in 1849 and 1850 under the presidency of John Hope Shaw, a Leeds solicitor whose father had been a surgeon in Otley. By the mid-1850s it could boast that 'the demands and the taste for literary and scientific achievement have increased in Leeds in a ratio far exceeding the numerical increase of population'.

Hope Shaw was a Whig churchman who was three times Mayor of Leeds as well as being seven times president of the Philosophical and Literary Society and for several years president of the Leeds Mechanics' Institution. He spoke to the Philosophical and Literary Society in October 1854 on the history of English municipalities. He was a close friend of Canon Hook, 'the Apostle of the Church to the great middle classes', who as Vicar of Leeds did much to influence for good the life of the city. Hook, who was in Leeds from 1837 to 1859, was president of the Society when the British Association visited Leeds in 1858. Among businessmen, the Marshalls and the Gotts were keenly interested in the Society. Business overlapped in both their cases with other cultural interests. Dr Gott, born and brought up in Leeds in a family of industrialists, became Vicar in 1873. It is said that he loved Leeds 'even to its smuts'. Henry Marshall divided his time between Leeds and the Lake District – he was Mayor of Leeds in 1845 – and James Marshall, who was a friend of Adam Sedgwick and Sir John Herschel, was a keen advocate of scientific education. Cordelia Marshall married William Whewell, Professor of Moral Philosophy in Cambridge, and Whewell was one of the distinguished outsiders who read a paper to the Leeds Philosophical and Literary Society in 1856.

Among the other interesting papers which were read to the Society during the early 1850s were one by J. I. Ikin, the Town Clerk, on 'the progress of public hygiene and sanitary legislation', one by W. B. Denison on 'the homes of the working classes' (Denison had just constructed the Leeds Model Lodging House for working men), one by Sir Joseph Paxton himself on 'the Growth of London and other Large Towns in the United Kingdom with Suggestions for their better Architectural Arrangements, Internal Communications and Sanitary Improvements', and one by Heaton on 'Town Halls'.

Heaton, born in Leeds (his father was a bookseller) and

educated at Leeds Grammar School and Caius College, Cambridge, was one of the distinguished band of Leeds doctors who initiated so much in the life of the city. He was elected physician to the Leeds Public Dispensary in 1843 and to the House of Recovery in 1846, and appointments of this kind gave him a genuine knowledge of the social problems of the growing community. He was as much interested, however, in an ideal which would inspire the cities as in the facts which dragged them down. When he visited the Continent, he greatly admired 'those famous old cities whose Town Halls are the permanent glory of the inhabitants and the standing wonder and delight of visitors from a distance'. He believed, moreover, as did people who thought like him, that 'if a noble municipal palace that might fairly vie with some of the best Town Halls of the Continent were to be erected in the middle of their hitherto squalid and unbeautiful town, it would become a practical admonition to the populace of the value of beauty and art, and in course of time men would learn to live up to it'.

A not dissimilar point had been made by Benjamin Disraeli on his visit to the Manchester Athenaeum seven years before, when, in the company of Dickens and Cobden, he held up before his audience the stimulating examples of the great merchants of Venice, who were the patrons of Titian and Tintoretto; the merchant family of the Medici who made Florence the home of genius; and the manufacturers of Flanders, who dwelt in such cities as Bruges and Ghent. A rich town like Leeds, Heaton maintained, should consider the Town Hall question 'in the most broad and liberal spirit, and ... incur that which might even seem to some to be an extravagant expenditure, rather than fail in a duty which it owed to the rest of the community and to posterity'.

The Town Council soon found that even when the problems of the Town Hall were approached in a cautious rather than a 'broad and liberal spirit', the cost of the venture increased year by year. In June 1852 the Town Hall Committee resolved to advertise an open competition for 'plans, elevations, specifications and sections' for a new Town Hall. Sir Charles Barry, who was still engaged at that time in supervising the building of the new House of Commons, was chosen as adviser. The first prize was to consist of £200, the second £100, and the third £50.

The Committee, advised by Barry, decided that the most effective plan was that proposed by a young Hull architect, Cuthbert Brodrick. He was only twenty-nine years old when he prepared his drawings, and it is said that his mother, fearing that he would be bound to fail, tried to dissuade him from entering the competition. He had previously served as a pupil with Messrs Lockwood and Mawson of Bradford, who had designed St George's Hall in Bradford and were engaged during the 1850s in the building of the new industrial town of Saltaire. Lockwood and Mawson were awarded the second prize in the Leeds contest, and Brodrick's distinction in beating them was undoubtedly a tribute to exceptional powers as well as to the fact that the Committee probably thought he would be less expensive.

Brodrick had entered the architectural profession in 1837 and terminated his articles in 1843. He specialized in Gothic building and had visited the Continent in 1844, where he saw the chief buildings of northern France, Paris, Genoa, Verona, Venice, Florence, Siena, and Rome. After such a visit, it was something of an anticlimax that his first commission in Yorkshire was for a small railway station in the East Riding. In May 1853 he watched the laying of the foundation stone of a new centre which he had designed for the Hull Literary Society and the Hull Literary and Philosophical Society, two kindred institutions of the same type as the Leeds Society to which Heaton belonged.

The Town Hall Committee was extremely cautious in the approach to Brodrick. First it sought an assurance from Barry. 'On being asked . . . whether he thought such a young man . . . might be entrusted with the construction of so large a building, Sir Charles replied that, previous to the competition he was not aware that such an architect existed, but he was fully satisfied that the Council might trust him with the most perfect safety'. Having secured this assurance from Barry, the Committee sought an assurance from Brodrick. In February 1853 it persuaded the Town Council to accept an estimate of £39,000 for the building and went on to insist on a clause in Brodrick's contract stating that he would receive no remuneration if his work exceeded this estimate. Brodrick protested against 'this very unusual clause', but said that he would agree to it 'provided that it does not hold good if the cost of the building is increased by means over which I can have no control'. The Committee accepted this qualification. At the same time a newly-appointed 'sub-committee to superintend the progress of the works' was designed to act as a watchdog.

It was during the course of 1854 and 1855 that lavish modifications were made to the initial scheme. The vestibule was extended, an organ was approved and, most important of all, a tower which had been rejected by the Council in February 1853 was again contemplated. Without a magnificent organ no Victorian public hall would have been complete, and details of the 'gigantic instrument' which was eventually installed will be given later. It excited 'considerable interest amongst organists and amateurs throughout Europe'. The tower, however, was an object of prolonged and at times bitter controversy. It had first been suggested by Barry, and Brodrick had produced a design which would cost £6,000 to execute. When the Town Council turned this down in February 1853 it was far from being the end of the story. The proposal was brought up again in September 1854 with a limitation of cost to £7,000, but it was defeated by seven votes. In February 1855 the quarterly meeting of the full Town Council decided as a compromise to allow for a form of roof construction which might eventually permit the erection of a tower 'if at any time it should be thought desirable to do so'.

The addition of a tower was strongly criticized by 'the economical section of the inhabitants on the grounds that a tower would cost money and would be only good to look at, not to use'. The 'cultured classes', of whom Dr Heaton was a spokesman – they included a large proportion of professional people – retaliated by pleading for a complete abandonment of a utilitarian attitude, however difficult that might be in Leeds, and at a meeting of the Philosophical and Literary Society in January 1854, Heaton boldly stated the non-utilitarian point of view. After discussing the town halls of the Continent, he urged that Leeds also should build an impressive 'outward symbol' of 'public government'. He went on:

> It is in such a spirit that I would have discussed the question of the propriety of adding a tower to this building. Were this a question to be decided on merely utilitarian grounds, I believe the tower must be condemned, for it is not my opinion that of the possible uses suggested, to which such an erection might be applied, are of sufficient practical importance to warrant the expense of such a structure, were these the only or the chief consideration. But let us ask what is appropriate to a building for the purpose of the one in question, and what will be conducive to its dignity and beauty? And should we decide that a tower may be made and indeed is essential to fulfil these conditions, let us not, after having nobly determined on the expenditure of so large a sum upon the body of the work, grudge a few additional thousands to give this completion to the whole.

In other words, functional criteria were explicitly set on one side, and emphasis was placed on 'nobility', 'elevating influences', and 'pretensions'. The Town Hall was to be a visible proof that 'in the ardour of mercantile pursuits the inhabitants of Leeds have not omitted to cultivate the perception of the beautiful and a taste for the fine arts'. It was to serve as 'a lasting monument of their public spirit, and generous pride in the possession of their municipal privileges'.

The language was tinged with Continental associations. Indeed, Heaton hoped that visitors would come to Leeds to see the Town Hall just as he had been to Ghent for that purpose. The Town Hall buildings, he hoped, might be 'famous beyond their own limits, and, like the noble halls of France, of Belgium and of Italy ... attract to our town the visits of strangers, dilettanti tourists, and the lovers of art from distant places'.

The advocates of the tower won the day, although the struggle was protracted. On one occasion a private citizen, J. E. Denison of Ossington, offered to contribute £100 towards its erection. It was not until March 1856 that the addition was formally approved by a majority of nineteen. The cost was to be £5,500. By then the building of the Town Hall had led to unanticipated difficulties, concerned not with the architecture but with contracting, and the cost of the whole venture had soared still further. Pride was having to be paid for in good hard cash.

4

The first stone of the new Town Hall was laid in August 1853 by John Hope Shaw, who was then Mayor of Leeds. The ceremony was attended by large crowds, and the procession 'of enormous length', led by a number of brass bands, included the vicar, the architect, the military officers stationed in the town, the committees of the Philosophical and Literary Society and the Mechanics' Institutes, the Friendly Societies, the Guardians of the Poor, and representatives of business and the professions as well as members of the Town Council and official visitors from other West Riding boroughs. After the stone had been laid, a choir consisting of members of the Madrigal and Motet Society (which had been founded three years before) then sang a rousing chorus which began:

> A blessing we ask on the work now begun,
> May it prosper in doing – be useful when done:
> May the Hall whose foundations thus broadly are laid
> Stand a trophy to Freedom – to Peace, and to Trade.

The celebrations continued with speeches from the Mayor, the Member of Parliament for Leeds, Brodrick, Canon Hook, and many of the visitors. After a civic banquet there were popular festivities on Woodhouse Moor, attended by a crowd of more than sixty thousand people. The day ended with fireworks.

A few weeks before this celebration, the contract for the building of the Town Hall had been awarded to a Leeds builder, Samuel Atack, who, in association with Benjamin Musgrave, a dyer, undertook to construct the building for £41,835, and to have it completed by 1 January 1856. The first increase in costs over the original allocation was caused by a rapid rise in the price of labour and of building materials in 1853. Leeds was unfortunate in that it built its Town Hall in a period of rising prices. It was also unfortunate that its contractor, like so many nineteenth-century contractors, lacked the capital to pursue his work continuously. He was also ineffective, partly because this was a year of full employment, in mustering a thoroughly reliable labour force. He was engaged at that time on a contract for building a barracks near Sheffield where he was employing three hundred men.

By November, Brodrick and Atack were on bad terms with each other, and for a time the excavation works were completely suspended because they were not up to Brodrick's specifications. Disputes continued throughout the early months of 1854. In February Brodrick complained of the small number of men employed on the work and told Atack that he would withhold any certificates for payment until the number of men reached 150, including 20 hewers and 40 dressers and wallers.

The Town Hall was built with a fluctuating labour force – for example, 125 on 9 February (when there was a dispute about extra rates for dressing wall stones) and only 70 on 20 February. The sub-committee visited the site on 1 March and expressed themselves 'satisfied with the work ... dissatisfied with the progress'. On 14 March, a day of bad weather, only 35 men were on the job.

The argument about the tower affected the composition and disposition of the labour force. 'Few men employed, being hindered on account of the Tower,' the clerk of works wrote on 29 April, a day when a joiner fell from the joists. In good weather on 27 June only 95 men were at work. 'This is on account of Quarries turning out badly. We have had little from Rawdon Hill for some weeks past.' Two days later the stone was said to be 'outrageous', and the clerk had to visit the quarries personally. By this time, Atack was on the site all the time himself. There was normal employment on 18 November, a fine day with no broken time, when 190 men were employed.

There are a few vivid pictures in the surviving log-book of James Donaldson, the clerk of works, of the state of affairs in 1855, a year when Britain was at war in the Crimea. In the middle of March, Brodrick visited the site and was 'so dissatisfied with the Rawdon Hill stone being used for cornices ... that he took a hammer and destroyed a cornice stone in order to prevent it being used in the building'. There were further disputes about stone in the next few months, and in October the Committee authorized Brodrick to get stone from Newcastle, Darley Dale 'or any other available place' to complete the building. In July the sub-committee visited the site and urged Atack, who was then employing 100 men, 'to get more men without delay'. The target date was not very far off. In September, Brodrick himself again complained to Atack of 'the slow progress of the works', and urged him to push them forward 'with more spirit'. The news from the Crimea made this more difficult. There was 'no work after dinner' on 17 September, to celebrate the fall of Sebastapol. The following day there were very few men at work: 'They have not all returned and are still keeping up the Illumination which was so bright last night'.

Sebastapol was on the eve of a local crisis. Atack informed Brodrick on 1 October that his bankers (Beckett & Company) had told him that they would not honour his cheques after the end of September. Brodrick replied sympathetically the following day that he was sorry to hear this news and would give him an additional certificate for £1,000 on his return to Leeds over and above what he had certified him. He appears to have been able to ease Atack's position until January 1856, when he informed him that the Committee had not given him instructions to issue any more certificates. In early April 1856 the works were standing still. 'The contractor', the clerk noted, 'is unable to proceed any further. He has been overpaid, and the architect will not certify for any more money. A little stir took place about the contractor having removed some scaffolding which was not allowed to be removed.... Policemen were sent to watch the place night and day until matters were settled.'

Work was still standing the next day when Brodrick formally reported the difficulties to his Committee. He and the chairman had a 'scene' on the site on 9 April when they ordered two workmen employed by a sub-contractor to leave their work. They reached some kind of agreement with Atack, however, and the major works were resumed the following day. Brodrick was doing his best to speed up the work when once again the Crimean War intruded. 'No work after dinner,' we read on 24 July, 'in honour of the entry of the 4th Dragoon Guards into Leeds from the Crimea.' On 2 September work was said to be unsatisfactory and many of the plasterers absent: 'some feast in the neighbourhood is the cause.'

In the autumn and early winter Atack and Brodrick were arguing once more about certificates for payment. Atack even made a bid for the tower contract, a separate contract, in order to have ready money in advance. His offer was turned down and the Committee showed that it had full confidence in Brodrick. He told them in December 1856 that he could no longer give any work certificates to Atack. 'With your concurrence I have assisted him as much as possible for many months back, and I cannot do so any further.' Atack's contract had been for £45,564: already £44,160 had been paid him. It would take an additional £4,740 to finish the work, and the arrears along with this considerable sum could not be covered under the heading of 'extra work' as he wished. 'Extra work', in Brodrick's opinion, amounted at most to £3,000. The Committee authorized Brodrick to make a temporary arrangement until after Christmas whereby payments were to be made to Atack 'by measuring the actual work done instead of by the time of the workmen generally as was formerly arranged.'

In January 1857 work stopped completely, Atack being 'unable to proceed further with any part of the work unless money is advanced to him which cannot be done as he is already overpaid according to the terms of his contract.' The chairman told Donaldson to be sure to forbid Atack from removing any materials or equipment from the site and ordered a policeman 'to look round in the night'. When Atack tried to give orders to a labourer and a few plasterers on 21 January, Brodrick intervened to send them away. Later in the month all Atack's plant and stock were finally seized, and he went bankrupt in March 1857.

Various other contractors were appointed to complete the Town Hall, and there was also a change in the clerkship of works when Donaldson left for India in the middle of June. The contract for the tower, about which there had been so much contention, was awarded to another Leeds firm. Even at this late stage, its cost exceeded the sum contemplated, and the deficiency had to be made up from an unexpected surplus on the contract for ventilating and warming the Town Hall. Further economies were made in the windows. In June 1856 it was decided that the windows should be glazed with three panes of glass throughout, instead of nine as originally intended.

The tower continued to engage the thoughts both of the Committee and of the citizens. In December 1856 E. B. Denison, Q.C., a distinguished local lawyer, delivered a lecture on Public Clocks to the Leeds Philosophical and Literary Society. In May 1857 the Council decided to install a clock and a bell. In the last stages of discussion, when the building was being completed, the Council voted unanimously the sums of money necessary. Not all the work had been completed, however, by the date of the official opening, and the building of the tower, which was suspended in the early summer of 1858, was also unfinished.

5

The official opening of the Town Hall on 7 September was intended to be a very special occasion in the life of Leeds, and so it proved to be. It was decided in 1858 to combine the opening with an exhibition of local manufactures and a music festival and to invite the Queen and the Prince Consort.

The Exhibition was to be held in the Cloth Hall. It was organized by the Leeds Chamber of Commerce, which had been formed, appropriately enough, in 1851. Its president, Darnton Lupton, had been a keen supporter of the Town Hall project. The object of the exhibition was to display the great diversity of the industrial products of Leeds, including the great variety of its machinery. To this variety John Jowitt, one of the vice-presidents of the Chamber, attributed the freedom of Leeds 'from these great fluctuations to which other manufacturing towns are subject.' He may have had Bradford in mind.

The musical festival was to be a tribute to culture in the interests of charity, the funds of the General Infirmary. There had been a growing interest in music in Leeds for several years before 1858, but the only room large enough for good concerts was the Music Hall in Albion Street, where Jenny Lind had sung and Robert Senior Burton, the organist of the Parish Church, and William Spark, the organist of St George's Church, had already arranged subscription concerts. The Town Hall was conceived of, among its many other roles, like St George's Hall, as a centre of music, and the festival was planned directly by the Town Council itself, which co-opted members of outside musical bodies on to its organizing committee. The festival was to begin with Mendelssohn's *Elijah* and to end with Handel's *Messiah*, and a great ball was to complete the programme.

The Queen's visit was to be very carefully planned. As Princess Victoria she had driven unofficially through Leeds on her way from Harewood House to Wentworth Woodhouse in 1835. To make sure that the formalities were properly handled in 1858, letters were exchanged with other corporations which had recently received the Queen, particularly Birmingham which she had visited in June 1858. Detailed arrangements were made by a special festival committee presided over by Councillor Lupton. Offers of gifts of plants, including three cartloads of evergreens, were accepted in June. An offer from a Bradford man to provide illuminations ('allow a Bradfordian to make a show in your good old town') may or may not have been taken up. It was decided to recolour the mayor's chain, bought twenty years before. The offer of a military band from Pimlico was refused. It was agreed that members of the Town Council attending the ceremony should pay for their own carriages. They were to wear full dress and official costume. Two carriages were to be provided for officers of the Corporation, and the town clerk was to have his servant on the box.

Platforms for Sunday School children were to be erected on Woodhouse Moor, where there was to be a children's demonstration, and medals were to be struck for the occasion in large numbers. The Leeds Friendly Societies, a very powerful force in the life of the town, were asked to contribute to the success of the occasion. There were 19,700 members in all, including a very large number of Oddfellows and 1,500 Foresters. The 300 members of the Leeds Corporation Flour and Provision

Society also offered to co-operate. Representatives of several of these bodies attended a special meeting of the Watch Committee to discuss arrangements.

Tickets for the Town Hall itself were in great demand and many applications were refused. The ladies of the Town Council had to ballot for seats. Among the men who were refused special admission tickets were the Medical Officer of the Leeds Infirmary, the Inspector of Schools for Yorkshire, the headmaster of the Leeds School of Art, the secretary of the Yorkshire Union of Mechanics' Institutes, the resident engineer of the Leeds and Great Northern Railway, the secretary of the Leeds Stock Exchange, the secretary of the Chamber of Commerce (this request was put up twice before the Committee), the secretary of the Leeds Anti-Slavery Society, the secretary of the Leeds Early Closing Association, and the Lord Mayor elect of London with his lady. Some of the requests were very persuasive. The secretary of the Holbeck Mechanics' Institute referred to the 'well-known liberality' of the chairman 'towards the cause of education amongst the working class'; the plea did not succeed. Another letter ran as follows:

Mr Mayor,
Dear Sir,

Having particular desire to see Her Majesty at the Town Hall I am applying to you for a Ticket as I understand you have the power to give your Friends a treat. I think I have some claim – I was born in Leeds 77 years ago last June and I hope have not been idle, I was overseer in 1812 of Marsh Lane Quarry Hill Mabgate when flour was 7s. per stone and when we had to coin palings to pay our Poor at the workhouse, and when 17 Men were hung at York for Luddism at Hudd[ersfield]. We had to pay our own expences even to our tea at the Workhouse. I was 2 years librarian at the Mechanics Institution which was over my warehouse in Basinghall Street. I was one of the first teachers along with my brother John and others, at the first Sabbath School. I am one of the Methodists to the Ebenezer Chapel belonging to the new Methodist connexion – 7 years before the Old Connexion had one. I am not weary of the employment yet . . . I was there last Sabbath and will attend as long as I am able, as I fully believe there would have been a revolution in this country but for Sabbath School and the benefits both Children and Parents have from them. As we go on the Voluntary Principle we have done 59 years for nothing but their good wishes – and Prayers – your compliance with my request will greatly oblige.

Yours respectfully,
Geo. Heap Senior.

It is refreshing to know that this request was granted.

So much spontaneous interest did not necessarily guarantee good order, and a bundle of papers survives about military and police arrangements. The chairman of the Watch Committee wrote to the Home Secretary, Spencer Walpole, for help and received a reply on 4 August from the Metropolitan Commissioner of Police, Sir Richard Mayne, promising 'any assistance in his power'. On 23 August Walpole wrote that Superintendent Walker of the Metropolitan Police would be sent down for the occasion to assist Read, the Leeds Chief Constable, and Superintendent Grauhan. The Leeds police force with its 221 members was to be augmented by 160 from the West Riding, 50 from Bradford, 93 from London, 2 from Birmingham and 17 others including 1 from Manchester, 1 from Liverpool and 1 from York. The Military were to be present in strength, chiefly four companies of the 22nd Regiment of the Foot and the 18th Hussars, and the Assistant Adjutant-General was to be in charge. Local pensioners were to be enrolled to keep order and the members of the Friendly Societies were to be used for this purpose also.

The last request before the ceremony took place came from a number of workmen. It ran:

We the undersigned workmen engaged at the Town Hall works humbly petition the Committee to take into consideration the propriety of a small grant being given to them to celebrate the successful erection and almost completion of so important and magnificent building. This being the custom in all new Buildings, either public or private, we hope will be sufficient apology for trespassing upon your valuable time at present. As the works are so nearly finished, many of the workmen must necessarily be immediately discharged, therefore we humbly and respectfully beg to solicit your earliest attention to this petition.

It was signed by paviours, plasterers, joiners, masons,

carvers, painters, gas-fitters, organ-builders, and decorators. The Committee granted the workmen £25.

While the letters were pouring in, the Committee was busy drafting a loyal address to the Queen. It recapitulated the whole case for the building of the Town Hall specially for her benefit:

> We venture to hope that so excellent a judge of art as Your Majesty may find something to approve in the Hall in which we are now for the first time assembled, and may be well pleased to see a stirring and thriving seat of English industry embellished by an edifice not inferior to those stately piles which still attest the ancient opulence of the great commercial cities of Italy and Flanders. For the mere purpose of municipal government a less spacious and costly building might have sufficed. But in our architectural plans, we have borne in mind the probability that, at no distant time, civil and criminal justice may be dispensed to an extensive region in this town, the real capital of the West Riding. We were also desirous to provide a place where large assemblies might meet in comfort to exercise their constitutional right of discussing public questions, listen to instruction on literary or philosophical subjects, or to enjoy innocent amusements.

It was a cogent statement, although its cogency would not have pleased everyone in Bradford. It ought to be added also that it was decided that a copy of the programme should be sent to the Town Clerk of York.

6

The Queen arrived in Leeds in the early evening of Monday, 6 September. The mills had been closed for the day 'almost universally', and there were dense crowds 'from an early hour until midnight'. It rained hard an hour before the Queen was due to arrive, but the few drops which fell as she arrived fortunately stopped just as she left the station. The Central Station was packed by an official welcoming party which included the Mayor, Peter Fairbairn, a self-made man who worked with his brother, the well-known engineer, William Fairbairn, in early-nineteenth-century Manchester, the Councillors and Aldermen in brand-new official robes, the Bishop of

Ripon, Lord Derby, Earl Fitzwilliam, Lord Goderich, Lord Hardwicke, M. T. Baines, M.P., R. Monckton Milnes, M.P., and Edmund Denison, the chairman of the Great Northern Railway. Both land and industry were represented on this occasion, therefore, as were Whigs and Tories. 'The appearance of the station at this time, if not very handsome,' it was said, 'was certainly attractive. The directors had not wasted the shareholders' money in elaborate decorations, but the gay uniforms of the military and the robes of the Council supplied the want, and gave to a scene which would otherwise have been very dull and uninteresting a sufficient degree of variety to make it pleasing and somewhat picturesque.' A royal salute added to the picturesqueness.

The route to Woodsley House, the home of Fairbairn, where the Queen was to stay, was lined with enthusiastic crowds behind barricades, and everywhere there were lavish decorations both on private houses and commercial buildings. The Corporation had appointed a sub-committee on street decorations. It had also provided limited funds for them, but these allocations were only a tiny fraction of the total amount spent. Flags, banners, elaborate wooden arches and colonnades, flowers and streamers were everywhere. 'The new styles of street architecture, improvised for the occasion, relieved very effectively the monotony of a protracted route, in certain portions through an unattractive district,' the *Leeds Mercury* wrote, 'whilst the profusion of banners . . . reminded one rather of some rustic fête or May-day festivity of the olden times, than of the rejoicings of a sober, money-making, mercantile community.' One chemist, Mr Trant, in Park Lane even perfumed the air outside his shop, 'and thus another sense was gratified'.

The comments made at the time in the local press suggest that a mood of quite unreal romance was being cultivated in Leeds for this royal occasion. Again the Town Hall was the symbol of it, in much the same way that the Crystal Palace had been the symbol of romance for the nation in 1851. Once the Queen had seen the 32,110 Sunday School children on Woodhouse Moor – a record gathering of this kind – and moved in gay procession down Woodhouse Lane and through the centre of the town, she was confronted with the Town Hall as a glorious climax. A giant arch had been built at the top of East Parade. Designed by Brodrick himself, it was constructed 'in imitation of stone in the style of architecture commonly called *Renaissance*'. The object of placing the arch at the top of East Parade was to hide the Town Hall from view 'so that the full effect of the noble structure might be realized by Her Majesty at once'. French, Prussian, and American flags were flying on the arch beside the Union Jack and the Royal Standard.

'Everyone was evidently proud of the Town Hall and felt that it was worthy of a Royal inauguration.' A statue of the Queen, the work of Edward Behnes and costing a thousand guineas, had been presented to the Council by the Mayor. It dominated the vestibule, so much so that the *Leeds Mercury* wrote that 'in our judgment the Queen ought for ever to have that noble vestibule, the gem of the Town Hall entirely to herself'. The words 'Europe–Asia–Africa–America' round the vestibule reminded the inhabitants of Leeds that they were part of an Empire, 'that Her Majesty's dominion extends to all quarters of the globe'. The Queen and Prince Consort paused to admire the statue as they came in. They also surveyed 'the beautiful decorations of the dome'. The organ then pealed out the national anthem, the Bishop of Ripon said prayers (Dr Hook wrote later that he felt quite out of it), the Hallelujah Chorus was sung, and the address which had been so carefully prepared was read by the Town Clerk. It ended with the words:

It is probable [in the future] that experimental science will have made great progress; that inventions of which we have seen the promising infancy will have been brought by successive improvements near to perfection; and that the material wealth of our island may be such as would now seem fabulous. Yet we trust that even then our Hall will be seen with interest as a memorial of a time when England already enjoyed order and freedom, profound tranquillity and steadily increasing prosperity, under a Sovereign exemplary in the discharge of every political and of every domestic duty; and that those who visit this building will contemplate it with double interest when they are told that it was inaugurated by the good Queen Victoria.

The Queen replied quite simply, praising 'the active industry and enterprising spirit' of Leeds as much as she praised 'the noble hall' itself. The Prince Consort also spoke before the Queen knighted Fairbairn. This was a popular gesture both with the middle class of Leeds and with the crowd. When a statue of him was erected by public subscription in 1868, seven years after his death, it is recorded that there was a huge crowd present 'chiefly of the working classes, with whom he was a great favourite'.

After the ceremony was over in 1858, the royal pair left for the station. It had been a remarkable visit. 'For a portion of two days, through the condescension of Her Majesty,' the *Leeds Mercury* wrote, 'this old and busy seat of industry becomes in a sense the seat of the Empire.' For once, the Tory rival of the *Mercury*, the *Leeds Intelligencer*, agreed. 'A novel had just now been issued from the press entitled *Every Man his own Trumpetor*. We have not read it; and are not quite up to the science of blowing our own trumpet, but are pleasantly saved the disaster in failing in the attempt to sound the praises of our native town ... by the more independent ... comments of others.... We could not have claimed such praises as *The Times* bestows though we are quite disposed to regard them as well deserved.' *The Times* spoke of loyalty and affection as well as energy. Leeds had been superabundant in the last of these qualities: it had now shown that it possessed the others in good measure too.

After the royal visitors had left Leeds, the Queen having approved of the 'entire arrangements' and having noted with appreciation 'the loyalty and affection' of the 'vast assemblages of people', a great luncheon was held in the Town Hall for nearly four hundred guests. Most of the speeches on this ceremonial occasion were concerned with the Town Hall. The Bishop of Ripon stated that the erection of the building was 'an indication of the prosperity of the borough' – a prosperity to which, he trusted, it was destined very largely to contribute. This was exactly the right note on which to start. The religious note came next. He had been concerned with the opening of many religious buildings in the Leeds area. Although the Town Hall was not designed specifically for the purposes of religious worship, it had been constructed so that 'within its walls justice might be duly administered, scientific inquiry pursued, knowledge advanced and developed'. These were high purposes, best associated with religion. The *Bradford Observer*'s comments on St George's Hall were relevant in this context. Councillor Beckett who spoke soon afterwards related the Town Hall a little more mundanely to the other improvements which had recently been made in the town, 'the supply of water, the drainage, the efficiency of the police, and the lighting of the borough'.

The two Members of Parliament for the West Riding, Edmund Denison, a Conservative, and Lord Goderich, a Whig, were particularly eloquent. Denison, who had earlier welcomed the Queen at the station as chairman of the Great Northern Railway Company, claimed that she had always evinced her readiness to visit any great town whose inhabitants were ready at their own expense to erect institutions and buildings like Leeds Town Hall, 'calculated to lead to the intellectual improvement of all those around it'. The citizens of Leeds had roused themselves 'from their lethargy with regard to intellectual pursuits . . . convinced, at last, that there were other matters well worth their attention besides manufacturing broad-cloth for the purpose of making money'. Not that making money was not necessary. The Prince Consort had that morning visited the Exhibition of Local Industry in the Cloth Hall. 'Beautiful as was their Town Hall,' Denison ventured to say, 'their Exhibition was better worth their study and attention.' The romance was not to turn their heads, nor were 'the intellectual pursuits'.

Goderich admired the Town Hall as a product of the wealth and energy of Leeds, but he brought out yet a further note, not an easy accomplishment at this late stage of the proceedings. The building showed not only the public spirit and liberality of the town but the vigour and vitality of the Corporation which had sponsored both the building and the festival. Goderich had always thought municipal institutions of the greatest value to the country. Long might England preserve and cherish them! 'In the Town Hall the Corporation', he felt sure, 'would discharge their duties for the administration of the affairs of the town with the same success which had crowned their efforts in the erection of that edifice.' The *Leeds Mercury* underlined the point made by Goderich. 'If there is anything of which Leeds might justly be proud in this municipal adventure, it is that it had been erected by the people's own means and representatives, and is not conferred upon us by a lordly proprietor or patron.'

One of the Members of Parliament for Leeds, M. T. Baines, echoed the views of his colleagues, adding, as if to show that the aspirations of Leeds were not yet fully satisfied, that he hoped that now that Leeds had good accommodation for courts of justice, it ought to be in a very strong position indeed to press its claims to 'assume the rank and character of an assize town'. A later speaker added that Lord Brougham had told him that the new court rooms in the Town Hall were 'unequalled in their arrangement'. Presumably this had been on the occasion of Brougham's visit to a great soirée of the Mechanics' Institute in November 1857, a visit which inspired Hook to dilate on the virtues of life in Leeds. Brougham had sung the praises of Leeds in 1830. The inhabitants of the great manufacturing towns, Hook now argued, were superior in morals as well as in intelligence to the inhabitants of the rural districts. 'There was a wonderful weight of energy in the manufacturing districts for counteracting vice which they in the country did not possess.' Crime was far lower than the critics of cities believed. Nevertheless, Leeds needed its courts at least as a symbol of its pride, and the local ambition to become an assize town was eventually satisfied in 1864, when the county of York was divided for assize purposes.

One of the last speakers at the luncheon of 1858 was Brodrick who was 'warmly applauded by the whole company'. It would be interesting to know what his thoughts were on this occasion. As it is, all that the reports say is that Brodrick 'briefly replied'. By 1858 he had become a genuine Leeds citizen. He lived in bachelor lodgings at Far Headingley among the great Victorian villas and was an active member of the Leeds Club, which was much frequented by the merchants and professional gentlemen of the town. He designed many other interesting buildings in Leeds, including the fascinating and unorthodox Corn Exchange of 1860, with a magnificent glass roof like the inverted hull of a ship.

7

The Town Hall itself remains an impressive architectural monument both to Brodrick and to his age. It covered an area of 5,600 square yards and was located in what is now a commanding position. The position was made more commanding in 1858 by a 'platform of earth' being specially thrown-up for the occasion.

The basic plan was a parallelogram 250 feet by 200 feet, conceived in the grand 'Renaissance' manner, symmetrical but essentially simple. A single order of Corinthian columns and pilasters was to support an entablature and balustrade just under 70 feet in height. The large Victoria Hall rises out of the centre of the building to a height of 92 feet. One hundred and sixty-one feet long by 72 feet wide and 75 feet high, it was quite deliberately intended to be bigger than other provincial halls, including St George's Hall in Bradford, and to vie with the Guildhall in the City of London. The inhabitants of Leeds might not have been able to argue for long about the merits of 'Renaissance' architecture, but they could appreciate statistical tables of the following kind:

	Feet Long	*Feet Wide*	*Feet High*
Westminster Hall	228	66	92
St George's Hall, Liverpool	169	74	75
Birmingham Town Hall	145	65	65
Durham Castle	180	50	36
London Guildhall	153	50	55
London Euston Station Hall	125	61	60
Leeds Town Hall	161	72	75

They could also appreciate the decorations. The Hall was 'enriched with ornament in relief and in colour in almost lavish manner, every portion being more or less decorated'. The sides of the Hall were divided into five bays by composite Corinthian columns and pilasters 'in imitation of Rosso Antico' with gilt bronze capitals and bases, standing upon a surbase 'inlaid with precious and rare specimens of marbles, executed in the most finished style of painting'. An enriched entablature ran round the hall, and from it sprang 'a fine circular ceiling, highly ornamented with conventional foliage'. The Hall was lit by ten semi-circular windows, the stained glass for which was made in Manchester. The cut-glass chandeliers were made in Birmingham. All the riches of Victorian England were thus being lavished on Leeds. The mottoes inscribed in various parts of the Hall were superbly Victorian also. 'Except the Lord build the House, they labour in vain that build it'. 'Except the Lord keep the city, the watchman watcheth but in vain'. 'Weave Truth with Trust'. 'Magna Charta'. 'Forward'. And from Bradford, '*Labor omnia vincit*'.

The coloured decorations in the Hall and vestibule were the work of John Crace of London. Over the tympanum of the entrance to the vestibule there was placed a striking emblematic group of figures, elaborately carved by John Thomas, one of the sculptors of the House of Commons. The group represented Leeds 'in its commercial and industrial character, fostering and encouraging the Arts and Sciences'. The central figure, which was 'almost colossal', was that of a female in free and elegant drapery holding in her outstretched right hand a wreath and in her left a distaff. Justice, the Fine Arts, Poetry and Music were represented by other figures. So, at least as appropriately, was Industry, 'looking with anxious care towards the principal figure holding in her hands samples of textile fabrics'. Mercury smiled on the scene, 'symbolic of Order, Peace and Prosperity'.

Contemporaries delighted in these features as they delighted in the magnificent organ, built in London and costing £6,000. They were impressed, too, by the Council Chamber with its rich ornamentation, marred a little at first by the fact that there had not been time to complete the coloured decoration before the inauguration and that consequently the walls and ceiling had been 'distempered with plain tints'.

The façade, the massive proportions, the flight of twenty steps, the sombre stone and the black lions are the features of the Town Hall which have most interested posterity. Yet the façade was changed from the original plan, and the stone, impressive though it remains, came from several places. The main quarries were not far from Leeds, but Darley Dale stone was used for the large blocks of stone in the south colonnade and the stone for the lions was Portland stone from Dorset. The lions themselves were an improvisation. At the time the Leeds Corporation was asking for estimates and models, Brodrick met a stone-carver working on the Town Hall at Hull. He was so impressed that he sent the carver, Noble, to the Zoological Gardens, Regents Park, to model four lions for Leeds Town Hall. Estimates were asked for by the Corporation and Noble's tender of £600 was considerably lower than his two rivals' £1,200 and £800.

The tower, about which so much argument had arisen, fittingly completed the edifice. The small towers, in reality ornamental ventilating flues, recalled the towers of Hanover Chapel in Regent Street, designed by C. R. Cockerell in 1825. The main dome-capped tower, however, was unique. It was not completed in September 1858, nor was it ready for the meeting of the British Association in Leeds later in the year. To have completed it for this great intellectual occasion, always a landmark in the history of nineteenth-century provincial towns, would have been truly symbolic in the light of all that had gone before.

So successful, however, was the general effect of the Leeds Town Hall that it provided inspiration for at least three other town halls, that of near-by Morley, usually profoundly suspicious of Leeds, Portsmouth, and Bolton. Brodrick was asked to submit a design for the last of these, but he refused to co-operate with a local architect as the Bolton Corporation wished. The result was that another Leeds architect, William Hill, got the commission and completed the work.

Perhaps the last word on Leeds Town Hall should be a word on cost. It was doubtless a great monument to business energy and to civic pride, but it cost far more, as most monuments do, than was originally intended. The structure and fittings cost

£122,000 or £80,165 more than the original estimate. The advocates of 'economy', so powerful in mid-Victorian local government, would never have supported the project had they known this, and there was an inevitable lull in civic spending in Leeds after 1858. When Edward Baines urged that a fund should be raised to decorate the new Town Hall with paintings by eminent Victorian artists, a subscription fund was opened, but the subscriptions did not come in. 'The times were not ripe for such a movement', he complained. 'The people of Leeds had been inclined to see the necessity of making their Town Hall more creditable to themselves ... but had not advanced far enough to feel emulous of the local patriotism which distinguished the good Flemish and German burghers of the Middle Ages.'

CHAPTER FIVE

Birmingham: The Making of a Civic Gospel

I only hope that Corporations generally will become much more expensive than they have been – not expensive in the sense of wasting money, but that there will be such nobleness and liberality amongst the people of our towns and cities as will lead them to give their Corporations power to expend more money on those things which, as public opinion advances, are found to be essential to the health and comfort and improvement of our people.

JOHN BRIGHT in a speech at
Birmingham (January 1864)

I

CIVIC pride in Leeds expressed itself in fits and starts: it inspired great events in the life of the city, but more usually it exhausted itself in local rivalry. In Birmingham, by contrast, civic pride was the driving force of a whole civic philosophy, known at the time and since as 'the civic gospel'. In eighteenth- and early-nineteenth-century Birmingham there was immense pride in the bare social and economic fact that 'there is scarcely a town in America or Europe that is not indebted for some portion of its luxury or its comfort to the enterprise and ingenuity of the men of Birmingham'. In the Victorian age, however, the pride went deeper and concerned itself as much with politics as with economics. The fruits of the civic gospel included a sweeping reorganization of the functions and finances of local government. Birmingham, already so widely known for its 'Brummagem' wares, not all of which were highly prized, acquired the international reputation during the 1870s and early 1880s of being 'the best-governed city in the world'.

The gospel did not depend on local rivalry, although contemporaries drew an illuminating contrast between society and politics in Manchester and Birmingham, and historians have since divided the nineteenth century chronologically with Manchester leading in the early part of Queen Victoria's reign and Birmingham leading in the last phases. 'In many ways,' G. M. Young has written in a memorable passage, 'the change from Early to Late-Victorian England is symbolized in the names of two great cities: Manchester, solid, uniform, pacific, the native home of the great economic creed on which aristocratic England has always looked, and educated England was beginning to look, with some aversion and some contempt: Birmingham, experimental, adventurous, diverse, where old Radicalism might in one decade flower into lavish Socialism, in another into a pugnacious Imperialism.'

Illuminating though this contrast is, it is important not to press it too far. Birmingham was more important than Manchester in national history during the seven years which preceded Queen Victoria's accession to the throne. Before there was an Anti-Corn Law League there was a Birmingham Political Union. Before there was a Manchester School there was a Birmingham School of political economists. Before Richard Cobden there was Thomas Attwood, whose power and influence depended on a platform agitation. Moreover, after Manchester's rise to national prominence in the late 1830s and the 1840s there was always, as we have seen, a substantial minority (at times a majority) in the city who refused to accept the doctrines with which the city was generally associated.

There was far less uniformity in Manchester than people in London believed, certainly far less 'pacifism' of all varieties. It was Bright who was burned in effigy during the Crimean War, not Palmerston or even Tsar Nicholas. There was also a very considerable if inadequately satisfied local interest in the collective well-being of Manchester, an interest which can be traced in local meetings, local newspapers, and costly local enterprises. At the same time, Birmingham for several decades lagged behind: the very vitality of the civic gospel in the 1870s was a measure, in part at least, of the extent of the leeway which the city had to make up after wasted years in the middle of the century. There was a long period of strict economy and of civic stagnation before the feeling of adventure began to dominate the men who mattered. Before the Birmingham Education Society, the precursor of the National Education League and indirectly of the National Liberal Federation, came into existence in 1867, there was a Manchester Education Aid Society. Before Birmingham opened its first public library, Manchester already had one. And as for 'aristocratic England', it had no great liking for either place.

The real contrast between Manchester and Birmingham was a contrast of economic and social structure, and in this respect the two cities were very different from each other during all periods of the nineteenth century. Four conditions of work in Birmingham set the terms of its social history. First, there was great diversity of occupation, far greater than in Leeds: more than five hundred classes of trade gave what a Board of Health Commissioner in 1849 called 'exceptional elasticity to the trade of the town'. Second, work was carried on in small workshops rather than in large factories, and economic development throughout the century multiplied the number of producing units rather than added to the scale of existing enterprises. Manchester was quite different in this respect. 'There are no large and crowded factories,' a factory inspector stated in 1843, 'such as abound in the other districts.' Relations between 'masters' and 'men' in Birmingham were close therefore, if not always good, and the economic and political philosophies which thrived locally were those which laid emphasis on 'mutual interests', 'interdependence' and 'common action'. Birmingham was a place, John Collins, the local Chartist, later remarked, where 'large manufacturers cannot shut up their men as they did in Manchester . . . for it was well known that [in Manchester] the working people were at the mercy of the manufacturers.'

Third, a large proportion of the Birmingham labour force was skilled and therefore relatively well-off economically: the city thus suffered far less from the introduction of machinery – as a contemporary argued in 1836 – than cities like Manchester where machinery was, in a great degree, 'an actual *substitute* for human labour'. There was less pressure, therefore, for 'factory reform' and less fear of women's and children's labour, more dependence on friendly societies and less on trade unions, and a far greater emphasis on education. Housing was better than in most English industrial cities, and the Select Committee on the Health of Towns had extolled the practice of 'each family living in a separate dwelling' as 'conducive to comfort and cleanliness'. The benefits of 'the age of improvement' were felt to be shared, if unequally. The People's Hall, sponsored by artisans and completed in 1846, was dedicated to the object of 'the educational, moral and political improvement of the people': it was in existence only three years, but its ethos lingered for the rest of the century.

Fourth, there was considerable social mobility in Birmingham, or at least considerable local optimism about the prospects of 'rising in society'. Faucher noted this. 'It was always a peculiarity of Birmingham', a London journalist declared in the early 1850s, 'that small household trades existed which gave the inmates independence, and often led – if the trade continued good – to competence or fortune.' Of course, if trade turned bad, as it often did in a city of marked industrial fluctuations, small masters might find themselves 'men' again. The mobility worked both ways. Distress, however, did not divide masters and men in Birmingham: it brought them together by encouraging common statements of grievances.

In such circumstances, there was ample scope for political co-operation in Radical causes. This did not start with Joseph Chamberlain and the creation of the Birmingham Liberal 'caucus' in the 1860s and 1870s: it was a persistent element in civic life. The Birmingham Political Union, founded by Attwood in 1829, was designed to bring together in 'harmonious co-operation' middle and working classes – together they constituted what he called 'the industrious classes' – to 'knock at the gates of government' and secure parliamentary and economic reform. Economic and social power was wielded by the local 'middle class', but they were quite prepared to share a militant Radical ideology, and to unite against common enemies. It was Attwood, a middle-class banker and industrialist, who pinned his trust in a million able-bodied unemployed and a bad harvest as conditions of a 'further reform of parliament'. He believed that it would be 'a much quieter and easier operation' than it had been in 1832.

Thirteen years later, Joseph Sturge's Complete Suffrage Union was a vigorous and high-minded attempt 'to unite two dissevered classes' pulled apart during the late 1830s by the rival pressures of Chartism and the Anti-Corn Law League, neither of which had its headquarters in Birmingham. Sturge, a Quaker corn factor, seemed to symbolize the dedicated Birmingham middle-class leader willing to serve the political interests of working men with whom he was associated economically. He demanded not only repeal of the corn laws but manhood suffrage. He even constructed a model ballot box so that electors might better understand the mechanics of the secret ballot.

Few leaders of the Birmingham middle classes went as far as Sturge in the turbulent years of national class conflict during the early 1840s, but many working men responded to his message. One of them, John Mason, a shoemaker, who had arrived in Birmingham from Newcastle-on-Tyne as one of Feargus O'Connor's Chartist lecturers, declared unequivocally in 1849, on the eve of emigrating to the United States, that 'the strength of democracy consists in reconciling the various classes of society, and inspiring every man with a just confidence of public order and security'.

By the end of the 1840s a working alliance had been re-forged in Birmingham, and it was to last throughout the middle years of the century. In due time it was to facilitate the rise of Joseph Chamberlain to local and subsequently to national power. The alliance was neither experimental nor adventurous, but it gave Birmingham the same position of primacy in relation to the struggle for the 1867 Reform Bill as it had exercised during the struggles of 1830 to 1832. A Committee of Non-Electors was active as early as the general election of 1847 in pressing for the return of the two Liberal candidates, and for their part the Liberal candidates pledged themselves to an extension of the suffrage. When John Bright changed his parliamentary constituency from Manchester to Birmingham in 1857, after being defeated in Lancashire, the non-electors supported his candidature as strongly as the electors: they had been active in all the elections of the preceding period and they remained so until 1867.

Not surprisingly, Bright, in his first address to his new constituents, electors and non-electors alike, meeting in a crowded Town Hall, had half to apologize for arguing the case for reform in a city which thirty years earlier had 'shaken the fabric of privilege to its base'. 'Not a few of the strong men of that time are now white with age.... Shall their sons be less noble than they?' he asked his excited audience. 'Shall the fire which they kindled be extinguished with you?... I see your answer in every face. You are resolved that the legacy which they bequeathed to you, you will hand down in an accumulated wealth of freedom to your children.' Birmingham had established a radical tradition.

It was about this time that Richard Cobden wrote that 'the state of society' was 'more healthy and natural in a moral and political sense' in Birmingham than in Manchester. 'There is a freer intercourse between all classes than in the Lancashire town where a great and impassable gulf separates the workman from his employer.'

The language of 'union' remained the favourite local mode of political expression, even when the vote itself, which had been envisaged by Attwood in 1832 and Sturge in 1842 as a necessary means of securing further economic reform, began to be thought of more and more as a crowning recognition of personal worth and responsibility among the working-class sections of the population. In 1849 a political meeting looked forward to 'a happy union of all classes for the purpose of securing their full and efficient representation in Parliament': when Bright launched his new crusade in 1859 it was the recently founded Reformers' Union which mobilized support to advance it. It soon gave way to a politically more broadly based Reform Association, but the new association devoted itself from the start to securing wide class support.

The Liberalism of Joseph Chamberlain gained sustenance from this soil. The Birmingham Liberal Association was founded in February 1865. It co-operated closely with the Reform League, a national organization which won widespread working-class support in the battle which led up to the

Reform Act of 1867. 'In Birmingham,' Bright exclaimed later in that year, 'I believe the "middle class" is ready to work heartily with the "working class", and I hope a thorough union may take place.'

James Baldwin, a Town Councillor who had long been a supporter of political alliance between middle and working classes, was one of the founders of the Liberal Association and the first president of the Reform League. The first secretary of the Association was George Dixon, a rich and philanthropic merchant, who became a Member of Parliament for Birmingham at a by-election in 1867. Another member of the committee was Councillor William Harris, 'the Abbé Siéyès of Birmingham', a leader writer for the *Birmingham Daily Post* and a most active and intelligent political wire-puller behind the scenes. He succeeded Dixon as secretary of the Association when it was reorganized on the eve of the general election in October 1868.

By the reorganization, the Association was finally transformed into the 'caucus'. It was open for membership to anyone willing to pay a nominal annual subscription of one shilling. It was divided into ward branches, 'the grass roots' of the organization, with permanent committees, each ward electing members to a General Committee, which increased in size as the population of Birmingham grew. A smaller Executive Committee managed day-to-day affairs. The Association proved its efficiency at the general election of 1868, when it ensured the return of three Liberal Members of Parliament even though each elector had only two votes under the new Act. Liberal voters voted 'as they were told'. In some wards they were told to vote for Bright and Dixon, in others for Dixon and Muntz (Bright's colleague as sitting Liberal Member), in the remainder for Muntz and Bright. They not only secured enormous Liberal majorities of three to one, but demonstrated their discipline by voting in such a way that there was less than five hundred votes difference between the first and the third Liberal victor. 'The whole credit of having initiated and carried out this new machinery', Joseph Chamberlain said later, 'belongs to my friend, Mr Harris.' A subscription list was prepared for him and a gift of £240 collected. He went on to serve as vice-president and president of the Association.

Chamberlain profited directly from the work of the 'caucus' and in time, as it provided a pattern for other constituency Liberal parties and the National Liberal Federation, came to be identified with it. He had arrived in Birmingham in 1854 at the age of eighteen, and very quickly established a reputation in a limited circle not only as a business man but as a forceful and unusual personality. He smoked endless strong cigars, and amazed hostesses by 'the effrontery with which he talked pure undiluted politics at social functions'. He once appeared at a public meeting in a seal-skin topcoat. 'This made people gasp', a local journalist reminisced more than forty years later. 'Any man daring enough to dress thus', he added, 'must be a Caesar or a Napoleon.' Another writer chose a different parallel. 'What Wellington was in military matters, Chamberlain was in politics.' Chamberlain was not a member, however, of the committee of the first Liberal Association of 1865 nor a prominent local politician in the struggles of 1867. His main local activity was concerned with the Vestry Committee of the Unitarian Church, and bodies like the local debating society.

He emerged into full public life only two years later when the Radical and Nonconformist National Education League was founded: he was elected chairman of its executive committee and soon became well known outside as well as inside Birmingham. The National Education League was in some ways more important in local Birmingham life than in the life of the nation. It could not direct or divert W. E. Forster, who was preparing the first great national Education Act, but it drew into local politics many people who otherwise might have stayed aloof. They argued the case for public control of education with the same passion that they had displayed in their Sunday School work and Nonconformist activity within their own denominations. Dixon was first president of the Birmingham Education Society: the secretary was Jesse Collings, an immigrant from Devonshire, who was to be closely associated with Chamberlain in national as well as local politics as the century went by. When Dixon resigned his seat on the Birmingham Town Council on becoming Member of Parliament in 1868, Collings took his place.

Chamberlain entered the Town Council a year later. He first spoke in the Town Hall in that year, attacking the opposition of the House of Lords to the disestablishment of the Irish Church, and characteristically condemning the feudal aristocracy for securing unearned income from land held 'in the vicinity of great towns, like Birmingham and Manchester'. It was said later that it was the bright idea of Francis Schnadhorst, a 'spectacled, sallow, sombre' Birmingham Nonconformist draper, who kept a tailor's shop in Bill Street, that Chamberlain should be pushed into local politics. Yet he did not need much pushing. When a deputation headed by Harris, 'the father of the Caucus', invited him to stand as a Liberal candidate for St Paul's ward, he immediately accepted. He was recommended to the electors as 'a large ratepayer, a man of thorough business habits, enlarged views and marked ability, belonging indeed to precisely the class of burgesses most desirable on the council'.

Four years later he was chosen as Mayor. The contests in St Paul's ward in 1873 just before he became Mayor were particularly bitter ones, and in 1872 he won by only sixty-one votes. Chamberlain was attacked as 'a monopolizer and a modern dictator' ('Now, lads, let's be equal and I will be your king'), and a key role in the victory was played by W. J. Davis, the secretary of the Brass-workers, who persuaded twenty-one members of his union who had signed a petition in favour of Chamberlain's Conservative opponent to change sides at the last moment. The tradition of co-operation between middle and working classes had been reaffirmed at a crucial moment, and the Working Men's Reform League merged itself with the Liberal Association. The tradition of co-operation was reaffirmed also in the School Board elections of 1873 which led to a Liberal triumph and placed Chamberlain in the chairmanship of the School Board as well as the mayoralty. When Chamberlain contested the general election at Sheffield in 1874, a group of workers from Birmingham went with him to help in the campaign. A year later Chamberlain told Davis, 'if you want to be on the School Board or the Town Council, come to me. As far as I can see, your principles are the same as mine.'

2

The choice of Chamberlain as Mayor was to have far more than local importance, yet it must figure dramatically in any study of Victorian cities. His three years of office from 1873 to 1876 saw the implementation of a civic gospel which had its origins not only in the economic and social alliances described above, but in religious idealism and mounting dissatisfaction with narrow conceptions of the proper scope of local government. The positive radicalism which Chamberlain put into practice in Birmingham was to be canvassed throughout the country, as was the caucus system of securing it. Both were wildly controversial, yet both forced the local problems of big cities into national prominence. City government was never quite the same again.

Chamberlain saw his task as that of governing Birmingham in the interests of 'the people', all the people. This objective was not in itself new. The Birmingham Political Union had prided itself, in the words of the *Birmingham Journal* of February 1830, on having 'a most salutary effect in our parish affairs. The Junta who have hitherto controlled the business of the town have, by a steady system of concert and combination, too frequently succeeded in carrying obnoxious measures which might otherwise have been easily defeated, if the parishioners had only adopted similar plans of resistance.' These words were written before the incorporation of Birmingham in 1838. The Union pledged itself in one of its formal objects to redress 'local public wrongs and oppressions and all local encroachments upon the rights, interests and privileges of the community'.

In the struggle to obtain a charter of incorporation which would transfer power to an elected Town Council, emphasis was placed in Birmingham, as in other and older places, on the total abolition of the 'oligarchical system'. The Street Commissioners survived in Birmingham until 1852, doing much good work, but their final disappearance was heralded as a 'victory of the people'. Chamberlain spoke in these terms when he laid the foundation stone of the new municipal buildings in 1873. 'I have an abiding faith in municipal institutions, an abiding sense of the value and importance of local government.... Our Corporation represents the authority of the people. Through them you obtain the full and direct expression of the popular will, and consequently, any disrespect to us, anything that would depreciate us in the public estimation necessarily degrades the principles which we represent.'

It was very similar language to that used by Lord Goderich after the opening of Leeds Town Hall. It was language which could come quite naturally to a Radical of the Manchester School, like Bright, as the motto of this chapter suggests. It did not necessarily imply a positive or constructive attitude to the tasks of local government: indeed stress on representation, the stress of the Municipal Reform Act of 1835, might imply relative lack of concern for function. Radicalism itself, in local or in national government, might appeal more to economy and retrenchment than to activity. Chamberlain, however, always spoke and thought in positive and constructive terms. He was a builder rather than a debater: this is why he was often accused, as he was in St Paul's Ward in 1872, of 'monopolizing' and 'dictating'. 'There is no nobler sphere for those who have not the opportunity of engaging in imperial politics', he believed to the end of his life, 'than to take part in municipal work, to the wise conduct of which they owe the welfare, the wealth, the comfort, and the lives of 400,000 people.'

Half way through his mayoralty, he talked of Birmingham within twelve months 'not knowing itself'. When it was over, he referred with pride to the 'new duties and extended work' which had been imposed on the Town Council and argued forcefully that 'increased responsibilities bring with them a higher sense of the dignity and importance of municipal work'. A few years later, when he became a Cabinet Minister in 1880, he wrote that unless he could secure for the nation the same social improvements which he had already secured in Birmingham 'it will have been a sorry exchange to give up the Town Council for the Cabinet'.

The sense of adventure in local government and of increased responsibility were learned by Chamberlain not only from advanced Liberals, like Harris, who served on the Town Council from 1865 to 1871, but from Nonconformist ministers in Birmingham who were the first people boldly to proclaim a 'civic gospel'. It is scarcely surprising that they should have been drawn into radical causes early in the century when they were always conscious of the fact that they were battling against the 'establishment' or that they should have been so prominent in the education controversies of the late 1860s, when the attack on Church privilege was a key theme in the agitation. What is more surprising is that they gave other grounds for their civic initiative and provided a richer kind of inspiration.

The most significant of the Nonconformist ministers, because he came first and because he always displayed striking originality, was George Dawson, born in London in 1821 and educated at Aberdeen and Glasgow Universities. Dawson began his ministry in Birmingham at Mount Zion Baptist Chapel in 1844. He was the Baptists' second choice, and if some of them were a little suspicious of their new minister, they were right to be so. His education, secular in tone, had diverged sharply from that of most Baptist ministers, and he was quite uninfluenced by evangelicalism and its 'scheme of salvation'. Yet whatever Baptist suspicions there were – and they quickly led to a complete break – Dawson made an immediate impact on a far bigger section of the numerically and socially strong local Nonconformist population. He was a striking figure to see and an appealing preacher to hear, conversational rather than rhetorical, practical, allusive and inspiring: Charles Kingsley later called him 'the greatest talker in England'. Congregationalists found his sermons startlingly original: Unitarians, the group to which Chamberlain belonged, were sufficiently impressed for one of them to say that this was the preaching for which they had longed all their lives. Collings, for example, became one of the most enthusiastic members of his congregation.

In August 1847 Dawson opened his own church in Birmingham, the Church of the Saviour, in the middle of the city. It had a 'preacher's platform' in place of a pulpit, a platform which Dawson occupied weekly until his death in 1876. From this platform, solely under his own control, Dawson could address the citizens of Birmingham on any subject he wished. Characteristically his first sermon in the Church of the Saviour was later printed with the title 'The Demands of the Age on the Church'. Dawson's congregation, which included many people who were or became influential in the civic life of Birmingham, beginning with Harris himself, was pledged to no doctrinal tests: its members regarded fixed creeds as 'productive of mischief' and appealed instead to 'the authority of conscience'. Religion was judged by its effects on practical conduct. Opinions might differ, but behaviour should not. The bond between the members of Dawson's congregation, therefore, was 'a common end and purpose – to clothe the naked, to feed the hungry, and to instruct the ignorant'. Dawson himself turned for many of his opinions to a Unitarian, James Martineau of Liverpool, the brother of Harriet: he preached his message from every platform available to him, in lectures as much as in sermons. In his lectures he set out 'to inculcate great principles' which he thought 'needful to the people's well-being. ... I regard this', he said, 'as my wooden horse, which I can get within the walls of Troy.'

Birmingham was his Troy. He urged his congregation – some of whom attended the Church of the Saviour once on Sunday either before or after attending another place of worship – to give all their talents to the service of the city. At the opening of the Birmingham Free Reference Library in 1866 he made one of his most memorable addresses on this theme. 'A great town', he declared, 'exists to discharge towards the people of that town the duties that a great nation exists to discharge towards the people of that nation.' In an age of nationalism this was a stirring pronouncement: it gained in force from Dawson's well-known sympathy with Continental movements. He was also an avowed admirer of Thomas Carlyle, whose concern for the heroic he related to the everyday life of a provincial city. 'A town is a solemn organism through which shall flow, and in which shall be shaped, all the highest, loftiest and truest ends of man's moral nature.'

Dawson went even further and compared the idea of a 'new corporation', providing numerous public libraries and education for all its citizens, with the old idea of a church. The public library movement was in his view 'the largest and widest Church ever established'. Like the Church of the Saviour, it demanded 'no test' and 'no articles': it offered 'a brotherhood removed from the endless grovellings and the bickerings which surround us'. The brotherhood was universal. Speaking of the Town Librarian, Dawson said that he envied him profoundly. 'I am glad', he went on, 'that the Corporation has given itself an officer who represents intellect – that it looks upward deliberately and says – "we are a corporation who have undertaken the highest duty that is possible for us; we have made provision for our people – for *all* our people – and we have made provision of God's greatest and best gifts unto men".'

The same point about '*all* our people' had been made, interestingly enough, in Manchester.'[1] 'The most hopeful feature about rate-supported libraries', the Manchester Mechanics' Institution had reported in 1853, 'is that when fairly worked, they are pre-eminently Institutions for *all classes*. It is doubtless a good thing that the rich, out of their abundance, shall give liberally for the education, the refinement and the rational amusement [of the poor]. . . . It is a better thing for them to unite their contributions, in such proportions as they can for such objects. But it is best of all that they should make a common effort for a common purpose; that they should continue to extend that public domain for mental culture which is the joint heritage and ought to be the common enjoyment of rich and poor.' Dawson's view of duty was grounded in a conception of common purpose – a city transcended the social classes into which it was divided. In this sense the 'civic gospel' was a true gospel. The ideals which lay behind it were greater than the men who brought it into being.

Dawson's friends were behind the 'civic renaissance' in Birmingham, which reached its culmination when Chamberlain was mayor. As early as 1861 they launched a satirical paper

1. For Chartist praise of the Manchester Library, see above, p. 136.

called *The Town Crier* which dealt with 'public affairs and with men in their public capacity'. Its object was 'the good government and progress of the town', and to achieve this the sponsors of the paper were prepared to press for the 'removing [of] stumbling blocks and putting incompetent and pretentious persons out of the way'. Among the sponsors were William Harris, a regular attender at the Church of the Saviour, Samuel Timmins, a well-known local writer and author of a large symposium on the industries of 'Birmingham and the Midland Hardware District' (1860), and J. T. Bunce, who had started active life as a Tory opponent of 'the rising Democratic spirit'. He was converted to Liberalism, and after a brief spell as editor of the *Birmingham Gazette* moved in 1861 to the *Birmingham Daily Post* and became one of Birmingham's most careful and informative historians. The *Town Crier* compared municipal government as it was – in incompetent hands – with municipal government as it might be.

Charles Vince, Dawson's successor as Baptist minister at Mount Zion Chapel, 'the best-loved perhaps of all the Birmingham ministers of his time', shared the same sense of purpose. He was interested in politics, and spoke on a Reform League platform and at public meetings of the Natural Education League and the Liberal Association. So too did H. W. Crosskey, Minister of the Unitarian Church of the Messiah, who did not arrive in Birmingham until 1869. His arrival – at a strategic moment – gave to Unitarianism, the religion of many of Birmingham's most influential families (including the Chamberlains), a new social sense. His predecessor had been unable to preach the kind of gospel that moved men to new social purposes: Crosskey by contrast pressed hard for educational reforms and sang the praises of the 'caucus'. 'The day had gone by', he wrote in 1877, 'for attempting to control a large constituency by a clique composed of a few wealthy men. A whole suburb could be outvoted by a couple of streets.' 'I cannot call to mind any other town outside Birmingham', he also wrote, 'in which Democracy has been so largely interpreted as the life of the people as an organized whole.'

Yet another Nonconformist minister was of outstanding

importance in the history of Birmingham's civic gospel, although he formulated it later than Dawson. Robert William Dale, the pastor of Carrs Lane Congregational Church from 1854 to 1895, was a truly Cromwellian figure. 'I never see Dale rising', Muntz once told John Bright, 'without thinking of the Church militant.' Chamberlain described him as 'before them all in strength of calibre'. Dale was far less clerical than Muntz's comment suggests: he looked like a prosperous merchant or manufacturer. He played a most active part behind the scenes in Birmingham life without seeking in any way to drag his congregation as a corporate body behind him. Yet he did not fear the exodus of wealthy Congregationalist families from the centre to the outskirts of Birmingham, outside the range of Carrs Lane. 'To prevent Carrs Lane becoming what it must become if it is to live at all – the church of the multitude – would be to stop one of the finest and most hopeful movements conceivable.' He loved Birmingham as a city and knew much about its business life. After seeing Lake Lucerne with its 'guardian mountains', he wrote, 'there is nothing in this magnificent view which makes me feel half the thrill I have sometimes felt when I have looked down on the smoky streets of Birmingham from the railway as I have returned to work from a holiday.'

Dale had listened to Dawson preaching when he was a young student, and he wrote much about him later in his life. Although he did not agree with Dawson on many religious matters, he shared his belief that politics was a high calling. 'Those who decline to use their political power are guilty of treachery both to God and to men.' He believed also that Christians had to be practical: 'the eleventh commandment is that thou shalt keep a balance sheet.' Yet collective action was as necessary in many aspects of policy as private enterprise. From 1867 onwards he urged the case for far fuller participation in local government. Birmingham Christians were told to work on the committees of hospitals, to become aldermen and councillors, 'to give their time as well as their money to whatever improvements are intended to develop the intelligence of the community. They ought to be reformers of local abuses . . . to see to it that the towns and parishes in which they live are well drained, well lighted, and well paved; that there are good schools for every class of the population: that there are harmless public amusements; that all parochial and municipal affairs are conducted honourably and equitably.'

This was a more comprehensive list of civic duties than Dawson had propounded in his comparison of the public library movement with the spread of a church. Dale did not accept Dawson's ideas of what constituted a church, but he continued to plead for dedicated service to the local community to work through the long agenda of uncompleted reforms. Speaking of Alderman White, a Quaker who was responsible along with Chamberlain for the making of the great Birmingham Improvement Scheme, he said that he felt that his friend 'was trying to get the will of God done on earth as it is done in heaven just as much as when he was fighting St Mary's Ward, just as much as when he was speaking in the Town Council, as when he was teaching his Bible class on the Sunday morning.' He believed that the conditions of urban life necessitated a new concern for up-to-date Christian ethics. Evangelicalism of the eighteenth-century or the early-nineteenth-century variety was not enough.

We are living in a new world and Evangelicals do not seem to have discovered it. The immense development of the manufacturing industries, the wider separation of classes in great towns – a separation produced by the increase of commercial wealth – the new relations that have grown up between the employers and the employed, the spread of popular education, the growth of a vast popular literature, the increased political power of the masses of the people, the gradual decay of the old aristocratic organization of society, and the advance, in many forms of the spirit of democracy – have urgently demanded fresh applications of the eternal ideas of the Christian Faith to conduct. But Evangelical Christians have hardly touched the new ethical problems which have come with the new time.

The vitality of the civic gospel in Birmingham derived from the abandonment of narrow conceptions of evangelicalism and the search for a more relevant and inspiring message. Dale was intensely interested in national issues, but he believed, with Chamberlain, that national politics could often do less than local politics to settle the critical issues of the time. He wrote in his still interesting book, *The Laws of Christ for Common Life* (1884):

> I sometimes think that municipalities can do more for the people than Parliament. Their powers will probably be enlarged; but under the powers they already possess they can greatly diminish the amount of sickness in the community, and can prolong human life. They can prevent – they have prevented – tens of thousands of children from becoming orphans. They can do much to improve those miserable homes which are fatal not only to health, but to decency and morality. They can give to the poor the enjoyment of pleasant parks and gardens, and the intellectual cultivation and refinement of public libraries and galleries of art. They can redress in many ways the inequalities of human conditions. The gracious words of Christ, 'Inasmuch as ye did it unto one of these my brethren, even these least, ye did it unto Me' will be addressed not only to those who with their own hands fed the hungry, and clothed the naked, and cared for the sick, but to those who supported a municipal policy which lessened the miseries of the wretched and added brightness to the life of the desolate.

This was powerful preaching by any standards. The influence of Nonconformist ministers in Birmingham would, of course, have been far less real had the city not been a Nonconformist centre since the seventeenth century. Pre-Victorian history influenced the pattern of Victorian religion, and hence of Victorian politics. 'In this town,' the writer of a local guide book noted in 1819, 'every individual worships his Maker in whatever way his individualism leads him without the least notice being taken or remarks made.' Old dissent was particularly strong, and Methodism, with its delayed response to civic needs, was relatively weak, certainly as an influence in local government. 'Birmingham for Primitive Methodism', one local Methodist complained, 'has been like the seed sown on hard and rocky places.' The Wesleyan Methodists were sharply criticized by men like Dawson, who accused Methodists, particularly when they were strong, of attaching exaggerated importance to 'what are technically called "experiences", thus drawing off attention from that great matter which absolutely must be insisted upon – good works'.

Once again Evangelicalism, Methodist, or Anglican, was not enough for the leaders of Birmingham Nonconformity. It was through the Labour movement rather than through mid-Victorian Radicalism that Methodism was to leave its chief mark on civic politics, particularly in the Durham coalfields and the Potteries.

Unitarianism, the religion of only a small minority of the population, had a far bigger impact on Victorian politics, not only in Birmingham but in Manchester, in Liverpool, and in smaller communities like Leicester where there were so many Unitarian mayors that the Unitarian chapel was known as 'the mares' nest'. In Birmingham a most impressive Unitarian Church – far removed from the eighteenth-century style of chapel – was opened in 1862. It was built in 'geometrical Gothic' and had a fine open timber roof and several stained glass windows. The Church of the Messiah, as it was called, was more than the centre of a small sect: it was a cultural and intellectual centre of a whole society, a place where ideas about society were openly and critically discussed. Crosskey's congregation included Joseph Chamberlain, Arthur, his younger brother, William Kenrick, his brother-in-law, and R. F. Martineau. In smaller Unitarian chapels, like that at Newhall Hill, other men were drawn into municipal service: they included Henry Payton, who joined the Council in 1871, was a strong supporter of Chamberlain, and in 1876 became chairman of the Public Works Committee. Crosskey, like Dawson, had been influenced by James Martineau, and it is interesting to note that James's famous sister Harriet, who did not share his views, nonetheless believed that 'civic economy' needed as much attention as 'political economy'. Where Unitarianism was weak in the nineteenth century, Liberalism lacked a social cutting edge. Birmingham Quakerism, so very different in mood and feeling, was also a significant element in Birmingham life, and seven of Birmingham's nineteenth-century mayors were Quakers. There was often uncertainty as to the extent to which they should commit themselves in political life, but Bright himself, the Member of Parliament for the city, had made his stand, like Sturge, on this critical issue. In the 1860s and 1870s the adult school movement was bringing most

Quakers into touch with the facts of poverty and disease, and between 1866 and 1873, the seed-time of the 'civic renaissance', five new Quaker Town Councillors were elected.

The Church of England in Birmingham, numerically quite powerful – it claimed almost half the Church attendance at the religious census of 1851 – was directly concerned with many good causes, most of them evangelical ones, but it did not shape Birmingham's civic gospel. Its most distinguished local spokesman, the Rev. J. C. Miller, for twenty years Rector of St Martin's (1846 to 1866), moved with the main stream of local Liberalism, but his own pastoral efforts were concerned primarily with 'missionary work' on his own doorstep. His *Church of the People* (1855), one of his many published sermons, set out his main objectives. The Rev. Sebastian Yorke was keenly concerned with Church of England education as were many of the other Anglican clergy. Some of them, however, lost in local popularity because of their direct association with Birmingham's dwindling but never non-existent Tory minority. It was not forgotten that one of Miller's predecessors had refused to allow the Birmingham Political Union to ring the bells of St Martin's for political purposes. Both the Rector of St Martin's and the Rector of St Philip's had signed a petition against the Reform Bill.

Anti-Tory feeling could easily be mobilized in Birmingham, and it usually burst against the Church. In 1868 the Liberals were celebrating a little prematurely the death of their rivals, when they circulated a card bearing the words, 'A Man that is born a Tory hath but a short time to live, and is full of Humbug: he springeth up like a fungus, and withereth like a cauliflower; and is seen no more; in the midst of life and hope he meets his death.' Two years later they were regretting these words when the Conservatives did well at the first School Board election, again in alliance with local churchmen.

The Roman Catholics were growing in numbers in Birmingham throughout the Victorian years – and Cardinal Newman was living in the Oratory in the Hagley Road, far apart in spirit from the bustle of the city – but there was a far smaller proportion of Irish Roman Catholics in Birmingham than in the industrial cities of the north. They played little positive part in local politics, although they were negatively important in 1886 when their small numbers made it far easier for Joseph Chamberlain to oppose home rule in Birmingham than if he had lived in Liverpool, Manchester, or Leeds.

Given this religious kaleidoscope, there was great scope for Nonconformist initiative in Birmingham. Its impact was strengthened by the fact that the prestige – and wealth – of the majority of Birmingham's most respected families were moving forces behind local dissent. Businessmen had not yet responded to the pressures to move over to the Church of England or to contract out of religion altogether, and they contributed generously to the work as well as to the finance of the Nonconformist congregations. Dale once described Birmingham as 'a great village'. So in a sense it was. Many of the important decisions about city life were taken by a small knot of Nonconformist families, who knew each other well, frequently inter-married, and continued until the middle of the twentieth century to dominate local social life. Many of them lived in Birmingham's most distinctive 'suburb', Edgbaston, a carefully-planned residential estate belonging to the Calthorpe family, and situated only one mile from the centre of the city. The idea of a great city as an 'anonymous' whole must be treated with as much caution in Birmingham as in Manchester: so must the idea, developed by Continental sociologists, of 'impersonal' urban relationships. The civic gospel in Birmingham was a personal affair, just as the relations between the Nonconformist ministers and the members of their congregations were personal. 'The men that took part in the great and successful movement for reforming our administration and ennobling it', Dale wrote in the 1890s, 'had learnt the principles on which they acted and caught the spirit by which they were inspired very largely in the Nonconformist churches of Birmingham.'

They were influenced too by the language and attitudes of business. If the sense of gospel was derived from religion, the commandments, as Dale and Dawson would have wished, were the precepts of efficiency. In 1892, after the 'civic renaissance' was over, Chamberlain wrote in an American magazine that 'the leading idea of the English system of municipal government' might be said to be that of 'a joint stock or co-operative enterprise in which every citizen is a shareholder, and of which the dividends are received in the improved health and the increase of the comfort and happiness of the community. The members of the Council are the directors of this great business, and their fees consist in the confidence, the consideration, and the gratitude of those amongst whom they live. In no other undertaking, whether philanthropic or commercial, are the returns more speedy, more manifest, or more beneficial.'

In saying this, Chamberlain was not merely writing for a business-minded American audience: he was expressing himself in language that would have been equally appreciated in Birmingham. The returns, however, had to be earned. When a member of the Calthorpe family, which owned the Edgbaston Estate, announced that he intended to stand as a Conservative candidate in 1897, the Birmingham Free Citizens' Committee, a Radical organization, warned the electors that in the opinion of this Committee Calthorpe belonged to a family 'taking tens of thousands a year from ground rents in Edgbaston, which have been quadrupled in a comparatively short time, not by the energy or skill or enterprise of the Calthorpe family, but by the energy, enterprise and skill of the people of Birmingham'.

The gospel of positive municipal action was preached most effectively in Birmingham between 1866 and 1873 because in an age when the national exchequer offered little direct assistance to local government the city was richer than it had been before, and more funds were available for civic expenditure. The fact that money was cheap during the later 1870s, when business conditions were far less favourable than they had been ten years before, enabled the initiative to be continued, with far more doubts and hesitations, until at least the main agenda had been completed. It is significant that Bunce in the monumental *History of the Corporation* stated simply that the great advances of the 1870s 'effected in so short a period' had been made possible by the increasing prosperity of Birmingham, its rapid extension, its growth of population, and 'the rise in the number and value of properties assessable to local rates'.

Dawson, Crosskey and Dale were capable of seeing the emergence of the civic gospel in largely secular terms. Crosskey referred back to Athens, and Dale, like Heaton in Leeds, made cross-references not to Jerusalem but to Florence. He wrote:

> Towards the end of the 'sixties a few Birmingham men made the discovery that perhaps a strong and able Town Council might do almost as much to improve the conditions of life in the town as Parliament itself. I have called it a 'discovery', for it had all the freshness and charm of a discovery. One of its first effects was to invest the Council with a new attractiveness and dignity. . . . Weaker and less effective members of the Corporation were gradually dropped, and their places filled by men of quite a new type. The November Ward meetings assumed a new character. The speakers, instead of discussing small questions of administration and economy, dwelt with glowing enthusiasm on what a great and prosperous town like Birmingham might do for its people. They spoke of sweeping away streets in which it was not possible to live a healthy and decent life; of making the town cleaner, sweeter and brighter; of providing gardens and parks and a museum; they insisted that great monopolies like the gas and water supply should be in the hands of the corporation; that good water should be supplied without stint at the lowest possible prices; that the profits of the gas supply should relieve the pressure of the rates. Sometimes an adventurous orator would excite his audience by dwelling on the glories of Florence, and of the other cities of Italy in the Middle Ages, and suggest that Birmingham too might become the home of a noble literature and art.

3

The transformation of the old Council, a body lacking in both dignity and vision, was achieved only after tough battles not only at election times, as in St Paul's Ward in 1872, but in the Council itself. It was known for years as the 'Old Woodman' Council, since many of its members used to meet in the Old Woodman Tavern in Easy Row. The Council Chamber in Moor Street was small and dingy, a remarkable contrast with Birmingham's impressive Town Hall, the idea of which had been suggested in the mid-1820s by the committee which managed Birmingham's triennial music festivals. The Hall was built on the orders of the Street Commissioners and completed in 1835. Its architects were Hansom and Welsh (a design by Barry was not accepted) and the building was in classical style, suggested by the temple of Jupiter Stator in Rome. As in Leeds, the contractors, in this case working closely with the architects, underestimated the cost of the work and went bankrupt in the course of building: in Birmingham, however, the Hall was not set aside for the purposes of local government, and while thousands of people could gather there for great political meetings – or music festivals – the Town Council met in a room which allowed space only for about a dozen of the public to stand and watch the frequently sordid proceedings.

The civic pride of Birmingham expressed itself before the late 1860s not in the Council but in other institutions and above all in the strong public conviction, maintained by politicians and press, that the local radical tradition was a formative element in national political development. 'There was nothing to attract, those days,' one alderman reminisced later, 'in the position of a Town Councillor or to lead the people to suppose that there was any dignity attaching to the position; or any sacrifices made in serving them by filling it.' There was no mayoral chain or mace, and much of the real work of the borough was conducted in a solicitor's private office.

This state of affairs was a mockery of the high hopes which the advocates of the incorporation of Birmingham, all of them Liberals or Radicals, had expressed during the early 1830s. When Conservatives had told them that Birmingham was already well-governed, better governed indeed by the Street Commissioners than it would be by a Town Council, they had retaliated with the argument, well expressed by R. K. Douglas, the editor of the *Birmingham Journal*, that 'local institutions alone generated and fostered a conviction amongst the people that government was a matter in which every man ought to take an interest'.

The setting up of a Town Council by the Charter of Incorporation of 1838 was a victory for the Radicals, but it did not mean that they had won this debate. The powers of the Town

Council were less great than the powers of the Street Commission, which continued in existence until 1852. There was less sense of genuine responsibility on the part of the Council than on the part of the Commissioners, and in face of a restricted municipal franchise and notable public apathy it could hardly be claimed that the cause of democracy had been advanced by the changes. Moreover, after 1852, when the powers of the Commissioners were taken over by the Council and the financial resources of the town were trebled, the worst period of Birmingham local government began. During the very years when John Bright was thundering on the platform of the Town Hall about the principles of Liberalism, or Dawson was arguing the case for the rights of foreign nationalities in the Church of the Saviour, the sixty-four members of the Town Council were bickering as much about private feuds as about public interest. There was certainly no shortage of talk. 'It is really desirable that at least a few members of the Council should be content to abstain from talk', the *Birmingham Gazette* stated in October 1856. 'Loquacity is the great vice of the Council: meetings are frequently protracted beyond all endurance by the delight taken by some members in listening to the sound of their own voices; and business is postponed to speeches.'

Most of the members of the Council were nominally Liberals or even Radicals, but their political stances on national issues proved less important than their caution on local questions. Their economic position was what counted most, and they were largely recruited, as a Birmingham writer put it, from 'the unprogressive tradesmen class – many of them worthy in their way, but of limited ideas. In their private businesses they were not accustomed to deal with big transactions and high figures, so that spending large sums of money, if proposed, filled the brewer, the baker and the candlestick-maker with alarm.'

Important historical inferences may be drawn about the civic gospel of the late 1860s and 1870s from this picture of what had gone before. First, as has been stated, it was an overdue reaction to a kind of political maladjustment – lively concern for national politics, sordid local politics. Second, a new and more aggressive Liberalism, placing more emphasis on the public good and on the democratic means of achieving it collectively, was needed to transform local politics. A party 'caucus' was exactly the kind of instrument which could best do this, for it could choose or reject candidates, strengthen general public interest, and relate local to national issues. Whatever the disadvantages of non-party government in local affairs, Birmingham needed party direction to destroy sloth and construct new policies. 'The aim of the caucus', Chamberlain argued, 'is essentially democratic. It is to provide for the full and efficient representation of the will of the majority, and for its definite expression in the government of the people.' Deeds were more important than talk.

Third, the idea of a 'gospel' was needed to raise the tone of local government: existing practices bore no relation to the idealism either of religious leaders or even of national politicians. Without such a gospel, of course, the 'caucus' itself would have been in danger of becoming a piece of mere machinery. Fourth, business habits, which gave so much vitality to the 'civic renaissance', when new men of business were called to power, actually held back progress during the earlier period: the business habits of what Cobden called the 'shopocracy', habits which were common to shopkeeper-councillors in all parts of the country, did not greatly assist the cause of effective local government. Fifth, Birmingham, which was so outstanding in the late 1860s and 1870s – it was a 'Mecca' of local government – was not very different from a large number of other towns and cities during the previous period. Indeed it was behind many of them, including Leeds, in certain fields and Liverpool and Glasgow in many. Sixth, in Birmingham as elsewhere, the financial aspects of local government were usually decisive, then as now. 'Economy' shaped the policy of the 'Old Woodman' Council, and it needed more willingness to spend as well as agreement that there were good things on which a Council might spend money before a 'renaissance' could happen. Seventh, there was a Chamberlain in Birmingham, a genuinely great man who was to stand out in national and imperial as well as local government.

The 'Economy' group had gained ground in the Town

Council soon after the Council's reconstitution in 1852. Their leader was a remarkable Birmingham character, Joseph Allday, son of a Digbeth butcher, who had begun his political career in the 1820s as editor of the *Argus*, a scurrilous weekly periodical. The *Argus* anticipated the popular appeal of late-nineteenth-century sensationalism within a framework of local scandal and gossip, taking as its motto:

> Yes I am proud – I must be proud to see
> Men not afraid of God, afraid of me.

Tory-Radical in politics, vigorously anti-Catholic and anti-Dissent, the *Argus* under Allday's personal direction revelled in vituperation. 'The canting cry of modern evangelism – the mock humanity of modern philanthropists – the folly, absurdity, and imposition of our modern political economists – it is our duty to *Lash and Expose*.' No two 'satirical' papers could have been further removed from each other in tone and in purpose than the *Argus* of the 1820s and the *Town Crier* in the 1860s.

Allday spanned the two periods of Birmingham's history, freely making enemies in both: he was the kind of 'character' – there was usually one – who was prominent in nineteenth-century local government in all parts of the country. Chamberlain was a genius: Allday a sham. For him local politics was a series of 'jobs': the less that was spent by the Council the better. All forms of idealism were dangerously expensive. At the same time Allday loved to expose 'scandals', and he distinguished himself locally in 1853 when he led a campaign to demand an official investigation into 'terrible atrocities at the Borough Gaol'. Although an Anglican and a churchwarden of St Martin's, he joined Dissenters in 1858 in resisting an attempt to re-impose Church rates. He was also chairman of the Board of Guardians. Elected to the Town Council in 1849, he served on it for ten years, becoming chairman of the Finance Committee in 1856. He resigned from the Council in 1859, and died at the age of sixty-two, two years later.

The rise to power of the 'Economists' should be seen against a background of rising prices in the early 1850s. While the Leeds Town Council was building the Town Hall, the

Birmingham Town Council was refusing to appoint a Medical Officer of Health and a stipendiary magistrate, cutting the costs of the jail, rejecting a public baths project, quarrelling with the Recorder and arguing noisily in public about the choice of a Town Clerk. In 1852 costly sewage schemes had been approved, and the Public Works Committee set about its tasks with vigour. Within a year, however, the city's finances showed that a borough improvement rate of two shillings in the pound – the limit set in 1851 – was inadequate to finance this and other schemes. The costs of reform had been badly underestimated. The financial position continued to deteriorate, and the excess of annual expenditure over income on the borough Improvement Account, which stood at £36,392 at the end of 1853, rose to £71,192 at the end of 1855. The 'Economists' believed that a borough improvement rate of two shillings in the pound and borrowing powers of up to £150,000 were quite adequate for a city the size of Birmingham, and they succeeded in 1855 in having the borough rate, which was levied separately from the borough improvement rate and the street improvement rate, reduced from one shilling and threepence to tenpence in the pound. They dubbed their opponents 'the Extravagant party', and used every opportunity to discredit them personally.

The climax came in November and December 1855 when a proposal of the General Purposes Committee of the Council to buy out the local Waterworks Company was withdrawn as a result of the pressure of the 'Economists'. A new Improvement Bill, which would have consolidated the two improvement rates and increased the Council's borrowing powers, was thrown out at a ratepayers' poll. Defeated in the Council, where they were still in a minority, Allday and his friends had insisted on a public meeting of ratepayers, one of the noisiest in Birmingham's history. 'It was a scene of indescribable confusion,' one observer wrote. 'So great was the noise that not one word of the resolution (in favour of the new Improvement Bill) was heard by anyone in the meeting.' At the poll the new Bill was rejected by the enormous majority of 3,232, only 170 votes being recorded in its favour and 3,402 against.

The immediate result of this poll was dramatic if not inspiring. The directors of the Birmingham Banking Company, whose manager, W. Beaumont, was Treasurer of the Corporation, refused to allow any extension of the Corporation's overdraft, which then stood at £26,000. Alarmed by this, the Finance Committee and the Public Works Committee of the Town Council both resigned *en bloc* at the next meeting of the Council. The 'Economists', although in a minority on the Council as a whole, took over both committees and standing orders were suspended to allow Allday to become chairman of three committees at the same time. This was 'monopolizing' with a vengeance, but Allday was then at the height of his power.

He used his power in 1856 and 1857 to reduce all kinds of public works expenditure. The cost of repairing, cleansing, and watering the roads fell from £23,280 in 1855 to £15,838 in 1856; no more street lamps were provided, although only just over 100 of the 150 miles of public highway in Birmingham were lit at night; and drainage and sewage facilities were cut as much as possible. It is easy to detect Allday's influence also behind a refusal to provide additional police, even though the refusal meant actually losing government aid. He had always opposed 'centralization', and he cared little for the Chief Superintendent's opinion that only a substantial increase in the size of the local police force would provide the means 'likely to detect and prevent the assaults and depredations in the Borough, of which such great complaints had lately been made'.

There must have been great tension behind the scenes at this time between the Council and its officials. The dispute concerning the Town Clerk in 1854 was followed in 1857 by the dismissal of J. Pigott Smith from his position as local surveyor. Pigott Smith had contributed much to the development of nineteenth-century Birmingham, but the 'Economists' felt that he was a hidden hand behind the schemes of the 'Extravagant' party. His dismissal followed his refusal to appear before the Council in committee for the purpose of an investigation of his conduct. His successor, W. S. Till, formerly his deputy, proceeded obediently with the economies

Allday and his friends desired. The Public Works Committee's estimate fell within a year by £10,685.

At the beginning of 1859 Birmingham's bank deficit had been wiped out, and outstanding liabilities on the Improvement Account had been severely cut. Yet at this point in Birmingham's civic history the 'Economists', who had carried all before them, began to lose some of their influence. Allday was defeated at the aldermanic elections and left the Council in a huff. He had often told his friends in the Woodman that he would '*never* betray the people of Birmingham'. Now he could argue that they had betrayed him.

In fact, new voices were being heard in 1859, 1860, and 1861. Robert Wright, an able solicitor with a flair for finance, had been elected to the Council in 1858: he made the arguments of the 'Economists' look silly. Others made them look narrow and restrictive. Two councillors pressed for a public library; a bigger group urged better lighting, better drainage, and large-scale street improvements. A few members of the Public Works Committee even went to Birkenhead to see the new tram system in operation and were 'fully satisfied of the utility, economy and comfort of the system'.

Older voices also began to assert themselves. Alderman H. Hawkes, who had been mayor in 1852, and was a vigorous supporter of the Reform Association, was a keen advocate of local government reform in 1860 and took a position of leadership as the 1860s went by. 'A brilliant speaker', he was to preside at the famous meeting which reconstituted the Liberal Association in 1868. Alderman Ryland, a Street Commissioner, a professional man, who was renowned as a devoted philanthropist, came more into his own again. The Town Clerk, Thomas Standbridge, chosen in 1854 and in office until his death in 1869, was invaluable to the reformers and highly respected by all. The climax of this new period in local government came with the successful passing of a new Improvement Act in 1861. Like the Bill of 1855 it did not have an easy passage, but this time the ratepayers supported it in a poll by 6,531 votes to 3,802. The 'Extravagant' party, not really a party at all but a collection of reasonably responsible citizens, had mobilized its full strength. The 'Economists' had more or less maintained their position.

The new Act permitted the Council to raise further loans not exceeding £150,000 for general town improvements and £50,000 for street improvements. The Council took advantage of these powers and carried out a very large number of necessary minor works. They were able to do this without increasing the rates because of the continued growth of the amount and value of property assessed for local taxation. A two-shilling rate had raised only £48,000 in 1853: by 1860 the figure was up to £63,000 and by 1865, on the eve of the 'civic renaissance', £74,100. If there had been a more realistic assessment of rateable values in the mid-1850s the worst excesses of the 'Economists' might have been curbed without excitement. As it was, not until the 1860s was Birmingham able for the first time in its history to draw upon adequate financial support for what its Council wished to do. Its vision, however, was still limited. The death rate in the city was still appallingly high – it rose sharply between 1849 and 1853 – but attempts to secure the appointment of a Medical Officer of Health were always defeated. 'Nature, geography and soil had done a great deal for the health of Birmingham and ... the governmental authorities of the town had done very little.' Some of the new members of the Council, men of greater wealth and public spirit than their predecessors, still felt that all public works should be proceeded with very 'slowly and deliberately'.

The public library movement, which so excited Dawson, was the one great manifestation of new initiative. It was in 1860, just as the tide was turning, that the Council decided to implement Ewart's Act and levy a penny rate to establish a central reference library with reading and news rooms, a museum and gallery of art, and four district lending libraries with news rooms attached. Dawson's speech at the opening of the Central Reference Library in 1866 was, as we have seen, a great landmark in the history of the civic gospel.

It was not books, however, but sewage which gave the makers of the civic gospel their greatest opportunity. The question of how to dispose of the town's sewage was often the main item on the Council's agenda in the late 1860s, when new men of influence, like Dixon, Collings, and Chamberlain, were being returned to it. The question was not a new one. Seaports like Liverpool were able to deal with this problem with little strain by dumping their sewage in the sea: Birmingham was troubled both by financial and technical problems. Although extensive drainage works had been constructed by the Council, Birmingham's sewage was piped, in its raw state, into the River Tame at Saltley. As early as 1854 objections were raised to this practice and in 1857, C. B. Adderley, Member of Parliament and public-spirited landowner (later Lord Norton) who gave Birmingham a public park in 1856 – the Town Council was remarkably slow in taking up his generous offer – complained of the pollution. A year later he was granted an injunction from the Chancery Court restraining the Council from depositing solid sewage on the land at the outlet of the sewers at Saltley. The Council was given a few months' time to remedy the situation.

The Public Works Committee, which, as we have seen, was perhaps the most controversial of all the Council's committees in mid-Victorian Birmingham, advised the Council to acquire a large tract of land in the Tame Valley on which to set up a vast sewage farm. Sewage could also be sold for a profit to farmers on 'the line of route'. A conduit and other sewage works would cost £275,000.

These proposals of the Public Works Committee were keenly challenged by Councillor Thomas Avery, who had retired early from his family firm of scale-makers, had entered the Council in 1862 and had become the chairman of the Finance Committee. As the old 'Economist' party had lost power, Avery had demanded economy in the name of efficiency and had greatly improved the financial condition of the Council by reorganizing its obsolete system of accounting. Although a Conservative in national politics, he had a Gladstonian approach to public finance. He did not like lavish civic spending, and while many of the items of civic expenditure to which he objected were far from lavish, he believed that no improvement was possible in the city unless there was far sounder administration.

Avery's attack on the Public Works Committee in 1870 was

in character, yet the consequences which flowed from it marked a genuine landmark in the transition from mid- to late-Victorian England. From it quite new departures in local government were to be made, departures which became associated not with Gladstonian but with Chamberlainite Liberalism. After prolonged debate – eight long and stormy debates in three months – a special Sewage Enquiry Committee was set up 'for the purpose of reporting to the Council, as early as practicable, their opinion as to the best mode of disposing of or dealing with the sewage of the Borough, with power to engage such professional assistance as they may deem necessary'. The members of the Committee consisted largely of the 'new men', almost all of whom were Liberals, who had been elected to the Council during the previous few years. Chamberlain excused himself from serving on it, not because he was out of sympathy but because he was fully occupied elsewhere.

The Enquiry Committee, convened because of Avery's insistence on efficient and financially sound administration, produced a long report of nearly three hundred pages, which was a most revealing and influential social document. Alongside detailed accounts of conflicting theories of sewage disposal, there was a devastatingly candid account of the sanitary state of Birmingham. The overall city death rate concealed the great variations in mortality in the different parts of the city and the exceptionally high mortality in wards like St John's and St George's. Evidence of differential mortality rates had provided a most effective stimulus to the movements for administrative reform during the 1840s: where there were such variations was there not an immediate case for social control? Chamberlain followed Chadwick in asking the question: 'Could any one doubt the evidence of the medical men that a large proportion of the death rate was distinctly due to the existence of pestiferous nuisances in the town?'

Questions of this kind were the leading questions Chamberlain continued to ask as Mayor of Birmingham. The civic gospel concerned itself increasingly with the disparities of life in a great city, with the contrasts between rich and poor, which had captured men's imagination in the Manchester of the

1840s. One immediate answer to the sewage question was to get rid of no fewer than 14,000 open middens and ashpits draining directly into the sewers. This was among the proposals of the Committee, which were accepted by the Council after a very long debate by thirty-three votes to twenty-three in October 1871. The same Committee went on to assume responsibility for the carrying out of a new plan of sewage disposal: although its plan was resisted by private interests, by 1875 the Council had satisfied the Court of Chancery that no further nuisance existed. In the same year the national Public Health Act, passed by Disraeli's Conservative Government, provided for the creation of 'united districts' for 'specified sanitary purposes'. As a result, Birmingham was able to join with its neighbours in establishing the Birmingham, Tame and New District Drainage Board. Chamberlain presided with pride at its inaugural conference.

Given that Birmingham was to take its health problems seriously, and to pay for ambitious sewage schemes, its finances needed to be thought out completely afresh, not merely set out in new form or audited more efficiently. Other cities had sources of revenue which they could fall back upon independently of the rates. Liverpool, for example, although it levied 'improvement' rates from the 1860s, had a large corporate estate, worth more than £600,000 a year in 1871 'if let at rack rent' and actually yielding more than £100,000, besides large profits derived from market fines, legal fees and other services. Bristol also had large outside income.

Other cities derived income from profitable municipal utilities. By 1870 there were forty-nine municipal gas undertakings in England and Wales, many of them in the industrial North of England. Manchester's Street Commissioners had built a gas works as early as 1817; in 1870 Leeds had just taken over its Gaslight Company, founded in 1818, at a cost (probably too high) of £763,225. Glasgow, which had set about pulling down its pestilential Frying Pan alleys after the formation by local Act of Parliament of the City Improvement Trust in 1866, acquired its gas company in 1869. Special Acts of Parliament were necessary to effect such transfers, until the Public Health Act of 1875 gave urban authorities powers to buy out gas companies by mutual agreement, subject only to the consent of the recently founded Local Government Board. Chamberlain did not wait for this legislation. In 1873 he approached the Birmingham Gas, Light and Coke Company, which had been founded in 1819 and had a share capital of £300,000. The acquisition of this and a bigger second company, the Birmingham and Staffordshire Gas Light Company, which had been founded in 1825 and had a share capital of over £600,000, was the first stage in his municipal programme as Mayor.

It was perhaps fitting that gas should now figure so prominently in the working out of the civic gospel, not for the more obvious reasons, but because gas lighting had always been taken as a symbol of 'improvement'. Cardinal Newman once made it the touchstone of a whole materialist philosophy of progress. He was not far wrong. A pamphlet had been published in Birmingham by William Matthews in 1830 with the eloquent title *A Sketch of the Principal Means which have been Employed to Ameliorate the Intellectual and Moral Condition of the Working Classes at Birmingham*: the pamphlet was originally written as the introduction to a historical sketch on the origins and progress of gas lighting. Years later in 1885, when Birmingham's new art gallery, costing £40,000, was opened by the Prince of Wales, it was judged a matter of pride that it should be situated above the offices of the municipal gas committee. The costs, it was said, had been covered by the profits on municipal gas, and there was a motto on the memorial in the entrance hall bearing the words 'By the gains of industry we promote art'.

Chamberlain gave three reasons for wishing to take over the gas companies. He placed the financial argument last, whatever priority it had in his mind. The new understanding would prove lucrative: its profits could be used to improve the health of Birmingham. 'When the purchase of the Water Works comes before you, it will be a question concerning the health of the town; the acquisition of the Gas Works concerns the profits of the town, and its financial resources. Both are matters of absolute public necessity.' The two other reasons for 'municipalizing' gas were more general. All monopolies in any way sustained by the State should be in the hands of the elected representatives of the people, to whom their profits should of right go. Municipalization would increase the power and influence of the local council, which should be encouraged to become a real local parliament, supreme in its own sphere of jurisdiction.[1]

4

Chamberlain's proposals to take over the two gas companies were put before the Council in January 1874. They involved raising the borough debt from £500,000 to £2,500,000. This was exactly the kind of proposal which Avery would have opposed bitterly in the mid-1860s, when he objected as forcibly as the old 'Economists' to an extension of the Council's power to borrow money. Chamberlain now argued boldly and unequivocally that 'a Corporation that is afraid to borrow is too timid to do its duty', and the Council, including Avery, supported him by the enormous majority of fifty-four to two. This was probably the biggest majority any Town Council ever had in introducing such drastic new measures. Why had there been such a volte-face?

To answer simply either that the civic gospel was at work or that Chamberlain was an outstanding leader would be true but inadequate. There were three other reasons – economic, social, and political. The year 1872 was a 'good year' in Birmingham, 'rarely equalled and never surpassed', one local businessman called it: there were few brakes on optimism. The years 1873 and 1874 saw the beginnings of a financial and economic crisis, which was to change businessmen's moods for the rest of the century, yet the fall of foreign investment, which was a feature of the crisis, actually facilitated domestic public investment by freeing funds and lowering interest rates.

The social reason was just as important. The advent of 'new men' to the Council between 1866 and 1873 raised its social

1. For a remarkable contrast of attitude, see the *Manchester Guardian* (5 November 1831). 'We see no good that can arise from the establishment of a mock parliament in every area of the kingdom, existing under no public responsibility, yet directing and acting on any public question.'

prestige, for many of the new men, such as George Braithwaite Lloyd, the banker, well qualified on account of 'his great intelligence in all business transactions', his 'great industry' and 'his enviable public character', came from the 'superior social strata' of the city. Like Chamberlain himself, they were 'substantial burgesses', whose credit was unlimited. Not only were they willing to borrow – as lesser men might not have been – and, even more necessary, able to borrow, but they were prepared also to devote their time to the affairs of the city because they believed with Chamberlain that the Council could become a 'real local parliament'. They made it such. 'Instead of the Town Council being a by-word,' the Town Clerk wrote more than thirty years later, 'it has been the pivot upon which the whole life of the community has turned.'

Attwood had often compared the men of Birmingham very favourably with the Members of Parliament he met at Westminster: William Kenrick, Chamberlain's brother-in-law, equally satisfied with the comparison, said that when he compared 'our little parliament with the big Parliament at Westminster, I compare the briskness of our pace with the slowness or – if I wished to be complimentary – the deliberateness, the tardy progress which characterizes the proceedings of the great Parliament.' Birmingham society, which for so long had tolerated its Town Council, now saw it as an instrument of collective purpose and, equally important, saw membership of it as a source of status. Cities which never achieved this sense – and most did not – always lacked the fullest feeling that they were taking part in a 'renaissance'.

The third reason, the political, was perhaps the most important of all. A majority of fifty-four votes to two was a tribute not only to social progress but to party discipline. The 'caucus' had pushed all its weight behind the Liberal Party at the local elections of 1873, not only in Chamberlain's ward but everywhere. 'In Birmingham,' wrote Schnadhorst, 'the improvement in the material and sanitary condition of the town since the application of political force to municipal life cannot be questioned, and has been accompanied by a marked change in the character of its governing body.' The reasons for the Liberal Association intervening in local political life – its counterpart in many other cities, Wolverhampton, Portsmouth, and Brighton, for example, did not – were bound up not only with concern for the issues mentioned above but with its particular concern for 'non-Anglicanized' education.

Next to the battle for the vote and the return of Liberal members to Parliament, the 'caucus' had the cause of education at heart. Some of its members had wished to see Town Councils empowered to levy rates for educational purposes. When, instead, Forster's Act of 1870 set up elected *ad hoc* bodies, the local School Boards, the 'caucus' realized that these bodies would be of great party importance. It failed, somewhat surprisingly, however, to win control of the new Birmingham Board at the first School Board elections of 1870. Only 29,183 voters out of an electorate of over 52,000 chose to vote, and since voting was cumulative – electors could give as many of their votes as they wished to each candidate – all eight Anglican candidates were returned as was the Roman Catholic. The Education Act of 1870 had been deliberately designed to allow for the representation of minorities, but the only effect of the Liberal defeat in Birmingham was to tighten Liberal Party organization. The Liberals were goaded, as a result of 1870, into fighting local political battles far more fiercely both for control of the School Board and the Town Council. One writer of the period went as far as to describe the 'caucus', in its most highly developed form, as 'the offspring of the cumulative and the minority vote'. The presence on the School Board of an anti-Liberal majority (nine members of the Education League had been defeated in 1870) seemed to make it imperative to tighten the Liberal grip on the Town Council, with which the School Board was engaged in almost perpetual conflict between 1870 and 1873. The conflict reached its height in February 1872, when the Town Council refused by a majority of thirty to carry out its legal duty of levying the School Rate demanded by the Board.

At the municipal elections of 1872 and 1873, therefore, party feeling ran very high indeed. In 1872 the Conservatives contested seven of the thirteen wards and, although losing almost everywhere, succeeded in defeating F. W. Schnadhorst. No defeat, except that of Chamberlain himself, could have more riled the Liberals. Almost inevitably, the General Committee of the Liberal Association, which had already intervened in earlier elections, decided formally in March 1873, on a motion of Chamberlain, 'that in consequence of the recent action by the Tory party in Birmingham [in fighting municipal and School Board elections], the Liberal Association should in future take part in such elections, and that whenever a Liberal candidate is opposed by a Tory candidate, the support of the Association should be given to the Liberal.'

The party feeling was further sharpened when there was talk in some circles of offering the mayoralty on the basis of seniority to Alderman W. Brinsley, an old-fashioned 'radical' in the Allday tradition. The approach to Chamberlain was a direct consequence of this. When the electors went to the polls they returned Liberal Association candidates, who were all militant Chamberlainites, in every one of the wards. They had been nominated by the Ward Committees and knew exactly how they were expected to vote. Not only were the Conservatives routed, but anti-Chamberlainite Liberals or 'radicals' were all defeated too.

The civic gospel was thus placed quite firmly in the trust of Chamberlain and his supporters. It was vigorously advocated also as the central issue of the election. When one Chamberlainite candidate, a Quaker, Richard Barrow, was told by an elector that he had favoured 'extravagance' in the Town Council, he replied that he was determined to vote for every measure that would make Birmingham a 'clean, healthy and model town'. He added also that 'the Council ought to have had the Waterworks and Gas Company in their hands years ago if the members had been far-sighted enough'.

Agreement with the gas companies was finally reached in March 1874. In describing the details to the approving Council, Chamberlain forecast an immediate profit of £14,800 in the first year. The money could be used for necessary civic purposes, for 'every day new duties are being imposed upon the Corporation'. In fourteen years' time he expected a profit of £50,000 'without in the slightest degree increasing the cost of gas to the consumer more than would have been the case had not the Corporation taken over the concern'. Once again he reverted to the public monopoly argument: 'It is intolerable that streets, for which we are responsible, should be likely to be torn up at any moment at the pleasure of a private company.' The Council accepted all these arguments, and although various local boards and large local consumers of gas opposed Birmingham's private bill when it came before a special committee of the House of Commons, which included Gladstone, the opposition was as unsuccessful at Westminster as it had been in Birmingham. The bill was passed in July 1875, and Chamberlain was chosen as the first chairman of the newly constituted municipal Gas Committee.

The profits on the first year's working were not £14,800 but £34,000. By the beginning of the next decade the *Birmingham Mail* could write that it was very easy for the members of the Gas Committee to present their annual accounts 'for the figures always seemed to be part of some fairy tale'. The members of the Gas Committee always included some of the best businessmen in Birmingham, who were attracted by the practical problems its work posed. Plant was extended and modernized, the cost of raising money fell, the price of gas was twice lowered during the first five years of municipal ownership, and the working conditions of employees in the two amalgamated gas works were greatly improved.

In turning from gas to water, Chamberlain was reverting to the health problem which had been forced to the forefront during the debates on the report of the Special Enquiry Committee into Sewage Works. He justified having first concerned himself with gas on the grounds that improved health amenities had to be paid for and the community was not willing simply to pay for them out of the rates. He was right about this, for at the height of the talk about the need for a civic gospel, a poll of ratepayers in March 1874 rejected a proposal to seek legislation to permit the improvement rate to exceed two shillings in the pound.

Whenever it had been suggested earlier in the century, as it had been during the early 1850s, that Birmingham might purchase the Water Works, financial arguments had always been raised against the suggestion. Chamberlain now felt he could take it up safely. 'What do you think of the inhabitants being compelled to drink water which is as bad as sewage before clarification?' he asked. The Birmingham Water Works Company, founded in 1826, was quite well run, but Chamberlain skilfully used statistics about wells and taps to compare Birmingham's experience with that of other towns and declared that poor people in Birmingham were so short of water that they were driven to steal it from other people. He made the most of the greatest social weakness of the existing system – the dependence of poor people on unhealthy and contaminated wells: Avery had directed attention to this in a pamphlet of 1869, *The Corporation of Birmingham and the Water Supply of the Town.*

Once again Chamberlain laid down general principles, as he had done in the case of gas. The first he had already stated on the earlier occasion. 'All regulated monopolies, sustained by the State, in the interests of the inhabitants generally, should be controlled by the representatives of the people, and not left in the hands of private speculators.' Second, and in this he followed the Royal Commission on Sanitary Reform of 1869, 'the power of life and death' should above all else not be left in private hands. 'Whereas there should be a profit made on the gas undertaking, the Water Works should never be a source of profit, as all profit should go in the reduction of the price of water.'

The health problem was in the news again in 1874, partly on account of a severe smallpox epidemic. A Medical Officer of Health, Dr Alfred Hill, had been appointed two years earlier – not as a result of local initiative but to comply with the terms of the national Public Health Act of the same year – and his reports began to influence local opinion. In addition an almost completely newly manned Sanitary Committee was set up after the municipal elections of 1873 with Dr Barratt, a member of the Sewage Enquiry Committee, as its first chairman. It undertook a large-scale sanitary survey of Birmingham in the winter of 1874–5. Chamberlain took advantage of all these signs of the times in presenting his case for taking over the Water Works Company: he could also point to the fact that sixty-nine local authorities owned their water works in 1870.

Whereas the two gas companies had been amenable to

pressure, the Water Works Company was financially strong and its property was increasing in value. The resistance did not frighten Chamberlain, however, and he rallied full local support. The Council was unanimous, and there was no demand for a ratepayers' poll. In the House of Lords the Bill was bitterly opposed as 'compulsory purchase', unjust to shareholders, but opposition from the Lords always helped rather than hindered the cause of radicalism in Birmingham. The Bill passed the House in August 1875 and the Works were transferred in January 1876. 'Without the additions which have been made,' the *Birmingham Mail* wrote lightly thirteen years later, 'the town would have been a desert of Sahara, while the Edgbaston horticulturalists would have been reduced to the necessity of moistening their lawns with beer.'

The acquisition of the water works was associated also with the setting up of Birmingham's first Health Committee in 1875. It was charged with many tasks from the disposal of sewage and refuse to the inspection of milk and food. Other cities had had such committees for years – Sheffield, for example, and Liverpool, which led the way, since 1842 – and Birmingham was now responding at last under the impact of the civic gospel to the facts of squalor and disease which had drawn into action the earlier spokesmen of the 'Sanitary Idea'. Additional inspectors were appointed – Birmingham had previously had only one for every 30,000 inhabitants, while Manchester had one for every 8,000 and Leeds one for every 13,000 – and with one inspector for each ward more 'nuisances' were reported. Within eight years more than 3,000 wells, used by 60,000 people, were condemned on the grounds that they were dangerously contaminated. As a result of these and other measures, Birmingham's death rate, which had been 25.2 per thousand for the years 1871–5, a higher death rate than that of 1849, before the Town Council acquired its greater powers, and 3.2 per cent above the national rate, was reduced to 20.7 per thousand for the years 1880–85, only 1.3 per cent above the national rate.

The averages for the whole city, always misleading, do not express the full measure of benefit reaped by the 'black spot' districts, where the death rate had been abnormally high.

'Birmingham', the Town Council was able to report in 1881, 'is now, as regards its health, first among all the large towns of Great Britain which are fairly comparable with it. ... The amount of work done by the department had gradually diminished during the last three years. This is not on account of any inadequate supervision or want of diligence on the part of the officers, but is to be accounted for by the fact that the town is now getting into a much better sanitary condition.'

These 'improvements' led to a decline in the influence of the old and controversial Public Works Committee, and it is significant that Avery, who had been made chairman of the reformed Sewage Committee, resigned his post to become chairman of the new Water Committee in 1875. In this year the crowning achievement of Birmingham's civic policy, Chamberlain's great Improvement Scheme, was started. The use of the noun 'improvement' in the title (with a capital I) also marked the peak point in the use of this word, a word which can be fittingly applied as a label to a whole age.

The Improvement Scheme was made possible by a piece of national legislation, again a Conservative measure, the Artisans' Dwellings Act of 1875, which Richard Cross, Disraeli's reforming Home Secretary, deliberately referred to Chamberlain for his approval during its passage through Parliament. The Act provided for the compulsory acquisition by specified local authorities of insanitary areas within their boundaries. After acquisition, existing properties could be demolished, new houses could be built, and general improvements could be carried out. Chamberlain admired the philosophy behind the act which he claimed 'recognized something higher than property'. He took steps at once to have set up an 'Improvement Committee' of the Council, and encouraged his friend William White, who represented the poorest and most insanitary ward in the borough, to become its first chairman.

The Medical Officer of Health was asked to prepare a map of a 'scheduled area'. He did so within a few weeks, picking out a crowded area of 'narrow streets, houses without back doors or windows, situated both in and out of courts; confined yards; courts open at one end only, and this one opening small and narrow; the impossibility in many instances, of providing sufficient privy accommodation; houses and shopping so dilapidated as to be in imminent danger of falling, and incapable of proper repair.' The evils ensuing were 'want of ventilation, want of light, want of proper and decent accommodation, resulting in dirty habits, low health and debased morals on the part of the tenants'.

White, who was a moving speaker, added his own verdict. 'The rubbish and dilapidation in whole quarters', he said, 'have reminded me of Strasbourg, which I saw soon after the bombardment [of 1870]. In passing through such streets as Thomas Street, the back of Lichfield Street, and other parts indicated in the plan before the Council, little else is to be seen but bowing roofs, tottering chimneys, tumbledown and often disused shopping, heaps of bricks, broken windows and coarse, rough pavements, damp and sloppy. It is not easy to describe or imagine the dreary desolation which acre after acre of the very heart of the town presents to anyone who will take the trouble to visit it. In houses, too, not of the worst class, but in front streets, and inhabited by respectable and thriving tradesmen, intolerable structural evils abound . . . which I have seen with my own eyes and have heard from witnesses. I am stating facts.'

White's speech recalls some of Charles Booth's comments fifteen years later on London or Seebohm Rowntree's comments twenty-five years later on York. Chamberlain, listening to White, spoke of the 'deep impression' which had been made by the disclosure of 'these terrible facts' on his own mind 'and that of the town'. It is scarcely surprising that the Council approved the scheme of clearing the scheduled district, an area of ninety-three acres, as the Improvement Committee had proposed. There was vociferous Conservative opposition not so much in the Council as at the Local Government Board inquiry, but a provisional order from the Local Government Board, later confirmed by Act of Parliament in August 1876, authorized its acquisition.

Of the ninety-three acres, the Corporation was to acquire about forty-three, at a total cost of £1,310,000. Proposed new streets to relieve central traffic problems would absorb nearly eight acres, and would cost £34,000 to build. The estimated improved value of the surplus land was £794,000. This left the estimated net cost of carrying out the Improvement Scheme at £550,000. The Corporation could borrow at 3½ per cent, repayable in fifty years. For the fifty years of the loan the annual cost to the Corporation would be £18,000, and at the end of fifty years the property would belong to Birmingham. Improved rateable value, however, could be set against annual cost, and Chamberlain estimated that when this element was taken into account, the annual cost of the Scheme would be only £12,000. 'Is that too heavy a burden for the town of Birmingham to contemplate?' he asked. 'I believe the town and, above all, the next generation will have cause to bless the Town Council if it ... exercises what I venture to call a sagacious audacity.'

Without resorting to the power of compulsory purchase, the Committee had begun at once to acquire as much land and property as possible within the improvement area. It employed funds raised by an Improvement Trust backed by prominent local people: Chamberlain himself guaranteed £10,000. The purchases were made without consulting the Council and without disclosing the price paid for the individual properties. Building did not begin until 1878: by then purchases of property totalling over a million pounds had been made. The main feature of the scheme was an imposing new street, called Corporation Street, which radically altered the whole topography of central Birmingham.

Civic pride was more obvious than the civic gospel in this venture, as Conservative critics pointed out. Both Chamberlain and White talked of the example of Paris and the creation of 'a great street, as broad as a Parisian boulevard from New Street to the Aston Road': they held that Birmingham was 'under-shopped' and lacking in 'dignity'. New Street was a 'veritable quagmire: to walk across it was something of an adventure'. The critics argued that 'the denizens of the crowded courts and alleys' would have preferred artisans' dwellings, as Cross had intended when he drafted his Act. Birmingham did not develop an enlightened working-class housing policy on the basis of the Improvement Scheme, and even the more far-reaching national Housing of the Working Classes Act of 1890 had few consequences in the city. The city was not exceptional, however, in its relative indifference to these questions. It was always far too easy to argue in the economic conditions of the late nineteenth century that the existence of empty houses in working-class districts 'proved' that there was no shortage of 'artisans' dwellings'. Moreover, the Birmingham Liberals could claim Cross's blessing on their venture. In 1876 he paid a warm tribute to Chamberlain when he attended a local Conservative demonstration. 'I must give the highest praise to the municipal authorities', he said – and it must have galled many of his hearers – 'for the way in which they have carried out my Act.'

Corporation Street was completed section by section, the Improvement Committee proceeding slowly as a matter of policy so as not to throw too much property on the market at any one time. As a result, the street, like all other Victorian streets, lacked architectural unity and consisted of what a critic called 'selected varieties of all sorts': it was quite different from Napoleon III's Paris. It is important to note that there was no shortage of criticism at any stage. According to one Councillor, much ridicule was heaped upon White and the area had been christened the new Utah, the new Jerusalem, and even the Promised Land: another Councillor said that the Improvement Committee was known locally as the Imprudent Committee.

A revived Municipal Reform Association complained perhaps more seriously in 1880 of 'the annihilation of all individual freedom, whether of judgment or conscience, by the caucus system'. Hawkes and Dixon had both come round to this view, and accused Chamberlain personally of manipulating other people. 'Greater men than Chamberlain', John Lowe, a former Conservative councillor, complained in 1877, had made the mistake of over confidence. 'Look at Napoleon. Where did he finish? In exile.' Avery, who had begun by supporting the Improvement Scheme, turned against it. Less politically committed critics of the scheme made fun of the inability of the Corporation to let all the sites, an inability which was real enough when economic conditions were as unfavourable as they were in 1879 or in the mid-1880s. As the *Dart*, a satirical magazine, put it in 1879:

> One end's begun, but who shall see
> The other end? – a mystery!
> 'Twill be a Herculean feat
> To make it so that both ends meet.

The administrators of the scheme were certainly conscious of their difficulties. By 1886 there was a deficit on the revenue account of £95,858, and the contribution from the rates had to be increased from £20,000 to £25,000. It was not until 1892 that the Improvement Committee was able to report for the first time that there was a surplus on its account. The economic and financial difficulties were closely associated with the trade cycle, and, as always the case in Birmingham, the social barometer followed the trade cycle as well. When times were good, satire withered away. 'We should scarcely need to take a nap as long as Rip Van Winkle's,' the *Birmingham Weekly Post* commented in 1881, 'to wake up and find Corporation Street complete, bustling with life and activity.'

Long before the street was completed, Chamberlain had left the Council to join the Cabinet. He had become a Member of Parliament for Birmingham in 1876 on Dixon's retirement, two years after Sheffield had rejected him. In 1880 he joined Gladstone's Liberal Cabinet as President of the Board of Trade. He expressed his feelings about local and national politics with customary candour both in 1876 and after 1880. 'What a fool I am to be willing to go to Parliament and give up the opportunity of influencing the only constructive legislation in the country for the sake of tacking M.P. to my name', he wrote to Collings in 1876. 'Unless I can secure for the nation results similar to those which have followed the adoption of my policy in Birmingham,' he wrote to Morley in 1883, 'it will have been a sorry exchange to give up the Town Council for the Cabinet.' At the same time, he was under no illusions concerning the significance of what he had accomplished in Birmingham. 'I think I have now almost completed my municipal programme,' he wrote just before he entered the House of Commons, 'and may sing *nunc dimittis*. The Town will be parked, paved, assized, marketed, gas-and-watered and *improved* – all as a result of three years' active work.'

5

Chamberlain's successful implementation of the civic gospel in Birmingham turned the spotlight on the city in a way in which it had never been turned before. Part of the interest was, of course, in Chamberlain himself. He was obviously a 'man of destiny', and both his personal contribution to the city's progress and his devotion to the Town Council were undeniable. He had deliberately given up commercial life, in which (unlike Cobden) he had been remarkably successful, for municipal life: what would happen when he gave up municipal life for national life? What would happen when, knowing Gladstone's dislike of 'programmes', he tried to work out a programme for the nation?

Another part of the interest in Birmingham was in the caucus. Was it an instrument of democratic freedom or of a new kind of oligarchical tyranny based on American or Australian rather than on British models? British periodicals were full of articles on this subject, particularly after 1877 when the National Liberal Federation was founded on 'Birmingham principles'. The authors of the articles fell into two groups, those who defended and those who attacked 'the Birmingham system', and even Liberals themselves were divided on this issue. The general election of 1880 was regarded as a test of 'the efficiency of the new democratic machinery of which Birmingham is the capital'.

At least some part of the interest in Birmingham, however, went deeper than this. It was interest in civic achievement as such. Writers from all parts of the world went to Birmingham to report on what they saw there. As Chamberlain himself said in his speech accepting nomination as candidate for Birmingham in 1876, 'Local government is increasing in importance while Imperial is diminishing'. That he himself would not have accepted this assessment twenty years later does not make it an untrue assessment on the eve of the great political storms of the late 1870s and early 1880s.

An American writer, J. Ralph, called Birmingham in 1890 'the best-governed city in the world'. He compared it not only with American cities, many of which were in the grip of corrupt bosses or machines, but with other English cities and with cities in Europe. Two features of Birmingham's local government appealed particularly both to Ralph and to other observers – first, the intellectual calibre and social status of the councillors, second the quality of the 'municipal civil service'.

The contrast in both these respects with the 'Old Woodman' Council is striking. It was symbolized in the opening in 1879 of the Council House. As early as 1853 the site of the future Council House, right in the heart of Birmingham, was bought by the town. Because of bickering and misunderstandings it remained undeveloped until 1870. In that year a proposal of the Estates Committee was at last accepted for the construction of 'town buildings', and Alfred Waterhouse, the celebrated Victorian architect, 'whose smile was worth ten thousand pounds a year to him', both in Manchester and in Birmingham, was appointed as consultant. H. R. Yeoville Thomason was finally chosen as architect – his plan was far less interesting architecturally than at least one of the rejected plans – and Chamberlain laid the foundation stone of the new buildings in 1874.

The completed building may be compared with the Leeds Town Hall, at least in its décor. Just as Leeds saluted its local industries, so Birmingham proudly placed on the central pediment over the principal entrance a sculptured group representing 'Britannia rewarding the Birmingham Manufacturers'. Other sculptural groups in the four pediments at each angle of the front of the building represented literature, art, and science in their relation to industry. The interior of the building included an impressive mayor's parlour, 'noble' reception rooms, and a 'handsome and commodious Council Chamber'. The Chamber, unlike the House of Commons, was semi-circular in plan with a spectators' gallery. The windows in the upper tier were filled with stained glass, and both the walls and the ceilings were ornamented with frescoes 'emblematical of Birmingham industry'. It is not surprising to learn that Mr Yeoville Thomason 'superintended every detail in its erection'.

The new Council House was given its name only after a characteristic burst of Victorian controversy. The Estates Committee favoured the name 'Municipal Hall' and Alderman Avery the 'Guildhall', but the title 'Council House' finally prevailed by thirty-four votes to twenty-six. Ten years after its opening the Chamberlain Memorial was unveiled – a Gothic fountain of Portland stone, with columns, arches, and water-jets. Chamberlain had warmly approved the proposal when it was first mooted. 'All this is good for the party, and good for municipal institutions which are daily becoming of more importance and more honoured.'

Unlike many cities, Birmingham continued to recruit councillors of standing and ability, although soon after the beginning of the twentieth century *The Times* noted a 'disposition to think that the same degree of credit can no longer be got out of local administration by the leisured or aspiring citizen as was the case a few years ago'. The same social groups – with a bigger proportion of professional men and a sprinkling of working men – continued to compete for municipal power, with political complications greatly increased after the Liberal split (on the Irish question) in 1886. There was less leadership, however, than in Chamberlain's time, and more complaints of 'extravagance'. In the year of the split a Liberal councillor complained that the rates were rising to an extent that Birmingham shopkeepers and traders could not stand. 'The expenditure meant a larger outlay year by year for interest and for the sinking fund than the town could afford. Money had been spent in the Council to an extent that was simply appalling.'

There was always a real danger that Birmingham would 'lapse into the languid indifference of the pre-Chamberlain era'. As early as 1883 the ratepayers threw out by a small majority on a low poll a proposed Birmingham Corporation Consolidation Act, and it was only after a legal judgment in the Court of Queen's Bench that this important measure was allowed to come into force: in 1907, this time successfully and in face of the advice of Neville Chamberlain, the ratepayers defeated a proposal to embark upon a new central demolition scheme and to build a useful new thoroughfare, even though it would add only one halfpenny in the pound to the rates. There was little sense of gospel in an unknown ratepayer's remark, 'one must cut one's coat according to the cloth at one's disposal. My grandfather did not spend five-twelfths of his income for my benefit, and I for one would strongly object to paying eight shillings and fourpence in the pound rates for the benefit of posterity.'

It is illuminating when considering the civic gospel to compare the balance of opinions on matters of this kind – the calibre and commitment of councillors and the financial basis of change – in Birmingham and other cities, with or without a civic gospel. In many cities the most active local citizens played little part in government. 'The richest capitalists in manufacturing towns', G. C. Broderick wrote in 1875, when Chamberlain was Mayor of Birmingham, 'are deterred ... from aspiring to civic dignities. Their sense of self-importance and their sense of responsibility find a far more complete gratification in the colossal operations of trade, and in the management of country estates far removed from their place of business than is offered by a career of municipal statesmanship crowned with knighthood, or baronetcy itself.' They might wish to become justices of the peace, but they felt no urge to become town councillors. A few influential Nonconformists with very strong views on education might be tempted to join the new School Boards of 1870, men like Sir John Brown in Sheffield, which had a quite remarkable first School Board, or Hugh Birley in Manchester, but the town councils were still outside the orbit of their concern.

There was an obvious contrast between Birmingham and some of the smaller parliamentary towns such as Derby or Nottingham where, in the words of a witness before a committee, the councils consisted not of 'persons of influence or positions in the town ... but of persons in the lower rank of life, who have accumulated a little property, and who wish to obtain a position in the town.' There was an equally real contrast between Birmingham and Manchester. The enthusiasm of the first Council members in Manchester had given way to the plodding inefficiency of 'second-rate men', the 'hard-headed shopkeepers' whom Beatrice Webb described. 'The social status', she wrote on her visit to Manchester at the end of the century, 'is predominantly lower-middle-class, a Tory solicitor and an I.L.P. journalist being the only men with any pretension to culture.' Beatrice Webb was a biased observer, but there is plenty of local evidence to support two of her other conclusions. 'Friction and petty scandals, accusations and recriminations, dog the Council's work.' 'There is no head of the concern [as Chamberlain had been in Birmingham], no one who corresponds to a general manager of a railway company, still less to its paid chairman. The mayor elected for one year has all his time absorbed by public meetings, social functions or routine administration; he is far more the ceremonial head of the city than the chief of the executive of the city government.'

Deficiencies of leadership were more serious than biases of social composition, yet the small numbers of working men on the Councils – Birmingham was like the other cities in this respect – sometimes gave the Councils an air of unreality. Working-class pressures were slow to mount, and when the secretary of the Birmingham Gasworkers' Union won a local election contest at Saltley in 1897 there was something curiously drab about the *Birmingham Daily Mail*'s comment – 'There is no reason why the secretary of the Gasworkers should not do as useful work in the City Council as a Lawyer or a Pork Butcher'. The apathy of twentieth-century local government politics is not a new phenomenon. Even in caucus-ridden Birmingham there was usually only a strictly limited interest in local affairs; in the towns and cities as a whole, as Broderick wrote, local government was in the hands of shopkeepers and struggling professional men, engaged in busy callings and with few hours to spend on detailed public business. 'The mass of the population take little part in political life of any kind, except when called upon to vote, to attend a town meeting or to sign a petition; and so far as they read the newspapers they probably gain more knowledge of national than of local affairs.'

The main battles in the cities, therefore, were battles about finance. The alternating periods of civic spending and 'going slow' did not always coincide in different places, for it needed inspiration as well as 'good times' to move from one period to another. In Liverpool, for example, just at the time that Birmingham was spending lavishly, there was great local pressure to 'go slow'. The spending initiative had come earlier than in Birmingham, and it was in 1859, not in the 1870s, that the Liverpool Borough Engineer argued boldly that it was 'only by a comprehensive scheme for the remedy of present evils and the preventing of their repetition, and by providing for future requirements that any plan of improvement really worthy of consideration can be made.'

He went even further and suggested the building of a 'great boulevard' which would serve as 'an elongated park passing through country affording ever-varying and charming prospects.' His plans were not fully accomplished, but they were indicative of a mood and a purpose. The improvement of streets and boulevards, as one Liverpool Councillor put it in 1858, was a subject 'seriously affecting the welfare of the burgesses at large' and directly of concern to 'our well-conducted and industrious working classes'. Yet during the 1870s 'the flood of improvements', as B. D. White has pointed out in his *History of the Corporation of Liverpool*, 'dwindled to a trickle ... and dried up altogether after 1883'. The Liberals, who gained ground in Liverpool against the previously powerful Tories – the Tories recaptured power later – were not interested in the civic gospel in Liverpool: they were quite content to fight their campaigns on the older slogan of 'retrenchment and reform'.

Even where the local Liberals copied, at least in their own way, the Birmingham caucus system of party management, there was no guarantee that they would follow its positive lead in local government. The Leeds Liberals, to take one example, intervened directly in local politics without producing the Birmingham result, so that Beatrice Webb could be just as scathing about the local government of Leeds as about that of Manchester. Financial restrictions could hold back all major reforms. It is significant that whereas Birmingham solved its sewage problem after Adderley's complaints about river pollution, the Leeds Corporation, faced with a parallel challenge in 1870 concerning the pollution of the River Aire, failed to deal adequately with its problems of sewage disposal until well into the twentieth century. In Sheffield, where the Town Council had resolved in 1860 that 'it is not expedient at the present time to consider the most efficient means of improving the sanitary condition of the Borough', there were complaints about river pollution as late as the 1890s. A combined sewage system was not decided upon until 1884. The foundation of a Town Hall was not laid until 1891, and Queen Victoria travelled to Sheffield to open it in 1897, nearly forty years after she had travelled to Leeds. Until then the Councillors had met in rented rooms or after 1857 in the Free Library, and the local government offices were scattered about 'the meaner streets of the town'.

Of course, there were genuine financial difficulties confronting most of the cities in the nineteenth century, and the greater the scope of civic action, the more pronounced the difficulties became. Battles about rates were sometimes dramatic in almost all Victorian cities, particularly when they raised questions of principle, whether, for example, the city should be thought 'clean' or 'dirty': often, however, they were merely squalid. Grants-in-aid from central government and loans, instruments which, as we have seen, gained tremendously in fiscal and administrative importance only during the last years of the century, never reduced the significance of the local struggle to keep down rates. What Dr McDonagh has called the self-sustaining and self-generating impulse of administration at the centre continued to operate, widening in scope, and assisting local efforts to reform. As for city borrowing, it was subject to many different legal limitations at different parts of the century. It reached a very high figure before the Victorian age ended. Whereas the total debt of all the 178 corporations in England and Wales was only £1,768,000 in 1838–9, of which Liverpool alone owed 60 per cent, and in 1872–3 the total still stood at only £6,613,095, by the end of the century Birmingham's debt alone was more than £10 million. Birmingham could compare itself not with other British cities but with 'small continental principalities'.

Liverpool, which under Conservative rule was to embark upon many schemes of 'daring municipalization', remained prominent among the borrowers.

The municipal 'civil service' of Birmingham was perhaps its greatest jewel, for the service remained in existence in good times and bad, both when 'principles' were in the ascendant and when 'economy' was the only watchword. The Finance Committee could not have carried out its increasingly complicated work had it not been for the assistance of a growing City Treasurer's Department. The co-ordinating General Purposes Committee would have been paralysed had it not included the Town Clerk. In 1867 when W. R. Hughes became City Treasurer of Birmingham, he was assisted by a book-keeper and a youth: in 1898 there were twenty clerks and a Deputy. In 1869 when E. J. Hayes replaced Thomas Standbridge as Town Clerk, there was a tradition that the Town Clerk carried on his private business as a solicitor as well: in 1898 the Town Clerk's office included eight committee clerks, a Deputy Town Clerk, a Chief Clerk and two Assistant Solicitors. The civic gospel depended on this administrative substructure, a fact which Chamberlain fully recognized. In a fascinating speech at Glasgow in 1897 he remarked that if ever corruption crept into the cities of Great Britain it would be when the higher officials were paid less and the lower officials more than the market value of their services.

In all Victorian cities, perhaps most in those cities where there was no civic gospel, the question of the quality of the sub-structure gained in importance. An American specialist in government, A. L. Lowell, concluded after visiting England early in the new century that 'the excellence of municipal government was very roughly proportional to the influence of the permanent officials.' Their influence was great in Bradford, Glasgow, Liverpool and Birmingham and low in Manchester, Bristol and London. 'This difference', he held, 'explains to some extent the shortcomings in the last three places.'

Manchester, however, for a very large part of Queen Victoria's reign, had possessed one outstanding local official – Sir Joseph Heron, Town Clerk from the town's incorporation in 1838 to his death in 1889 (he was knighted in 1869 and served only as consultant Town Clerk after 1877). Heron was a 'consummate ruler of men', a dominating personality who was always far more than a legal adviser. Once when an angry councillor asked him by what right he intervened in a Council debate – 'What ward do you represent?' – he replied briefly, 'A larger ward than yours, sir. I represent the entire city.' Such official power could become intolerably bureaucratic, yet its existence was a measure of the change in the organization of civic life. The restraints on bureaucracy were always less strong than in nineteenth-century Birmingham just because the councillors were never of sufficient calibre to earn the respect as well as the service of their officials. Heron's grip on Manchester was strengthened rather than relaxed when the councillors spent most of 1859 and 1860 wrangling as to whether his salary should be increased from £1,500 to £2,000.

The same trends could be traced in national and imperial as well as local government, and it was the final consequence of Birmingham's civic gospel that it was applied in Whitehall and the Empire. Chamberlain was careful to insert into the unauthorized Radical programme of 1885 the same ideas which had guided him in Birmingham: he stated then that 'the most fruitful field before reformers' was 'an extension of the functions and authority of local government' as a means of 'equalizing the condition of men' and limiting 'the extremes which now form so great a blot on our social system'. After the split of 1886 he dropped many of these ideas, but continued to express his belief in 'constructive local government' in a wider setting. His attitude, for example, to 'Home Rule for the Rand' in 1896–7 has been described by his biographer, J. L. Garvin, as 'calling up on every side reminiscences of his administration of Birmingham'.

It is for this reason, if for no other, that G. M. Young's contrast between Manchester and Birmingham remains extremely apposite. Just as the ideas of the Manchester School had a universal reference, so the ideas of Birmingham, as expressed by Chamberlain, had an imperial reference. 'Cobden, the international man', had his counterpart in 'Chamberlain, the imperialist'. The tone of late-nineteenth-century argument about Empire was coloured by Birmingham just as the tone of mid-nineteenth-century argument about The World had been coloured by Manchester.

The point has been made not only by G. M. Young but by Sir Keith Hancock in his masterly *Survey of Commonwealth Affairs*:

> From the time of the Fair Trade movement to the days when the Chamberlain family takes the lead [after 1903] in the struggle for national protection and economic preference, Birmingham had the same symbolical importance which Manchester possessed in the middle of the nineteenth century.... One might almost dramatize the past century of British commercial policy as a struggle between free-trade Manchester and protectionist Birmingham – or better still as a three-cornered struggle, with the old industrialist-cosmopolitan City of London joining forces with Manchester to keep Birmingham in check. Birmingham was destined in the end to win.

CHAPTER SIX

Middlesbrough: The Growth of a New Community

This remarkable place, THE YOUNGEST CHILD OF ENGLAND'S ENTERPRISE.... It is an infant, gentlemen, but it is an infant Hercules.

W. E. GLADSTONE on his visit to Middlesbrough (October 1862)

I

DURING Joseph Chamberlain's mayoralty, the rateable value of Birmingham was £1,229,844: that of Middlesbrough at the same date was £130,255. The population of the two communities was around 344,000 and 40,000. Yet it was Middlesbrough which Gladstone compared with Hercules, an infant Hercules, no doubt, but 'an Hercules all the same'.

Within the reign of Queen Victoria itself, Middlesbrough grew from a very tiny rural community to a very large town of over one hundred thousand people. There were cities outside Britain, in the United States or Australia, which grew from nothing even faster during the nineteenth century, but there was no other English town. By comparison, Birmingham was old, old enough to have been called 'the toyshop of Europe' by Edmund Burke, reputed to be old enough in the boast of William Hutton, its first historian, to have manufactured the wheels for Queen Boadicea's chariot. The great engineer, Thomas Telford, had described it long before Queen Victoria came to the throne as 'famous for its buttons and its locks, its ignorance and its barbarism'.

Middlesbrough was a town 'which had won a name without history, an importance without antiquity'. The other new English communities of the nineteenth century, the railway town of Crewe, for example, or Barrow-in-Furness, with which Middlesbrough had much in common, were smaller than Middlesbrough and, despite many claims to continuing interest, left a less vivid impression on contemporaries. 'The outcome of present century enterprise and discovery', the Victorians called Middlesbrough, and went on to claim that it occupied 'an unique position in the annals of our native land'. It was known throughout the world, too. 'The iron it supplies furnishes railways to Europe; it runs by Neapolitan and Papal dungeons; it startles the bandit in his haunts in Cilicia; it streaks the prairies of America; it stretches over the plains of India; it surprises the Belochees; it pursues the peggunus of Gangotri. It has crept out of the Cleveland Hills, where it has slept since the Roman days, and now, like a strong and invincible serpent, coils itself round the world.'

This romantic language demonstrates how the 'magic of industry' fascinated the Victorians. It did not, however, inhibit them from being didactic too. The story of Middlesbrough, like all good Victorian stories, had a moral. 'Middlesbrough, the delineation of whose growth and development forms the subject-matter of the following pages', a historian of the town began in 1899, 'must ever present to the mind of the thoughtful a most striking illustration of England's enormous industrial progress during the nineteenth century.' Another writer spoke proudly of 'a modern progressive spirit working upon old materials'. Middlesbrough was felt to be 'unparalleled in its proofs of rapid and genuine progress', a creation both of individual enterprise and of the powerful 'associative principle', the supremely practical product of 'a beautiful system of interwoven interests and mutual dependence'. 'In towns such as this, you see the secret workings of that indefatigable machine of spirited and patriotic industry, which goes on forcing this tight little island steadily ahead, and far ahead, of all competitors.'

The origins of Middlesbrough can be traced back before Queen Victoria's reign. Yet it contained only four houses and twenty-five inhabitants in 1801, and only forty inhabitants in 1829. At the census of 1831 the number had risen to 154, and in 1841 to 5,463. The ten years from 1831 to 1841 saw the planned development of the community by the 'Middlesbrough [or Middlesburgh] Owners' as a port for the shipment of coals at the terminus of the famous Stockton and Darlington Railway. The railway, opened in September 1825, had been sponsored by a little group of 'Quaker gentlemen' in Darlington and the surrounding countryside, and it was nicknamed in consequence 'the Quakers' line'. They were anxious to export local supplies of coal from the River Tees to London and other markets, and it was with this end in view that they extended the line to Middlesbrough, six miles nearer the sea where the river was deeper. Stockton, an older town, was difficult to navigate, and Middlesbrough, which at that time consisted of five hundred acres of bleak salt marshes, was developed instead. It says much for the quality of vision of the leading personality in the enterprise, Joseph Pease, not to speak of his initiative, that in 1828 after he had looked at the one farmhouse which then constituted 'Middlesbrough', he wrote in his diary that 'imagination here has very ample scope in fancying a coming day when the bare fields . . . will be covered with a busy multitude and numerous vessels crowding to these banks denote the busy seaport.'

Pease and his associates, Thomas Richardson, a relative, Henry Birbeck, Simon Martin, and Francis Gibson, all of them Quakers, bought the Middlesbrough estate for £30,000 in 1829, and they set out resolutely to develop it as a rival to large and well-established ports, like Sunderland and even Newcastle. They talked eloquently of 'taking the lead of both Tyne and Wear'. There was also a pronounced local rivalry of a more immediate kind with Stockton, a quiet country town which boasted of a roll of mayors covering a period of nearly four hundred years; good feelings were scarcely improved by the fact that Middlesbrough's mail arrived for several years at the Stockton Post Office addressed 'Middlesbrough, near Stockton-on-Tees'.

In 1826 Pease had made the modest estimate that ten thousand tons of coal could be exported each year from Teesside. The actual figure in 1830–31, the first year after the Stockton and Darlington Railway had been extended to Middlesbrough, was over a hundred and fifty thousand tons. The first load of coal included one immense block of 'black diamonds' which it was calculated would make, when broken, two London chaldrons. By 1840 the total of coal exports had risen to over one and a half million tons. The early prosperity of Middlesbrough was thus guaranteed. The building of superior shipping staiths was followed by the making of a new cut in the Tees and the construction of docks, and with the staiths and the docks came the first local industry. A Middlesbrough pottery was started in 1834, and the first order shipped to Gibraltar in the same year. In 1840, the year that the first public market was opened (on the site of the old farm pond) and the first church consecrated, John Harris, one of Pease's colleagues in the management of the Stockton and Darlington Railway Company, persuaded two ironfounders, Henry Bolckow and John Vaughan, to settle in Middlesbrough and open a foundry and rolling mill.

It was this early growth, continuing through the 1840s, which inspired J. W. Ord, the first historian of the Cleveland district, to describe Middlesbrough in 1846 as 'one of the commercial prodigies of the nineteenth century'. Anticipating the lyrical language of the later century, he added that, to the stranger visiting Middlesbrough after the lapse of a few years, 'this proud array of ships, docks, warehouses, churches, foundries, wharves, etc., would seem like some enchanted spectacle, some Arabian Nights' vision, "such stuff as dreams are made of"'. The 'etc.' is hardly such stuff as dreams are made of, but it is very easy to see what Ord meant when he referred to Middlesbrough's population in 1841 as an 'amazing number'. He usually preferred to dwell not on the statistics set out in the census returns of the nineteenth century, but on the evidence of Domesday Book: Middlesbrough was impressive enough to shift the focus of his attention. It was also impressive enough for its first royal visitor, the Duke of Sussex, who was taken to see Middlesbrough by the Lord Lieutenant of the North Riding in 1838, to congratulate the inhabitants on the 'spirit of progress' they displayed. William Fallows, agent of the Stockton and Darlington Railway Company and later, among his many other duties, first postmaster of Middlesbrough, Justice of the Peace, and Mayor, replied appropriately to the Duke that though the town could not boast of 'the ancient and valuable institutions' which might be seen in the older towns around them, 'yet we have far greater pleasure in seeing those institutions rising up in the midst of us, by our own industry and exertions, growing with our growth and strengthening with our strength'.

The Middlesbrough owners were interested, somewhat paternalistically, like the Railway Company at Crewe or at Barrow-in-Furness, in the creation of social institutions. They set out some of their plans in a deed of covenant entered into in February 1831. In order to 'produce some uniformity and respectability in the houses to be built', they laid out a 'new town' behind the wharves on a strictly symmetrical plan with a central square from which four main streets – North Street, South Street, East Street, and West Street – each moved out at right-angles. It is a tragedy that in an age of deliberate 'new town' building, this fascinating example of nineteenth-century town planning has been almost destroyed in recent years.

Church and market were at the centre of a planned community, which, as Middlesbrough grew, ceased to be the effective centre of the Victorian city. The planning was concerned with spiritual welfare as well as with material well-being. The Quaker owners did not hesitate, to the delight of the Bishop of Durham, to give high priority to the building of the Parish Church of St Hilda. They provided land: £500 was provided by the Church Building Society and £1,200 was raised by a grand bazaar and lottery. That care for spiritual welfare was needed in Middlesbrough was suggested by the high incidence of drunkenness among the new population. 'A large part of the inhabitants', one Middlesbrough veteran reminisced later in the century, 'was given up to intemperance.'

Middlesbrough was on a turbulent urban frontier, despite its Quaker inspiration. It is said that in the very early days one publican did a roaring trade with no other seats for his customers than a few planks supported on beer barrels. 'Seafaring men – living next door to each other in what was soon to form a street, but separated by a few unoccupied building sites – used to talk to one another from their own doors, when at home, through their speaking trumpets, same as they did at sea, because they could not travel between the two houses without sinking up to the calves of their legs in mire.' In a letter of January 1838, Thomas Richardson was told 'Very lately a person was relating to us what a rough set you were in Middlesbrough, *not one gentleman in the place*, but correcting himself, "Yes, there was one gentleman, Mr Holmes."' (J. G. Holmes, a shipbuilder, was a well-known teetotaller, who had helped to found the first temperance society in 1837.) The letter writer added, 'You must not place yourself too high, mind, when he is thought to be the only *gentleman* among you.'

During the 1840s Middlesbrough acquired its first complex of urban institutions. A Centenary Wesleyan Methodist Chapel was opened in 1840, and Richmond Street Primitive Methodist Chapel in 1841. A Mechanics' Institute was founded in 1840, and a separate Oddfellows' District was carved out in 1842. Friendly societies had been active in the town from the start. In 1843 the first new school buildings were erected by the British and Foreign School Society: there had been schools in existence in the 1830s, although it had proved difficult 'to prevail or to compel the attendance of the children'.

The government of the town passed in 1841 to twelve Improvement Commissioners, who by an Improvement Act of that year were given power to deal with watch, paving, lighting, cleansing and drainage. Hitherto government had been by annual general meeting: now the twelve commissioners included Fallows, Holmes, Otley, a proprietor of the pottery, William Blenkinsop, an innkeeper, Isaac Sharp, the local agent of the Middlesbrough Owners, and Henry Bolckow. They were empowered to levy a rate not exceeding two shillings in the pound (the same as the Birmingham figure) or two shillings and sixpence with the consent of a majority of ratepayers at a town meeting, and they could borrow up to £5,000. They took their work most conscientiously and by 1843 had set up a sanitary committee as one of their five standing committees. It was a sign of their energy that they were soon involved in disputes with the local gas company, formed in 1838: these disputes led to its early municipalization.

Government in general was tough but cheap, as it passed from a paternalistic to a representative phase. The clerk to the commissioners was a local solicitor, and R. Ord held the combined posts of chief of police, surveyor, and collector of rates and tolls at a salary of £60 a year. When in 1846 a Town Hall was built in the central square of the 'new town', it was 'a very unpretentious pile ... designed evidently with an eye to utility rather than to ornament'. Later in the century it was used as a branch police station and for market offices: in the late 1840s a fire engine was kept there. The engine had been bought for £15 from another local authority.

2

Middlesbrough was incorporated in 1853, and by then a big leap forward in its economic life had further guaranteed its future prosperity. Middlesbrough could hardly have captured the inspiration of men like Gladstone had it simply been a coal-exporting centre: indeed, its coal trade declined sharply in the mid-Victorian years. Ironically the completion of the national railway network hastened the decline, for it became more profitable to move coal by rail than by sea. What coastal trade was left passed back into the hands of Newcastle or to near-by Hartlepool. This decline, which might have reduced Middlesbrough to a ghost town, was completely overshadowed, however, by the growth of the local iron industry, so much so that the first modest phases of Middlesbrough's urban life before 1850 were almost forgotten in the light of what came afterwards. A population of 7,431 at the census of 1851, living in 1,262 houses, had risen in 1861 to a population of 19,416, living in 3,203 houses. In 1871 there was a further rise to 39,563, in 1881 to 55,934, in 1891 to 75,532, and in 1901 to 91,302.

People were attracted to Middlesbrough from all parts of the country in the same way as they were attracted to Liverpool and Birkenhead. In 1861 73.2 per cent of its population was born in Yorkshire, but by 1871 both ironworkers from

Durham, South Wales, Staffordshire, and Scotland and labourers from Ireland had flocked to the town in such numbers that the native county element had sunk to 50.1 per cent. During the next decade immigration continued but at a diminished rate. There were even immigrants from the British Colonies, the East Indies, and the United States, with 551 people being described as coming from 'foreign parts' at the census of 1871. Middlesbrough had a very different demographic pattern from that of most English towns, with West Bromwich, Norwich, Ipswich, Leicester, and Northampton the most 'intensely English towns', as Ravenstein called them, at the other end of the scale. Indeed, in his view, Middlesbrough's 'rapid growth, the heterogeneous composition of its population, and the preponderance of the male sex, recall features generally credited only to towns of the American West'. The 'preponderance of the male sex', so long a feature of Australian demographic history, deserves as much attention as the mixture of origins, for certainly it left its mark on the ways of life of the growing town. The only other British towns which proved more attractive to male than to female immigrants were West Ham, St Helens, Airdrie, Hamilton, Greenock, Hawick and, an interesting overlap, West Bromwich. Whereas female immigrants, seeking jobs in domestic service, were prominent in most Victorian cities, they were far less prominent in essentially working-class Middlesbrough.

The religious mix was interesting also. It was a sign of the times that a Jewish Synagogue was opened in 1874. The Roman Catholics had built their first church in 1838. Before that they had worshipped in a room later taken over by the Unitarians, the first of Middlesbrough's religious groups to have a meeting room – as early as 1833. The Catholics built up a huge congregation, largely Irish, during the sixteen years of Father Burns's priesthood from 1854 to 1870, and in 1878 Middlesbrough became the centre of a Roman Catholic bishopric with a new cathedral church described as 'the handsomest and largest ecclesiastical edifice in the town'.

The preponderance of males and the variety of religions were two signs only that Middlesbrough had many of the features of a 'melting-pot' community. Bradford woolcombers, sent to Middlesbrough in the 1850s, praised their 'marsters' and acknowledged that the workmen were 'very civel to us': at the same time, they warned their comrades back in Bradford that 'if you send men hear in Large Numbers and the Marsters begin to turn the irish of[f] it will very likely lead to a disturbance'.

Against this background it was appropriate that Henry Bolckow, who transformed both the economic and social life of Middlesbrough, and thereby made possible the great leap ahead of population, was himself a Mecklenberger, who had arrived in Newcastle in 1827 at the age of twenty-one. He worked for a time as accountant, foreign correspondent and commission agent. He settled in Middlesbrough in 1841 with a capital of £50,000 to invest. His partner, John Vaughan, was also an outsider, a man who looked at several places before he settled in Middlesbrough. Born at Worcester in 1799, he had been employed at the famous Dowlais iron works in Wales before becoming a manager first at Carlisle and then at Newcastle. He was a remarkable man, a perfect hero of self help of the type extolled by Samuel Smiles. The two men formed an impressive partnership. 'For a number of years they were nearly as much part and parcel of each other as the Siamese twins. They had one object in common; they lived not together, but next door to each other; they were continually in each other's company, consulting, controlling, planning, advising for the same ends.' The site of their future iron works was a piece of waste land by the river side; at low tide, part of it was a dreary waste of mud on which sailors had discharged their ballast.

From 1841 until 1850 Bolckow and Vaughan were engaged in an arduous and small-scale enterprise in Middlesbrough, looking laboriously to places miles outside Middlesbrough for the ironstone they needed. Ore might be collected from Whitby, for example, carried by sea to Middlesbrough, taken by rail to blast-furnaces twenty-five miles away at Witton Park near Bishop Auckland on the South Durham coalfields, converted into pig-iron, and brought back by rail to the Middlesbrough foundry. This complicated economic chain was broken by what has usually been called 'a great stroke of luck' in the year 1850. Vaughan is said to have discovered a magnificent supply of workable ironstone in the near-by Cleveland Hills at Eston. The local ores, the existence of which had been known for centuries, had generally been thought to be of poor quality and had been dismissed by J. W. Ord as 'of little value except as ballast, and scarcely of sufficient importance to encourage speculation'. Vaughan, who was advised by John Marley, a competent mining engineer, proved Ord and a number of distinguished geologists to be completely wrong. He did not, however, stumble over a block of ironstone while out shooting on the Cleveland Hills. This legend, which he always denied, concealed the care that was taken to find good sites for iron works.

Extremely advantageous leases were acquired from the owner of the land, a trial quarry was begun in August 1850, a temporary tramway was laid down in September, and the first lot of seven tons of iron transported within three weeks after discovery. It is said that Vaughan, excited as he was, had as little sense of the ultimate quantitative significance of his discovery as Pease and his colleague had had of the volume of coal exports when they first built Middlesbrough. He talked of a thousand tons of ironstone being taken from Eston each week: in fact, that quantity was exceeded in a few months, and before very long three times the amount was extracted daily.

This story has an American or an Australian ring to it, for it was about this time that gold was discovered first in California (1849) and next in Victoria (1851). Whole new communities came into being with a rough but vigorous life of their own. Middlesbrough was, in a sense, the British Ballarat. Certainly, despite the inferior popular appeal of iron to gold, the Cleveland statistics were felt to be breathtaking by all the writers on the British economy in newspapers and periodicals. Production of pig-iron increased tenfold in the five years after 1851, by 1861 had leapt to half a million tons, and by 1867 to nearly a million tons. By 1873 the North Eastern ironfield, with Middlesbrough as its capital, was producing over five and a half million tons of ore and making over two million tons of pig-iron, about one third of the total British output. A great wave of mid-Victorian prosperity pushed the price of iron to unprecedented heights.

The region was completely transformed in appearance as a result of these economic advances. In 1851, the year of the Great Exhibition, the first blast-furnace in Middlesbrough was blown in: before ten years had elapsed there were over forty furnaces in Cleveland and Tees-side. In 1862 there were fifteen at Eston alone. Changes in technique were as exciting and important as these spectacular quantitative changes. Both the height and capacity of the furnaces were raised dramatically, waste was reduced, and daily output increased to as much as five thousand tons a day. The lavish praise bestowed on Middlesbrough's 'progressive enterprise' was deserved: techniques were greatly ahead of those of other places.

Bolckow and Vaughan had led the way; other ironmasters, some of whom very quickly became powerful men in the life of the town, followed quickly. The first were Edward Gilkes and C. A. Leatham, both Quakers, the former an engineer with the Stockton and Darlington Railway Company, the latter the son-in-law of Joseph Pease. Their 'Tees Furnaces' passed later into the hands of Wilson, Pease & Company, again a Quaker concern. Isaac Wilson, who had settled in Middlesbrough in 1841 and had been one of the owners of the pottery, was also connected by marriage with the Pease family. Joseph Pease died in 1903, but there were four distinct local businesses directed by members of the Pease family during the later nineteenth century – Joseph Pease and Partners dealing in coal; J. W. Pease & Company in ironstone and limestone; J. and J. W. Pease in banking; and Henry Pease & Company in manufacturing. This remarkable concentration of economic power in the hands of one family was converted into social power locally in the nineteenth century and nationally in the twentieth, when members of the Pease family acquired a bundle of titles. An aristocracy was in the making. Such extended influence somewhat disturbed Edward Pease, the aged head of the family, who lived from 1767 to 1858 and was known as 'the father of the railways' for his work in connexion with the opening of the Stockton and Darlington. In his diary for November 1851 he wrote that 'now there are prospects of great advantages from the discovery of iron ore in the Cleveland range of hills, I feel a great anxiety that none of my beloved family may be caught in its enticings; they have quite enough of this world's engagements'.

Distinct from the Peases were Isaac Lowthian Bell and his two brothers, the sons of Thomas Bell, an ironmaster of Newcastle, yet in this case also there was an odd link with Vaughan, who had been superintendent at the Bells' Newcastle works. The Bells leased ironstone deposits at Normanby in 1853 and built the Port Clarence furnaces on the north side of the Tees opposite Middlesbrough. They used not the Stockton and Darlington Railway but the West Hartlepool Railway, in which the lease owner was financially interested. This provided an additional element of rivalry in the local situation. The Bells progressed, however, and built up a huge enterprise by efficient, up-to-date methods. Lowthian Bell had had an exceptionally good scientific education for a nineteenth-century British businessman and throughout his life he was keenly interested in science: he was also interested in the economic and social statistics of his industry. He became the acknowledged spokesman of the North-east as he built up his business power.

The other local pioneers included William Hopkins and Thomas Snowdon, two men who were associated with the Stockton and Darlington Railway interest and opened the Tees-side Iron Works in 1853; the Cochranes, a family of ironmasters from Staffordshire, who built their first furnace at Ormsby in 1854; and Bernhard Samuelson, son of a Liverpool merchant and head of an agricultural engineering works at Banbury, who after building furnaces at South Bank in 1854 leased a ten-acre field there at a rent of £5 an acre and set about creating yet another new community of his own.

In Middlesbrough itself Henry Bolckow was an outstanding figure in this dynamic phase of the community's history. When the town was incorporated in 1853, with a population which was still less than ten thousand, Bolckow became the first Mayor. He was also the first President of the Chamber of Commerce when the Chamber was formed in 1863 and the first Member of Parliament for Middlesbrough – returned unopposed – when it became a Parliamentary Constituency in 1868. He had to have a special Act of Parliament passed to qualify him as a British subject. His rugged Liberalism was a by-product of his business career, and he is remembered more by his deeds than by his speeches.

Disraeli understood the type better than Gladstone. 'They say we all have our hobbies,' he made his Mr Trafford say, 'and it was mine to improve the conditions of my workpeople, to see what good tenements, and good schools, and just wages paid in a fair manner, and the encouragement of civilizing pursuits would do to elevate their character. I should find an ample reward in the moral tone and material happiness of this community; but really, viewing it in a pecuniary point of view, the investment of capital has been one of the most profitable I ever made.' Certainly Bolckow had much in common with other businessmen who founded new communities and almost automatically took their place in Parliament. John Laird, the Conservative shipbuilder, who became first Member of Parliament for Birkenhead in 1861, and Ralph Ward-Jackson in near-by West Hartlepool were similar types. There was something of the same strain also in Sir Titus Salt.

Bolckow talked like a benevolent proprietor when he gave Middlesbrough its first public park in 1868 and in the same year new schools capable of providing for nine hundred children. He headed local subscription lists for every good cause while he lived, and left generous benefactions when he died. He talked the language, too, of 'pride in his order'. He was chairman of the Middlesbrough Exchange Company, which was as much a symbol of business pride in Middlesbrough as the Town Hall was of civic enthusiasm in Leeds. He laid the foundation stone of the Exchange in 1866, Middlesbrough's most ambitious building to that date: it cost £28,000 and was deemed, without undue boasting, to constitute 'a pile of buildings which would do credit to any town'. The architect was a Stockton man, C. J. Adams, but this did not seem to matter.

A statue of Bolckow, unveiled by Lord Frederick Cavendish in 1881, depicts him handing over to the people the charter of incorporation of Middlesbrough. It had always seemed to be in his gift to offer, for as Prince Arthur said in opening the park Bolckow gave to the town, he had stood by the side of the iron cradle in which Middlesbrough was rocked and had watched over the child with care as it grew. 'He knows what it wants, and what its interests are.' Bolckow may well have chosen Middlesbrough's motto, *Erimus*, which may be compared with Robert Bruce's *Fuimus*. It seemed particularly appropriate to Gladstone. When Bolckow died, the *North Eastern Gazette* appeared with wide black borders around its columns.

The influence of other ironmasters was strong also in the life of Middlesbrough. When Bolckow was Mayor in 1853, Isaac Wilson and John Vaughan were two of the four aldermen. Wilson succeeded Bolckow as Mayor (and later as Member of Parliament) and he was succeeded the following year by Vaughan. William Fallows, Edgar Gilkes, William Hopkins got their chance during the next twelve years. Thomas Hugh Bell got his in 1874. The constitution of the Town Council changed – it was elected on a ward basis from 1858 and was increased in size after a new Improvement Act in 1866 – but effective power continued to reside in a small group of men, who controlled the local economy. They were mostly Liberal in politics – Hopkins and Cochrane were exceptions – and they formed a Liberal Reform Association in 1867. The Association pressed Wilson to stand as Liberal candidate for Middlesbrough at the first election of 1868, but when Henry Bolckow decided to stand with Wilson's support, the position was willingly accepted.

There was considerable intermarriage within this group of ironmasters, and sons and nephews were drawn in to join their fathers and uncles while they were still very young. The ramifications of the Pease connexion have already been mentioned. Other families were interconnected, too. Henry Bolckow and John Vaughan, for example, were married to sisters, and Bolckow's sister was the first wife of William Hopkins. Family ties continued to sustain the expanding economy which was based on partnership, not on dependence upon an outside and impersonal capital market.

Obligations to Middlesbrough's growing working class were stated almost in family terms during the 1850s and 1860s, although the language did not always necessarily conform to the facts. More important than the language in determining the pattern of relationships was the prevalence of high wages, the unprecedented boom conditions of the late 1860s (there were years of slump also at the troughs of the cycle) and the shared sense of growth. As a local poet sang proudly, before the town became too big:

> Then streets se cliver scan increased;
> Smash man! they numbered fifty;
> Thor's thirty butchers, man, at least,
> An' twenty tailors thrifty,
> Thor's sixty shops for rum an' beer;
> Thor's four prime shavers too, man;
> Thor's sailors, smiths and cobblers here,
> An' Cleveland poets two, man.

The two Cleveland poets were pillars of local 'culture': its patrons were the ironmasters. Yet there were many cultural developments during the middle years of the century which duplicated developments in the new cities of America or Australia. Chapel-building was the biggest single corporate enterprise: the 'propensity to give' expressed itself most notably in this form. Churches were less popular, at first, and although one of the early non-resident incumbents had been Cobden's tutor, until the Rev. Richard Bradley arrived in 1854 'it was considered hardly respectable [according to the Additional Curates' Aid Society] to be a member of the Church'. Sunday Schools were the most powerful educational influence from the start, and the Sunday School Union one of the most carefully organized local voluntary bodies. Yet the Mechanics' Institute, which acquired a new building in 1860, flourished rather longer than the Mechanics' Institutes of older towns, and its work was supplemented in 1863 by the Middlesbrough Athenaeum, 'a society for the cultivation of Literature, Science and the Arts': in 1875 the Athenaeum took the old and respected name of 'Literary and Philosophical Society'. It had held its meetings before that date in two dingy back rooms: now it had its own premises, which were opened by

Sir Stafford Northcote, the Conservative Chancellor of the Exchequer.

Two years before this, an Orpheus Music Club had been formed in Middlesbrough, and during the late 1860s both a choral society and a philharmonic society were in existence. Music was usually the first of the manifestations of popular culture: it was believed by the middle classes also – in Middlesbrough as elsewhere – that it was a perfect instrument for 'soothing the weary brow'. It is interesting to note that G. M. Tweddell in his excellent account of Middlesbrough in Bulmer's *North Yorkshire* (1883) noted with pride that the new School Board, which supplemented the schools presented by Bolckow, had just bought a piano. This, he added, was 'to be principally used for teaching the pupils vocal music, which cannot but have a civilizing influence'.

In 1870 a reading room and free library were opened under the Public Libraries Act, after inquiries had been made by the Town Council about the management and financing of libraries in Manchester and Birmingham. The Library Committee dreamed of an Art Gallery too, but it was not able to start a museum until 1890, after several years of intermittent discussion.

'Social activities' were far easier to organize. The Cleveland Club was opened in 1868 in the east end of the Exchange Building, and another middle-class club, the Erimus, was founded in 1873 with a limited membership of three hundred. The clientele of these clubs consisted largely of 'gentlemen in the iron industry'. Also in 1873, however, a working-men's club was opened by Bolckow; it had a quarterly subscription of two shillings, and its philosophy was stated in very stilted language: 'those who contributed so largely towards the means of civilization shall partake more truly of the culture and refinement which it entailed by having opportunities afforded them for rational and civilizing pleasures'.

Fortunately, the usual language of the Middlesbrough press was hardly as stilted as this. The first newspaper, the *Middlesbrough Chronicle*, a monthly, was started in 1853 by Joseph Richardson, who had first arrived in the town in 1841 and had worked as a cabinet maker: an earlier venture of his was a magazine, *The Literary Pilot*. In 1855 Richardson transformed the *Chronicle* into a weekly, the *Middlesbrough Weekly News and Cleveland Advertiser*. It was a Liberal paper, but had a brief period under Conservative editorship. A further Conservative paper, the *Weekly Exchange*, challenged the most lasting of Middlesbrough's papers, the Liberal *Weekly Gazette*, which became the *Daily Gazette* in 1869.

Newspaper comments were often acrimonious: there were also local satirists. W. W. C. Seymour in 1864 wrote his *Who's Who: How is Middlesbrough Ruled and Governed?* It attacked 'the disloyal church-detesting town councillors of Middlesbrough', the 'tramp skinflint journeymen painters, penny wise and pound foolish', and 'the ranters and teetotal lecturers' who dominated Middlesbrough's life. There is evidence too that the rule of 'Middlesbrough's two kings – King Coal and King Iron' – was sometimes resented. A Parliamentary Debating Society, which flourished in the late 1870s, as in several other Victorian towns, allowed considerable scope for criticism and speculation. The resentment could not go too far, however, for there was no other basis at all for the existence of Middlesbrough.

3

It was impossible for Middlesbrough to preserve its mid-Victorian character. The sheer growth of the town made it more and more difficult for either one man or a group of families to control it. Quite apart from technical difficulties – the difficulties which led Birmingham men both to preach a civic gospel and to recruit an efficient civil service – there were many signs that the will to control of the ironmasters was being blunted as they followed the pattern of other English businessmen and chose to live in the country rather than in the town. Henry Bolckow, who in his early days in Middlesbrough had lived in Cleveland Street within five minutes' walk of the old Market, himself moved to Marton Hall, where he collected rare books and pictures. While he lived in Middlesbrough he had attended the Centenary Wesleyan chapel: in Marton he worshipped at the local parish church. John Vaughan, who died in 1868, long before the exodus was far advanced, lived in Gunnergate Hall; Isaac Wilson, who had formerly lived in 'the old town' in Sussex Street, now lived in Northope Hall, and W. K. Hopkins at the newly built mansion of Grey Towers. Their children continued to be linked in marriage, but neither the children nor the managers who succeeded them in their works, when their enterprises grew in size and were transformed into local limited liability companies, necessarily shared the feelings of the older generation about the links which bound them to the town.

The new generation certainly ceased to be as interested in the Town Council as the pioneers had been. As their influence declined – it did not by any means disappear – 'intermediate social classes' came into greater prominence, particularly the local shopkeepers, who gradually acquired the kind of social and political authority that they already possessed in most other Victorian cities. They had been numerically important on the Council before the 1870s. but they did not provide the leadership. After 1875 the position changed. Hugh Bell did not retire from the Council until 1907, but by then it had become a very different kind of Council from that of 1870. Of the eighteen mayors from 1893 to 1912 only two belonged to the class of large manufacturers. In 1872 there were ten ironmasters and seven shopkeepers on the Council: in 1912 there were fifteen shopkeepers and one ironmaster. In short, there had been a quiet local revolution.

The revolution did not pass completely unnoticed. The *Daily Gazette* complained as early as 1874 of 'the men with the largest stake ... withdrawing from the Council'. Two years later it was commenting on the same kind of civic ineptitude which had been complained of in Birmingham during the rule of the 'Old Woodman Council'. 'What we deplore are the constant bickerings and personal abuse which of late years have been introduced. Scarcely can any question be settled without a scene; and too often the worst possible accusations are freely made and the business obstructed for no conceivable good.' An article of 1877 was headed: 'Decay of Municipal Life'. It asked the question, 'Where are our great manufacturers and old inhabitants now? They are fast disappearing.'

In 1880 it complained of 'sectional representation'. 'Now the butchers are to the fore with some unsavoury grievance; then the publicans bumptiously demand to be heard; next the teetotallers put forward exclusive pretensions to dominate. All this is worse than absurd. It is an utter perversion of the first principles of municipal representation. Unless some great political principle is involved, the one consideration should be to elect men who by their intelligence, respectability and knowledge of the town's requirements, are fitted for a seat in the local Parliament.' Six years later the composition of the Council was again condemned as 'a byeword and a reproach'.

Whatever the justice of such complaints, little attempt was made in Middlesbrough to forge a constructive plan of civic development. Improvement had depended for so long on the paternalism either of the 'Owners' or of the ironmasters that once their influence was removed the zest for improvement was reduced. Liberalism in Middlesbrough always lacked a municipal programme. A few Liberals believed during the 1880s that the day was not far distant when municipal elections, 'as in Birmingham, Leeds and other large towns', would be contested solely on political issues, but neither the old ironmasters nor the new shopocracy cared to convert Liberalism into an instrument of positive social action. The only time that they were induced to press their politics locally was when the licensed victuallers seemed to be pulling the strings of the Conservative party too tightly. Teetotalism remained a far livelier issue than civic reform.

Even in national politics the Birmingham model was not copied until 1881. When in 1876 an attempt was made to construct a 'strong, broad and comprehensive Liberal Association', there were eight ironmasters on the provisional committee of fifteen, and no provision was made either for ward organization or for a 'general committee'. Membership of this Association never exceeded two hundred, and it disappeared after the general election of 1880. A new association, formed in 1881, and affiliated to Chamberlain's National Liberal Federation, was representative of lower-middle-class groups and looked to Birmingham, Leeds and Darlington. It had five hundred members, but it failed to win substantial support from the ironmasters.

When home rule split the Liberal Party in 1886, some of the ironmasters turned against Gladstone. Wilson remained loyal, but Bell, who had been thought of as his successor, became Unionist (he returned to the Liberal fold later on the issue of protection). Carl Bolckow moved in the same direction. The Pease family was divided against itself, the greater and more influential element remaining Gladstonian. The increase in the Conservative and Unionist vote in Middlesbrough during the 1880s and 1890s – a Unionist actually won by fifty-five votes in the 'khaki election' of 1900 – was a sign that the new community had lost its 'instinctive liberalism'. A few young Liberals at the end of the century tried in vain to break the spell by preaching a more active policy, concerned in particular with improvements in housing, health, and education.

By then the challenge to Middlesbrough Liberalism came from the left as well as from the right. In mid-Victorian Middlesbrough 'labour' had been thought of solely as an economic force: in late-Victorian Middlesbrough it began to acquire an active political personality of its own. At the general election of 1892 a 'Lib-Lab' candidate, Joseph Havelock Wilson, the general secretary of the Sailors' and Firemen's Union, won a memorable victory over W. S. Robson, the official Liberal, who was a barrister. Long before this, in 1874, John Kane, a member of the Iron Workers' Association, a nominee of the Labour Representation League of 1869, and a supporter of the trade union 'Junta' in London, polled 1,541 votes against Henry Bolckow's 3,719, with Hopkins, the Conservative ironmaster, polling only 996 votes.

Neither Kane nor Havelock Wilson was completely independent of the Liberal Party – neither was in any sense a socialist – but their achievements, particularly Havelock Wilson's, brought to the surface new elements in Middlesbrough's political life. Havelock Wilson was reconciled with the local Liberal Association later in the 1890s – he was the sole Liberal candidate in 1895 and 1906 – but independent Labour began to emerge as a separate force on his left. Tom Mann supported the idea of an independent Labour candidate in

1891 and attacked Isaac Wilson for his opposition to a statutory eight-hour working day, the public building of artisans' dwellings and the provision of work for the unemployed. In 1906 George Lansbury was to poll 1,484 votes as a Socialist candidate. The Trades Council, founded in 1879, was for long a Lib-Lab stronghold, but a local branch of the Independent Labour Party was active in the late 1890s and there were moves after 1900 to associate the Labour movement in Middlesbrough with the Labour Representation Committee.

'Lib-Labism' was a very different phenomenon from mid-Victorian paternalism, even when it was patronized by businessmen. Its influence in local politics, however, was small, and the attempt to keep rates down or to defend Nonconformity and temperance remained the main elements at municipal elections. There was little working-class representation, and it was not until 1904 when a very short-lived Municipal Reform Association came into existence – with a Unitarian minister, W. H. Lambelle, on its executive committee – that Middlesbrough heard much local talk of 'civic reform'. Some attempts were made, however, particularly during the late 1880s, to raise the prestige of the Council as a whole. In October 1881, Middlesbrough had celebrated its jubilee, but there was so much local 'distress' – the newspapers called the decline of the iron rails industry 'the death of a staple industry' – that the celebrations were somewhat muted. The Corporation refused to associate itself with the preparations for the event, which included the unveiling of Bolckow's statue, a great banquet for notabilities, and a firework display.

In 1887, however, the Corporation was directly responsible for the official proceedings which took place to commemorate the opening of the new Town Hall, the foundation stone of which had been laid – after long delays – in 1883. The land for the building had been acquired in 1872, when the ubiquitous Alfred Waterhouse, bobbing up once more, was appointed architect, but there had been great changes in Middlesbrough by the time that the building was started with a local architect in charge. The Prince and Princess of Wales accepted a civic invitation to open the impressive Gothic building which was described as being 'in the style of the thirteenth century suffused with the feeling and spirit of the present time'. Waterhouse was the assessor on this occasion and the chief title to fame of the architect, George Gordon Hoskins, was that he 'had designed numerous villa residences in the counties of Durham and Yorkshire'. The Hall had a clock tower, 170 feet high, a large assembly room and a Council Chamber embellished with full-length portraits of Joseph Pease, William Fallows, Bolckow, Vaughan, and Bell. Bolckow and Vaughan figured also in the décor of the triumphal arches which were built specially for the opening.

The most active supporters of the idea of a new Town Hall – many of them were Conservatives – had used language not unlike that of the 1850s in Leeds. 'We hope the Council in framing their new scheme', the *Weekly Gazette* stated in 1881, 'will have under consideration the wants of the borough for fully one hundred years to come. It is also wise and prudent to enforce upon them that the building itself must be of an imposing character, befitting a go-ahead community which proposes to have as much reverence for culture as for power. ... We have every reason to believe that there are men on the Council who will say that a ship is not spoiled for want of the proverbial half-pennyworth of tar. We congratulate the town upon the fact that it has at last been placed in a position to crown its civic edifice by providing a suitable home for its civic institutions.' The building, it was argued, would have to be of the kind that would inspire future citizens to enjoy 'the refining influence of art' and to say gratefully:

> Everywhere I see around me rise the wondrous world of Art,
> Buildings bright with richest sculpture standing in the common
> mart.

To disarm obvious criticism, it was pointed out that the building did not need to be financed from the rates; it could be paid for by a 'civic loan'. This procedure was followed, although final sanction for borrowing the money was not obtained until three years after the Town Hall was opened.

At the opening ceremony the Conservative Mayor, Major

Dixon, Middlesbrough's largest shipbuilder, who lived in Vaughan's old home, Gunnergate Hall, and whose family was related by marriage to the Bells, the Bolckows and later the Dormans, was eloquent in his praise of municipal government. 'Though our municipality is young in years, we have to the best of our ability carried on the noble traditions of freedom and self government which have ever distinguished the Towns of England.' He went on to talk of municipal institutions. 'In a Corporation which has existed for a very few years, we have institutions of all kinds to create and develop, and it has been, therefore, the pride and the ambition of Middlesbrough to furnish such institutions.' Lastly, he reverted to what may be called the main Leeds theme of the 1850s:

> Up to this time all the Public Buildings that have been erected in Middlesbrough have soon proved themselves utterly inadequate to the wants of the place, and have not been able to keep up with rapid development. In erecting these Buildings we are doing something permanent. We have not much of a past to speak of, but we look to having a great future.

In his reply the Prince of Wales had little alternative but to extol Middlesbrough's 'Municipal Patriotism'. He could not resist saying also, however, that he had expected to see a smoky town. This remark provoked a characteristically candid comment from the mayor, which catches the spirit of late-Victorian Middlesbrough far more than the heavy rhetoric:

> His Royal Highness owned he had expected to see a smoky town. It is one, and if there is one thing more than another that Middlesbrough can be said to be proud of, it is the smoke (cheers and laughter). The smoke is an indication of plenty of work (applause) – an indication of prosperous times (cheers) – an indication that all classes of workpeople are being employed, that there is little necessity for charity (cheers) and that even those in the humblest station are in a position free from want (cheers). Therefore we are proud of our smoke (cheers).

Such pride would probably not have been expressed in this crude form and with such gusto had not Middlesbrough, like other industrial communities, passed through anxious days after the high summer of Victorian prosperity. In late-Victorian England, as G. M. Young has written, there was a chill in the air. The changes in the approach to local government in Middlesbrough can be understood only in the light of changes in the economic sub-structure of the town. The transition from iron to steel meant greater vulnerability to foreign competition: it meant also that business fluctuations, the cycles of good and bad years, were international in character. The smoke registered full employment for the worker: for the manufacturer it indicated that he was holding his own against competition. He was holding his own, however, as he well knew, in a far more interdependent world. The surviving iron industry in Middlesbrough came to depend more and more on the importation into Middlesbrough of foreign quality ores. In 1870 pig-iron production in Cleveland was self-contained: by the end of Queen Victoria's reign it was dependent on the world overseas.

The steel industry, with its large-scale plant, depended not only on foreign imports of material but on extensive outside capitalization. The partnerships of mid-Victorian Middlesbrough gave way, in consequence, to limited liability companies. Bolckow and Vaughan became a limited liability company as early as 1864 with a capital of £5½ million. The two great partners had a large financial interest in the new company, but Manchester businessmen, quite unconnected with Middlesbrough, were drawn into the flotation and were represented on the new Board of Directors. 'Capitalized by Manchester, but dominated by Welsh technicians' was one verdict on the incorporation. The trend towards limited liability continued throughout the 1880s and 1890s, and was associated also in its later phases with tendencies towards integration of businesses and amalgamation. Small partnerships disappeared: large integrated concerns on a national rather than a local scale became the effective business units.

This story has many different facets. In 1850, when John Vaughan discovered rich supplies of ironstone at Eston, steel was slow and expensive to manufacture. It was not used for large-scale construction, railways or ships, for example, but for tools, springs and weapons. The iron age was still at its height, and the building of the Crystal Palace in 1851 marked the triumph not only of a new material, glass, but of an old one, iron. Five years later Henry Bessemer, challenged by the military demand of the Crimean War, developed the converter process which made it possible to produce high-tensile steel in large quantities. The ore used, however, had to be free of phosphorus. Sheffield was the first British centre of the new industry, and Middlesbrough, with plentiful local supplies of phosphoric ore, lagged behind in the middle years of the century. As late as 1872 it was stated that 'no steel of any kind' was manufactured on the North-east coast. The great mid-Victorian boom of the late 1860s and the early 1870s came and went in Middlesbrough with the iron industry still supreme.

Middlesbrough had to develop its late-Victorian steel industry with imported raw materials at a time when economic conditions were unfavourable. Dividends slumped and many greatly respected firms actually went into liquidation. The local press wrote ominously of 'careless and incompetent management, reckless speculation and extravagant living'. The Bolckow-Vaughan concern, which had been founded on luck, was the first to adapt itself to the new conditions. In 1876 the first Bessemer steel plant was built by the company at Eston – it had previously owned a small steel works at Gorton, near Manchester – and 10,000 tons of steel were produced during the first year of operation. By 1879, a year of heavy depression, when there were many bankruptcies in the iron industry, steel output had risen to over 85,000 tons and the works were 'engaged to their fullest capacity'.

In the same year an important new process of steel-making was demonstrated on Tees-side at the Bolckow-Vaughan works. The Gilchrist-Thomas open-hearth process permitted steel to be made from phosphoric iron ores. Enormous plant was required, and the Bolckow-Vaughan concern with Carl Bolckow, nephew of Henry Bolckow, as chairman, was ready to transform itself to meet the new opportunities. The process ultimately benefited foreign producers, however, far more than it benefited Britain. 'Middlesbrough', wrote Lowthian Bell, 'was soon besieged by the combined forces of Belgium, France, Prussia, Austria and America.' The local failures continued, Carl Bolckow himself suffering so severely in the collapse of one of his subsidiary concerns in 1891 and 1892 that he sold his uncle's collection of paintings and *objets d'art* at Christie's and disposed of his life interest in the Marton estates.

One of the new Middlesbrough firms which had the greatest stake in the future had been founded in 1870 by Arthur Dorman, born at Ashford in Kent, and Albert de Lande Long. They originally set out to manufacture iron bars and angles for shipbuilding, the most prosperous branch of the iron industry, but they acquired the Britannia Works from Samuelson in 1879, became a limited liability company ten years later, and by the end of Victoria's reign were employing three thousand men in the iron and steel industry. In 1899 when Bell Brothers, which had remained an iron-producing concern, became a limited liability company, half the ordinary shares were held by Dorman-Long. Three years later Sir Lowthian Bell became chairman of Dorman-Long, and in the very distant future, after a sequence of amalgamations, Dorman-Long amalgamated with Bolckow-Vaughan in the strange and unforeseeable economic circumstances of 1929.

Financial and technical elements contributed to this prolonged process of integration and amalgamation. From the point of view of the citizens of Middlesbrough the changes had three important social effects. First, the increasing size of plant meant a new pattern of relationships at work. The employer receded from the workshop, and his place was taken by managers, ranging in grade from the general manager or works manager down to the foreman on the shop floor. The terms of work were set increasingly by bargaining between trade unions and employers, the employers being associated collectively in the Cleveland Ironmasters' Association and the workers in national trade unions. Second, the contribution of employers to the life of the community outside the factory was inevitably curtailed. It was not only, as we have seen, that they were usually living outside Middlesbrough. More important still, they were not as familiar with daily life there as their parents or uncles had been. A number of their managers were active in municipal politics – men like E. T. John or F. W. Mildred of Bolckow-Vaughan or T. F. Ward of Samuelson's –

but as a group they were less homogeneous in outlook than their employers had been, and far less able to provide effective financial patronage for local causes. Third, the fortunes of Middlesbrough depended more and more on financial initiatives taken outside. The capital market began to count in the life of the town as its local economy was drawn more and more into the national economy. In Middlesbrough, even more than in the country as a whole, the neglected 1890s were years of change in national life, particularly in relation to the balance between provincial and national. The provincial, both in the field of economy and culture, counted for less and the national (or generalizing) for more.

Although all these changes were noted, however sketchily, by observers at the time, it is remarkable that the best account of the texture of Middlesbrough's urban life in the new conditions was provided by Lady Florence Bell, the wife of Sir Hugh Bell, Middlesbrough's greatest ironfounder, in her brief but vivid study, *At the Works*, which was published in 1907. What she wrote of Middlesbrough then must have been true of Middlesbrough throughout the last part of the century, for she seized, like the French sociologist Le Play, on the central social relationships connected with 'work, place and home'. The necessity of living near the works meant renting cheap houses in unattractive rows of 'little brown streets'. 'It is a side-issue for the workman whether he and his family are going to live under healthy conditions; the one absolute necessity is to be at work.' 'There springs, and too rapidly, into existence a community of a pre-ordained, inevitable kind, the members of which must live near their work. They must therefore have houses built as quickly as possible; the houses must be as cheap, must be as big as the workman wants, and no bigger; and as they are built there arise hastily located, instantly occupied, the rows and rows of little brown streets. . . . A town arising in this way cannot wait to consider anything else but time and space.' Long working hours meant scarce leisure; and what leisure there was often was not well employed. The roughness of Middlesbrough persisted into the twentieth century. The public house was the main social institution, and drunkenness was its most common offence.

More than a quarter of the workmen read books as well as newspapers, nearly a half read the newspapers only, and a quarter did not read at all. The more educated people of the country did not usually set them an example. 'Those who should be able to bring a leaven of art, of literature, of thought, to the toilers around them, are toiling also themselves; they are part of the immense machine, and it is impossible for them to judge of it with a free mind.'

The pattern of urban life in Middlesbrough seemed to her to be of a 'pre-ordained, inevitable kind', yet she discerned variety in the pattern. Some working men were tolerably secure; others, as Booth and Rowntree showed in London and York, were in poverty and want; 'the great majority were on the borderline between the two'. Social insecurity was at the heart of the industrial and consequently of the urban system. The fortunes of families depended not only on the income of the wage-earner but on the size of his family and the administrative capacity of his wife. Lady Bell was the first of the writers on Middlesbrough to turn the spotlight on the housewife. The community might appear on the surface to be aggressively masculine, but everything depended on the women. There was more variety inside the individual houses than the general vista of the street promised. 'The husband's steadiness and capacity to earn are not more important than the wife's administration of the earnings.'

Housing conditions in Middlesbrough were bad at the end of Queen Victoria's reign and the death rate was high. There had been a 'dirty party' during the middle years of the century, which argued that since Middlesbrough was 'new', it did not need extensive health legislation. 'Property owners,' wrote *Veritas* to the *Middlesbrough Weekly News* in 1859, 'away with this insidious foe – that will not allow you to build a pantry without submitting plans and specifications for the approval of an authorized architect.' The inhabitants of Middlesbrough would suffer more from eating American bacon than keeping pigs in the Mechanics' Institute garden. Baths and wash-houses, which were advocated at this time by the 'clean party', were not built until 1884. 'The great unwashed go unwashed still,' the editor of the newspaper remarked, 'and the Tees [will] receive its usual quota of bather victims, and the new cemetery its consumptive and steam-destroyed sacrifices.' It was axiomatic to the 'clean party' that 'we not only want to see factories acquired by our manufacturers and a comfortable independence for our tradesmen but to surround all classes with aids to health and longevity.' The 'permanent prosperity' of the town depended 'almost as much upon its acquiring the character of being a healthy and salubrious locality as upon its skill and industry'. What Lady Bell wrote in 1907 was anticipated nearly fifty years before by a writer who emphasized that 'healthy habitations' were necessary if people were to secure 'the attraction of their leisure hours and solace of their eye'.

Little was done, and Middlesbrough, new though it was, was distinctly unhealthy. For the years 1871–3 the death rate averaged 23.96 per thousand of the population for the borough as a whole, and it was far worse than this in the most crowded working-class districts. The infantile mortality rate was, as always, an index of lack of social control. Forty per cent of the total recorded deaths in Middlesbrough in the years 1871–3 were of children under the age of one year: deaths of children between the ages of one and five accounted for another 20 per cent.

The building of a more effective drainage system during the 1870s was a sign of 'improvement', but there were prolonged battles about rates which held back progress. In 1874, for example, after the Finance Committee of the Town Council had recommended a rate of two shillings in the pound, the Council as a whole amended it to one shilling and sixpence. The Finance Committee protested, but the Mayor had to give his casting vote in full Council in order that the decision to set the impossibly low rate of one shilling and sixpence could be rescinded. A compromise was struck, and by fourteen votes to eleven the Council agreed on a vote of two shillings. Four years later, ratepayers who claimed that they represented '£76,500 of the rateable value of Middlesbrough' petitioned the Council to cut its capital expenditure on such items as water and drainage. 'These changes must inevitably cause an increase in the rates, and the subscribers ... respectfully submit that such an increase at a time of unprecedented commercial depression, is neither expedient nor warrantable.'

From the late 1890s onwards, the annual reports of the Medical Officer of Health provided full statistics of differential mortality rates by age and by district. There was far less public interest in Middlesbrough, however, than had been shown in Birmingham twenty years before. It was not until 1900 that the Trades Council organized a large-scale conference on the housing question, which recommended that local use should be made of the Housing of the Working Classes Act of 1890. A Sanitary and Housing Reform Association, which was founded as a result of this conference, was unable to make much headway. Middlesbrough remained an unhealthy town with inferior working-class housing conditions. Geography, which favoured the town economically, did not help it socially: 'few worse sites on which to found a large and increasing town could have been found', wrote the first Medical Officer of Health. The land development of the new community had rested on speculation not on service. The Grange Farm at Linthorpe containing just over 140 acres was sold to a Manchester company for £70,000 in 1866: two years earlier three acres in the same township were sold at a price of £600 per acre for building sites. 'The price of building land', a local writer remarked in 1881, 'has more than tripled within the last twenty years, while corner sites and small lots are difficult to obtain at exorbitant prices.' The Middlesbrough Estate had proved 'a princely land speculation'. Similar comments were being made at the end of Queen Victoria's reign, when most of the development of the town centre was complete.

The face of the town reflected its history and the urges which brought it into being. A Middlesbrough guide to the town stated in 1899:

> At first sight Middlesbrough is not calculated to create a particularly favourable impression upon the visitor. Its utilitarian aspect is somewhat too pronounced. With its numerous ironworks lying between the town and the river, the town itself being built upon a low level stretch of country on the south side of the river, and its streets composed for the most part of plain brick houses, it presents

essentially a business town, and little that is picturesque to attract and please the eye.

The Victorian contrast between 'utility' and 'pretensions', which is implicit in this self-assessment, represents far too simple a view of the proper relationship between art or architecture and business. It led the writer also to praise some of the more pretentious and costly late-nineteenth-century buildings in Middlesbrough and to overlook both the more simple appeal of the early buildings and the savage power of the industrial scene itself. It obscured the nature of the historical process which had made Middlesbrough look as it did. Lady Bell was more percipient. She saw that at twilight and in the night, when the sky was lit up by the furnaces, Middlesbrough could be a most impressive place to see. There was nothing in Middlesbrough to 'appeal to a sense of art or beauty' except, in its strange way, Middlesbrough itself.

The growth of the town made the first planned settlement of the 'Middlesbrough Owners' seem like a tiny frontier encampment strategically placed alongside the river. The railway line separated this Middlesbrough from the new town centre which developed around the new Town Hall and principal buildings, which were opened in 1887. When the plan for a new Town Hall was being mooted it was already known, as a newspaper put it, that 'the town is extending southwards, the iron and other works having taken possession of the ground at the east and west'. 'Should the growth go on,' the newspaper concluded, 'as there is very little doubt it will do, the new Town Hall and Municipal Buildings will in a few years be in a central position.' They were. The chief business thoroughfares of the 1840s and 1850s were Commercial Street and the streets running off Market Place to the north of the railway. After 1850, however, the area between the railway and Grange Road was developed, and after 1860 the Newport district, a factory area with long rows of working-class houses and a railway system of its own. By 1870 the main shopping centre was on both sides of the Middlesbrough railway station, and a grid-iron pattern of streets was taking shape which still gives Middlesbrough a curiously symmetrical appearance. The conditions of ownership and development dictated the form of layout, which, as W. G. Hoskins has pointed out, links Middlesbrough with very different English towns of other centuries, like Salisbury and Winchelsea. 'The planned town is an aberration, not the norm.' The absolute ownership of the first site was associated with the optimism about the future which remained strong in mid-Victorian Middlesbrough. 'The planning of a new town – laying out the lines of streets, lanes, markets, churches and house plots over a considerable area – required the investment of a large amount of capital and a greater degree of optimism than most landlords could contemplate.' *Erimus* was a very appropriate and necessary motto.

Yet the planning of Middlesbrough lacked the single purpose and persistence which had characterized the planning of Saltaire in the 1850s, and once the town spilt out of the original rectangle there was no inducement to retain homogeneity of style or architecture. There was no inducement either to relate working-class housing to any other criterion than nearness to work. Three main arterial roads, wider than most nineteenth-century English urban roads, cut through the rows of working-class streets south of the railway line – Linthorpe Road, the chief business street in the town, linking the railway station with the old village of Linthorpe, which was soon swallowed up in Middlesbrough itself; Newport Road cutting across Middlesbrough from the extreme west; and Morton Road on the opposite boundary, leading to Grove Hill where 'most of the gentry' who continued to live in or near Middlesbrough had their residences. The cricket ground was at Grove Hill: the football ground, one of the best in the country, was in Linthorpe Road just beyond the point where the old large middle-class houses of early Middlesbrough were being pulled down and replaced by shops. Electric trams were not introduced until 1898, but there were horse trams along the main routes from 1876.

The large new railway station, completed in 1877, was within easy reach of the centre of the 'old town' and the new. The street names on each side of the track revealed two layers of history – Stockton Street, Wellington Street,

Brougham Street and Sussex Street lying to the north between the old rectangle and the railway; Wilson Street, Bolckow Street, Vaughan Street, and Gilkes Street to the south. The name of Albert, however, was ubiquitous. A northern street, graced by the Theatre Royal (1866), was named after him, a southern road, bisecting Corporation Street, and both the new Town Hall and the old Exchange as great urban landmarks, and the park which Bolckow presented to the town was called Albert Park.

Many of the most Victorian of the local institutions were located on the moving southern boundary – the old cemetery, opened by the Corporation in 1854 (the first burials there were victims of the cholera), the fever hospital (there must have been almost as many writers of Victorian novels about fever hospitals as readers of novels inside them) and the 'palatial' workhouse, *the* Institution both to the Victorians and the men and women of the early twentieth century. The Prince Consort was more favoured in Middlesbrough than the Queen. Victoria Square, lying between the municipal buildings and a group of new Board Schools, was considered so uninviting – as late as 1899 – that it was nicknamed 'the Dark Continent'.

In the twentieth century Middlesbrough continued to move farther south, with housing estates flanking the most prosperous middle-class areas. 'The extremes of poverty', as Ruth Glass wrote in 1948, 'are on the northern and southern edge espectively.' The result was a social segmentation which was mplicit in nineteenth-century history. The specific urban menities of Middlesbrough, the 'urban equipment' of late-Victorian England, remained in the north – the railway tation, the major shopping area, the clubs, cinemas, estaurants and public houses, the General Post Office, and the Town Hall – but a 'new town' without social institutions had rown up on the southern side of Albert Park. Two ways of fe, as different as the contrasting ways of life within Victorian ities, were co-existing. 'People in the north live under conitions which almost compel them to be "matey"; people in ie south have chosen conditions which make it possible for iem to be secluded.' The complex of institutions, originally designed in some sense for all, was not at the centre of Middlesbrough but at the periphery.

Much of Middlesbrough's public building in the north was constructed during the same period that Chamberlain and his successors were remodelling the centre of Birmingham. The railway station cost £100,000 and was often compared with St Pancras: in the same year that it was opened, 1877, the Temperance Hall in Gilkes Street was also opened. Its large hall which seated two thousand people was the biggest in Middlesbrough until the new Town Hall was built. The Town Hall cost £130,000 to build: it is interesting to compare this figure with the £2,000 which had been spent by the Middlesbrough Owners on the first Town Hall, 'a neat edifice of stone, designed by Mr Moffatt of Doncaster' and opened in 1846.

The shift of taste and more profound transformations of economic and social structure within the short span of Middlesbrough's Victorian history are fascinating themes for the historian. The real interest of Middlesbrough's nineteenth-century history lies, indeed, not so much in the newness of the community which was created there as in the speed with which an intricate and complex economic, social, and political sequence was unfolded. Historians of Continental cities, like Genoa, Venice, Bruges, or Amsterdam, have devoted huge monographs to sequences of change far less dramatic in character and stretched out not over sixty years but over several centuries.

Contemporary interpretations of the sequence are almost as interesting as the sequence itself. Some of them have been quoted as an introduction to this essay. There was one other interpretation which deserves special attention because of its author, Joseph Cowen, the Newcastle newspaper editor, who, as we have seen, was one of the most eloquent panegyrists of the claim of city against countryside. Cowen's *Newcastle Chronicle* was read everywhere 'from Tees to Tweed': his powerful platform speeches and spirited lectures delivered for such bodies as the Northern Union of Mechanics' Institutions and the Co-operative Congress, were as influential in the North of England as his articles. He was a remarkable orator at his best in great halls before large audiences, where it was said he obeyed the injunction of Demosthenes and relied upon 'continuous action' – 'action while stating his case, action in the discussion of it, and action when making his appeal'.

At the Middlesbrough Jubilee celebrations of 1881, Cowen proposed the toast of 'the Mayor, Aldermen and Burgesses of Middlesbrough and Prosperity to their Town and Trades on this Jubilee'. Surprisingly, not everybody could hear him on this occasion, but people crowded around the platform to catch his very congenial message. Wherever the British flag was flying, he began, and to whatever corner of the world English enterprise had penetrated, the fame of Middlesbrough was known.

> The story, the marvellous story, of its rise is admiringly recited, and the fame of its factories is dwelt upon. The idea symbolized by its history is force – the physical, mental and moral force which enables communities to wrestle with and overcome the obstacles which circumstances cast in their way as they struggle upwards and onwards to a better state of living.

Not only Middlesbrough but nineteenth-century urban life in general was the subject of this comment. Cowen was born in 1831, about the same date that Middlesbrough was founded: his father had been largely involved at that time in the formation of the Northern Political Union, which, like Attwood's Birmingham Political Union, quickened the pace of radical agitation during the critical months leading up to the passing of the Great Reform Bill. Joseph Cowen senior started his life at the forge, and the metaphors of the forge appealed to him throughout his political career. So they did also to the son. Mental and moral force had made reform inevitable. The threat of physical force had usually been there, too. Urban life generated force, and that was its strength. 'In the great battle between movement and stagnation the cry was ever onward; and before that cry many cherished convictions and many tender prejudices had to go down. The towns of which Middlesbrough was a type were the leaders of this advance; they recorded the rise of the nation.'

Six solid 'broad-brimmed, broad-fronted, broad-bottomed' Quakers had cleared a swamp and made a city. They had not been inhibited by history. They trusted not in precedent but in the future. 'The steam engine had no precedent, the locomotive was without ancestry, and the telegraph centred on no heritage.' Middlesbrough was genuinely 'new', like them. 'He had a sneaking sympathy with the plaintive wail that Mr Ruskin and others so oft, so touchingly, and so eloquently raised o'er a vanished and irrecoverable past. But the facts were against them. The minister of civilization preached from the railway car and the telegraph.' There was no need to bemoan the biggest of all facts, that 'Arcadian association and romantic solitude' had retreated before the era of hammers and anvils, of looms and furnaces.

Few of Cowen's many public speeches sound more Victorian than this. But then all the accounts of the Jubilee are impressively evocative. Before the Mayor could reply to Cowen, there were loud cries from a section of the audience for John Vaughan's son, 'the son of the puddler' who had made the development of the town possible. Fallows, who, with the Mayor, acknowledged Cowen's toast, had been in Middlesbrough since its beginnings and he felt 'too touched to say a single word'. The proposer of the next toast to the 'Iron and Steel Trades of the District' referred to iron not only as the material upon which Middlesbrough's prosperity depended but, in defiance of Manchester and its cotton, as 'the great civilizer of the world'. The Lord Mayor of York, who was present as a guest, must have pondered deep on all these sentiments. The firework display in Albert Park which rounded off the festivities included Bengal Fire, Aladdin's Oriental Tree and the Falls of Niagara, but the *grande finale* consisted of 'a magnificent flight of two hundred coloured rockets and a monster piece of pyrotechnic art in the form of "Scenes of Middlesbrough"'.

CHAPTER SEVEN

Melbourne, a Victorian Community Overseas

Twenty years ago the site of the metropolis of Victoria was a forest, ten years ago it was covered with a straggling village, today it has assumed the aspect of a city of magnitude and importance; and who shall define the limits of its future dignity and splendour? The prophetic eye beholds its wide and spacious thoroughfares fringed with edifices worthy of the wealth of its citizens and corresponding in architectural pretensions with the greatness of the commercial transactions of their occupants.

The *Australian Home Guardian*, 'Local Progress' (8 November 1856)

I

MIDDLESBROUGH was rightly regarded as a remarkable product of Victorian enterprise. In distant parts of the Empire, however, far bigger communities developed from humble beginnings to become great cities during Queen Victoria's reign. Toronto, for example, grew from a small town of ten thousand at the time of its incorporation in 1834 to a characteristically Victorian city of over two hundred thousand people by the end of the century. Bombay, bedecked with the most 'imposing', certainly the most exotic, examples of Victorian architecture, was the third most populous city of the Empire, coming after London and Calcutta. By the beginning of the 1880s it had a population of over seven hundred thousand: ten years later the population was 821,764, including over eleven thousand Europeans. The ravages of plague caused the death rate to leap to sixty-nine per thousand in 1899, and the total population fell, but the city was to continue to grow rapidly in the twentieth century. Of the various groups who contributed to its progress, the influential Parsees possessed many of the favourite Victorian virtues. In social texture as well as in architecture Bombay belonged unmistakably to Queen Victoria's world.

One of the most interesting of the cities of the Empire, younger than Bombay, Toronto, or its nearest rival Sydney, was Melbourne, the chief city in a state named after the Queen. In 1850, when the independence of Victoria was proclaimed with a salute of twenty-one guns and the blaze of tar barrels and bonfires, the total population of the new self-governing colony was only 97,000. Twenty-five years later it had risen to over a million. Melbourne itself grew from a town of 23,000 people, the capital of a pastoral and agricultural district, to a great city – a collection of over thirty separate municipalities – with more than half a million people at the end of the reign.

The rateable value of Melbourne in 1891 was surpassed in the Empire only by London and, only just ahead, by Glasgow. During the great urban boom of the 1880s, Melbourne was described by a distinguished visitor, G. A. Sala, as 'marvellous Melbourne'. Other people called it 'the Paris of the Antipodes' or 'the Chicago of the South'. The stock Victorian phrases were once more employed: in the language of the trade directories and the newspapers, the rise of Melbourne was 'unparalleled in the annals of the world'. 'From a few wattle-and-daub huts and weather-board shanties', wrote J. Freeman in 1888 in his *Lights and Shades of Melbourne Life*, 'has risen the magnificent city to which we are all so proud to belong.' Another local writer of the 1880s, having exhausted superlatives, turned to Shakespeare for the motto of his chapter on Melbourne:

> There are more things in heaven and earth
> Than are dreamt of in our philosophy.

Like Middlesbrough, Melbourne was developed on the basis of a very simple ground plan. The site was first occupied by free white settlers in 1835 when it was considered to be a good 'place for a village'. They were acting without an governmental sanction, but Governor Bourke of New South Wales visited the settlement in March 1837, authorized it existence as a township, and christened it Melbourne afte

Britain's Prime Minister. The fact that he named a near-by settlement at the mouth of the River Yarra 'Williamstown' after the reigning monarch showed that he miscalculated the future importance of the two communities. Melbourne became a metropolis; Williamstown a suburb. The reasons for this were topographical, but the 'plan' for Melbourne paid little attention to physical features. The layout of the future city in ten-acre squares followed 'a plan in the Sydney office generally approved as suitable for laying out a new township'. It was the Assistant Surveyor-General of New South Wales, Robert Hoddle, who introduced the main modification to the office formula. He pressed the Governor hard, on the grounds of advantage to 'health and convenience', to be allowed to construct exceptionally wide streets, ninety-nine feet across. There were to be three main east–west streets, four 'little' east–west streets or 'lanes' only thirty-three feet wide (Hoddle had to yield to the Governor on these) and seven main north–south streets. A site was reserved for a market to the west of the settlement. Bourke went on to name the streets as he had named the new town.

This was the simplest of all plans, and it was later followed in other parts of what became the metropolitan area of Melbourne. Such grid-iron development took no account of physical contours, and allowed neither for crescents, as in the great eighteenth-century towns, nor squares, even of the kind that the Middlesbrough Owners had provided. It offered the quickest way of disposing of new land, however, and, as the settlement grew, it brought with it huge speculative gains in land values. The first land sales took place in June 1837, when Hoddle auctioned a hundred city lots at an average price of £38. The two he bought himself – for £54 – were worth £250,000 when he died in 1881. There were quicker returns than this. Three allotments bought for £136 at the first sales fetched over £10,000 three years later. There were inevitable slumps in values, as in 1841, when the first boom broke, but there were windfall gains which not even the most optimistic prophets of progress could have forecast, after the discovery of gold in 1851. For a time Melbourne was deserted for the Victorian gold fields. Then, as the European invasion gathered momentum, the town trebled its population in three years. In the ten years from 1851 to 1861 it increased five-fold to 126,000. At the height of the boom, small allotments cost more than in London and shops were rented at sums of up to £2,000 a year. 'It then appeared', a writer in the *Australian Home Companion* exclaimed dramatically in 1856, 'that the gliding years of the past were like the gentle and almost unobservable movement of the mountain glacier, which suddenly rushes down a precipice with the crash of ten thousand storms.'

W. S. Jevons, the British economist, described the early 1850s less poetically as years of 'wonderful circumstances'. Already he noted in 1858 that Melbourne had acquired what he called a 'metropolitan' character. It was a commercial centre with 'two or more primary productive operations', and people from the whole of Victoria flocked into it for business and for entertainment. It was a very British kind of metropolis. The city centre included well-stocked and well-lit shops 'equal to the best in London'; bank buildings, described in 1856 as 'of considerable architectural pretensions'; a Theatre Royal, built in 1842, where you could see 'Italian opera in a style worthy of the English metropolis itself'; and a new Melbourne Club, opened in 1858, which 'though it has not the Corinthian pillars and fine architectural proportions of the Conservative at home ... would not at all disgrace St James's Street'. The suburb of Carlton was laid out on the model of London's Bloomsbury, and the new University, the foundation stone of which was laid in 1854, was appropriately located there.

Melbourne's rapid suburbanization was very British also. It was regarded as a matter of pride – 'evidence of progression' was the contemporary phrase – that from the start 'commodious and elegant mansions and villas' were being built in the suburbs. East Melbourne and Richmond appealed to the wealthier inhabitants, who also crossed the river and settled in South Yarra, Hawthorn and Kew. '*Rus in Urbe*' was their ideal. St Kilda, established in 1842 and named in 1843, was thought of as a 'refuge, away from the turmoil, the daily battle, the busy bartering of Melbourne'. There, 'with much wisdom', men of property 'built their homes and deposited their household gods'. 'A race of Spaniards or Neapolitans ... would never have dreamt of doing more than establish their abiding places in Melbourne proper.' More distant than St Kilda was Brighton, named like dozens of seaside resorts in all parts of the world after the most celebrated of all seaside resorts, the symbol, indeed, of the new seaside town.

The suburbs were not entirely elegant, however. At the height of the gold rush, in order to reach St Kilda, you had to pass by the huge 'canvas town' near the river where thousands of the poorer immigrants camped. The suburbs of Collingwood and Fitzroy, although they were very different from the working-class districts of Hunslet and Holbeck, were occupied by people of lower incomes. The nature of the land and the method of development encouraged exceptionally low-density housing. Unlike Naples, or for that matter Glasgow, Melbourne was a town of houses and low-storeyed buildings rather than flats or tenements, and no matter what the 'social tone' of the suburb, there was a marked preference for detached houses over terraces. The consequences were far-reaching. After the Second World War, Melbourne had fewer persons to the acre than in any of the great cities of the nineteenth century – only half as many as Greater London or Birmingham, a quarter as many as New York: only Los Angeles, the automobile city of the twentieth century, had a lower density.

This aspect of Melbourne's layout, so proudly proclaimed in the 1850s, entailed long-term problems. As the Town Planning Commission of 1929 reported:

> the relatively low average density of population in Melbourne, however beneficial it has been in other respects, has presented many problems to those charged with the responsibility of supplying the various public services. ... It is obvious that the cost of transport, water, sewerage, power, lighting, road construction, and maintenance generally must fall much more heavily upon those residing in a metropolis where the density of population averages about six to the acre as compared to a city where there are 20, 40 or more people to the acre.

Transport, water, sewerage, power, road construction and maintenance generally were all being identified as major urban problems in Melbourne during the 1850s, when the sheer pace of growth overwhelmed the administrators as it overwhelmed the primitive administrative structures of early-nineteenth-century British cities. Transport problems were handled with greatest dispatch. The first permanent bridge across the River Yarra (in bluestone and granite) was opened in 1850: between 1850 and 1860 a number of suburban railways were built, the first, the oldest railway in Australia, from Flinders Street in the centre of the city to Port Melbourne, the rest a simple network of lines which extended to Brighton and Williamstown.

Speculation played a big part in this railway development – which helps to explain the dispatch – but it laid the foundations for later urban development in the 1860s and 1870s. In the meantime one of the special features of Melbourne was the horse-drawn omnibus system. The omnibus was 'a kind of *dos-à-dos* conveyance, holding three in front and three behind'. It had a waterproof top, supported by four iron rods, and oilskin curtains to draw all around as a protection from the rain or dust. Clara Aspinall in 1862 wrote:

> Ladies, when they first arrive in the colony, look somewhat scornfully at these conveyances, and imagine that they would never condescend to appear in one of them; but it is astonishing how soon they become not only reconciled to them, but thankful to get into one of them after an exhausting walk into the town.

Good water was one of the secrets of Melbourne's early growth. A supply of fresh water above the Yarra Falls was a great attraction to the early settlers. As Melbourne grew, however, the water proved both inadequate in quantity and unsatisfactory in quality. 'Colonial fever' claimed many victims as early as 1840 and 1841, and attempts to set up a public water supply company failed. Its distribution of water was in the hands of 'a race of men' who might be seen plying their vocation, all day long, through the streets of Melbourne, 'without the stranger being perhaps aware of how great are the profits of an occupation as simple as theirs seems to be'. Exactly the same points were being made about Melbourne's water supply during the early 1850s as in any European city. The turning point came in 1853 when Commissioners of Water Supply and Sewerage were appointed and work was begun on the Yan Yean Water System, which was said to surpass in scale similar schemes in New York. In 1857 Melbourne for the first time had water 'laid on', and the event was celebrated with a great procession of plumbers, firemen and members of the town's temperance societies.

Sewerage facilities caused more difficulty and delay. In 1848 a committee of the Melbourne Corporation had recommended 'a proper system of sewerage' and an act to allow the town to levy a sewerage rate; but nothing came of the initiative. Ten years later the issue was being raised more vigorously, but only by an active minority. Medical men, divided though they were into factions, were ahead of public opinion, some of them expressing the opinion that it needed cholera (an epidemic disease which did not attack Australia) to stimulate general interest. They pointed out that they had the inestimable advantage in Australia of being able to follow European examples rather than to engage 'in a long series of experiments before arriving at the conclusion of what is the best method to be adopted'. At the same time, as the President of the Medical Society of Victoria noted in 1861, 'the magnificent water supply which this city enjoys will prove a curse instead of a blessing if a thorough system of underground drainage is long delayed'. The pollution of the River Yarra, the Saltwater River, the Albert Park Lagoon and the Port Melbourne Lagoon was serious enough as late as 1889 to stimulate a Victorian royal commission to use language similar to that used by Chadwick and his colleagues in Britain in the 1840s.

Sewage was carried away in huge open gutters, at their worst in the centre of the town. Mortality in the suburbs, varying from suburb to suburb, was greater, however, than in the centre and greater than in London. And there was no excuse. 'In a city of recent growth, without any intense overcrowding, with a population well fed and well clad, and with a climate generally favourable, the death rate should be decidedly lower.' Two years before the Commission reported, a Victorian politician had written to Sir Henry Parkes, the outstanding

Australian politician of his age, pleading for 'needful legislation'. All the public health bills previously introduced, he said, had been deficient in different ways, and it 'went to his heart' to note the differential mortality statistics of the suburbs. 'When I see the flagrant disregard of the simplest laws of health, I had almost added decency, in the suburban locality I often wonder that we are not worse off.'

In 1891 the Melbourne and Metropolitan Board of Works came into existence, with powers to manage water works, sewerage and drainage. By its efforts it did much to improve health conditions in the city, particularly in the late 1890s and first decade of the twentieth century. Satirists still talked of the city as 'marvellous Smelbourne', but in 1898 central Melbourne was at last connected with the metropolitan sewerage system. The chairman of the Board of Works, Edward Fitzgibbon, who had been Town Clerk for thirty-five years, echoed Joseph Chamberlain: 'it was not a question of how much the scheme was going to cost in money but how much it was going to save in the lives of the citizens'. Melbourne would henceforth be one of the 'sweetest cities in the world'.

The problems of transport, water and sewerage were as serious in Sydney as in Melbourne, and progress just as tardy. Jevons had compared unfavourably the 'miserable tenements and shanties' of Sydney's Rocks with some of the worst parts of London and Liverpool. 'Nowhere are the bounty and the beauty of Nature so painfully contrasted with the misery and deformity which lie to the charge of Man.' In 1856 a subcommittee of the Philosophical Society of New South Wales had reported that the sanitary state of Sydney was worse than that of London, which actually had a lower rate of mortality in a year of cholera and a lower infant mortality rate. Men like Dr Bland, Christopher Rolleston, the Registrar-General, and Dr Aaron, who had been a doctor in Birmingham in the early 1830s and was appointed Medical Officer of Health in 1856, familiarized their contemporaries with the social significance of the 'Sanitary Idea'. 'We must put our shoulder to the wheel, and only then may we properly appeal to the Throne of Grace for a blessing on our endeavours.'

Early Melbourne, in its first years a town of energetic young men, made the most of its rivalry with established Sydney, the distant administrative capital of the colony. It emphasized that it was the creation of 'ardent, intelligent and persevering men' who had triumphed 'without any Government assistance' and 'in defiance of all the impediments thrown in their way by the influence of rich and designing landed proprietors of Sydney'. The granting of municipal government in 1842 and separation of Victoria from New South Wales in 1850 were hailed as relief from 'tyranny'. Yet the problems of government loomed just as large after these two landmarks as before. The young Corporation of the 1840s found it difficult to collect rates: the new colony of Victoria was plunged into the politics of gold. Between 1856 and 1860 central government was tidied up and a new Parliament House built, one of the finest examples in the world of Victorian architecture, but municipal government became more complicated after a Municipal Act of 1854 allowed municipal districts to be scheduled and councils elected on a petition of 150 householders.

Later legislation permitted the districts to be called boroughs and eventually, after 1869, cities. As Melbourne grew in size, its local government thus became increasingly decentralized. The City of Melbourne was merely the central part of the metropolis, about twelve square miles in area. The Duke of Edinburgh might lay the foundation stone of its Town Hall in 1867, but the Town Hall was to be one of many. The imposing Town Halls of the separately managed communities, the first of which was built in 1880, were status symbols rather than centres of good administration. They might cost anything from £10,000 to £100,000. With their towers and clocks, they were considered locally as 'one of the features of the city', 'visible proofs' – so at least the *Argus* claimed – 'of the success and popularity of self-government here'.

'It may be questioned', the *Argus* admitted (20 November 1880), 'whether sub-division has not been pushed to excess.' This was the opinion of some at least of the most far-sighted supporters of 'self-government'. As in Britain, the main local battle in the municipalities raged about the rates. The primary purpose for which the local authorities were constituted was the construction and maintenance of roads and streets: many of the other purposes of positive local government were in Victoria left to the state government or not pursued at all. The advocates of a 'Greater Melbourne' with a large Council of its own were never able to redress the balance. They found it impossible to preach a civic gospel with the same kind of success that Dawson and his colleagues had preached it in Birmingham. The same was true of Sydney also. By 1895 Sir William Manning, Chancellor of Sydney University, was arguing the case for the creation of a Greater Sydney County Council along the lines of the recently founded London County Council. He discovered that it was impossible, however, to convince either the cluster of municipal councils or the ratepayers who elected them that co-ordination and strong local government were desirable objectives.

2

The story of Melbourne's growth and of public responses to it is full of interest. There are three aspects of it which deserve special attention in any study of Victorian cities. First, within a short space of time Melbourne underwent surprisingly diverse experiences, far more so than Sydney. If Middlesbrough's history is revealing in this sense, that of Melbourne is far more so. The change from primitive settlement to great city was the fundamental change, but the change from boom city in the 1880s to depression city in the 1890s involved within a far shorter period extraordinary switches of mood and policy. As a local poet wrote of Melbourne during the 1890s:

> Hers is a people ever in extremes,
> Or in a nightmare, or in golden dreams.

The urban boom of the 1880s, which influenced every aspect of the city's life – employment, population, income, leisure, social leadership, and, not least, taste and style – collapsed dramatically during the early 1890s. Buoyant optimism gave way to staid frugality. As the economic foundations of prosperity collapsed, there were profound transformations in family fortunes, municipal plans and moral attitudes. It is scarcely any exaggeration to say that the 'personality' of Melbourne – certainly its image – changed at this time. Its population fell also. It had passed the half-million mark in 1892 when the boom had clearly broken: it did not reach that figure again until 1900. In the meantime Sydney, with its growing suburbs, increased in population from 399,270 in 1891 to 487,900 in 1901. The tale of two cities, a main theme in Australian history, was passing through another chapter.

The origins of the boom were complex. Gold-mining, which had accounted for the great boom of the 1850s, had lost its importance during the 1870s. By that time, however, Melbourne had become the greatest Australian centre of trade and finance. A huge International Exhibition, which was held in 1880 and 1881, put Melbourne 'on the map'. It was also a gesture of confidence, for its opponents claimed that it was inappropriate to spend large sums of public money when trade was bad. The confidence proved justified when British capital poured into Victoria during the 1880s, attracted by higher rates of interest than could be obtained at home. Both farming and industry boomed. Melbourne benefited directly and disproportionately from the inflow of capital and the rise in incomes. The growth of a centralized railway system favoured it economically; the willingness of rich Victorian farmers to spend their money in Melbourne, even for a minority of them to lease or to own villas in its fashionable suburbs, favoured it both economically and socially. Increasing wealth was diverted into the city's building industry, and this in turn forced up the price of land. The financing of the boom encouraged, indeed it depended upon, an increasing amount of speculation.

Critics of the 'speculative mentality' were given short shrift by the men of power in the city. These men, many of whom had arrived in Victoria during the gold rush, were proud of their power, and they did not worry about their debts. 'Without debt,' said one, 'civilization was a failure.'[1] They combined belief in many of the underlying shibboleths of Puritanism – extremely narrow sabbatarianism, for instance, or teetotalism – with aggressive self-assertiveness. It is

1. cf. Chamberlain's comment on debt, p. 219 above.

scarcely surprising that foreign observers called Melbourne an 'American-style' city at this time. They contrasted what Francis Adams, a most percipient social critic, called the 'general sense of movement, of progress, of conscious power' in Melbourne with the dilatory, much more complacent, far more old-fashioned mood of Sydney. Sydneyites were 'quieter, less assertive, more civilized'. Melbourne was the 'phenomenal city of Australia' with people whose pride in it amounted to passion. 'The old Anglo–Australian generation which founded its prosperity is quietly but swiftly passing away.'

There was nothing 'phenomenal' about Sydney, 'a city of charm with an element of the ideal'. It had what another observer, Stanley James alias Julian Thomas, the famous journalist who also used the nickname 'the Vagabond', called in 1877, 'an essential respectability', even 'a respect for constituted authority, typical of an old-established crown colony'. It was 'a sleepy hollow'. Its business habits were different from those of Melbourne also. 'There is a bustle and life about Melbourne which you altogether miss in Sydney', wrote R. E. N. Twopeny in 1883. 'The Melbourne man is always on the look-out for business, the Sydney man waits for business to come to him.' Even the Melbourne girls, according to Adams, were 'more American than English'. 'Restless, frank, energetic, they have little prudery, and are well able to look after themselves.'

The Melbourne boom reached its height in 1888. By then the city had been provided with its first electric light, with telephones, with new suburban railways, with cable trams, 'neat little trams that glide with a swan-like motion', with lavish new shops, complete with hydraulic lifts, with busy highly decorated arcades, with new theatres, hotels and restaurants, and with dozens of opulent new mansions in the suburbs, particularly in the fashionable suburb of Toorak. Queen Victoria's jubilee in 1887 had been celebrated in Melbourne 'with an enthusiasm that was not excelled in any part of the Empire': it was followed in 1888 by a dazzling Centennial Exhibition to commemorate the centenary of the first British settlement in Australia. The scale of its planning was so extravagant that the chairman of the Planning Commission, Chief Justice Higinbotham, resigned in protest and had to be replaced by a politician. When the boom was over, the Exhibition was to be remembered as a 'costly blunder', but at the time 'no money spent ever gave so much direct enjoyment to so many people'.

Enjoyment was the keynote, and there seemed to be no reason to fear that the boom soon would be over. On 20 January 1888, the day's transactions on the Melbourne Stock Exchange exceeded £2 million. In just over a month in the spring of the year, sixteen land companies, fourteen trading companies and three coal and copper companies published their prospectuses in the Melbourne papers. Real property deals reached unprecedented figures. The Equity Insurance Co., for example, bought land in Collins Street at £2,300 a foot. On 2 August 1888, the *Argus* wrote that 'possibly in describing what we are now doing, when a twentieth-century journalist or historian refers to the issue of today's paper ... he will hold it to be not the least of the merits of the men of 1888 that they had a profound belief in the Australian future.'

The historian will concentrate rather on the historical residue of this buoyant age, particularly on the surviving architecture of the Melbourne of the late 1880s. Seldom can domestic architecture have produced such a rich variety of 'imposing' styles. Many of the mansions of Melbourne were older than the 1880s; 'Como', for example, gracious and well-balanced, with plain iron pickets guarding its verandas and balconies, was built in the late 1850s. The mansions of the 1880s followed local tradition in their generous use of decorative cast-iron, but they emphasized size rather than balance and had a special, and at their best, enchanting exuberance. Following the fashion set by the Governor in Toorak before he moved to new Government House (modelled directly on Osborne), they often had large towers. The towers were embellished with turrets, garlands, spikes, urns and statuettes. Melbourne was reaching upwards: the shops, coffee houses and hotels, equally ornate, were reaching upwards for different reasons. In the suburbs there was leafy space: in the centre pressure on restricted sites.

Some ten years gone this town too flat appear'd:
No Prell nor Fink colossal piles had rear'd.
Now land's so dear that Dives bids Vetruvius
Upraise an edifice to mock Vesuvius.

Yet Victorian Melbourne did not reach very high in an age when Chicago was already building skyscrapers. Municipal legislation limited building heights, and it was left to the mid-twentieth-century builders to re-set Melbourne's skyline. The profusion of styles was what dazzled during the 1880s – Scots Baronial at Hawthorn Glen, the home of a wealthy music seller; rich baroque in the huge house in East Malvern known at the time as 'Davis's Folly' (Davis was one of the great land speculators); Spanish, Moorish, Oriental, or elaborate Gothic. No wall outside or inside the house was allowed to be bare. Outside the house there were lawns, conservatories, shrubberies, summer houses and fern houses, 'all that wealth and taste can gather to make a home look seductive'. Inside the houses there was ostentatious comfort and the same confusion of period, huge private ballrooms and even chain mail and four poster beds. Antiquity had made its way to the Antipodes. So too had armies of domestic servants, many of them Irish: without domestic servants 'mansion economy' would have been impracticable.

In working-class houses also there was emphasis on both external and internal decoration. The number of houses in Melbourne increased by more than forty thousand between 1881 and 1891 and most of them were for people with limited incomes. Locally made cast-iron (there were several foundries by 1880) was prominent in the small houses of Fitzroy and Collingwood as well as in the mansions of South Yarra and Toorak. There was no marked divergence of taste between the men of power and the men without property. Stucco decoration – with heads, urns and flowers – was not reserved for the rich. Much of this work fortunately still survives, and it is beginning to be properly appreciated.

There was a sharp reaction against it during the 1920s when Victoriana were condemned indiscriminately in both Australia and England. 'Towards the middle of the nineteenth century,' the author of the article on Architecture in the *Australian*

Encyclopedia (1926) wrote, 'when taste was at a low ebb and cheap ornament popular, commercial firms made a speciality of building accessories such as veranda pillars, railing and roof crestings, in cast-iron of the poorest design, and the simple style of domestic architecture degenerated into an over-ornamental type of which many examples still exist.' Recovery of genuine delight in many of these condemned Victorian buildings is a measure of the Victorian revival. The reaction against the style started, however, long before the 1920s. When the boom of the 1880s was followed by depression, the uses of iron dwindled. Terracotta and timber displaced cast-iron so generally that, as E. Graeme Robertson has written in his beautifully illustrated *Victorian Heritage, Ornamental Cast Iron in Architecture* (1960), 'the styles before and after the depression were so dissimilar as to seem many years apart'.

What happened to styles happened to much else besides. The end of the boom destroyed many of the families who had behaved most ostentatiously. As early as 1888, the peak year of the boom, there were the first sensational insolvencies. The following year there were more insolvencies and alarming legal actions which revealed the scale of fraudulent practices behind many of the financial operations of the boom. Some of Melbourne's most prominent citizens in this and in later years were appearing in the law courts. When British capital ceased to flow to Victoria in 1891 the number of insolvencies further increased, and the situation was made worse in 1892 when there was a sharp fall in wool prices. The collapse of the banks followed the collapse of the land speculation companies, and the Federal Bank had to close its doors in 1893. The Government was driven to declare protracted bank holidays in an effort to avert ruin. 'People gathered in crowds about the temples of Mammon asking themselves and each other what was to happen.' From the more solid earth of Sydney, the *Bulletin*, itself a portent of a new age, noted coolly in November 1893 that 'the policy of the continent at large should be to declare Victoria an infected province until its moral character has been renovated and its reputation restored.'

3

The *Bulletin* had been founded in 1880, but it was not until the 1890s that it became a great social force. It began to serve as the chief instrument of a new kind of aggressive Australian nationalism, preaching the cause of labour, attacking the obsolete social distinctions and hierarchies of England, encouraging the emergence of a new group of Australian 'nationalist' writers interested in Australian people and in Australian landscapes, and, above all, proclaiming distinctive Australian values.

The values were believed to be most genuine and least tainted when they were found not in the cities but in the outback. The most important of them were tough masculinity, lack of affectation, the effortless ability to be 'practical', independence, a sense of equality, contempt for displays of authority, loyalty to 'mates', and hatred of 'scabs'. These values were expressed in ballads, in short stories, in newspaper articles, and in education: they soon coalesced to form a national mystique. They sustained – and continue to sustain – an orthodox interpretation of Australian history, in which the 1890s appear as the great creative decade when the Labour movement acquired new momentum and meaning, during and after the maritime strike of 1890, when the greatest Australian writers like Furphy, Lawson, and Daley struck a new note in poetry and prose, and the first real Australian painters found inspiration in their native landscape, and when Britain ceased to be the general provider of institutions and culture.

Vance Palmer's essay, *The Legend of the Nineties* (1954), was a suggestive perspective study of the light and shade of this period: more recently Russel Ward's brilliant *The Australian Legend* (1958) with its detailed description of the origins of the cult of 'the noble bushman' from convict days onwards, has greatly enriched Australian historiography while at the same time raising as many questions as it answers. Is it not significant that during a decade when two thirds of the Australian people lived in towns and cities, a proportion which was not matched by any other new country, including the United States and Canada, until the third decade of the twentieth century, the source of values was not the city but the bush? The lure and love of the bush continued to grow after the decade. 'Everyone knows what the true Australia is', a reviewer of Russel Ward's book in *The Age* of Melbourne remarked. 'It is the Bush – where most Australians don't live.' 'The city environment, unbalanced by nature, is a dead end for the human race', wrote Bishop Burgmann in his fascinating little booklet, *The Education of an Australian* (Sydney, 1944). 'All our architects and town planners . . . should be sent to school for a very long time in the Australian bush.' Is this kind of identification merely an Australian version of the British preference for country over town or has it got a particular framework of reference of its own, set by conditions both of immigration and of urbanization? The answers to the questions are central to any general interpretation of Australian history, but they will only be complete when far more systematic study has been made of the Australian city.

Leaving on one side the captivating question of whether Australian attitudes towards the city would have been different had New South Wales and Victoria been peopled not by immigrants from Britain but from Italy, with its ancient urban traditions, there are many distinctive factors in Australian experience which must be taken into the reckoning. It is just as necessary to relate the new pattern of the 1890s to the eclipse of Melbourne in the years that followed the boom, to the increasing pull of Sydney as a 'cultural centre' and to the changing images of Melbourne and Sydney, as it is to relate it to what was happening or what had happened in the outback. In order to examine critically the role of 'the legend' in Australian historiography it is necessary too to re-evaluate Melbourne's urban culture in the 1880s at the flowering of the boom. This is interesting both in itself and in its implications and bearings. If the first main interest of Melbourne's urban history in the Victorian age is the drama of its changing fortunes, the second is that the nature of those changing fortunes helps to provide a unifying explanation for nineteenth-century Australian history as a whole.

Something may have been lost in the 1890s as well as gained through the processes of transformation – the sense, for example, of the cultural possibilities of the city and of the need to master its problems from inside. Comparative history is relevant in this context. Russel Ward turned to F. J. Turner's famous hypothesis about the historical role of the American frontier for insights into Australian experiences: the student of Australian urbanism can turn to the writings of Professor A. M. Schlesinger and others for the attempt to explain American history in the late nineteenth century in terms of the 'rise of the city'. At a time when the 'muck-rakers' were exposing the evils of American cities and American civic reformers were seeking to remedy them, Australian interest was diverted from the city altogether. A poem by Henry Lawson, published in the *Bulletin* in 1892, caught the mood:

Ye landlords of the cities that are builded by the sea –
You toady 'Representative', you careless absentee –
I come, a sweat from Borderland, to warn you of a change,
To tell you of the spirit that is roused beyond the range;
I come from where on western plains the lonely homesteads stand,
To tell you of the coming of the Natives of the Land!

Melbourne in the 1880s was proud of its increasing 'urbanity': Sydney in the 1890s lived on rural values. Four aspects of Melbourne's urbanity deserve to be noted. First, it had much in common with British provincial experience. Second, it depended on immigrants from Britain, who used very similar arguments in Melbourne to the kind of arguments which were being used in Britain. Third, it was characteristically 'Victorian' in temper, using Victorian in its general and not in its geographical sense. Fourth, it had within it tendencies which were already making for divergence from Britain. Some of these have already been noted – the 'Americanism', for example, which was commented upon by Adams: others were 'nationalist' in feeling, although the nationalism was a very different kind from that of the *Bulletin* during the 1890s.

The feeling that there was a distinctive Australian future was nurtured in the cities: culture not nature was to make it. At a time when the Australian landscape was felt to be greatly inferior to that of Britain, the cities were already believed to have a superiority of their own. Their inhabitants were far better off, it was argued, than the men and women of London compelled to 'pine and starve and die, in courts and alleys'. They were relatively free, too, of a 'snob class'. At their best, they felt that they were making history. 'Are we not ourselves the realization of More's *Utopia*?' one magazine writer asked in 1881, adding by way of qualification that the difference between Melbourne and More's ideal state was that in Utopia all the streets were kept clean. Even this, of course, could and would be remedied. 'Our posterity will no more resemble us than the luxurious Venetians resembled their hardy forefathers who first started to build on those lonely sandy islands of the Adriatic,' Fergus Hume predicted in his readable book *The Mystery of a Hansom Cab*.

The culture of Melbourne, like the culture of other Australian cities, had a predominantly British cast. This had been true from the start. 'To the immigrant from the United Kingdom this is not a *foreign* land', the *Home Friend* noted in 1853, not, of course, completely innocently. 'The novelty to him is the familiar aspect presented by everything around – in fact, by the absence of novelty.' The cultural institutions which grew up during the 1840s and 1850s all had British counterparts: the friendly societies, which were to be found in every procession in Adelaide or Melbourne and Birmingham and Leeds, the Philosophical Institution, the Mechanics' Institutes, the Society of Arts, and the Young Men's Mutual Improvement Association (with lectures in alternate weeks on 'Geology in Victoria' and Dickens's *Dombey and Son*) were all products of an age of improvement which was common both to Britain and to Australia. 'St Kilda is to have an Athenaeum and Emerald Hill a Mechanics' Institute', the *Australian Home Companion* noted in November 1856. 'The friends of the people have used much diligence and tact in the accomplishment of their initiating plans [which] mark an advancing state of *social progress*.'

The same pressures could be traced behind the growth (and decay) of such institutions. There were complaints in 1857, for example, that 'the minds of Melbourne people have not yet been sufficiently disengaged from politics to allow for their according to music, the drama and other branches of amusement their usual attention'. When Shakespeare was being performed at the Theatre Royal, there were too many 'wide spaces' in the auditorium. There was a healthy reaction, however, to Verdi's *La Traviata*: 'the daily journals of Melbourne are to be entitled to the highest praise for having anticipated the London *Times* in a worthy endeavour to abolish any latent taste for the drivelling compositions of a certain school of French dramatic authors'. There was a pat on the back for the founders of the Trades Hall Literary Institute opened on the Queen's birthday in 1859, the year of the publication of Samuel Smiles's *Self Help*: 'as a sign of the habits and wishes of the working classes, this building is worthy of notice'.

The opening of the Public Library in 1859 inspired similar thoughts to those which Dawson expressed in Birmingham not long afterwards: not dissimilar thoughts had been expressed in Sydney when the Mechanics' Institute library was opened in 1843. 'A country may grow rich and powerful without the cultivation of the mind, but no nation can ever remain permanently great or respected, without learning be diffused.' The Melbourne Library, which had over 111,000 volumes by 1880, collected the best that was available from Britain until the depression of the 1890s led to a cut in its income. Its appeal was an extension of the same kind of appeal public libraries made in Britain. Henry Hyndman, the British Socialist leader, in praising Melbourne for the range of its cultural activities, with 'the people at large' as well as 'the educated class' taking part in them, said that there was only one drawback. He quoted a nineteenth-century London wit who, when asked how he liked Melbourne, replied: 'Immensely, but don't you think it is a little far from town?'

It was certainly much farther from town than the British provincial cities with which it had so much else in common. The pattern of cultural activities, however, depended much upon the free entry of British ideas and of British people, particularly professional people. Protection might be imposed against foreign goods – in this policy Victoria diverged sharply from Britain – but the cultural life of Victoria depended on personal initiatives with genuine British inspiration. The medical profession of Victoria sought to create the same kind of moral drives – for sanitary reform, for example – as the medical profession in Britain. The Victorian Institute of Architects copied the Institute of British Architects. University teachers sought to carry forward the same notions of popular as well as of academic education, which were responsible for the development of university extension work. The career of Professor C. H. Pearson, for example, illustrates the influence, limited but persuasive, of a 'liberal' mind upon a great city. Journalists might pass from one press to another, like Julian Thomas, 'the Vagabond', who insisted on describing everything in Melbourne, stage and pulpit, school and hospital, public platform and parliament itself, as if it were London.

The periodical press as a whole echoed British controversies. In 1851 the *Australasian* appeared from the *Argus* office in Melbourne to furnish a supply of material from the 'fountain head of British Literature': four years later a Melbourne *Punch* appeared with Frederick Sinnett, a friend and disciple of John Stuart Mill, and James Smith, a former correspondent of the London *Punch*, as its two main writers: from 1876 to 1885 the *Melbourne Review* represented all that was best in the culture of the city. Significantly, most of its contributors were amateurs, not professionals. They wrote about subjects which they felt were important as well as interesting.

The *Melbourne Review*, its rival the *Victorian Review*, and the short-lived *Centennial Magazine* remain fascinating repositories of Victoriana, as interesting in their way as the surviving Victorian mansions in Toorak and South Yarra. The 'Victorian' element in Melbourne's culture was demonstrated before bigger audiences at the time in the Great Exhibitions of 1880 and 1888, which may be compared in their tone and organization with the exhibitions in London and the British provincial cities.

There had been popular inter-colonial exhibitions in Sydney and Melbourne during the 1850s and 1860s, when they had been conceived of as means of 'imparting information to the juvenile population', 'elevating public taste', and 'bringing together, with one common object, people of all ranks and classes'. Melbourne had its own Exhibition building with fluted columns and imposing façade as early as 1854. An International Exhibition held at Sydney in 1879 set the stage for a more lavish kind of performance. It took place in its own 'Crystal Palace' and, although too far from London to attract the Queen, gained in prestige at least from the presence of her statue in the midst:

> The image of the Mighty Queen,
> Her people's love, her people's pride,
> Shone in the midst, and far and wide
> Gave life and sanction to the scene.

Vocal critics of governmental extravagance described the New South Wales Exhibition as an 'enormous swindle': agricultural Members of Parliament, who disliked the city, called it an attempt 'to dupe the country by causing a drain upon the pockets of the people for the express purpose of aggrandizing Sydney at the expense of the country'. The language recalls the language in Britain of the opponents of the Great Exhibition.

The Melbourne International Exhibition of 1880 was just as controversial, since it provoked all the many enemies of Graham Berry's 'red' regime, some of them confirmed free-traders, others socially superior pastoralists. The Exhibition was mooted as an idea long before it became a practical possibility. *Punch* called it a 'white elephant': the *Argus* described the Commissioners as 'impudent time-servers'. For all the bitterness of its controversial background, however, the Exhibition had a high-sounding moral invocation. Sir William Clarke, the chairman of the Commission which planned it, proudly told the Governor that the site on which the 'palace of industry' would be built was 'within a generation part of an unknown forest in an unknown land'. 'It is now the site of a populous and well-built city, presenting all the evidences of wealth and civilization, ranking with the foremost cities of the world.' The same theme was taken up in a cantata *Victoria* specially written by Leon Caron. Part I described the past. 'Victoria, sleeping amidst the primeval solitudes, is aroused by voices which foretell the speedy discovery and development of the country.' Part II described the present. Victoria, the 'Queen of the South', is 'discovered engaged in various pursuits – pastoral, agricultural and industrial – and is approached by a company of Nymphs, representing the various nations of the earth.'

On the opening day of the Exhibition, twenty thousand people were in the streets, watching the great procession led by nine brass bands. The *Argus*, changing its language, described it as 'a triumphal march of ... industrial battalions proceeding to celebrate the completion of a temple erected to contain the achievements of skilful labour, the trophies of science, and the achievements of art'. The most abiding evidence of the achievement was the temple itself. A huge Exhibition building had been completed in twenty months. With a dome, which it was proudly announced was higher than that of St Paul's, and a confusion of French and Italian styles, it became a great landmark in the city. It was there that the first Federal Parliament of Australia met in 1901.

The success of the 1880 Exhibition, which defied all expectations, was not merely rhetorical. The objects on view were ordered enthusiastically by Melbourne householders: some of them came from France, and in the opinion of one of Victoria's early historians helped to dispel 'provincialism'. On a different plane it was hailed as a great 'national' achievement, for home-produced and (against the British grain) protected Victorian manufactures were not disgraced when they were placed alongside the products of Europe. The knowledge of them would spread, it was believed, in potentially lucrative markets overseas. The Exhibition would be a good economic proposition for the state.

The Centennial Exhibition of 1888 was on an even bigger scale. There could be no complaint that the times were unpropitious, as there had been in 1880, and there was an even greater emphasis on 'culture', particularly music and painting, than there had been at the earlier Exhibition. A choir of five thousand sang music old and new, and half a million people attended symphony concerts. There were two landscape paintings on display, Frederick Leighton's 'Hercules

Struggling with Death for the Body of Alcestis' and Anton von Werner's life-size painting of Bismarck addressing the Reichstag. The Exhibition building was already there, and full attention could be devoted in 1888 to what to do with it. Over two million people visited the Exhibition, admiring the display of exhibits from ninety-three different countries (with Germany far more prominent throughout than in 1880). The Victorian Government spent a quarter of a million pounds on the Exhibition, ten times the amount originally estimated. The boom made such over-spending seem almost natural. It was never to seem natural again, however, for once the boom broke, exhibitions on this scale were not repeated in Melbourne.

On the surface Melbourne's culture, as expressed in the *Melbourne Review* or in the Exhibitions, was characteristically 'Victorian'. The British historian J. A. Froude, who visited Melbourne in 1885 and, as in all his travels, saw only the surface, wrote complacently that 'it was English life over again: nothing strange, nothing exotic, nothing new or original, save perhaps a greater animation of spirits. ... All was the same – dress, manners, talk, appearance.' Francis Adams saw deeply that there were 'dissimilar natural and social conditions'.

There were, indeed, differences of texture which made the city different from a British provincial city. There was poverty in Melbourne, particularly in hard times, of which there were plenty, but there was less hopeless destitution than in London or Leeds. 'Here,' in Victoria, we read in the *Victorian Review* of 1880, 'we are exempt ... from ... the complications of the Mother country, the poverty and crime bequeathed by the dark ages.' Contrasts were frequently drawn between Australia's well-paid working class and London's 'residuum', 'pining and starving and dying in courts, alleys and mouldy garrets of cheap lodging houses'. The contrast was one of attitudes as well as of fortunes. The gold rush had produced a state of affairs when, as the *Argus* wrote, 'society' was turned topsy-turvy in Victoria. 'Jack is not merely as good as his master, but is a great deal better in a pecuniary point of view.' Money was spent with greater prodigality. This was a fundamental difference. Luck was known to be a lever of the system, however much British (or Australian) social philosophers might write about character, thrift, and improvement.

As a 'well-to-do class' emerged (this term was used far more often than 'middle class'), it showed little instinctive understanding for the delicate nuances of English social status, although it had a cliquishness and a marked stratification of its own. The absences of familiar nuances shocked those British visitors who were particularly sensitive to them. They freely contrasted 'colonial' and 'British', and thereby demonstrated their own kind of insensitivity: 'inferior English' or more often 'inferior Scotch' were cutting terms which were often used. What Francis Adams called 'worldly Presbyterianism' was as unattractive to them as the 'crude cosmopolitanism' it covered over. Some of the writers in the reviews echoed their distaste. 'With the growth of cities,' a writer in the *Australian Review* remarked in 1886, 'their inhabitants should become urbane. . . . But close observers will see that courtesies and sweet graces of manner are becoming rarer among us each year.' Examples were given:

Let any gentleman take a walk in our public promenades, for instance the Botanical Gardens [Melbourne's pride] let us say on Sunday afternoon – let him be so particular about his dress as to don, among other things, a white waistcoat, a well-brushed tall black hat, and let him wear gloves. In a quarter of an hour's walk, simply because he happens to be well-dressed, he will attract to himself a disagreeable amount of attention from groups of flashily clad 'larrikins' whose overheard fragments of conversation among themselves are quite offensive enough. . . . Pedestrians need not pray for temporary deafness as they stroll through Battersea Park, the Bois de Boulogne, the Vienna Prater, or the Pincian Gardens in Rome.

The Melbourne larrikins were just as contemptuous of authority as the bushmen, noble or otherwise. They were 'lawless', 'nomadic', and 'uncomfortable under the roof of a house', as different from the London or Birmingham 'roughs', Adams thought, as angry tigers were from bears at play, worse even than the 'Bowery boys' of America. 'In Europe,' wrote Julian Thomas, 'the "rough" avoids the neighbourhood of police courts. He looks not to be known by magistrates or detectives. But here, the larrikin not only chaffs and annoys the policeman on his beat, but daily crowds the police court, and manifests the liveliest interest in the fate of male or female friends who may be on trial.' The 'larrikin tradition' may be as much of a clue to the Australian *mystique* as the tradition of the outback.

Another aspect of Melbourne's life which seemed different from that of Britain was the general interest in sport among all sections of the population. Australia led Britain in this direction of social history, and Melbourne led Australia. Twopeny, with Melbourne in mind, called Australia 'the most sporting country in the world'. Adams endorsed the verdict, and Melbourne's own 'Juvenal' wrote in 1892:

> Australian natives are too much inclined
> To honour muscle at the expense of mind.

Sir Charles Dilke forgot British parallels altogether and compared the excitement of an Australian Rules football championship match in Melbourne with that of a bull fight in Madrid: Julian Thomas said that after seeing a match between Melbourne and Carlton a boxing match seemed very tame.

> The six or seven thousand spectators comprised representatives of nearly all classes. It was a truly democratic crowd. Ex-Cabinet Ministers and their families, Members of Parliament, professional men and tradesmen, free selectors and squatters, clerks, shopmen, bargemen, mechanics, larrikins, betting men, publicans, barmaids (very strongly represented), working-girls and the half world, all were there.

Similar comments were made about the bigger crowds which watched the Melbourne Cup race, first run in 1861, 'a mixture of a Fourth of July celebration, *Mardi Gras*, an Italian carnival, the Derby and Goodwood Race meetings, and the Agricultural Show at Islington. No race meeting in England will compare with it'. The stake reached over £2,000 in 1883 and rose to over £10,000 in 1890. Mark Twain, who thought that larrikins were simply an 'old species' met elsewhere, conceded that the Melbourne Cup was unique, 'the great annual day of sacrifice'.

The entertainment element in sport was exploited in Melbourne along with all other forms of entertainment. The city was called 'a city of spectators'. The chronology of this development pre-dated the rise of the football leagues in England and the general provision of working-class entertainment for leisure. The music halls developed side by side. It was in the music halls that the ballads were sung which were to provide the richest expression of those rural values which were to be written about with pride during the 1890s. That the virtues of the country were being tacitly accepted at least by some people in Melbourne was demonstrated in an interesting Melbourne review of *A Century of Australian Song* published in 1885. The reviewer wrote:

It contains excellent samples of the craft, many of them redolent of the bush and the diggings; but the greater portion betray a town origin and are in no wise distinguishable from the ordinary effusions enshrined in the poems of the older country.

The demand for something genuinely 'Australian' could be heard in Melbourne throughout the whole of the period. It implied more than the demand for something genuinely 'provincial' which could be heard in Britain outside London. In the last resort, it was a demand not for equality of esteem or achievement but for distinctiveness of expression. Julian Thomas might attack 'half fledged *littérateurs* . . . whose only knowledge of life has been that of bush houses . . . and whose inspiration has been derived from the contemplation of a gum tree and a kangaroo', but there was vocal if intermittent request from the 1850s onwards, even from people who read British periodicals, for 'magazines written for Australians by Australians'. *Australian Christmas Chimes* published in 1881 printed next to each other 'Lost in the Bush' and 'Jack, a Romance of the Melbourne Exhibition Ball'. The *Centennial Magazine* said that a 'Bush Court' ought to have been added to the attractions of the Exhibition of 1888. The beauties of the Australian landscape were debated before they were accepted. J. R. Ashton in an article on 'An Aim for Australian Art' (1888) condemned the view that Australia should have an art 'which no one can mistake for that of any other country than Australia', and he found it necessary to condemn specifically 'those who see no beauty in any subject unless it comes from the back blocks, treeless plains covered with parched grass, kangaroo and emu, men dying of thirst or being speared'.

When Melbourne's growth came to an end in the 1890s, and Sydney continued to forge ahead, the *Bulletin*, read by an enthusiastic audience, provided an increasing volume of 'up-country' material. *The Man from Snowy River* (1895), the title of Paterson's first book of verse, was symbolic. Men from Melbourne joined in the venture. They included Victor Daley, who wrote about wine and roses not 'up-country stuff', Julian Ashton and Norman Lindsay. Arthur Streeton, the artist, wrote significantly in 1891, 'I'm not a bit tired of Australia. . . . I want to stay here, but not in Melbourne. . . . I intend to go straight inland (away from all public society) and stay there two or three years and create some things entirely new.'

Melbourne seemed stale and inhibiting. The fact that the capital of the new movements, the bustling Sydney of the 1890s, was wild, badly managed, almost totally lacking in civic spirit and openly corrupt, gave point to the rural values which seemed to represent an imperfectly articulated but for that very reason more attractive integrity. Not that Sydney was thought to be unexciting. It was the place, indeed, for a good time, a centre for gaiety and gossip. This became the ultimate *rationale* of the city in Australia: it was a very old *rationale* of cities which can be discovered even in the testimony of the Ancient World. The historian of Australia's part in the First World War writes that 'before 1914 it was observed, even in the Far West, that the new generation of Australians managed to preserve its cheque in the country towns, and to reach Sydney or Melbourne – and lose it there'.

The sobriety of Melbourne's reaction to the slump made for a new kind of contrast between the two cities. Talk of private thrift and public economy, of hard work and contrite hearts, of clearing up and cleaning up gave Melbourne a new and unfamiliar tone. There had been plenty of such talk during the 1880s, but it was always swallowed up in ostentation and exuberance. Bankruptcy, unemployment, labour troubles, a drift from city to country, the reorganization of Victorian agriculture, all these and other factors gave such talk compelling relevance after 1891. A new emphasis was placed on 'respectability' just at the time that respectability was being questioned in Britain and mocked at in Sydney. The members of the *Bulletin* staff were known, indeed, as the 'Bohemians'. While Melbourne was becoming more 'stuffy', they were rebelling most enthusiastically against all forms of stuffiness.

It is scarcely an exaggeration to describe the change in Melbourne as a change of urban personality. No longer was Melbourne called the most American of Australian cities: instead, and with an equal amount of inaccuracy, it was called the most British of Australian cities. Its new ruling groups were thought to be hierarchical in their attitudes, less democratic than the people with money in Sydney: by a surprising turn of judgement, less interested in the social power which money provided than in other and older forms of social power. Its professional people were thought to constitute a kind of hereditary élite. Its institutions, many of them bold ventures of an unsettled and enterprising society, were thought to be 'established', 'conservative' and even 'rigid'. Adams's comment that Sydneyites were 'quieter, less assertive, more civilized', 'exempt from the wilder excess of enthusiasm' in time came to be applied to the inhabitants of Melbourne. Eventually it was Sydney, the old colonial capital, which was said to be 'Americanized'.

J. D. Pringle's *Australian Accent* (1958) should be set alongside Francis Adams's *The Australians* (1893) to gauge the full extent of this historical contrast. Pringle writes:

> Melbourne is outwardly by far the most English and class-conscious of Australian cities. Sydney, which is regarded by the rest of Australia with something of the same half-amused, half-shocked disapproval with which a citizen of Boston regards Chicago or an Edinburgh man regards Glasgow, is turbulent, crude, vital and grossly materialist.

The truth or falsity of such observations is not what is interesting, at least to the student of Victorian cities. What is remarkable is the force of the contrast. The turning point was the economic collapse of the 1890s. A mythical Chinese scholar, said to have visited Melbourne in 1900, reputedly wrote that the people seemed to be always in a hurry, but they appeared also 'to be flying in all directions, like hungry ghosts seeking peace and rest'. When he asked his cousin if the 'look of anxiety on their eager faces' meant that some 'public calamity' had befallen the city, his cousin misleadingly answered no. There had been such a calamity, and it was of profound importance not only in the history of Melbourne, but in the history of Australia.

4

The calamity, of course, could scarcely have been avoided, given the conditions of the great burst of prosperity. The strength of the reaction owed something at least to the fact that there were people who could say 'we told you this is what would happen'. 'Of late,' a writer in *Table Talk* remarked in June 1888, the peak year of the boom, 'I have heard very serious misgivings expressed by sagacious and far-seeing financiers as to the permanence of the inflated value of city property.' There were other writers who questioned the moral values of some of the bigger speculators.

Undoubtedly such questioning reflected the feeling that Melbourne was sharing disproportionately as well as dangerously in the growth of Victoria. The third aspect of Melbourne's history which is of particular interest in the study of nineteenth-century cities concerns both demography and values. Melbourne concentrated within its own metropolitan area an exceptionally large proportion of the total population of Victoria – 26 per cent in 1861, 28 per cent in 1871, nearly 33 per cent in 1881 and over 43 per cent in 1891. Only in the last decade of the nineteenth century, when Melbourne's population remained static, did the proportion of country dwellers to townsfolk increase.

This concentration produced much the same shocked reactions from one school of writers as urban concentration did in Britain itself. Herman Merivale, the British professor of history who specialized in recent colonial history, wrote that 'the power of the few great towns' in Australia was 'exorbitant' in 1861. Twenty years later it was far greater. H. Mortimer Franklyn in his *A Glance at Australia in 1880*, published in Melbourne in 1881, argued that the future of Australia depended on the ability 'to promote the decentralization and distribution of those huge aggregations of men and women which are now to be met with in all metropolitan cities' and 'to encourage the growth of a feeling in favour of rural life, of the pursuits of husbandry, and of country sports and pastimes'. He believed that already in Victoria the power of city demagogues was being undermined by 'the rapid settlement of the soil by tens of thousands of freeholders ... a powerful body of permanent colonists who are Conservatives in the best sense of the word'. They would be sufficiently strong in numbers 'to offer a successful resistance to the policy, hitherto in force, of making the country tributary to the towns. The centre of gravity will shift from the latter to the former'.

At the end of the decade E. W. Beckett, writing on 'Australian and English Politics' in the *Fortnightly Review*, blamed the continuing growth of Melbourne on Victoria's pursuit of protectionist policies. Wages were higher at the point of import of materials. Hence labour was attracted to one place and 'the country was denuded of the men who ought to be irrigating the plains or clearing the trackless bush'. Beckett quoted a Melbourne newspaper's question: 'What may be the effect of an overgrown capital, with its army of labourers, who look to the government for support in times of distress, on the morals, the physique, and the prosperity of the people?' He added four points of his own. First, the position was much worse in Australia than in Britain, for in Britain limited space also accounted for the gravitation to the cities. Second, Australia was worse than the United States. 'It is only within the last fifty years that American cities have so enormously increased.' Third, Australia was sacrificing 'greatness' by excessive urban growth. 'A nation will never become great by adding house to house and street to street.' Fourth, Sydney was more favourably placed than Melbourne. 'It contains about a hundred thousand fewer inhabitants. If this difference is not to be attributed to the diverse results of Free Trade and Protection what then can be the cause? Yet Free Trade in New South Wales has not killed manufacturing industry. It has merely left it to grow where it can grow naturally.'

The prognostications of Mortimer Franklyn and the complaints of Beckett were exaggerated, but they were not simply pleas for a resident squirearchy or even a 'squattocracy', as so many English visitors and some Australians had advocated earlier in the century. They pointed to genuine divisions of interest between city and country and to the ultimate development of a 'country party' in Victoria which, although representing minority sectional interests, would be strong enough to have the chance of holding office.

In the meantime, within the cities there were other conflicts of interest also which visitors were slower to comprehend. They might lament the 'demagogy' of the Radical protectionists who had fought keen constitutional and fiscal battles with the more conservative free-traders – Victorian protectionism was always held to be a betrayal of all that was best in British Victorian life – but they did not usually note the rise of the urban Labour movement. It was the Labour movement which gave new significance to Sydney and New South Wales politics during the 1890s. There was greater militancy in Sydney during the maritime strike than in Melbourne and more concern for federation of labour and direct parliamentary representation. By the end of the 1890s the growth of a New South Wales Labour Party – the Labour Electoral League returned thirty-six members to Parliament in 1891 and held the balance of power in the Legislative Assembly – marked a strategic change in the Australian political pattern. Victoria, where the Labour Party appeared later and in 1894 entered into a compact to support a number of Victorian Liberals, including the great new political figure, Alfred Deakin, was not at the centre of the new Labour history which was to become such a basic ingredient, like the 'legend' itself, in Australian historiography.

The main danger of much of the historiography is that it overlooks as much as it affirms. Concentration on Sydney (or the outback) in the 1890s leads to an imperfect understanding of the urban texture of Melbourne in the 1880s: study of the working class leads to a glossing over of the complex class history of the middle nineteenth century: preoccupation with the 'nationalist' literature of the outback leads to a serious under-valuing of the most fascinating of all Australian novels about nineteenth-century Australia, Henry Handel Richardson's *The Fortunes of Richard Mahoney*, which deals sensitively and profoundly with the relationship between British and Australian experience during the Victorian age; commitment to the nationalist case encourages a narrowing of historical perspective. If Melbourne's culture in the 1880s is studied in detail as a particular kind of 'provincial culture' within a wider cultural context, then the denouement of the 1890s takes on a deeper meaning. Provincial pride and Australian nationalism had much in common with each other in their earliest origins. They diverged sharply and decisively during the 1890s. During this critical decade London won the final battle with the older English centres of provincial culture just at the time that it was losing it in the Empire. The dominance of Sydney may well have been a precondition of the eclipse of London.

The values are complex: the facts of demographic and economic history must be interpreted first. The process of Australian urbanization, which explains so much of Australia's history, must be studied statistically before it can be interpreted fully in social and political terms.

Many of the statistics have recently been collected and set in perspective by N. G. Butlin. He has shown, for example, that the building of cities during the last forty years of the nineteenth century absorbed the greater part of Australian resources devoted to development; that industry played a very small part in Australia's urbanization, a far smaller part than in Britain, for instance, or even in the United States; and that urbanization stimulated industrialization rather than the reverse – as if Manchester had come into being as a great city before it became an industrial capital.

In this setting Melbourne's growth was a major Australian economic enterprise. The extremely rapid growth of the 1880s during years of boom entailed not only a great rise in population, but a shift in its occupational structure (with a sharp rise in the number of government employees and professional people and workers concerned with commerce, manufacturing, transport, and construction), a great pressure on particular industries, notably the building industry, and an increase in the relative importance of others, notably metals and machinery. It also entailed substantial migration into Melbourne not only from country districts and smaller towns but from across the border in New South Wales. Victoria had more or less stopped its policy of assisted immigration before the boom began, and there had been a net loss in migration in the decade from 1871 to 1880. After the boom decade was over, there was once more an excess of departures over entries.

Throughout the whole period the proportion of native-born Australians was increasing. At the height of the boom it was estimated that over one half of Melbourne's population was Australian-born and rather less than one third had been born in the British Isles. For the six Australian colonies as a whole the proportion of native-born Australians increased from just over 60 per cent in 1881 to 77 per cent by the end of Queen Victoria's reign.

The more sedate population of the 1890s was an older population, robbed by death of some of the energetic leaders who had first arrived in Melbourne in the days of the gold rush. In the meantime Sydney was continuing to attract new immigrants. The differences between its demographic history and that of Melbourne must be taken into account in telling the tale of the two cities. Sydney had not enjoyed a great speculative boom in the 1880s, but it continued to grow rapidly during the 1890s while Melbourne stood still. It was Sydney's turn to claim in 1901 that 'it now stands as the second city of the British Empire, as estimated by the annual value of its rateable property'.

CHAPTER EIGHT

London, the World City

So far from the smoke of London being offensive to me, it has always been to my imagination the sublime canopy that shrouds the City of the World.

BENJAMIN HAYDON, *Autobiography* (1841)

Great city of the midnight sun,
Whose day begins when day is done.

RICHARD LE GALLIENNE (1895)

I

'HISTORY is nothing to him,' Francis Adams wrote of the characteristic inhabitant of the Australian sea-coast cities, 'and all he knows or even cares for England lies in his resentment and curiosity concerning London, with the tale of whose size and wonders the crowd of travelling "new chums" for ever troubles him.'

It was not only the Australians who expressed resentment and curiosity concerning London during the last twenty years of Queen Victoria's reign. London captured as much of the attention of thinkers and writers, social critics and prophets, as the provincial cities had done in early-Victorian England. Interest in the provincial cities had been associated with interest in the 'onward march of industrialism'. The growth of the cities, first the great industrial centres and then the outports – the centres of international trade – could be discussed straightforwardly in economic terms. Even the social consequences of this urbanization could be predicted – so it was claimed – from economic premisses. The rapid growth of London both in area and in population was fascinating in itself because it seemed to obey no known laws. Certainly industrialism by itself provided no adequate explanation. During the early nineteenth century London had declined in industrial importance in relation to the provinces. In economic activities like textiles, shipbuilding, and chemicals, it fell behind. The triumph of Manchester over Spitalfields, chronicled in parliamentary select committees, was plain for all to see at the beginning of Victoria's reign.

Some trades prospered, of course, if only by reason of the size of the London market. Soap, food, drink, and bricks were obvious examples. Commerce, domestic and international, set the pace. London as a port and storehouse retained its hold even when the provincial cities were leaping forward. It also employed an increasing number of people in the administration both of business and of government.

During the late nineteenth century London's numbers rose rapidly. The population of the administrative county of London increased from three million people in the early 1860s to four and a half million by the end of the reign: 'Greater London' (the term was used in the 1881 census) grew far more rapidly still. While the inner areas of London were losing people – after 1881 their continued population growth depended on natural increase and not on gains from migration – the Greater London area was attracting increasing numbers of people from the 'inner ring' as transport facilities improved.

The population of the 'outer ring' beyond the administrative county increased from 414,000 in 1861 to 1,405,000 by 1891 and to 2,045,000 in 1901. Even beyond the outer ring of London there were contiguous urban areas which raised the total population of London still higher. Between 1871 and 1901 the population of Greater London rose faster than that of any of the biggest provincial conurbations and far faster than the national population as a whole. It began to be difficult to say where London ended or, even more portentous, to say where it would end. 'Long avenues of villas, embowered in lilacs and laburnums', wrote Macaulay, 'extended from the great centre of wealth and civilisation almost to the boundaries of Middlesex and far into the heart of Kent and Surrey'. Questions already asked in the seventeenth and eighteenth centuries about the 'parasitism' of London acquired new point. The provincial cities no longer posed the most exciting and alarming riddles about present and future. Henry James, for all his appreciation of London, wrote of its 'horrible numerosity'. Arthur Sherwell in his *Life in West London* (1901) talked of the pathos and remorselessness of growth: 'a city is like a great, hungry sea, which flows on and on, filling up every creek, and then overspreads its borders, flooding the plains beyond'.[1]

Growth, however, was merely the first of the themes which fascinated contemporaries during the 1880s and 1890s. The social relations of London became more interesting as they were set out by Charles Booth and others in sober factual statements. Henry Mayhew and a number of other journalists in the 1850s and 1860s had made the dark side of London live in the minds of their readers, describing vividly the remarkable contrasts of fortunes. Booth, who admitted that he liked 'the essence' of 'great metropolitan cities' like London and New York, engaged both the intelligence of his readers and their consciences. Poverty was not merely a consequence of particular developments in industry: it was the biggest single fact of contemporary existence, 'the problem of problems'. His detailed statistical investigation of the facts of poverty in London was preceded by or accompanied by the publication of pamphlets and books on London's poverty, like the Congregationalist minister Andrew Mearns's *The Bitter Cry of Outcast London* (1883) or his namesake General Booth's *In Darkest England and the Way Out* (1890).

General Booth, like so many of the writers on provincial cities in early-Victorian England, began with the contrast between 'darkest Africa', which had just been penetrated by Stanley, and 'darkest London' with its 'submerged tenth'. 'The lot of the Negress in the Equatorial Forest is not,

1. cf. *Bentley's Miscellany* (1838): 'The ocean stream of life flows down the Strand, whose courts, lanes and alleys, are so many creeks, and inlets.... The rolling masses that flood a living tide along London streets ... have a character peculiarly their own, bearing no analogy to ... [those of] the great provincial towns'. Dickens also in *Nicholas Nickleby* (see above, p. 74) wrote of 'vehicles of all shapes and makes' mingling 'up together in one moving mass like running water' and lending 'their ceaseless roar to swell the noise and tumult'. Carlyle also compared the awakening of Manchester on a Monday morning to 'the boom of an Atlantic tide'.

perhaps, a very happy one, but is it so very much worse than that of many a pretty orphan girl in our Christian capital?' Charles Booth used his statistics more precisely than his namesake but with just as real a hope that the statistics would quicken feelings and become levers of social change. Over 30 per cent of London's population lived in poverty. The significance of this proportion was neither local nor metropolitan: it was national. In 1886, Booth wrote:

> My only justification for taking up the subject in the way I have done is that this piece of London is supposed to contain the most destitute population in England, and to be, as it were, the focus of the problem of poverty in the midst of wealth, which is troubling the hearts and minds of so many people.

The contrast between East End and West End in London, which reflected what the *Quarterly Review* called 'the complete separation of the residences of different classes of the community', was the great contrast of the 1880s and the 1890s. At the beginning of the century it had already been noted that the inhabitants of the 'extreme east' of London knew nothing of the western districts of London 'but from hearsay and report'. 'There was little communication of sympathy between the respective classes by which the two ends of London were occupied', wrote the Rev. John Richardson in his *Recollections of the Last Half Century* (1856). 'They differed in external appearance, clothes, pursuits and pleasures.' A witness before the Select Committee on the Health of Towns in 1840 had said of social conditions in the worst districts of the East End of London that 'none but the medical men and the parish officers know anything about them: they are as much unknown as the condition of a district in Otaheite'. Twenty-five years later, the London Diocesan Building Society reported that the East End was a vast region 'as unexplored as Timbuctoo'.

During the 1880s and 1890s the term 'East End' began to be used generally: it suggested a different world, an unknown world, within the same city. 'Who knows the East End?' Arthur Morrison asked in his *Tales of Mean Streets*, a collection of stories about London which provided an inspiration to housing reformers and welfare societies. 'It is down through Cornhill and out beyond Leadenhall Street and Aldgate Pump, one will say: a shocking place, where he once went with a curate; an evil plexus of slums that hide human creeping things; where filthy men and women live on penn'orths of gin, where collars and clean shirts are decencies unknown, where every citizen wears a black eye, and none ever combs his hair.' Morrison's description of each day in the life of the East End being like every other day recalls Dickens's comments on Coketown. Both men had been struck by exactly the same feature of Victorian urban life.

General Booth and the home missioner's comparisons with 'darkest Africa' were echoed, surprisingly enough, not only by social reformers and leaders of the 'settlement movement', some of whom dreamed of establishing a residential squire-archy in the East End, but by one of the Salvation Army's most scathing critics, the great scientist, T. H. Huxley, who wrote that the Polynesian savage 'in his most primitive condition' was 'not half so savage, so unclean, so irreclaimable as the tenant of a tenement in an East London slum'.

Such statements reveal not 'the truth' about the East End but rather the deep gulf in experience and values between observers and observed in the late nineteenth century. The glitter of the West End in the 1880s and 1890s sharpened the sense of contrast with the East. The statistics of poverty, mortality and deprivation were unchallengeable. Often, however, the elaboration of the contrast rested, as in Huxley's case, on the same kind of ignorance about how other people lived which Mrs Gaskell had noted in early-Victorian Manchester. Stepney and Wapping had nothing in common with Park Lane and Belgravia. Topographically, even, the wayward growth of the East had contrasted with the relative orderliness of the West, the alley with the square, the thicket with the garden, the railway embankment with the mews. Although there was poverty in the West End, within the region of Belgrave Square, for example, it was hidden from view: in the East End it was open, omnipresent and dominating.

Socially there were even greater contrasts, which Charles Booth was sensitive enough to discern and to appreciate. Not all the advantages were with the West. Starting with the moral premiss 'that the simple natural lives of working-class people tend to their own and their children's happiness more than the artificial complicated existence of the rich', Booth recognized that the social habits and institutions of the East End had their own colour, vitality and excitement. H. L. Smith, one of his fellow-authors of *Life and Labour*, wrote appreciatively of 'the contagion of numbers, the sense of something going on, the theatres and the music halls, the brightly lighted streets and the busy crowds – all, in short, that makes the difference between the Mile End Fair on a Saturday night and a dark and muddy country lane, with no glimmer of gas and with nothing to do. Who could wonder that men are drawn into such a vortex, even were the penalty greater than it is?' Gertrude Bell, a Bell of Middlesbrough – in her voluminous writings she wrote nothing of interest about the town which gave her family its livelihood – took up the same strain when she visited Whitechapel in 1891 and not only found it 'fascinating to watch' the people and to shop cheaply in the market but enjoyed the many glimpses of a quite different way of life. Her writings pass beyond the limits of observation: they display a genuine desire to get inside the minds of people different from herself.

George Lansbury has left an intimate insider's account of 'the unreasonable and unexpected happiness in the middle of sordid conditions' in the East End in his *Looking Backwards and Forwards* (1935). It is a matter of regret to historians that people from the East End of London have left few outsiders' accounts of the West. The reason is simple: most of them never visited it. They were separated from it not so much by distance as by privilege. Their criticisms would be illuminating, even if they were shallow. The West End too had its problems. While comparisons between Polynesian or African savages and East-Enders were being made so freely by Salvationists and scientists alike, Park Lane was being invaded by South African diamond and gold kings, who were accused by their West-End enemies of appropriating it exclusively for their own use. 'It is the patronage of Colonial plutocrats, not less than of American millionaires,' wrote the outstanding social commentator of late-Victorian England, the journalist T. H. S. Escott, 'which has contributed to brighten the brilliance and increase the expensiveness of life in that polite world' which revolved around the West End of London and later around the court of King Edward VII.

The two worlds of London, one dark and mysterious, the other dazzling and ostentatious, were of increased public interest just because late-Victorian London was being thought of more and more as a world city. This aspect of its existence was stressed more frequently during the 1880s and 1890s than ever before, partly because of the growth in international travel, partly because of the greater attention paid to London as the capital not only of a country but of an Empire, and partly because of the rise of mass-circulation journalism. The two Jubilees encouraged large numbers of visitors from overseas to see London for the first time. Many of them came from the Empire. Yet even before the Jubilees, international travel was increasing. The Australian-born Australian was just as enthusiastic as the 'new chums' were to talk about London and if possible to visit it. 'The astounding fact [was] that this modern Babylon is inhabitated by nearly twice as many people as the continent from which he comes', J. F. Hogan, one of the most perceptive Australians, wrote. 'The world's metropolis', an American writer in New York's *Century Magazine* called London in 1883: 'We may talk of our Western empire and our admirable ports, of our growth and our growing wealth; but here is and will remain for generations, the centre of the commercial and political world, the focus of intellectual activity and the mint of thought. Here ferments the largest and most highly developed humanity which as yet the universal mother has given birth to, and here the whole world's intellect comes to pay homage.'

Comments of this kind in the magazines, foreign and British, were more effective than the most lavishly sponsored efforts in twentieth-century public relations. Not all the comments, of course, would have been approved by public relations agencies. The facts of poverty were often set alongside the facts of Empire. London's reputation as a world city was not simply a reputation for brilliance. A little later Will Crooks's well-known remark about the same sun which never set on the Empire never rising on the dark alleys of East

London directly linked the preoccupation with poverty and the consciousness of imperial power. The Boer War with its evidence of malnutrition and physical unfitness underlined the connexion.

Railways and steamships had united the Empire. They had made possible the rise both of the industrial cities of the provinces and the great international seaports. By the 1880s and 1890s they considerably magnified the importance of London. The railway network centred on London, as all provincial travellers had long known to their cost, and the capital had always been, of course, a great international seaport in its own right. In 1880 the total value of its trade was greater than that of Liverpool, its nearest rival. It had an advantage in the import trade, while Liverpool had an advantage in exports. As centre of the great importing warehouses, London was as much a symbol of free trade as Manchester had been in the 1840s: its great warehouses, which could store more than two hundred thousand tons of goods, were picked out by Baedeker as one of the sights of the city. 'Nothing will convey to the stranger a better idea of the vast activity and stupendous wealth of London than a visit to the warehouses, filled to overflowing with interminable stores of every kind of foreign and colonial products.' An increasing amount of passenger traffic was also moving through London in the late-Victorian age. It was appropriate, indeed, that the station which linked Britain with the continent was named after the Queen.

Again there was ambivalence. Railway building, notably the building of Victoria, meant turning people out of their homes. The building of the docks also had been achieved only at considerable human cost, and there were heavy social costs involved in their business-like operation throughout the century. In good times they were crowded and prosperous. In times of bad trade they were idle and deserted, visible proof of the fluctuations of international commerce. In both good and bad times there was a tradition of industrial unrest. It was particularly active in the boom year of 1872, when the unions made attempts to organize dock labour, and in another 'good year', 1889, the year of the great dock strike. What was happening at the London docks in 1889 was known then throughout the world. Australia, indeed, was one of the countries which helped the dockers to carry their struggle for the dockers' tanner to a successful conclusion in 1889. Social relationships in the most international sector of the 'world's metropolis' were bound to interest anyone who was trying to read 'the signs of the times'.

The internationalism of London was mirrored not only in its trade and in its overseas connexions but in its population. Baedeker, in describing the docks, directed attention to 'the large and motley crowd of labourers, to which numerous dusky visages and foreign costumes impart a curious and picturesque air'. He also pointed out that there were more Scotsmen in London than in Aberdeen, more Irishmen than in Dublin, more Jews than in Palestine, and more Roman Catholics than in Rome.

After 1881, although the administrative county of London might be losing more and more emigrants to the surrounding region of Greater London – the population of the county actually fell after 1901 – it still attracted many immigrants from all parts of the world. The central parts of London, indeed, were the places where many of the foreign groups congregated. They made their home there as other groups moved out. People from other parts of Britain often chose these parts also. The conclusions of the census of 1861 had suggested that migration out of London was usually short-distance in character while migration into London obeyed different rules, following step-by-step along human trade routes. Throughout the rest of the Victorian age this pattern repeated itself. London as a whole had a fairly young population with relatively few old people. There were marked demographic differences, however, between its various constituent parts, and the demographic facts always reflected basic differences in economic and social conditions and opportunities.

2

It was the question of the relationship of the constituent parts to the whole which gave point to most of the other questions contemporaries were asking about London. What was the whole? Did its constituent parts have a real life of their own? Was there any real sense in which London was one? These were questions about society which were intimately bound up also with questions about government.

The largest city in the world, it was often said, in the 1860s and 1870s, was anonymous. It had been left outside the range of the great local government reforms of 1835 and such pioneer social and administrative legislation as the Public Health Act of 1848. In 1843 Lord Brougham had expressed the opinion that it was utterly impossible 'that many months should elapse before municipal reform should be extended to the City of London'. Forty years later people were still waiting. No government had dared to grapple systematically with its problems, and private attempts at reform had always broken down in face of the stubborn resistance of vested interests. G. M. Young, who placed Chamberlain's Birmingham firmly in the mainstream of national history, argues that London also had a very special place. 'The conversion of the vast and shapeless city which Dickens knew – fog-bound and fever-haunted, brooding over its dark, mysterious river – into the imperial capital, of Whitehall, the Thames Embankment, and South Kensington, is the still visible symbol of the mid-Victorian transition.'

A colourful anthology of complaints about mid-Victorian London could be collected without difficulty. The inner square mile, known as the City, retained its centuries-old form of government by lord mayor and corporation. It had long been ceasing to be a place of residence, however, and increasingly it was ceasing to 'represent' the bigger (and far less precisely demarcated) 'city as a whole'. Large parts of the bigger area were administered by parish councils and vestries, assisted by special commissions for lighting, paving and drainage, grand juries and petty sessions. Dickens poked fun at London government, because he was a serious supporter of a reformed system of administration. Supporters of decentralization were often as keen in their criticisms as reforming Benthamites. Edwin Chadwick was determined to hand over London's sanitary government (water supply and drainage) to a small executive Commission appointed by the

Crown. His anti-centralizing opponents wanted to develop full parochial or municipal control. 'The present condition of this huge metropolis', remarked Toulmin Smith, one of the most enthusiastic defenders of local self-government, 'exhibits the most extraordinary anomaly in England. Abounding in wealth and intelligence, by far the greater part of it is yet absolutely without any municipal government whatever.'

No fewer than 250 local Acts of Parliament had been passed relating to particular districts of London, and 10,000 commissioners were exercising varying functions and degrees of authority. Muddled government had grim consequences. 'The metropolis', wrote John Hollingshead in *Ragged London in 1861*, 'is not managed, not cleansed, not relieved from the spectre of starvation which dances before us at our doors.' These words were written after the first attempt at reform had been made.

Chadwick lost his battle to combine the administration of the water supply and drainage of London in the hands of a small Commission: the opposition of metropolitan interests was at least as responsible for his downfall as provincial suspicion of centralization. In 1854, however, the same year as he fell, a Royal Commission on the Corporation of London was as adamant as he had been – though not for quite the same reasons – that the idea of a gigantic new elected local authority for London was unwise and impracticable. London was not so much the great anomaly as the great exception. 'It is a province covered with houses; its diameter from north to south and from east to west is so great that persons living in the furthest extremities have few interests in common: its area is so large that each inhabitant is in general acquainted only with his own quarter and has no minute knowledge of other parts of the town. Hence the first two conditions for municipal government, minute local knowledge and community of interest, would be wanting if the whole of London were, by an extension of the present boundaries of the city, placed under a single municipal corporation. The enormous numbers of the population, and the vast magnitude of the interests which would be under the care of the municipal body, would likewise render its administration a work of great difficulty.'

The Commission recommended, therefore, neither a single municipal corporation nor a small executive 'dictatorship' of the kind which Chadwick hankered after, but a Metropolitan Board of Works consisting of delegates from the vestries of the larger London parishes and from groups of the smaller parishes. The delegates were to be elected indirectly by vestry or district boards and, with a constitution totally unlike that of the governing body of any other city in the country, the Board was to have a paid chairman.

These main recommendations of the Commission were accepted by the government and put into effect in the important Metropolis Local Management Act of 1855. Thereafter a considerable part of London was administered for certain limited purposes by the Metropolitan Board of Works. The definition of the area of the Board was determined neither by the facts of civic history nor by human geography but by the network of drains and sewers. The preamble to the Act spoke only of provision for 'the better management of the metropolis in respect of the sewerage and drainage and the paving, cleansing, lighting and improvements thereof'. This was eighteenth-century language, the language of the improvement Acts rather than full-blooded Victorian language of civic reform. Chadwick's controversial but constructive proposals about public policy which had led to the bitter disputes of the early 1850s were put on one side, much to his disgust. He never forgave Sir Benjamin Hall, who sponsored the Metropolitan Management Act – 'a huge impostor of a man', he called him – or placed his trust in the Metropolitan Board of Works, which he believed was deliberately designed to prevent London's sanitary services from being managed intelligently and efficiently.

Chadwick's zeal for 'public consolidation' and control of all metropolitan sanitary arrangements led him into distrust of all popular democratic remedies. Yet the new Board itself was not a democratic instrument. Its full name was as hard and institutional as any of the poor-law institutions with which Chadwick had been connected. It spoke in administrative terms for a 'metropolis' and not for a particular place called London. The thirty-nine vestry and district boards, which elected the forty-five members of the Metropolitan Board, had genuine local names, one of them, the venerable but archaic Corporation of the City of London, still appropriating the name of London itself. The Board as a whole, however, derived its authority not from local pressure but from reorganization from above. It was to serve the needs of a 'metropolis' rather than to speak in the name of London. The greatest 'city state' in the world, reformers maintained, was thus denied, even after 'reform', the common organization and corporate powers of the smallest English borough.

Although the Metropolitan Board of Works soon became far more than a sanitary authority, it could never hope to mobilize the same kind of civic pride that Joseph Chamberlain mobilized in Birmingham. It carried out great improvements, among them the building of Shaftesbury Avenue, Charing Cross Road, Clerkenwell Road, Victoria Street and Queen Victoria Street. It introduced the first building regulations, acquired a large number of parks, gardens and open spaces, a twenty-fifth part of the whole metropolitan area, and freed the river bridges of tolls. Its loan transactions set a pattern in local government finance. Its horizons were far wider than those of the vestries or the Corporation of the City of London itself, and it had at its disposal a rateable value which rose from £11,283,663 in 1856 to £27,386,086 in 1882. It often showed imagination in its work. Yet what it could never do was to fire the imagination either of Londoners or of people contemplating London from outside.

The system of indirect election inevitably kept the Board remote from the ordinary elector, while the members of it tended to regard their membership as a privilege for all time, not as a term of office for three years. It was calculated by one of the critics of the Board that it would take twelve years to change a single member. The perpetuation of vestry rule made for inefficient diversity – 'anarchy' was the usual contemporary description – and cheese-paring economy. Many functions of local government which inspired the reformers of the provinces were weak or non-existent in London. The water supply of the capital was in the hands of eight or nine monopolistic companies which made considerable profits and during the 1880s paid an average of 7 per cent to their shareholders on their swollen nominal capital. Gas supply was in the hands of three non-competing private companies. Little positive was done, as in the provinces, to develop new services – for example, the service of public libraries. 'The local government of London', Gladstone told the House of Commons in 1884, 'is, or if it is not, it certainly ought to be, the crown of all our local and municipal institutions.' It was not, and many people behaved as if it never ought to be.

The result was frustration. London was the seat of the government, the home of the sovereign, the centre of the legal system and the learned profession, the hub of the literary and scientific world, a world metropolis, but it could not speak in its own name except through the City of London, which was an institution which defied the 'march of improvement'. 'Is the capital of the British Empire to be the only space in that Empire in which the nation cannot speak through its local representatives?' critics asked. For all its practical achievements the Board could never satisfy its critics. It faced other difficulties, too. During its last years it was engaged in a somewhat desperate attempt to improve its financial position. Its income was derived from vestry rates and from the proceeds of duties on coal and wine. The sums raised from duties dwindled in an age of increasing free trade, but successive governments offered the Board no compensation. It could scarcely have been an encouragement to its chairman when Lord Randolph Churchill in his brief spell as Conservative Chancellor of the Exchequer in 1886 not only criticized the Board's expenditure but reminded him that it was, after all, not chosen directly by the electors.

Interest in the reform of the government of London redirected attention back to the capital city during the 1880s. How was London to be managed? The answer given during the 1850s had proved inadequate. Could a new answer be given which would take into account what Joseph Chamberlain's unauthorized programme called 'new conceptions of public duty, new developments of social enterprise, new estimates of the natural obligations of the community to one another'? Many of the old issues of the 1850s were reconsidered, but there were new issues too. The interest was largely political because the administrative patterns of London could only be tackled in political terms, and there were obvious enough political differences between the age of Palmerston and the age of Chamberlain. During the 1880s the old radicalism of London reformers, which had its origins in the battles for control of the London vestries in the early nineteenth century, was being either extended or challenged by the 'new radicalism' of young social reformers who were more interested in programmes than in theories of representation.

The setting up of the London County Council in 1888 – by a Conservative government – did not mark the climax of the reform movement but rather its emergence as an active political force. Direct election of 118 councillors allowed for the pressure of public opinion. The greater range of functions permitted increased civic initiative. The desire for even greater functions stimulated the demand for 'an untrammelled County Council'. At the same time, the continued power both of the vestries and of the City of London and the continued existence of 'vested interests' outside local government meant that there was tension and struggle. The struggle took political form and it enlivened both local and national politics. For the first time in the century London could contribute directly to the national debate on what good city government really meant. Because the contribution was made in political terms, it had national significance also. What London was doing with itself was for the first time news in Manchester and Birmingham.

Yet the change of constitution in 1888, which was the subject of hundreds of articles in newspapers, usually hostile, and in magazines, both British and foreign, did not resolve the fundamental question of the relationship between the parts of London and the whole. How strong should London's central government be? The issues emerged again in controversial political form in 1899 when Balfour created twenty-eight metropolitan boroughs each with its own mayor and council. Asquith led the Liberal opposition on this occasion, and attacked Balfour's Bill as an attempt 'to surround and buttress the unreformed city with a ring of sham municipalities'. When

Balfour's Bill was passed, the comment was made that it would create not one London but twenty-nine Birminghams. The sense of civic obligation in London, it seemed, was once again being deliberately sub-divided.

No one knew whether the sub-divisions reflected any existing sense of civic consciousness. What were the new London boroughs anyway? G. K. Chesterton, who had asked the question 'Where did London end?' also asked the question 'What did London mean?' in *The Napoleon of Notting Hill* (1904). The fantasy of his story was the kind of fantasy that grew out of frustrated hopes. The King in the novel has 'the noble conception' of 'a revival of the arrogance of the old medieval cities applied to our glorious suburbs. Clapham with a city guard. Wimbledon with a city wall. Surbiton raising a bell to raise its citizens. West Hampstead going into battle with its own banner.'

The story unfolds from this point. The 'idealism' of Notting Hill fired the civic pride of other places in London. Although it ended in wild conflict, for Chesterton 'it lifted the modern cities into that poetry which everyone who knows or mankind knows to be immeasurably more common than the commonplace'. Other writers were more sceptical. Graham Wallas in his brilliant but neglected *Human Nature in Politics* (1908) was just as interested as Chesterton in loyalties, affections and rivalries. His conclusion, however, was that, despite Chesterton, very few Londoners had learnt to feel and think primarily as citizens of their boroughs. 'Town Halls are built which they never see, coats of arms are invented which they would not recognize; and their boroughs are mere electoral wards in which they vote for a list of unknown names grouped under the general title adopted by their political party.'

3

Chestertonian paradox was one literary reaction to late-Victorian London, as different from Booth's sociology as the politics of the London Fabians were from the vestry politics of the bleak age of the Metropolitan Board. Yet, leaving Chesterton on one side, London had a special place, both in the literature of late-Victorian and early-Edwardian England and in its politics.

London was not, of course, discovered for the first time, as Manchester had been during the 1840s. There was a vast eighteenth-century literature about its many aspects, with Gay, Fielding and Johnson, among many others, as superb social commentators. In the nineteenth century Taine had written of its size[1]; Doré had illustrated its ways of life; Dickens and Mayhew had lingered on many aspects of its society; George Godwin in *Town Swamps and Social Bridges* (1859) and John Hollingshead in *Ragged London in 1861* had anticipated Mearns and Booth in turning to the facts of London poverty to try to answer 'the one domestic question at present uppermost in the public mind'. Even the politics of London had been of strategic importance in national political history in 1848, when the middle classes of the capital, 'peaceful, prudent and loyal', showed their intense fear of the Chartists, and in 1866 and 1867 when economic depression and political agitation in London pushed the Reform League into a noisy campaign to secure a new measure of parliamentary reform. Class divisions in London politics were clearly demonstrated not only during the Chartist period but in 1866 and 1867, when the *Standard* told working men that they were on trial to redress 'the pitiable episode of 1848' and *Blackwood's* urged 'all the respectability of London' to defeat Mr Beale of the Reform League as it – a superb collective – had defeated Feargus O'Connor nearly twenty years before.

Two facts made London's role in national history more dramatic during the 1880s and 1890s. First, the changes which were taking place in it were more striking than in any other part of the country. Second, it was acting in politics not merely as a national capital but as a centre of home-produced specifically London discontents.

Before 1880 the workers of London had been far less well organized in trade unions than the workers in most of the great industrial cities of the provinces. Some of them belonged to skilled crafts, which were well represented in the Trade Union Congress and in the 1850s and 1860s had their

1. See above, p. 86.

headquarters in London, but most of them were engaged in jobs concerned with road transport, dock work, railways, shops and offices, which were either largely unorganized or very poorly organized at the beginning of the 1880s. The attempt to organize workers in occupations of this kind after 1880 inevitably centred on London. When, for example, Will Thorne started the Gasworkers' and General Labourers' Union (later the National Union of General and Municipal Workers) at Beckton Gasworks in the early summer of 1889, 'the news', he wrote, 'spread like wildfire; in the public houses, factories, and works in Canning Town, Barking, East and West Ham, everyone was talking about the union.... The men at the works could talk about nothing else but "the union" and what it was going to do.' When Dickens wrote about a trade union in *Hard Times* – on the basis of very imperfect knowledge – he chose Lancashire as his setting: in the 1880s he would have chosen London. Annie Besant's organizing activities with the girls employed at the Bryant and May match factory made national news: they drew on middle-class sympathies by appealing to 'social compunction'. The story of the Dock Strike, as we have seen, excited the world.

There was another aspect of London's economic discontents in the 1880s which had general political significance. Many of the London trades, casual, sweated and economically vulnerable in an age of mounting foreign competition, were trades with a high incidence of cyclical unemployment: so, in particular, was London's greatest single large-scale enterprise, the docks. The most vocal complaints of the unemployed had been heard in Lancashire, Yorkshire and the Midlands earlier in the century. Although they were strong and insistent in London in 1866 and 1867, they gained in intensity during the 1880s. The unemployed were always inclined to demand political remedies, and during the 1880s the unemployed of London increased both in numbers and militancy. A crowd of 120,000 people had gathered in Hyde Park in 1884 to offer support to the government when its reform proposals were being approved in the House of Lords. This was described as 'the greatest Reform demonstration ever held'. More novel and more ominous, to Conservatives and Liberals alike, were the Socialist demonstrations of the later 1880s. The riots in Trafalgar Square in 1886 and 1887 were riots of London's unemployed, and the animosities which they roused were animosities against the propertied and privileged people in London. The East End met the West End in a social struggle which was far more meaningful than Chesterton's battle of Notting Hill.

The events of 'Bloody Monday', 8 February 1886, led to a jump in the Lord Mayor's Relief Fund for the unemployed from £3,000 to £80,000 in forty-eight hours. Yet charity could not buy social peace. 'Bloody Sunday', 13 November 1887, was the most exciting day in London's nineteenth-century political history. 'No one who ever saw it', wrote J. W. Mackail, the biographer of William Morris, 'will ever forget the strange and indeed terrible sight of that grey winter day, the vast sombre-coloured crowd, the brief but fiery struggle at the corner of the Strand, and the river of steel and scarlet that moved slowly through the dusky swaying masses when two squadrons of the Life Guards were summoned up from Whitehall.' Morris himself wrote a moving death chant on Alfred Linnel who died in hospital as a result of injuries received from the police on 'Bloody Sunday': it included the refrain:

> Not one, not one, nor thousands must they slay,
> But one and all if they would dusk the day.

Throughout this period of discontent and agitation, the most important of the London Socialist organizations, the Social Democratic Federation, quite deliberately based its tactics on the theory that the metropolis should lead the country. 'London, with its enormous concentration of wealth, population, and active commerce,' Henry Hyndman declared in 1888, 'must lead England safely along the path to a new period.' It was he who suggested that the Chartist failure to mobilize the metropolis had been the chief cause of the downfall of Chartism. His 1887 pamphlet *A Commune for Socialism* was a vigorous plea for municipal socialism. The Fabian Society also, which provided a non-revolutionary approach to reform, was London Socialism, not the metropolitan version of a provincial agitation. One of its first influential publications was *Facts for Londoners*, a fifty-two page pamphlet which came out in 1889 nine months after the first elections to the London County Council. When the Fabians went to the provinces, they found just as unfamiliar a world awaiting them as the Anti-Corn Law League had found when it went from Manchester to London.

The consequences were historically interesting. This was not the first time that London had taken the lead in attempting to shape national attitudes, but it was the first time for many years, almost the first time since Wilkes. The fact that the London Socialists of the 1880s and 1890s were more interested in 'theory' than the labour leaders of the provinces was to lead both to resistances and to complications. And there were at least as many difficulties in diffusing the 'secularism' of many of the London Socialists in the provinces during the 1890s as there had been in pressing the 'nonconformity' of the League on the London of the 1840s. The secularists were in a small minority even in London, but, as Dr Hobsbawm has written, 'secularism is the ideological thread which binds London labour history together, from the London Jacobins and Place, through the anti-religious Owenites and co-operators, the anti-religious journalists and book-sellers, through the free-thinking Radicals who followed Holyoake and flocked to Bradlaugh's Hall of Science, to the Social Democratic Federation and the London Fabians with their unconcealed distaste for chapel rhetoric.'

In all parts of the country it was recognized during the 1880s and 1890s that London politics 'counted', congenial or uncongenial though they might be held to be. When writers in periodicals wished to talk of the 'politics of the future', as they often did, they looked closely and carefully at the politics of London. Chamberlain had given Birmingham the international reputation of being the city with the civic gospel: the Socialists, divided though they were, dreamed of turning London into a great 'commune'. They gained inspiration not so much from the earlier record of agitation in the English provincial cities as from the revolutionary struggles in foreign capitals, the mayoral campaign of Henry George in New York in 1886, for example, or the successes of French Socialists in Parisian municipal elections. The Christian Socialists caught the contagion. When Scott Holland, the Christian Socialist, talked of the need for a 'municipal heart', he meant in the first instance a municipal heart for London.

The setting up of the London County Council should be seen against this background. So long as London was managed by the Metropolitan Board of Works, it could not canalize its discontents through constitutional channels nor could it provide its citizens with the opportunity of participating fully in the politics of social control. A County Council would be a forum. The leader of its dominant party, the Conservative critics of their own government feared, might become more powerful than 'any prime ministers and some monarchs'.

The path to reform led through the thickets of popular discontent. All mid-Victorian attempts at reform had always failed – in 1858, 1863, 1868, 1869, 1870 and 1875. They had been characteristic mid-Victorian exercises, with a Municipal Reform Association, founded by James Beal in 1866, using Radicals like John Stuart Mill as their spokesmen in Parliament. Mill had described the Corporation of the City of London in his *Representative Government* as a 'union of modern jobbery and antiquated foppery'. The language was memorable, but the only result of Mill's efforts was the usual parliamentary impasse. The very delays meant paradoxically that once London's reform was tackled seriously by a government, it would be bound to create considerable public controversy: the debate about the local government of London would be caught up in the debate about the 'advance of democracy'. The London Municipal Reform League, founded in 1881, with the barrister J. F. B. Firth as chairman – he had written a book called *Municipal London* five years earlier – was determined to apply every kind of democratic pressure.

In 1884, however, when Sir William Harcourt introduced his official London Government Bill, he was backed only listlessly by Gladstone, who could be eloquent about local government in general but was slow to see its needs in particular. The two men disagreed about the police clauses of the

Bill and the priority which should be given to it. The Liberal government was heavily over-committed in 1884, and Egypt and Ireland pushed London to the periphery of cabinet discussions. Harcourt urged that 'unity of government in the metropolis' was the only method of achieving real reform, and his enthusiasm created a far greater measure of alarm among Conservatives than any previous government had ever done. 'Had this Bill become law,' the *Quarterly Review* maintained, 'the consequences would have been almost revolutionary. A representative body, elected by the direct vote of the mass of electors, the majority of them ignorant of public affairs, and many of them extremely poor, would have held control over the richest and the most important urban area in the world.' Such fears went far beyond concern for administrative efficiency or dislike of centralization. They touched the jangling social nerves of late-Victorian politics. There was such great opposition to Harcourt's Bill inside and outside Parliament, particularly in the City of London, where vast sums were spent on an anti-reform campaign, that the Bill was withdrawn at a late period of the session.

The withdrawal did not satisfy either side. Harcourt's Bill had not only 'done much to awaken interest and nurture opinion on the question of the practicability of the government of London by a single municipality': it had focused attention on the social question. Mass meetings of protest against its withdrawal were held throughout London: only low attendance in the House of Commons demonstrated the apathy provincial Members of Parliament could still display when they were confronted with the affairs of the capital city.

Four years later, after a number of officials of the Metropolitan Board of Works had been accused, quite exceptionally, of questionable dealings in connexion with the letting of land, a Royal Commission was appointed to investigate the allegations and a Conservative government decided, at last, to change the government of London. It was part of a general change in the framework of local government. 'We cannot shut our eyes', C. T. Ritchie, the government's spokesman, said in March 1888, 'to the fact that whereas every other borough in the country possesses a body directly representing the ratepayers, no such body exists in London. There is no one elected by or responsible to the ratepayers.' Governments had kept their eyes firmly shut for decades, but at a time when local government as a whole was being reformed, it was difficult to allow London to remain the great exception. Ritchie proposed, almost incidentally, that London should be made not a borough but a county, with the same political and administrative apparatus as the other counties which were being given new constitutions at the same time. London, like Middlesex or Yorkshire, was to have its Lord Lieutenant, its Bench of Magistrates, and, above all, its elected County Council.

The strength of the Conservative Government was sufficient to carry the Bill, despite the fact that it had not figured in election programmes and that fears had only very recently been expressed by Conservatives that London, once it was given an elected Council, would become 'a popular and democratic community with enormous powers of taxing the richer classes, a gigantic seat of intense and interested agitation, a mighty fulcrum and lever for popular force'. There was a vague echo in Ritchie and Salisbury's legislation of 1888 of Disraeli's Second Reform Bill of 1867, 'the leap in the dark' which the young Salisbury had so bitterly opposed.[1] The views of Joseph Chamberlain and the Liberal Unionists seem to have influenced both the content and the timing of Salisbury's legislation.

At the same time, although the Metropolitan Board of Works disappeared, unlamented, under a cloud of suspicion, the new Act could scarcely be described as a radical measure. The forty-one vestries and district boards survived intact. So did the City of London, which A. G. Gardiner, the great Liberal journalist, called 'a sort of obsolete appendix at the centre'. Another Member of Parliament described it as 'a sort of strange animal pickled in spirits of wine'. The survival of vestries and City meant that there was continuing doubt about who spoke in the name of London. And many other Victorian institutions survived alongside the City – the Metropolitan Asylums Board, the thirty-eight Boards of Guardians, the Burial Boards, the Thames and Lea Conservancy Board, and

1. For the episode of the leap in the dark, see *Victorian People*, Chapter X.

the School Board, the last of which, unlike the rest, had introduced a breath of democracy into London in 1870. All the critics of the Bill in the House of Lords argued not that it was too extreme, but that it did not go far enough.

Radical or not, the Bill had possibilities, particularly for reformers. Mrs Besant said that it provided 'the machinery of social democracy', and reformers had long complained that they lacked proper machinery. It certainly gave scope for militancy. The presence of powerful vested interests in London which had gone untouched for decades necessarily involved the reformers in a sequence of fierce contests. They welcomed the opportunity. They disdained all the trappings of civic power – coats of arms, robes and maces, even entertainment allowances – and concentrated on the substance. In their contests they were bound to become public figures if they were not public figures already. Men like Lord Rosebery, who was elected as the first Chairman of the London County Council, were already public figures – the Council attracted a relatively large number of people who were: others, like Sidney Webb, stepped into the limelight from small Fabian Society meetings and propounded a philosophy of municipal reform for the millions.

The outlines of a militant programme were stated in a new paper, the *Star*, in 1888, the year that the reform act was passed. 'To rich and poor alike,' the *Star* complained, 'the present system of government is inimical, leaving the greatest and wealthiest city in the world the most helpless and impotent before any emergency. One fall of snow, a single fog reduces London to chaos.' A 'distinct radical policy for London', financed by the taxation of ground rents, was needed at once. The Fabians claimed that they helped to formulate the programme. The music critic of the *Star* was the Fabian, George Bernard Shaw, who, according to the first Fabian historian, promptly 'collared' the paper and wrote in it 'on every subject under the sun except music'. In fact, the *Star* was the voice of a broadly based 'radical revival', pressing for housing and land reform as well as progressive taxation three years before the Fabians. Sidney Webb drafted the influential *The London Programme* of 1891, which was commented upon in all the newspapers and periodicals. Webb demanded the abolition of the vestries and district boards, the equalization of London's rates and the creation of a 'municipal common fund', the taking over by the Council of the monopoly of water, gas, markets, trams and docks, the 'municipalization of hospitals' and a large-scale municipal housing programme. The last proposal, Webb stated, was already being put into effect in Glasgow, Liverpool, Dublin, Nottingham and Huddersfield. Why should London fall behind? 'Here, as in other matters, London's problem is too vast to be coped with except by London's powers; and it must now be pretty clear to all serious students, that London's poor can only be rehoused by London's collective effort.'

Just as Chamberlain referred to the example of other cities in his advocacy of reform, so did Webb in London. Many of the examples were foreign, but London could not be left out. 'Is it not time', Webb asked, 'that some of our individualist friends learned a little of the municipal history of their own country?' He was frequently compared with Chamberlain. 'Since Mr Chamberlain arose in Birmingham', wrote W. T. Stead, the editor of the *Pall Mall Gazette*, 'there has been no man so much like him as Mr Sidney Webb, who aspires to be Mr Chamberlain of London – only more so.' Beatrice Webb, who might have married Joseph Chamberlain, did not see much likeness 'in character, opinion or circumstances' in the two men who figured so prominently in her life: Stead was right, however, in suggesting that with the advent of the Fabians and their allies the cause of municipal reform passed from Birmingham to London.

The Fabian philosophy of municipal reform went much further than that of Chamberlain.[1] *Facts for Londoners* (1889) was

1. One of the least satisfactory parts of J. L. Garvin's *Life of Joseph Chamberlain* is his completely inadequate account of the years 1888 to 1891. He reveals none of Chamberlain's thoughts on the reform of London government, and provides only a bare summary of events year by year. His remark that the details 'have long since lost their interest, except for specializing historians' is an extremely curious comment in a work of this scale. In the *Radical Programme* (1885) Chamberlain urged that London should be split up into several 'cities' of the size of Birmingham, federated merely for common purposes in a central body.

full of ideas as well as facts. Throughout *Fabian Essays* (1889) a sense of the need for strong 'municipal action' was expressed, and the 'municipalization' of industry was bracketed in the same clause with 'nationalization'. It was their concern for municipal enterprise which gave the Fabians the nickname of 'gas and water socialists'. The phrase is meaningful only when it is remembered that London, unlike many of the provincial cities, controlled neither its gas supply nor its water supply and that disease and death were proven results of ineffective private administration. What was taken for granted in many parts of England was still contentious in London.

'The municipal history of the century is yet unwritten', Webb remarked in the first of his Fabian essays: he obviously believed that it had important lessons for London. George Bernard Shaw in one of his essays spelled out what some of the lessons were. He condemned the Manchester School for its protectionist concern for protecting private enterprise from the competition of public enterprise (he was unfair to Manchester's local government system in saying this) and told London ratepayers that they would be free from the fear 'of hungry mobs, nuclei of all the socialism and scoundrelism of the city' if only they would elect councils which would deal boldly with land speculation and unemployment. He started his survey with the experience of London in mind. 'Lord Hobhouse and his unimpeachable respectable committee for the taxation of ground values are already in the field claiming the value of the site of London for London collectively; and their agitation receives additional momentum from every lease that falls in.' The process of growth in London was, according to Shaw, directly related to its political and administrative needs. Just as Birmingham Nonconformists had carried over from religion into politics their belief in the need for a gospel, so the Fabians carried over from political theory into party action their belief in the need for public control. In the eyes of their opponents they were 'crudely collectivist'. 'To the Fabians the governing body of London, by whatever name it may be called, stands in the position which the "State" assumes in the eyes of their Continental teachers. It must be large enough and strong enough to accumulate many varied powers and duties in its own hands; and it must exercise extensive functions, which are not merely civic, but also ethical, social, and political.'

When the first London County Council, with its 'Progressive' majority, was elected in January 1889, the Fabian Society played little part in the story. Very soon, however, the Fabians were encouraging the Progressives, some of whom needed no encouragement, to think in large terms. Webb maintained that although the London County Council had been 'born in chains', that is to say its powers were far smaller than those of a provincial city, it could and should formulate objectives which would transform its role. Rosebery agreed with this approach. At the first meeting of the Council in March 1889 he said that as time went on the Council should ask for larger powers 'on the ground of the vast population that we, their freely elected members, represent in this Council'. The first years of the Council were spent in trying to wrest additional powers from the government. 'The L.C.C.', wrote one of its first members, 'is the local Parliament, absorbing all the functions and organs of local government.' To their opponents, the Progressive majority, which remained in control of London politics until 1907, consisted of 'Reds, Cads and Fads'. They included in 1889 J. F. B. Firth, who had won the support of old radicals, like Thomas Hughes, author of *Tom Brown's Schooldays*,[1] and new radicals, like Sir Charles Dilke, Sir John Lubbock, later Lord Avebury, cultured and intelligent, John Benn, a leader of outstanding ability who was anxious 'to give London a soul', and G. W. E. Russell, whose brilliant portraits of late-Victorian society, along with the writings of Escott, recapture mood and atmosphere far more effectively than most historical monographs. To the left of the Progressives was John Burns, 'the man with the red flag', who had been one of the trade-union leaders in the great dock strike of 1889: he had stood for the Council on a platform of 'practical socialism'.

Although Rosebery said that he was anxious that the new Council should not be divided on rigid party lines, it very quickly became a party council. The Progressives took all but

1. See *Victorian People*, Chapter VI.

one of the nineteen aldermanic places for themselves – they had keenly criticized the institution of aldermen in Ritchie's Bill – and when the press attacked them the only effect of the attacks was to strengthen the sense of solidarity of the group. The attacks were often unfair and far-fetched: they were accused, for example, of being 'inferior to the old-fashioned type of candidate who was sent up by the vestries to the moribund Board of Works', and their political programme was branded as 'extreme' and even 'confiscationist'. Much play was made of the argument that rates would increase after the change of constitution and that ground rents would be taxed.

In fact, despite the Fabian stiffening, many of the Progressives were moderate Liberals in outlook, and the quality of service and leadership they provided was far superior to that in most provincial cities. They had much leeway to make up in certain necessary and uncontentious matters of local government, like the fire brigade service, and they were no more ambitious in their attitude to other services, particularly gas and water, than many provincial local authorities had been for decades. Ten per cent of their members sat in Parliament as well as in the London County Council, a very high proportion, and those who did not sit there represented what Frederic Harrison called 'a new force in English politics, a popular power of which we have yet no experience'. They worked with zeal, the most lively of them holding that a County Council 'ought to be driven night and day like an Atlantic liner between New York and Liverpool!' Rosebery himself presided at forty-four public sittings of the Council in a year and attended 280 regular meetings of committees, a total commitment at least as great as that of a Minister of the Crown.

Criticisms of service of this kind were obviously misplaced, and Burns clearly turned the flank of the attack on the Council by declaring that the Council was being howled down by a 'corybantic press' and 'thwarted by politicians'. Far from leading a conspiracy, it was in danger of becoming the victim of a Conservative conspiracy. The first history of the London County Council, written by W. Saunders in 1892, was quietly and cautiously favourable to the new body. 'For three years, it seems, London has been governed by a Council two-thirds of whom are "Radicals and Socialists". The result might inspire confidence even in the minds of those who originally felt some distrust. Is there a single particular in which the government of London can be shown to be worse than it was three years ago? In numerous cases it has certainly improved.'

The Progressives stood on a more definite party programme at the elections of 1892 than they had done three years before. They were spurred on by the Fabians whose *Fabian Municipal Programme* and *Questions for Town Councillors* were very widely circulated. Sidney Webb wrote a number of articles for *The Speaker* in 1892 which were subsequently published under the title of *The London Programme*. The objects of the programme have already been stated: they also included a 'fair wages' clause in municipal contracts, a trade-union objective. The tone of the articles was militant. They contrasted the 'anarchy' and 'spoliation' of the past with the rich promise of the future. 'We dare not neglect the sullen discontent now spreading among its [London's] toiling millions. If only for the sake of the rest of the Empire, the London masses must be organized for a campaign against the speculators, vestry jobbers, house farmers, water sharks, market monopolists, ground landlords, and other social parasites now feeding upon their helplessness. Metropolitan reform has become a national, if not an imperial question.'

Webb hoped to appeal to 'all good citizens', whether Liberal or Conservative: he knew that the demand for municipalization, which was a main objective in the Fabian case for Socialism, could also be related to the need for efficiency and, as in Birmingham, to the demand for lower rates. For good or ill, however, the whole tenor of his argument was to widen the gap between the parties in the London County Council. Beatrice might boast about the way in which the most enlightened 'Moderates' were being converted to parts at least of the Fabian programme, but the increasing reliance of the Progressives on an intricate apparatus of party discipline, complete with whips, encouraged the Moderates to turn increasingly to the Conservative Party. In addition, there were a number of Fabians in the Council who shocked the Conservatives by putting forward the full Fabian case. Webb himself was returned for Deptford: he retired from the Colonial Office in order to devote most of his time to the Council's work. Associated with him were other Fabians who had been returned with big majorities ranging from 600 to 1,500. They all agreed with the answers Webb once gave to a Royal Commission's question – 'What limit would you put to the extension of municipal taxation?' 'I have no limit.' 'Supposing it had to go as far as twenty shillings in the pound?' 'That is a consummation I should view without any alarm whatever.' Their zealous activity inside the London County Council riled Salisbury, who described it in November 1894 as 'the place where collectivistic and socialistic experiments are tried ... where a new revolutionary spirit finds its instruments and collects its arms'.

As leader of the Opposition in Parliament – the Conservatives were out of office from 1892 to 1895 – Salisbury told his party not to be shy of using all its political power and machinery 'for the purpose of importing sound principles into the government of London'. The response was almost immediate – the founding of a London Municipal Society which linked Moderates and Conservatives. It went to work eagerly, backed by the press, and at the third elections for the Council in 1895 the electors returned an exactly equal number of representatives from the Moderate and Progressive parties. 'Many of the working-class voters and the small tradesmen', the Moderates claimed, 'had begun to see that the most tangible result of the activity of the Progressive Party was likely to be a great rise in the rates.' The Progressives remained in power only with the support of the aldermen who stayed in office from the former Council. Beatrice Webb consoled herself with the thought that Sidney's majority at Deptford had scarcely fallen and his poll increased. She also admitted that the Moderate successes had raised the standard of good looks of the London County Council and made it 'the most accomplished, distinguished, and even the most aristocratic, local government body in the world'.

Party division made London's government more exciting. It also shifted the debate about London from interest to principle. Even the Moderates were forced to suggest specific policies in 1895, notably support for the social reforms advocated by Joseph Chamberlain in his new guise as a leading figure in an essentially Conservative ministry. The Moderates were very strong in some of the vestries where they were subject to far less publicity than the London County Council received, and at the elections of 1898 they 'strained every nerve' to win power. The contest was especially heated because the Conservatives were now firmly entrenched at Westminster – they won the general election of 1895 – and there was a notable sense of rivalry between 'the two Parliaments', the one national and the other metropolitan. Salisbury went out of his way to attack the London County Council, and he was backed by his Liberal Unionist allies. The Progressives won a substantial victory, however, and the Fabians were left musing whether it was not a better guarantee of social advance to have a Conservative government in power and Progressives capturing local authorities than to have a weak Liberal government in power alongside a 'provincial shopocracy'.

One of the chief effects of the Progressive victory in 1898 was a renewal of Conservative determination to reorganize the constitution of the London County Council. It had been known for several years that the Conservatives contemplated creating new local authorities in the metropolitan boroughs to reduce the power of the London County Council. They totally rejected the advice of a Royal Commission appointed by the short-lived Liberal government in 1893 to inquire into 'the Proper Conditions under which the Amalgamation of the city and the county of London can be effected'. The Commission, which was presided over by Leonard Courtenay and included an ex-mayor of Liverpool and the Town Clerk of Birmingham, advised that the old City of London should form part of a greater city of London with its own Lord Mayor and Corporation. This was anathema to the Conservatives and to the London Municipal Society, who were anxious not only to preserve the City but to delegate 'the real municipal work' of

London to 'local councils' to whom 'the dignity and status of municipal corporations' should be given.

Their anxiety was welcomed by a number of large London vestries, notably Westminster and Kensington which presented petitions for charters of incorporation in 1897. Kensington pointed out that it had a population of 170,165 and a rateable value of £2,107,901; Islington's rateable value was higher than that of Leeds or Sheffield; St Pancras had a bigger population than Bradford, Bristol, Hull or Nottingham. In February 1898 twenty of the largest vestries presented a petition to the government urging that they should have conferred upon them 'greater civic dignity, at least commensurate with that possessed by numerous municipal boroughs of far less importance'. A conference of these vestries was held under Conservative enterprise at Westminster, and a later conference of Radical vestries was held at Islington.

The Unionist Bill of 1899 met the demand of the large vestries by introducing a dual system of government by County Council and a second tier of authorities, all of which were to be full municipal boroughs. In doing so, it seemed to the Progressives to be following a policy of 'divide and rule'. Such a policy had been advocated quite openly, indeed, in 1888 by Earl Fortescue, a former secretary of the Poor Law Board and chairman of the Commission of Sewers. The London County Council, he warned his readers in the *Nineteenth Century*, would have too much power, and it would be better to have two Councils, one north and one south of the river. '*Divide et impera* is a sound maxim.'

The Conservatives followed the advice, but altered the formula. Their decision in 1899 to create twenty-eight new metropolitan borough councils as a 'counterweight' to the power of the London County Council led to a bitter fight which the Council was bound to lose. The government's case, however, was not a strong one. London's unity was unquestionable, yet Balfour specifically rejected all suggestions that special machinery should be devised for linking together officially the London County Council and the new municipalities. Any system of liaison, he maintained, would 'inevitably drag these councils into the political vortex in which the

London County Council appears to flourish'. The Conservatives were more afraid of London's 'Radical complexion' than they had ever been.

Asquith mused on those more profound questions about the identity of London which arise, as we have seen, in every generation. 'When you call these new authorities municipalities,' he said, 'you are giving them a false name.... What is a municipality as we here in England understand it? A municipality is a community of spontaneous growth, self-governed and self-contained: a whole in itself. There is only one community in the metropolis which answers that description, and that is London as a whole.'

G. K. Chesterton could scarcely have dissented, yet in his fantasy he gave to the municipalities the flags and banners which the London County Council had scorned. He chose deliberately, as so many critics of utilitarianism had always done, to separate romance and efficiency. He once paid tribute to the Fabian Society for preaching the cause of 'cleanliness and common sense' and asked to be given 'the drainpipes of the Fabian Society rather than the pan-pipes of the later poets', but, given his general philosophy of life, he was bound to prefer 'municipalism' to 'metropolitanism'.

The Fabians believed that London's 'metropolitanism' had a provincial relevance also. When they turned to the Saxon past and, like Patrick Geddes and C. B. Fawcett, wrote of creating a 'new heptarchy', a union of provinces, there were many of them who wished to see the provinces of England governed by superior London County Councils. Instead of Birmingham in London, it was to be London in Birmingham. The age of gas had been the age of the city: the age of electricity would be the age of the 'region'.

4

Beatrice Webb took the chair in March 1903 at a Fabian meeting, when one of the most remarkable recent recruits to the Society, H. G. Wells, spoke along these lines in an address with the formidable title of 'The Question of Scientific Administrative Areas in Relation to Municipal Undertakings'. Wells, who believed that the Victorian age had been an age not of achievement but of waste,[1] became a member of the Fabian Committee on the Reform of Local Government which produced the 'New Heptarchy' series of Tracts.

Wells created more crises inside the Fabian Society than inside local government, but whatever he did, he remained a passionate Londoner. He might argue, as he often did, that Englishmen were losing their 'sense of place' and becoming 'de-localized', but as a writer he was as fascinated by the city of London as the leading characters in his first novels were. Its size appealed to him. So did its metropolitan character. He strongly disliked the provincial cities, which he did not know at first hand. Once he drew a distinction between what he called 'de-localized man', a man with a wide range of interests, and 'localized man' who was caught up in 'party politics'. Late-Victorian London is mirrored in his work, particularly the Greater London of the outer suburbs. He was born at Bromley in Kent in 1866, and as a young man he got to know most of London intimately, exploring it suburb by suburb and writing about his explorations in his 'real-life novels'. It is for this reason that he is as interesting to the student of late-Victorian cities as Mrs Gaskell or Disraeli to the student of the late 1840s. The political imagination in his novels – above all his desire to peer into the future – and his assessment of urban experience and of the significance of such factors as transport in urban life guarantee him the attention of historians. And for all his criticisms of the Victorians, he was in some sense a Victorian himself, not least, as G. V. Ellis has noted, in his unquenchable thirst to accumulate knowledge and in his conviction that knowledge thus accumulated may be assimilated by any person of moderately intelligent mind.

In *Love and Mr Lewisham* (1900) Wells described the student world of Exhibition Road which he had discovered, like Mr Lewisham, as a prize scholar at the Normal School of Science at South Kensington. This was Prince Albert's London, the by-product of the Great Exhibition of 1851. Late-nineteenth-century South London lives in this book also, with the 'grand fogs' of Clapham, 'horses looming up sud-

1. See above, p. 17.

denly out of the dark', 'street lamps, blurred, smoky orange at one's nearest' and 'the glare of shop windows'. *Kipps* (1905) went back further in Wells's life to the routines of life in the retail shops which he had known so well since his boyhood. (One of his first jobs was in the 'Manchester' department.) From Folkestone, where many of the chapters are set, London appeared to be 'a distant country'; when Kipps got there, London became 'his third world'. At first it was 'vast and incomprehensible', a place of 'intricate complexity'. Yet it was full of wonders. He compared the stiff narrowness of provincials in Folkestone with the *savoir-faire* of metropolitans in London. Three days before his marriage Kipps showed his bride-to-be the mighty terraces, the stucco tanks and the prehistoric monsters of the Crystal Palace gardens at Sydenham. The brief description of their visit should be set alongside the innumerable descriptions of visits to the Great Exhibition of 1851: it brings out the difference between mid- and late-Victorian England.[1]

Kipps ends, however, not in London but in Hythe, and it was *Tono Bungay* and *Ann Veronica*, both published in 1909, which first probed fully into the 'vast endlessness' of London from 'the miles of streets of houses' in central London, designed and erected for the prosperous middle classes 'in a perfect futility of building in the 'thirties, 'forties and 'fifties', to outer suburbia, where improved means of transport were encouraging a huge late-Victorian wave of speculative building. In *Ann Veronica* we read of 'Morningside Park . . . a suburb that had not altogether, as people say, come off'. 'It consisted, like pre-Roman Gaul, of three parts. There was first the Avenue, which ran in a consciously elegant curve from the railway station into an undeveloped wilderness of agriculture, with big yellow brick villas on either side, and then there was the Pavement, the little clump of shops about the post office, and under the railway arch was a congestion of workmen's dwellings. The road from Surbiton and Epsom ran under the arch, and like a bright fungoid growth in the ditch there was now appearing a sort of fourth estate of little red-and-white rough-cast villas, with meretricious gables and very brassy

1. For the Great Exhibition, see *Victorian People*, Chapter I.

window blinds.' This was neither East End nor West End: it was the new London which belonged unmistakably to the late nineteenth century. Victorian London was in danger of submerging the rest.

Wells followed Dickens in describing the process of muddle whereby London grew. Dickens had noted in *Dombey and Son* the 'disorderly crop of beginnings of mean houses, rising out of the rubbish, as if they had been unskilfully sown there'. Wells drew conclusions. In *Tono Bungay*, which he later described as his most ambitious novel, he wrote scornfully of the notion that 'it was nobody's business to see that people were well-housed under civilized conditions'. London as a city was a place of contradictions. George Ponderevo, the hero, is told by his uncle that London takes a lot of understanding but is nonetheless 'the richest town in the world, the biggest port, the greatest manufacturing town, the Imperial city, the centre of circulation, the heart of the world ... a whirlpool, a maelstrom'. George himself discovers, however, that London can be dingy, 'slovenly, harsh and irresponsive'. He even formulates what he calls 'a kind of theory of London'. He thinks that he can discern 'lines of an ordered structure out of which it has grown' and 'detect a process that is something more than confusion of casual accidents, though indeed it may be no more than a process of disease'.

George starts with 'the Great House region', which includes nineteenth-century Belgravia and finds 'its last systematic outbreak round and about Regent's Park'. Quite mistakenly, he attributes not only South Kensington but 'the museum and library movement' throughout the world to the example set by the elegant and leisured gentlemen of taste who graced the great London houses of the past. More percipiently he notes that the great railway termini had been kept as far as possible from the 'Great House region'. South London, however, has no protecting estates and it sprawls shapelessly, as Sir Walter Besant also noted, without any real centre of its own. East London suggests to him 'something disproportionately large, something morbidly expanded, without plan or intention, dark and sinister toward the clean clear social assurance of the West End'. Greater London also implies disproportionate growth, 'endless streets of undistinguished houses, undistinguished industries, shabby families, second-rate shops, inexplicable people who, in a once fashionable phrase, do not exist'.

George's theory, like the 'theories' of Manchester in the 1840s, ends with the same kind of doubts about the future balance of threat and opportunity. 'All these aspects have suggested to my mind ... the unorganized, abundant substance of some tumorous growth-process, a process which indeed bursts all the outlines of the affected carcase and protrudes such masses as ignoble, comfortable Croydon or tragic, impoverished West Ham. To this day I ask myself will those masses ever become structural, will they indeed shape into anything new whatever, or is that cancerous image their true and ultimate diagnosis?' To this question about growth, which revealed Wells's intense passion for plan and order and his distaste for all manifestations of disease, there was a further question about London which held dangers for the future. How would London respond to the 'invasion' from overseas, the pressure of foreign immigration? Would it be able to assimilate 'elements that have never understood and never will the great tradition'?

As George meditates on his 'theory' of London, which he elaborates on omnibus rides 'east and west and north and south', he begins to revise his first impression that London is a 'smoke-stained house wilderness'. 'The whole illimitable place teemed with suggestions of indefinite and sometimes outrageous possibility, of hidden but magnificent meanings.' Coningsby might well have mused in similar fashion about Manchester. Indeed, in all Wells's early real-life novels the education of the main character starts not with books but with London. In George's words, 'London took hold of me and the Science, which had been the universe, shrank back to the dimensions of tiresome little formulae.'

Beatrice Webb called Wells 'a romancer, spoilt by romancing': she added, however, in language which would have been appreciated during the 1840s, that 'in the present state of sociology, he is useful to Gradgrinds like ourselves'. Wells certainly served the same purpose as the social critics of early-Victorian England in directing attention in his novels to what he felt were the main social issues of his day. The business system with which late-Victorian London was associated, however, was quite different from the industrial system of early-Victorian Manchester: its instruments were neither mill chimneys nor mill hands but prospectuses and bank clerks. The dockworkers and the unskilled new unionists were part of history but not part of fiction. Advertising and credit kept the business system moving. When George's uncle told him that in his patent medicine enterprise he was minting faith, George concluded that the whole commercial system was no more than his uncle's career writ large. It was a 'swelling, thinning bubble of assurance' and its arithmetic was just as 'unsound, its dividends as ill-advised, its ultimate aim as vague and forgotten'. Perhaps it was drifting on to some treacherous circumstance which would parallel his uncle's personal disaster.

Wells's characters came for the most part neither from the established middle classes nor from the working classes. They were caught up not only in the sprawl of London but in the dubieties of social mobility – 'the career ouvert to the Talons'. London's geography mirrored the mobility. The second chapter of *Tono Bungay* is called 'Our Progress from Camden Town to Crest Hill'. The progress was from shabby impecuniosity to marble staircases and a golden bed, the facsimile of a bed in Fontainebleau. Beckenham was a 'transitory phase'. Chislehurst had grounds rather than a mere garden: it was associated in George's mind with asparagus, plovers' eggs, a butler and week-ending in hotels. Crest Hill was a palace at the top, a 'delirium of pinnacles': like the mansions of Melbourne, its indefinite extension was abruptly halted by the financial collapse of its owner. The owner was 'the symbol of this age ... the man of luck and advertisement, the current master of the world'.

The end of the novel suggested new twentieth-century themes – the replacement of luck by science, the struggle of truth against advertisement. It even mentioned journeys by aeroplane. The aeroplane was to consolidate the Victorian revolution in transport. Just as suburban railways had united the great urban province of London, so aeroplanes, Wells believed, would unite the world. The last chapter, however, dwelt on the 'symphony of London' itself. We move back to the beginning, to the disorderly present – to a London without plan, intention or comprehensive desire. 'This', Wells concluded, 'is the very key to it all.'

The New Machiavelli (1911) repeated these themes. Wells could never escape from them: they even provided the scaffolding of imagery for his science fiction. Bromstead in *The New Machiavelli* had been transformed during the Victorian age, transformed for the worse in an age of 'slovenly and wasteful experiment'. Like London itself, it demonstrated for Wells the inadequacies of 'headlong, aimless and haphazard methods'. 'It is as unfinished as ever; the builders' roads still run out and end in mid-field . . .; the various enterprises jumble in the same hopeless contradiction. . . . Pretentious villas jostle slums, and public houses and the tabernacle glower at one another across the cat-haunted lot that intervenes.' Penge, to which the hero of the novel moved after Bromstead, introduced him to 'the interminable extent' of Outer London – the Crystal Palace grounds were a frontier region – and also to its streaks of beauty, dark walls reflecting moonlight, the steam and sparks of railway trains, and the bright colours of railway signals.

On a visit to Switzerland, the clean prosperity of Basel made London seem ill-organized and dirty. 'Muddle' was the enemy, and the hero, like the Fabian Wells of 1903, thought of working in the Local Government Board and 'had great ideas about town-planning, about revisions of municipal areas and reorganized internal transit'. Order and planning were always the twin points of Wells's socialism. The difficulties of achieving it were discussed in the last part of the novel, which concerns a far more sophisticated London – intellectual and political London – than that to which Wells had introduced his readers in his earlier books.

It would be easy to dismiss Wells as a quite exceptional writer, new both in his preoccupations and purposes, if it were not for the novels of his friend George Gissing, which link the

London of Dickens with the London of Edwardian Fabianism. Gissing, who was born in Wakefield in Yorkshire in 1857, shared none of Wells's hopes. For a brief time he was a socialist, but he quickly abandoned all belief in the creation of socialistic utopias. He had no faith in science, either, approaching it with dread, almost with terror. Abroad, Wells might find inspiration in Basel: Gissing found it in Naples, 'the most wonderful and fearful place in Europe'. He was profoundly thankful that he had seen it before it became completely 'modernized and sanitarized'. In the last years of his life he stated frequently, both in his novels and his letters, that he preferred the country to the town. As early as 1885, indeed, he had written to his brother that he would surrender a year of his life for six months in the country 'with leisure to read Homer under a cottage roof'. In the last of his works, the autobiographical *Private Papers of Henry Ryecroft*, published in 1903, the year of his death, Gissing's hero wishes to add a new verse to the Litany praying God's blessing on 'all inhabitants of great towns, and especially for all such as dwell in lodgings, boarding houses, flats or any other sordid substitute for Home which need or foolishness may have contrived'.

Yet Gissing, like Wells, was pre-eminently a London novelist who dwelt on the detail of social circumstances in the capital. By a fascinating inversion of early-nineteenth-century experience he approached London from Manchester, with Chicago *en route*. As a youth he had spent a time at Owens College, Manchester: like Wells he was a scholarship holder. From Manchester he was sent down for a breach of discipline, consorting with a prostitute. After living for several years in America – he wrote short stories in Chicago – he moved to London for most of the rest of his life. Nearly all his characters are London characters, and when he talked about social problems, as he often did, he saw them in a London context. London provided him with his facts, his experiences, and his ideas.

The experiences were those of a sensitive artist, often a lonely artist, struggling in a great city, at times seeking to identify himself with the great social forces of his day, at other times searching for neutral ground from which to observe them. Many of his books deal with the alienation of the creative artist in 'modern' society. There are hints not of Wells but of Baudelaire in Gissing's feeling that the city kept the artist free and yet enslaved him. 'Multitude and solitude', Baudelaire had written, are 'terms that an active and fertile poet can make equal and interchangeable.' The city, particularly the city by night, made the equation possible. The reaction of the artist to the city was a welter of sensations. Baudelaire talked of 'bathing himself in a crowd': Gissing made the familiar comparison of London with an ocean. He held to the comparison when he talked not of the artist's sufferings but of his opportunities. 'Struggling for a living in London', he once wrote, 'is very much like holding yourself up after a shipwreck first by one floating spar and then by another; you are too much taken up with the effort of being yourself, to raise your head and look if anyone else is struggling in the waves.'

Gissing's facts, political and social, were meticulously observed. In 1887 he spent Sunday evenings on Clerkenwell Green to see what happened at Radical demonstrations. He went to Mile End Waste in 1888 to hear Annie Besant addressing a street meeting of the girls at Bryant and May's match works. 'I am bound to be in London,' he wrote characteristically in 1889, 'because I must work hard at gathering some new material.' On another occasion in 1893 he describes in his diary how he got up at 3.30 a.m. to explore the city to find an idea for a short story and went to Waterloo to see the 5.50 train off before having breakfast.

He was just as careful an observer as Wells was of the growth of greater London. In his novel *In the Year of Jubilee* (1893), he described how an enclosed meadow, part of the land attached to a country mansion, had become a new and unfinished housing area. 'London, devourer of rural limits, of a sudden, made hideous encroachments upon the old estate, now held by a speculative builder; of many streets to be constructed, three or four had already come into being, and others were mapped out, in mud and inchoate masonry.... Great elms, the pride of generations passed away, fell before the speculative axe, or were left standing in mournful isolation to please a speculative architect; bits of wayside hedges still shivered in fog and wind, amid hoardings variegated with placards and scaffolding black against the sky. The very earth had lost its wholesome odour; trampled into mire, fouled with builders' refuse and the noisome drift from adjacent streets, it sent forth under the sooty rain, a smell of corruption, of all the town's uncleanliness. On this rising locality had been bestowed the title of "Park".' For Gissing the symbols of progress could always become symbols of decay. It was not only artists who became alienated: suburbs could become alienated too.

Wells found railway trains genial: he admired the beauty of the coloured signals, but reserved his excitement for aeroplanes. Gissing, like Dickens, found locomotives frightening: hurrying crowds, black fumes and demon engines went together. 'Over the pest-stricken regions of East London, sweltering in sunshine which served only to reveal the intimacies of abomination, across miles of a city of the damned, such as thought never conceived before this age of ours . . . the train made its way at length beyond to utmost limits of dread, and entered upon a land of level meadows, of hedges and trees, of crops and cattle.' That was at the far end of the line. At the London termini Gissing noted the new facts of social and economic life which added to the dimensions of fear. 'High and low, on every available yard of wall, advertisements clamoured to the eye: theatres, journals, soaps, medicines, concerts, furniture, wines, prayer meetings – all the produce and refuse of civilization commenced in staring letters, in daubed effigies, base, paltry, grotesque. A battleground of advertisements, fitly chosen amid subterranean din and reek.' Before *Tono Bungay* was written, Gissing looked closely and in misery at the people and the problems Wells was to describe: there is little in Wells's social criticism that had not already been anticipated.

Gissing's ideas were relatively simple. The London crowds fascinated and horrified him as much as the masses of Manchester had fascinated and horrified the writers of the 1840s. He compared 'the thud of footfalls numberless' on the London pavements to a huge beast purring to itself in stupid contentment. Like the writers of the eighteenth century, he called the beast a mob, and expressed alarm that it was growing in extent and influence. 'As a force, by which the terror of the time is conditioned, they, the crowds, inspire me with distrust, with fear; as a visible multitude, they make me shrink aloof, and often move me to abhorrence. For the greater part of my life the people signified to me the London crowd.' At the same time, Gissing detested conventional middle-class ways of life, whether they were associated with confident possession or with shabby gentility.

Some of his conclusions were conservative, but at heart he was a late-Victorian rebel against the power of convention. His rebellion was muted because he was preoccupied with failure. He had collected as great a store of specialized information about people who failed as Samuel Smiles had collected of people who succeeded. He was keenly concerned also to depict people who suffered from educational or social deprivation. While he distrusted all general theories of class, he was acutely sensitive to all tensions of status. In what is probably the best of his novels, *New Grub Street* (1891), the very unromantic hero's wife (he is really an anti-hero) breaks with her husband because she cannot tolerate being the wife of a clerk 'who is paid so much a week'.

The novelist was in a strategic position to observe such facts of metropolitan social existence. In early life Gissing seems to have believed that he should go further and attack 'highly condemnable' evils and seek to influence 'thinking and struggling men'. 'I mean to bring home to people the ghastly condition (material, marital and moral) of our poorer classes, to show the hideous injustice of our whole system of society, to give light upon the plan of altering it, and, above all, to preach an enthusiasm for just and high ideals.' This approach aroused the interest of Frederic Harrison, the Positivist leader. Later, however, Gissing deplored such political attitudes and scorned the identification of the artist with political movements. He came to believe that the novelist should avoid all exaggeration. He should describe and argue, not preach or exclaim: above all, he should not identify his own individual suffering with the social suffering which lay behind political protest movements. One of the characters in *New Grub Street*, Biffen, a very unsuccessful novelist, condemns all drama in novels which springs from 'stage necessities'. 'Fiction hasn't yet outgrown the influence of the stage on which it originated. Whatever a man writes *for effect* is wrong and bad.'

Gissing was a great admirer of Dickens, about whom he wrote an interesting critical study, but he pointedly contrasted Dickens's desire to please as many of his readers as possible with his own unflinching determination to present the truth of life, even if the truth were 'savage' and its presentation made him unpopular. He also admired Carlyle who, among others, had taught him that it was the truth about life which really mattered. The link with Carlyle is itself a link with the 1840s. There were many other links. A novel like *The Nether World*, written in the year of the great dock strike, has as its theme 'those brute forces of society which fill with wreck the abyss of the nether world'. Even the language, the mould in which the novel is set, recalls the 1840s. Gissing was criticized for exactly the same reasons as Mrs Gaskell – leaning to one side in the social struggle rather than the other. He pushed the criticism aside by accusing his critics of attributing to him as author all the opinions which he put into the mouths of his characters. 'It is not I who propagate a doctrine,' he had to say on more than one occasion, 'but the characters whose lives I tell.' When sentiments expressed by Waymark, one of the characters in his interesting novel *The Unclassed* (1884), were treated as if they were the author's own, Gissing was at pains to point out that 'if my own ideas are to be found anywhere, it is in the practical course of events in the story; my characters must speak as they would actually, and I cannot be responsible for what they say.'

Such criticisms and rejoinders were unusual. For the most part Gissing's work left far less of a mark on his contemporaries than the social novels of the 1840s had done in their own generation. It is the social historian who can find most of interest in the novels, particularly about London, its social texture and the new influences which were changing it. So far, however, his novels have received far less attention from historians than the factual surveys of Charles Booth, the social and religious pamphlets which awakened the public conscience, and even the novels of H. G. Wells, which are themselves less popular today than many of the mid-Victorian writings Wells despised.

Gissing knew more about the social texture of London than most of the early-nineteenth-century writers on Manchester knew about the social texture of industrialism. Very occasionally also, like Booth, he was able to capture the excitement and fascination of London as well as its distresses. Booth had frankly admitted that one of the reasons why he preferred life in big cities was that the individual counted for less and the community for more: he felt that the liveliness of people in the city was not destroyed by the crushing weight of 'ruthlessness' and 'heartlessness'. Gissing, for all his talk of the superior charms of the country, admitted that there was no help in visions of Arcadia. He lingered over what he once called 'the dear old horrors of London', even the foggy, gas-lit 'labyrinth' between Tottenham Court Road and Leicester Square. 'The atmosphere of Wakefield', he admitted, 'would soon make the completest dullard of me.' After his sister had visited London with him, he wrote to her in 1886, not, I believe, with irony – 'I don't think that you will ever forget that first peep of London, shall you? That walk about the City, the first glimpse of St Paul's with the sun on it. . . . You remember too that glorious concert in the Albert Hall. . . . You will never hear "I dreamt I dwelt" sung more splendidly than it was that night nor perhaps, "Come into the garden, Maud".'

5

A book on Victorian cities could well end in the Albert Hall with this unexpected reference to two of the favourite songs of the age which were sung, perhaps not so well, in every city in the country. There was a further aspect of London, however, which added to its dominance in the 1880s and 1890s and which Gissing realized more clearly than most of his fellow-writers. He could realize it just because he was in a position to compare life in Wakefield with life in London as well as life in London with life in a rustic cottage in Devonshire.

Much as he loved London, Gissing feared its increasing hold on the literary world. He noted also in *New Grub Street* (1891) how it was becoming the undisputed centre of the new trade of writing for 'the quarter educated; that is to say the great new generation that is being turned out by the Board Schools, the young men and women who can just read, but are incapable of sustained attention'. *New Grub Street* is the first important novel to describe the beginnings of 'mass communication', 'the whole new development of journalism' which was associated with *Tit Bits* (Gissing called it *Chit-Chat*) and Lord Northcliffe. His analysis may not have gone very deep at this point – as Raymond Williams has suggested – but he was surely right to draw attention to the new hold which London was beginning to acquire over the provinces. The year 1896, when Lord Northcliffe founded the *Daily Mail*, was also the year when Oscar Wilde started his prison sentence, a critical date in the story of the late-Victorian revolt. In the same year young Marconi arrived in London to sell his wireless inventions to the Post Office, the first cinema show was presented in the West End, a critical date in modern social and cultural history, and the 'red flag' era of motoring came to an end. The 'Yellow Press' was to have more long-term significance than the 'Yellow Book': significantly the adjective 'yellow' had earlier been applied to the cheap railway novels or 'yellow backs' which first appeared on the book-stalls in the mid-1850s.

The 'communications revolution' has gone through many phases. In the late nineteenth century it was firmly centred on London. It was to alter profoundly the relations between provinces and capital, as Gissing perceived. 'I dislike the immense predominance of London,' he wrote. 'Whoever saw a book worth having come from anywhere but London? . . . Yet, of course, this is altogether wrong. London is increasing in size past all reason, her evils growing simultaneously.' It was not only the 'quarter educated' whom London was addressing. The *avant-garde* movements of the 1890s depended on London too. 'Town life nourishes and perfects all the civilized elements in man,' Wilde wrote in 1891. 'Shakespeare wrote nothing but doggerel verse before he came to London and never penned a line after he left.'

Between the age of *Grub Street* and of *New Grub Street*, between the age of Wilkes and Webb, the provinces had come to enjoy a vigorous life and a considerable measure of social and political power. Moreover, the provincial cities had developed as cultural centres, however limited their conceptions of culture sometimes were. During the 1890s the pattern was changing again. The decay of the provincial press, which rose to great heights in the mid-Victorian years and down to 1890, was implicit in the rise of the cheap national press, subsidized by advertisement. The power of advertisement threatened the independence of local markets and often the independence of the small producer. Other economic tendencies also were making for co-ordination, concentration and impersonalization. Socially the days of autonomous regional sub-cultures were doomed. The amateurism that lay behind much provincial culture was being made to look archaic in an age that turned increasingly to 'professionals' and 'experts'. The founding of new local societies which had reached a peak in the mid-Victorian years was beginning to decline.

The changes were, in a sense, all part of the same process. The geographical smallness of England made it difficult to maintain that 'decentralization' of which de Tocqueville had made so much. Small towns and country villages were being drawn into the orbit of regional capitals before the regional capitals were themselves drawn into the orbit of London. The provincial newspapers – as the *Yorkshire Post* noted in 1866 when it began as a daily – broke down 'the line of demarcation between town and country'. 'Railways and the electric telegraph have established a frequency of locomotion and a circulation of ideas which rob country society of all that inertness and stagnation which were once its peculiar characteristics; and the highest questions of politics and literature are discussed with as much knowledge and vivacity in a country town or a secluded manor house as in the smoking room of a London club. A precisely analogous change is visible in journalism. London newspapers have grown less exclusively metropolitan. County newspapers have grown less exclusively provincial.'

It was too soon in 1866 – or in 1890 – to predict the ultimate decline of the provincial press. The number of provincial papers had increased from 375 in the mid-1850s to 1,225 in the mid-1880s. An article in the *Fortnightly Review* in 1890, indeed, spoke of the 'distance' between the London papers and the 'bettermost provincial papers' diminishing 'at a rapid rate'. The provincial papers were often cheap and they were quick to take up new inventions, like the new linotype process, with the *Leeds Mercury* leading in 1889. What was overlooked by the spokesmen of 'provincialism' was that in time cheap national papers would find it possible to appeal to the same groups in all parts of the country by cheaper and more direct journalism. Popular papers like *Reynolds Weekly* and the *Telegraph* already pointed the way by 1866. London was to call the tune, increasingly after 1890, if need be by harnessing the provinces. To maintain its supremacy in circulation the *Daily Mail* soon established an office and printing works in Manchester. Its editor boasted that it was read simultaneously in Brighton and Newcastle-upon-Tyne. This was nationalization of news and opinions long before the nationalization of industry.

Political programmes in the 1890s were beginning to be nationalized also. The formation of the Unionist ministry of 1895 was a turning point, and the 'imperialism' which was so generally discussed during the next six years in all the towns and cities of the country pulled national opinion together, for or against, more effectively than any of the domestic issues of the previous sixty years. All older domestic issues, particularly parliamentary reform, had immediate local implications: imperialism had not. It is interesting to note that Victor Branford, Patrick Geddes's brilliant and formidable colleague, held that the growth of imperial bureaucracies was an active agent transforming the industrial town and leading it to yield in power and influence to the metropolis. Socialism, too, with its demand for national 'minimum standards' and for national control of industries, was an agent. It was a nation-wide phenomenon in the 1890s, although the different shapes that it assumed were determined, in part at least, by local factors – the 'metropolitanism' of the Social Democratic Federation, for instance, against the 'provincialism' of the Independent Labour Party.

Given these changes in the formulation of national objectives, it is scarcely surprising that there were many signs in the 1890s, as we have seen in the case of Middlesbrough, that enthusiasm for specifically local politics was declining among men of intelligence and leadership. The same was true of Manchester. In Birmingham also there were complaints in the early years of the twentieth century that there was a 'deterioration' in interest in local politics. *The Times* commented that 'there is a disposition to think that the same degree of credit can no longer be got out of local administration by the leisured or aspiring citizen, as was the case especially in Birmingham a few years ago'.

Certainly fewer initiatives in late-Victorian national politics were traceable to local provincial pressure groups. There was a marked contrast with the 1830s and 1840s when Bulwer Lytton had written that 'society in the Provinces is often more polished, intellectual, and urbane, than society in the Metropolis'. Lytton talked of 'drawing-room gossips' affecting to speak in 'the tone of Birmingham liberalism'. 'While social habits descend from the upper class to the lower class,' he went on, '*political* principles, on the contrary, are reverberations travelling from the base to the apex of society.' By the 1890s the 'base of society' was at least as articulate in London as it was in the provinces, and what was being said in the capital was being echoed in Manchester or in Middlesbrough.

The full history of the relations between London and the provinces remains to be written. It will be a more tangled history than that history of the municipalities which Webb asked for when he was formulating the *London Programme*. Relations between metropolis and provinces have gone through many different phases: they may not remain static in the future. The techniques for studying them will need to be carefully investigated before any conclusions are generally acceptable. There will have to be cross-references to what happened to Chicago in relation to New York. There seems to be a marked contrast with French experience where, as a recent French historian has put it, the provinces came into their own after 1871 and the dominion of Paris, which had lasted since 1789 and had been most pronounced under Napoleon III, had been broken.

This much is clear. At the end of Victorian England, London, the London of the Jubilees, of the Empire, of the great political movements, was in the ascendant. What Webb and Gissing said, Arthur Conan Doyle attempted to corroborate, employing techniques which scarcely bear a moment's scrutiny but which were also being employed in the United States. Turning aside from Baker Street and Sherlock Holmes, he wrote a remarkable article on 'The Geographical Distribution of British Intellect' in the *Nineteenth Century* for August 1888, a similar article to one composed in the United States showing that localities with a population of 8,000 or more gave birth to almost twice as many men of note as their proportionate share. For Britain Conan Doyle compiled a 'roll of honour' of 'the various men who have during the latter part of the Victorian era attained eminence in literature, poetry, art, medicine, sculpture, engineering, law and other walks of life'. This is his conclusion on London:

On analysing the English roll of honour, it will be found that out of the 824 names, 235 belong to men who are of London birth. Putting the population of London at one-seventh of that of England proper, it has clearly produced very much more than its numerical share of the intellect of the nation. To reduce it to figures, the proportion of celebrities amongst the born Londoners is about one in 16,000, while in the provinces it is not more than one in 34,000. This is as might be expected when one takes into account the centralization of wealth in London, and the way in which for centuries back the brightest intellects in every walk of life have been drawn towards the metropolis.

CHAPTER NINE

Epilogue: Old Cities and New

From Exeter last year to Liverpool this is a great change for the British Association. It is from the cloisters to the mart; from silence and past memories to the noise of tongues and active present occurrences.

DR JOHN DORAN, F.S.A., in *The Athenaeum* (1870)

Exeter is ancient and stinks!

ROBERT SOUTHEY (1799)

I

THERE were many complaints from the provinces during Queen Victoria's reign both about the facts of London's growth and the increasingly vociferous claims Londoners made concerning the superiority of metropolitan over provincial ways of life. The most bitter complaint in the last years of the reign was that Londoners did not know anything at all about the provincial cities. Social and parliamentary circles in London were linked with the country, with Trollope's Barsetshire, for example,[1] but they had few links with 'large and populous places'. Curiosity about the new ways of life in Manchester or Birmingham had long withered away. 'The life of a provincial city', wrote T. Wemyss Reid, the journalist and biographer, in 1888, 'presents no charms to the cultivated but superficial observer. Biography has nothing to say of the men who have had most to do with the building up of the fortunes of Birmingham and Manchester, of Liverpool and Leeds. The local reputation must acquire the stamp of metropolitan

1. Note Taine's notes on the London season during the 1860s – 'During the London season the Sunday night trains carry away a great number of land-owners who are going forty, eighty, a hundred miles to attend committee meetings, deliver "lectures", hold meetings, fulfil the duties of their unpaid offices on the bench, in the council, or in the church.'

approbation before it is thought worthy of notice even by the most thoughtful of social students.'

The African parallel came to mind yet once more. 'Those who are diligent in observing and investigating the manners and customs of some tribe in the heart of Africa, or of the inhabitants of some island in the South Seas, are altogether ignorant of what is passing at their own doors, under their own eyes, in towns which, although they cannot boast of the historic glories of the great capitals of Europe, are even now superior to them in wealth and population, and are laying broad and deep the foundations of a future destiny which may vie in interest and importance with that of some of the most famous cities of the ancient world.' The complaint was a legitimate one, and historians have done little more to offer redress than contemporaries did. They have continued for the most part to ignore 'local biography' and even local main-springs of national policies. The result of negligence has been persistent misunderstanding.

At the same time people in the great provincial cities have often contributed to their own neglect. They frequently destroyed their papers and in some cases failed to pass on to their heirs the oral record of their experience. They were just as likely to misunderstand London as Londoners misunderstood them. Certainly they were always ready to condemn London as being disastrously different when it suited them to say so. G. J. Holyoake, the Birmingham Radical, who grumbled about London's ascendancy, was himself criticized in the provinces for transporting with him wherever he went dangerous 'metropolitan' ideas. It is interesting to set alongside his views of London the comment made about him in a Newcastle paper, the *Newcastle Journal*, in 1851. He had just given a lecture on secularism in the 'capital of the north' after a debate lasting three nights. 'The town of Newcastle-upon-Tyne', the local newspaper complained, 'has been for some time past infested with a succession of low, scurrilous vagabonds, too lazy to work and too illiterate to earn an honourable livelihood. . . . It would seem as if there were to be no end of this abomination – that the inexhaustible channels of vice and immorality in the metropolis were to be distributed in innumerable streams over the provinces, and that this town was destined to receive considerably more than its proportionate share.'

Perhaps the fiercest abuse of London came from the oldest provincial cities, those with a tradition of civic pride which antedated not only the Victorian age but the industrial revolution. Some of them perpetuated the tradition of 'country' versus 'capital', a tradition which was far older than the word 'provinces' itself, a word which only came into general use during the 1780s. One of the most colourful eighteenth-century historians of York, Francis Drake, who published his *Eboracum or the History and Antiquities of the City of York* in 1736, argued, for example, that the 'overgrown bulk' of London was the consequence not of trade but of political and administrative aggrandizement. He bemoaned the 'melancholy prospect' of York declining still further unless it could increase both its trade and its social and political functions. Liverpool, he said, was gaining in importance in the North of England, while the privileged York merchants 'locked themselves from the world'.

The same point was made by John Bigland in his *Topographical and Historical Description of the County of York* in 1819. 'The genius of trade is too often cramped by the spirit of exclusion.' It was no surprise when the Parliamentary Boundary Commission of 1832 concluded that York was no longer 'a northern metropolis' or when a York alderman a year later bemoaned the fact that it was no longer true 'that there could be no stir in any part of the county but what it was felt in York'. Ten years later even the local inhabitants themselves were said to be suffering from decay; the city was not only ceasing to attract, it was failing to hold. 'This much neglected city,' one local writer called York in 1843, 'which the citizens have suffered in this age of improvement to be eclipsed in advancement by many a younger and less noted town.'

By the nineteenth century many of the older towns and cities of England were echoing complaints of this kind about 'overgrown' London, 'pushing' and 'resourceful' provincial rivals, and local 'decay'. The detailed story of the older cities remains to be told. No general account of Victorian cities would be complete, however, without some consideration of the relationship between the rapidly growing Victorian cities and those which changed far more slowly. York and Wakefield must be set alongside Leeds and Bradford, Coventry against Birmingham, Bristol against Liverpool, and old cathedral cities, like Exeter, Norwich and Lincoln, against Oldham or Middlesbrough or Barrow-in-Furness.

Yet the 'old' towns and cities did not form a homogeneous group. Some, like Exeter and Norwich, had been centres of industry: as their staple industry declined, the vitality of urban life diminished also. The provincial culture of Norwich when Harriet Martineau was a young woman there shone brightly compared with the culture of the mid-Victorian years. In Exeter a local newspaper could regret in 1881 that 'we do not grow, simply because the process of growth, as a city, ceased many generations back'. Other old provincial centres had owed nothing to the presence of a staple industry; they had carried out religious or marketing functions and in some cases had stood out as county capitals, like Lincoln, for centuries, and they passed not so much into eclipse as into torpor, 'bells ringing, clocks striking, men drinking, women talking and children dancing, eternally' as one Lincoln diarist put it in 1771.

Again it is impossible to generalize fairly. Some old towns failed to benefit from the 'railway age', a number of them by choice: others participated directly in its blessings and derived new importance and prosperity from the railway. Some old communities grew quite rapidly in population in the nineteenth century. Northampton, for example, more than doubled in numbers between 1801 and 1831: Carlisle almost doubled. Norwich, however, increased only from 61,304 to 62,294 in the exciting decade from 1821 to 1831 and in 1871 it had only just over 80,000 inhabitants. York grew very slowly from 23,692 in 1801 – a sizeable population by the standards of that day – to 36,303 in 1851, with the coming of the railway and the railway workshops offering new hope to the city, while Wakefield, once so much more important a market centre than Bradford, rose from 16,597 only to 22,065 during the same period. These rates of growth were dwarfed not only by new industrial communities such as Huddersfield, which grew by more than 30 per cent in every decade in the first half of the nineteenth century, but by Cheltenham which increased more than eleven times and by Brighton which increased nine times.

The pride in progress which animated the growing communities even when it did not guide them was not, of course, entirely absent in all the older cities. In Exeter, which had been intemperately criticized by Southey, James Cossins, a local writer, stated in 1877 that 'persons who had been absent from *Semper Fidelis* for many years, on revisiting the old city, declare that it is improved and so much altered that they cannot recognize some of the localities.' In Norwich, which faced many difficult problems as its industry contracted and its wealth diminished, there was genuine pride in the fact that the city very quickly adopted Ewart's Public Libraries' Act in 1856.[1] In the same year it opened its new cemetery, 'the greatest improvement effected in Norwich during the present century', one local writer called it. Norwich had its own triennial Music Festival, the first of which had been held in 1824, and although its sponsors attached special importance to the interchange of good feeling and hospitality between the city and county, they admitted, like the sponsors of the Birmingham Festival, that they were seeking to make a particular contribution to the 'cheerfulness and happiness' of the whole body of citizens.

In Bristol, where the adaptation and reorganization of the docks to meet new needs was difficult and protracted and the great industries which have made the city such a thriving centre in the twentieth century were either in their infancy or unborn, frequent hymns to progress were sung. 'It is very gratifying to know', the *Bristol Times and Mirror* noted in August 1869, 'that our ancient and well-beloved city is getting on in the world; and that in despite of business depression and the various discouragements which beset commercial affairs at present, we are in a state of vigorous life and progressive advancement.' Although the writer conceded that 'we cannot, perhaps, expect to compete with Liverpool, with its

1. Like Bristol, it had offered free library services to its citizens in the seventeenth century.

enormous manufacturing background of Lancashire and Cheshire', he ended boldly: 'Onward movement is the universal order of the day, and our good city is resolved not to be a laggard in the competitive race.'

Many comparisons with Liverpool were made in nineteenth-century Bristol. They reflected a more distant but economically far more real rivalry than that between Liverpool and Manchester. During the first decade of Queen Victoria's reign harbour charges at Bristol were higher than at Liverpool, and there was increasing local opposition to the Dock Company. Caricatures of a completely derelict Bristol harbour appeared, and the case for transferring the docks to the Corporation was argued with increasing passion on lines not dissimilar to those put forward in the battle for the repeal of the Corn Laws in Manchester. The chairman of the Free Port Association was called Bright: this was the most coincidental of the parallels.

The docks were acquired by the Corporation in 1848, and dues drastically reduced. Physical improvement was slower, however, and in 1851 a disgruntled local citizen complained, not unlike Drake in eighteenth-century York, that the corporation of Bristol was still falling far behind that of Liverpool in ideas and energy. He suggested 'with the utmost deference' that the whole corporation should travel *en masse* to Liverpool to make a personal inspection of the docks and commercial buildings there. Arguments about what form improvement and physical development should take continued to dog Bristol's progress, but the tonnage of foreign vessels using the port increased more than four times between 1846, when the Free Port Association sprang to life, and 1874. 'There is every year', the *Bristol Times* remarked in 1870, 'a steady forward, not flashy, spirit of enterprise growing up amongst us. While the old firms are more than holding their own, new ones are settling in the city and a healthy and competitive activity is producing results of which we have substantial proof in the new and splendid houses and villas that girdle our town, and the enlarged outlay of their inhabitants.'

Bristol, like Coventry, had to wait until the twentieth century for an unanticipated burst of new growth. In Newcastle-upon-Tyne and Nottingham, however, old and new co-existed, supplying two different ingredients of local pride – tradition and the sense of what a historian of Newcastle called in 1827 'the improving spirit of the age'. Richard Grainger, the builder, John Dobson, the architect, and an intelligent and sensitive town clerk, John Clayton, son of the previous town clerk and member of an influential local dynasty, worked out what would now be called a central development plan, completed in 1839, and bequeathed to the city a fine collection of handsome buildings which gave it a distinctive air of dignity and grace. Grey Street, which its admirers preferred to London's Regent Street, was described by Gladstone as the best modern street in Britain. The Central Exchange with its domed, colonnaded and rounded corners was as fine an edifice as any town hall. The railway station also was an impressive monument to early-Victorian progress. Although Dobson's original plan for it was completely modified, it was rightly hailed as 'the first example of railway architecture in the kingdom' and Dobson's conception of the role of the railway station architect should be set alongside Barry's conception of the role of the architect of town halls. As 'public works, structures seen by thousands of people', Dobson argued, railway stations might do much 'towards improving the taste of the public'.

Newcastle's golden age was over by the last years of Victoria's reign, when the city grew fastest, from less than 100,000 in 1851 to 215,000 at the beginning of the new century. Old city though it was and centre of perhaps the oldest industrial region in the country, the problems it bequeathed to the twentieth century were Victorian problems. If the richest part of its legacy was its cluster of nineteenth-century buildings, the chief social consequence of its precocious industrialization was that it had managed to keep its Town Moor before younger industrial cities lost their 'green lungs'.

By contrast, the lateness of enclosure in Nottingham, which, like Newcastle, was an industrial centre before the industrial revolution, added, as we have seen,[1] to nineteenth-century

1. See above, p. 29.

urban pressure and increased the seriousness of social problems. Nottingham had been described by Defoe as 'one of the most pleasant and beautiful towns in England'. By 1845, however, when an Enclosure Act was at last passed, the streets and courts of old Nottingham, 'cribbed, cabined and confined', presented 'a spectacle of the most lamentable description'. According to a government commissioner, they were as unhealthy and unpleasant to live in as 'anything within the entire range of manufacturing cities'. 'The entire quarters occupied by the labouring classes form but one great nuisance.' The absence of enclosure had also had the effect of driving out population to industrial villages on the periphery – 'colonies' they were sometimes called – such as Sneinton, Radford and Lenton.

The effect of the 1845 Enclosure Act was 'magical', according to two of Nottingham's Victorian historians. 'Factories, warehouses, and residences sprang up all around, as if by the wave of a magician's wand. Land and building societies were formed, by means of which persons of limited means were enabled to purchase small allotments at a moderate price and to build upon them on the most favourable terms. The transformation wrought upon the town as to its extent and aspect surpasses anything which has been witnessed elsewhere in Britain within the same brief space of time.' This was the new face of Nottingham, yet with no Dobson or Grainger or Clayton to see to its beauty. Even at the time, a local editor was driven to write that 'a man may ... ask what sort of exhibition this New Nottingham will make when its irregular streets are fully occupied by their equally irregular edifices.' There was some improvement in standards of working-class housing, yet for the most part contemporaries were satisfied by the rhetoric of urban pride rather than by its substance. On the one hand, they were flattered to hear from outsiders that 'Nottingham is become the Manchester of the Midlands ... with regard to its warehouses Nottingham cannot fail to astonish any visitor.' On the other hand, they continued to extol the antiquity of their inheritance. The same local historians who extolled Victorian magic were insistent that Nottingham was 'no creation of the present: it is a growth of ages. Gradually, by painful and laborious steps, by slow, measured degrees, it has been built up into the form of mingled strength and beauty which we now behold [1893]. Amid the unresting roll of our modern machinery and the din of today's business we may hear, if we only listen, the voices of a venerable past.'

2

The detailed study of older cities and their success or failure to adapt themselves to changing circumstances would require an examination of demography, economic and social structure, politics, administration and regional influence. Three general points stand out. First, the reform of municipal corporations in 1835 had different results in different places. In some cities it had the air of a revolution: in others little changed. Second, the urgent problems of urban life which are usually associated with the growth of new industrial towns – particularly problems of health, housing and public order – were just as acute, and sometimes more acute, in the old communities. Third, failure to adapt or inability to adapt successfully to the Victorian 'age of improvement' was not necessarily a once-and-for-all failure. Many of the older cities have enjoyed a twentieth-century renaissance, economic and political. The 'newest' of Britain's post-war cities, Coventry, at the very heart of twentieth-century history, is an old city. With the recent erection of new universities at York and Lancaster a medieval pattern of rivalry may be restored. Nottingham's great growth was sustained not by its old industries, like framework knitting, which were in a critical state in the 1840s, but by what Professor J. D. Chambers has called 'vast economic reinforcements' – chemicals, tobacco and cycles. Bristol likewise has owed much of its new prosperity to new industries. In all these cases pre-Victorian amenities contribute to the appeal of old cities in twentieth-century conditions. So great, indeed, is the appeal that many of the most interesting and impressive Victorian landmarks are in danger of being totally destroyed. A whole age could well be blotted out.

The wind of reform which blew through the older cities on the eve of 1835 has never been fully examined by historians.

What is certain is that while in new communities like Manchester and Birmingham the demand for parliamentary reform in the years 1830–32 was associated with economic pressures – for free trade or currency reform – in old communities one of the most powerful forces was the demand for a change in the structure of the old corporations, often for both political and religious reasons. A Select Committee of the House of Commons reported in 1833 that 'Corporations as at present constituted are not adapted to the present state of society', and the Whig barristers who constituted the Municipal Reform Commission were appointed to travel around the country to collect evidence which would substantiate the need for change. Their secretary was Joseph Parkes, a shrewd and extremely well-informed Radical, who had served his political apprenticeship in Birmingham during the Reform Bill struggle of 1830–32. Parkes was born in Warwick and knew the contrast between closed corporations and incorporated industrial cities: he considered the Municipal Reform Act to be 'the postscript to the Reform Bills'.

The same emphasis can be traced in the old corporation boroughs themselves. One hundred and seventy-eight boroughs scheduled for reform in the 1835 Act out of the 285 places which were examined included places as small as Arundel, Blandford, Llandovery and Tenby – all with less than 2,000 inhabitants – and Bath, Bristol, Coventry, Exeter, Hull, Leeds, Leicester, Liverpool, Newcastle, Norwich, Nottingham, Plymouth, Portsmouth, Preston, Stockport and York – all with more than 25,000. In many of these places there were fierce local attacks on what a Plymouth writer called 'a shabby mongrel aristocracy' that was dominating urban life. Nonconformity sharpened the attacks, deepening the sense of moral righteousness without necessarily widening civic horizons.

The story of Leicester, which was virtually taken over by the Nonconformists in 1836, has been ably told by R. W. Greaves and A. Temple Patterson. At the dinner to celebrate the passing of the Reform Bill in Leicester a local Radical speaker explained to the assembly that their next goal must be 'municipal reform and an electoral magistracy within five years'. The same speaker remarked three years later that if the House of Lords threw out the Whig Municipal Reform Bill 'we will act in concert with Birmingham and other great towns; we will re-form our unions.' While Radicals planned concerted action with groups of Radicals in the new cities, the defenders of the old order also sought to combine together. The Town Clerk of Leicester, Thomas Burbridge, circularized other closed corporations, like Coventry and Norwich, to offer co-operation in opposition.

Although the Municipal Reform Act of 1835 did not revolutionize the functions of local government – this was not its intention – in a community like Leicester it did involve a genuine transfer of power. The 'ascendancy of Nonconformity' determined Leicester's municipal history for the rest of the Victorian age. It could be a destructive as well as a creative or critical force. Much has been written in this book of Victorian civic pride. One of the first actions of the new elected Leicester Corporation (with only sixteen churchmen out of fifty-six) was to sell the plate, crockery, glass-ware and mace, the symbols of older civic pride. The rebuilding of Leicester was carried out in this spirit. 'Few towns', wrote the compiler of a local gazetteer in 1846, 'have been more extended and improved than Leicester in the last ten years . . . by the formation of new streets and the erection of elegant public edifices.' He added that 'the old street architecture of Leicester is rapidly vanishing . . . the greater part of the half-timbered lath-and-plaster houses, remarkable for their grotesque gables and picturesque appearance, have given place to plainer but more convenient dwellings.'

In Exeter also the struggle for parliamentary reform and the struggle for municipal reform were intimately associated. The power of the Cathedral was involved, and the controversial personality of its Bishop, Dr Henry Philpotts. The report of the Commission on Municipal Corporations was less severe on the local oligarchy in Exeter than on some others – the Corporation was condemned chiefly for not having gained 'the confidence of the inhabitants' – and the consequences of reform were less drastic. Part of the story of the city has been set out vividly by R. S. Lambert in his book on Thomas

Latimer, *The Cobbett of the West*, a crusading reformer who arrived in Exeter in 1827 to work as a journalist for the *Devonshire Chronicle*. Appointed editor of the *Western Times* in 1831, Latimer thundered against closed corporations of every variety, believing that they were in any case doomed once Parliament itself had been reformed. Yet in Exeter the newly elected council which was brought into existence by the 1835 Act remained under Tory control. Whereas in Leicester and Norwich there was a visible 'revolution', in Exeter the most important result of the setting up of the new Council was the increased pressure of publicity which its affairs received. This increased publicity for a time added a new excitement to local life, but there was no transfer of power. Latimer's motto 'Tempora Quaeram' was the motto only of a minority. There was only one Liberal mayor in Exeter between 1835 and 1868. In such circumstances journalism of the kind which Latimer provided until his death in the 1880s was a necessary ingredient in the just management of local affairs.

Nottingham, unlike Leicester, Exeter and Norwich, had a closed Whig Corporation under the 'old system' with little will or intelligence to perform the limited functions expected of it, despite the influence of Dissenters and Evangelicals. The new voting arrangements in 1835 actually reduced the size of the electoral roll. Six of the seven former aldermen were returned once more to assure continuity. The Town Clerk also was reappointed, and it was left to the new Councillors – three out of twenty-four were new to local government – to represent the 'revolution in local government'. The new Council achieved very little until after the passing of the Enclosure Act of 1845.

In practice, in all the old communities which were reformed in 1835, the 'revolutionary' impetus behind new demands for representation provided little incentive to improved local government. The narrowness of the ratepayers' franchise and the Radical emphasis on retrenchment and economy inhibited civic action. So too did the dislike of many Dissenters for what the *Nonconformist* in June 1846 dismissed contemptuously as the demand for 'parks, museums and well-ventilated houses' in place of 'civil rights'. Nor did the fact that vested interests were well entrenched and often well represented on the Council make crusading easy.

In Leicester, which provides a particularly interesting example, the vigour of the attack on 'privilege' was not matched by vigour in improvement. During the late 1840s the most significant division in local government was that between the 'Economy Party' or 'Economists' and the 'Improvers'. The 'Economists', led by Joseph Whetstone, the chairman of the Finance Committee of the Town Council, were as radical as their 'improving opponents', one of whom was William Biggs. Both Whetstone and Biggs were Nonconformists, and both had been active in the battle for parliamentary and municipal reform before 1835. Whetstone was anxious to improve Leicester's sewerage, drainage and water supply, but he bitterly resisted Biggs's attempt to associate 'improvement' of this kind with the building of a new town hall, the widening of the High Street, the extension of the Market Place and the provision of recreation grounds for the working classes. The *Leicester Chronicle* protested against 'Brummagem' town halls and accused Biggs of preferring 'embellishment' to drainage. It was left to the Tory *Advertiser* to point out that Biggs was as entitled as Caesar to find his town brick and leave it marble.

The fierce debate between the two radical factions in Leicester illustrates how in old towns, like new ones, questions of economy became central in local political argument. Biggs might refer to the 'merchant princes' of near-by Derby as 'the Medici of their day', but in Derby also the first mayor of the newly elected Town Council of 1835, Joseph Strutt, stated plainly at his first public dinner that the Council's duty was first to establish an efficient police force and second to be as economical as possible. When the Derby Improvement Commissioners, given their authority by an act of 1792, sought to use their powers to improve Derby's water supply in the early 1840s their early efforts were vigorously resisted by the Council. The fact that the Council was Whig and the Improvement Commissioners mainly Tory gave a party cast to the differences, but in matters of substance the debate turned as much on economy as did the debate in near-by Leicester. 'The town councillors', the Commissioners complained in 1842, when there was a threat to the continued existence of the Commission, 'are elected by the small ratepayers, and are greedy persons who will not be found to co-operate in the removal of nuisances and other evils.... It is safer and wiser', they went on, 'to leave the expenditure of money to those whose properties are affected, and who are the best judge of what should be done as to general improvements and the promotion of health and happiness.'

The Derby Improvement Commissioners and the Council made their peace with each other during the later 1840s and acted 'conjointly' in many matters. Even then, however, there was a limit to the improvements they could carry out. In the opinion, probably exaggerated, of a government inspector in 1849, the town was more in need of having applied to it the provisions of the Public Health Act of 1848 than most towns in the country. The struggle about economy continued, however, long after 1849. When the attempts were made to carry a comprehensive new Improvement Bill in 1852 a Ratepayers' Association was founded to defend the interest of the small property-owners and the Council had to yield. It was not until national legislation had been carried in 1858 that Derby was able to achieve reforms which its most public-spirited citizens had wished to achieve a decade before.

The debate about improvement in Derby cut across political lines. So too did the debate in Exeter and Norwich. During the 1840s antagonism between Radicals and Tories which had dominated Exeter during Latimer's early years there gave way to new disagreements. By 1845 when the first borough rate was levied, 'the Reformers', R. S. Lambert concludes, 'were distinguished from the Tories by little more than a zeal to prevent wasteful expenditure.' The Victorian historian of Norwich, A. D. Bayne, is even more terse in his judgement. Referring to the elections of 1871 which led to Conservative gains after a long period of Liberal ascendancy, he remarks that 'there was, however, a wonderful unanimity on both sides of the Council Chamber, when questions of expenditure came under consideration.'

Given the stress on 'economy' in many of the old cities,

the local leaders found it at least as difficult to deal with the problems of public order and public health as the local governments of the new communities. Many of the problems of urban life were common to both. Some of the least healthy districts in the country were to be found in the old districts of old towns, districts which were ravaged during the cholera outbreaks. It needed the jolt of cholera in old communities to stir opinion: in newer cities opinion in favour of reform usually developed more gradually and with less drama. Exeter was particularly hard hit by the cholera epidemic of 1832 when there were 1,200 cases and 400 deaths among a population of 28,000. York had 185 deaths in 1832 and 176 in 1849. The disease hit the poorest sections of the population most severely: it was, in more than one sense, as the *Economist* noted in 1849, 'a disease of society'. It also served, as another writer put it a year later, as 'a health inspector who speaks through his interpreter, the Registrar-General, in a language which reaches all ears'.

Its uneven incidence was not the least remarkable of its features. Newcastle was hard hit in 1831, much less affected in 1849, and a centre of horror in 1854: Liverpool as a seaport was always vulnerable. Yet Nottingham escaped very lightly in 1849 and Birmingham, with plentiful supplies of good water, was scarcely disturbed by cholera at all. Certainly old communities with their crowded courts and alleys and their often appalling sanitary conditions were as likely to suffer as the new industrial communities. The only variation was the duration of the outbreak. In Dr Snow's words: 'The duration of cholera in a place is usually in direct proportion to the number of the population. The disease remains but two or three weeks in a village, two or three months in a good sized town, whilst in a great metropolis it often remains a whole year or longer.'

The Health of Towns Association, which was founded in 1844, was at pains to stress in its propaganda that the battle for public health had to be fought just as vigorously in small towns and cities where there was no factory smoke as in crowded cities where the sky was black with smoke. There was one common sanitary 'law' which applied to both. The answers to a questionnaire which one of its sub-committees drafted in 1848 reveal a pattern of civic action and inertia which was uninfluenced either by the oldness or newness of the civic authorities or by their political affiliations. To the question 'Have the authorities of the town given any indication of their knowledge of the kind and degree of influence which the condition of suburban districts exercises over the health of the town?' the correspondent in Birmingham replied 'Not at all: the suburban districts are entirely neglected', and the correspondent in Canterbury remarked 'a few of the Town Council are quite aware of the influence which defective drainage has upon the public health, but a large number will not acknowledge it; and the greater number are so much opposed to public expenditure for any purpose that there is no hope of effectual means being resorted to by them for the public good.' To the question 'Have the authorities of the town done anything to obtain an abundant and economical supply of water: and are they aware of the advantages of the constant over the intermittent supply?' Brighton replied that the authorities had not yet tried and Oxford, 'never, and not likely to do so till compelled by parliamentary interposition'. Of the forty-two correspondents who replied 'no', only a minority were living in industrial communities. It was from Oxford, not from Manchester, that the reply to a further question ran, 'the *laissez-faire* system prevails, and nothing but the interference of government will change it.'

Nearly all the correspondents agreed that the opposition to sanitary reform was bound up with 'economy' at least as much as with opposition to 'centralization'. 'There is great unpopularity connected with town improvement,' was the reply from Nottingham, 'and popular men will not hazard their popularity by voting money for such purposes, though convinced of the necessity for such improvements.' This was a far cry from the attack on closed oligarchic corporations outside the range of public judgement. Both Leeds and York struck the alternative note: 'There is a strong feeling in Leeds that the local authority can manage their own affairs . . . better and more economically than if they were placed under government inspection.' 'There is here a very strong feeling against centralization', was the response from York, coupled with an expression of the hope that York would 'rank as high for its sanatory [*sic*] condition as it justly does for its many antiquarian remains'. Some of the leading local newspapers echoed these grumbles when the 1848 Public Health Bill was being debated. 'While we are most anxious that every town in the Kingdom should have the benefit of good sewerage and pure water,' an editorial in the *Leeds Mercury* stated, 'we could not consent to purchase these blessings by a permanent infringement of the rights of municipal bodies, and through them of the people at large.' The colourful and eccentric Colonel Sibthorp, who cared little for the benefits of either good sewerage or pure water, doubted whether old and new cities should be lumped together at all. 'Why should the pure city of Lincoln', he asked, 'be mixed up with the impure cities?'

The impact of national legislation on the local conditions of different kinds of community in mid- and late-Victorian England is a research study in itself. Before the coming of the national press, however, and the invention of the automobile, the country was already being pulled closer together. A recognition of common problems was the beginning of the process. Cobbett had described Frome as 'a little Manchester'[1]: it was not necessary to be a little Manchester to be drawn into urban debates in the Victorian age. All the moral problems of urban underworld, of 'the dangerous classes', were as evident in the older cities as in the new, even though their scale was much smaller. Visitors noted the incidence of prostitution in Salisbury as well as in Manchester. The same complaints were made about religious apathy whether or not a community basked in the shade of a cathedral. Rioting was just as prominent in the old cities as in the new: indeed, it had been much more prominent there during the Reform Bill struggles of 1830–32, when the disturbances in Bristol and Nottingham, even in Canterbury, were far more serious than those in Manchester or Birmingham.

In politics, the smaller and older cities and historic boroughs exercised a considerable influence over the political doctrines

1. See above, p. 88.

of the country. Most of the great new cities were strongholds of Liberalism from the beginning of the Victorian age: the main political questions which arose there in the late-Victorian years were, first, whether Conservatism could capture an urban foothold – this was the crucial question of 1867[1] – and second, whether Socialism would ultimately threaten Liberalism – this was one of the unsolved questions of 1901. In the smaller and older places there were always opportunities for Liberal gains. In Exeter, for example, there was a renewed sense of local Liberal triumph in 1868 when two Liberals were returned by small but enthusiastic majorities. Nottingham had an extremely interesting electoral history, not least on account of the tradition of corruption which existed there. A city which in 1847 returned Feargus O'Connor, the Chartist leader, along with John Walter, the son of the proprietor of *The Times*, was clearly idiosyncratic, and there were further signs of unorthodoxy in the return of the 'anti-oligarchic' Sir Robert Clifton, an Independent, in 1861 and of Ralph Bernal Osborne and Lord Amberley in 1865. 'Liberalism' in Nottingham was never allowed to pass unchallenged either on local or national issues. Liverpool also, the greatest of all the cities not dealt with in detail in this book, was markedly idiosyncratic: religion shaped political affiliations, and the presence of large numbers of Irishmen in the city gave a special twist both to Conservative and later to Labour politics. In Norwich, where electoral corruption survived the Corrupt Practices Act of 1883, there was a particularly interesting electoral situation when the claims of the agricultural labourer were being actively canvassed during the 1880s.

3

For all the political importance of some of the older cities in Victorian England, it was their distant past rather than their contemporary significance which drew most attention from writers, and even the newer cities could not escape their pedigrees. 'Manchester, as its name proclaims,' wrote J. Tait in his *Medieval Manchester*, 'is a place of high antiquity, though

1. See *Victorian People*, Chapter VIII.

time and the effacing finger of modern industry have left but scanty traces of its long past.' Tait was a scientific historian. The antiquarians, as we have seen, not only stopped short in their studies at the beginning of the Victorian age: they discovered or invented historical pedigrees for new cities with the same enthusiasm that they discovered or invented historical pedigrees for *nouveaux riches*. It is wrong to suggest, as Mumford does, that the 'new masters of society' in the city 'scornfully turned their backs on the past and all the accumulations of history and addressed themselves to creating a future.' In a country like England where the past remained a source of values, however contaminated, it was never wiped out. Some of the new cities, indeed, made more of their remote medieval origins than they did of the 'facts' of their economic progress. The author of an interesting series of articles in the *Athenaeum* on places about to be visited by the British Association said virtually nothing in any of his articles about the nineteenth century. He most enjoyed writing about Exeter, Norwich or York, but when he came to Bradford he concentrated on the Civil War of the sixteenth century and on Birmingham said little if anything of events after the departure of Dr Priestley. Fortunately for him the British Association did not hold a meeting in Crewe.

The same emphasis is traceable in the remarkable series of volumes on 'Historic Towns' which was edited by E. Freeman and W. Hunt and which first appeared in the year of the great dock strike, 1889. The past was to revivify the present. It could also be used to criticize the present. Carlyle made the most of the contrast between past and present in all his writings. Ruskin, who condemned Victorian London, drew inspiration from old cities. William Morris in his *News from Nowhere* produced a Utopia where London was more like the London of the Middle Ages than the town planners' dreams of the twentieth century. Starting with the same facts as Gissing, he countered Victorian sprawl with medieval compactness, a stinking River Thames with a beautiful and unpolluted navigable waterway, a city of tenements with a city of gardens. The squalor of the Middle Ages was overlooked, as the writer of a Utopia is entitled to overlook it, particularly when, as in

News from Nowhere, something more than an interpretation of medievalism was at stake. Raymond Unwin drew much of his early inspiration from Morris: W. R. Lethaby, who had many interesting ideas about London's future, was a medievalist by inclination and training.

Alongside the Victorian dream of an ideal city, therefore, there was Victorian interest in the cities of the past. Many of them had a special affection for Oxford, described by de Tocqueville as the English city which provided the clearest idea of the feudal cities of the Middle Ages. 'She lies steeped in sentiment,' wrote Matthew Arnold, 'spreading her gardens to the moonlight, and whispering from her towers the last enchantments of the middle ages'. Her dreaming spires were contrasted with the smoking mill chimneys of Leeds and Manchester, her tranquillity with the bustle of Birmingham or London. Her 'spirit' was evoked in Melbourne, much to the disgust of some of the more practical Australians, and in the university extension movement she colonized many of the newest centres of English industry. Her buildings were copied even in the United States. To some Victorians Oxford was the ideal city, as it was to Morris until he felt that parts of it were being threatened. Not all the Victorians fell under its spell, but for those who did the idea of the city carried with it many un-Victorian associations.

How many of them foresaw that in the twentieth century Oxford would be transformed by the motor car just as profoundly as the railway transformed the eighteenth-century city? Even in the nineteenth century 'speculative builders set the ancient city', as one Oxford historian put it, 'in an unattractive frame of brick. Villa-dom fringes her approaches. ... Municipal and private enterprise decorates the High Street and the Cornmarket and St Aldate's with buildings which reconcile ornateness with efficiency by superimposing a blend of half a dozen incongruous styles on the practical necessity of a shop front.' The Victorians gave Oxford not only a deplorable and badly managed railway station (there were fears at one time that there would also be a railway works) but Keble, a Gothic Museum, and perhaps the most quintessentially Victorian of all England's suburbs, not a West End but North

Oxford. They added without taking away. We have added Cowley, but how much of old Oxford is left?

4

With alarming appropriateness, Cowley was an agent of the automobile age which separates us from our Victorian ancestors as much as the railway age separated them from their ancestors. The automobile was to play havoc with the Victorian pattern of cities, and already by the end of the Victorian age the United States was beginning to forge ahead in the automobile industry and in all the consumer goods industries which were to revolutionize the urban way of life. European cities lagged far behind American cities in introducing electric transit. By 1900 there were twice as many telephones in the United States as in the whole of Europe. Elevators were in general use, and the skyscraper had established itself as a new American phenomenon. Defined in the *American Slang Dictionary* (1891) as 'a very tall building such as now are being built in Chicago', by the end of the decade it was being saluted as a creation of 'daring, wisdom and genius' brought into being 'without reference to any other nation on earth'.

Despite all the political and administrative difficulties confronting American city planners and reformers, there were many signs of a genuinely new approach to urban problems in the United States at the end of the Victorian period. It was in the United States, indeed, that the real new cities of the world were located. New York might stand in the eyes of the world for Tammany Hall, a huge municipal debt and corporation domination, but 'the omnipresence of electricity' was what struck most of the English visitors. The city seemed 'a magnificent embodiment of titanic energy and force'. Chicago might be condemned as 'Satan's invisible world displayed', but, as we have seen, it was also thought of as 'the city of destiny'. Richard Cobden in the distant days before the Great Fire of 1871 had already told Goldwin Smith on the eve of the latter's departure to the United States, 'See two things in the United States, if nothing else – see Niagara and Chicago.'

Philadelphia might strike American city reformers as 'corrupt but contented' and Cincinnati as a centre of 'cynical civic degradation' – these were the words of Delos F. Wilcox – but he went on to add, 'The very vigour of their [the cities'] growth has enabled them, like mad striplings, to defy the laws of civic health and squander with apparent immunity their native strength.'

There was no doubt that by the end of the Victorian age American cities were more vigorous by nature – concern with ecology perhaps starts at this point – than most English cities, however difficult the Americans were finding it to deal with health, order, planning and civic efficiency. The times had long since passed when American as well as English writers had been content to note that features of American cities were up to English or European standards, with remarks like 'the best society in New York would not suffer by comparison with the best society in England', or 'this locality must surely be the Birmingham of America'. In the early part of the nineteenth century the city makers of the expanding West had looked to the Eastern cities when they had not looked further beyond them to Europe. Pittsburgh, for example, which had its own bustling suburb of Birmingham long before the founding of Birmingham, Alabama, was accused of copying other places and finding out in the process that 'to imitate the evils and defects of other cities' was all that was in its power. By the end of the century several cities of the West, particularly Chicago, were in the vanguard of urban change.

The glitter of material wealth and the proliferation of ingenious urban gadgetry were not the only elements in the new urban equations, along with the old elements – slums, conflict, high mortality. The artefacts of Chicago pointed forward towards a new urban world. In an age of continuing architectural eclecticism in England, Henry Hobson Richardson in the United States offered a sense of structural form and an emphasis on the intelligent use of materials in place of ornate display and ponderous monumentalism. 'Some of the new residential streets of places as recent as Chicago or St Paul', the editor of the American *Baedeker* commented in 1898, 'more than hold their own ... with any contemporaneous thoroughfares of their own class in Europe.' The same point was made by Lewis Mumford in his *The Brown Decades*. While recognizing the continuing pull of eclecticism in American cities and analysing the reasons for urban failure, he argued at the same time that 'between 1880 and 1895 the task and method of modern architecture were clarified through the example of a group of American architects whose consistent and united efforts in this line antedated, by at least a decade, the earliest similar innovations in Europe.' He includes with Richardson J. W. Root, who, like Daniel Burnham, was drawn to Chicago in response to the immense architectural opportunities created by the Chicago Fire, and Louis Sullivan, an architect big enough and bold enough to jettison older cultural forms and start afresh.

Root translated the sense of new American opportunity into words as well as buildings. 'In America,' he wrote, 'we are free of artistic traditions. Our freedom begets license, it is true. We do shocking things; we produce works of architecture irremediably bad; we try crude experiments that result in disaster. Yet somewhere in this mass of ungoverned energies lies the principle of life. A new spirit of beauty is being developed and perfected, and even now its first achievements are beginning to delight us. This is not an old thing made over; it is new. It springs out of the past, but it is not tied to it; it studies the traditions, but it is not enslaved by them. Compare the best of our recent architecture – some of Richardson's designs for example – with the most pretentious buildings recently erected in Europe. In the American works we find strength and fitness, and a certain spontaneity and freshness, as of stately music, or a song in the green woods.'

The ending of Root's statement is almost as revealing as its main points. Songs in the green woods and songs in the cities were not to synchronize. The American city was to expand, to grow rich, to clothe itself in new garments, often to forget its 'Victorian' past, but it was to find it increasingly difficult to maintain 'spontaneity' and 'freshness'. The Chicago World Exhibition of 1893, the Columbian Exposition held to celebrate the four-hundredth anniversary of the discovery of the United States, is as appropriate an event to bring to a close a book on *Victorian Cities* as the London Great Exhibition of 1851 was to begin a book on *Victorian People*. Root had little to do with it, Sullivan designed only one notable building, the Transportation Building, and although F. L. Olmsted, the great landscape architect who had gleaned some of his first ideas about urban parks ('People's Gardens') in England, was drawn into consultation, the 'White City' and its surroundings failed to live up to the best that was already apparent in urban American architecture and design. Yet the mood was one of pride. Twelve million visitors enjoyed an unforgettable spectacle. How many of the visitors recalled that the Mayor, Carter C. Harrison, who was five times elected mayor of Chicago, had ended his address in 1879, when he first took office, with the words 'A good sanitary condition is indispensable to the prosperity of the city. But sweet scents may not be its necessary concomitant.... Too many are alarmed at an unpleasant but innocuous odor, and inhale with pleasure a sweet perfume laden with disease. I shall endeavor to foster healthfulness, yet not to destroy our great commercial interests'? If the English in 1851 had two faces, one looking back and one forward, so too did the Americans in 1893.

Perhaps an even better way of completing the circle is to examine the comments of H. G. Wells on a visit to New York in 1906. Wells was horrified by Victorian Cities just as he was horrified by Victorian People.[1] For this reason he had dreamed of a new urban order, and had contrasted London unfavourably with Basel.[2] When he visited New York, however, he had little doubt that 'this is the way the future must inevitably go'. The effect remained with him of 'an immeasurably powerful forward movement of rapid, eager advance, a process of enlargement and increment in every material sense'. This was one man's epilogue to 'Victorian Cities', yet in this as in all the judgements of Wells there is at least as much brashness as there is ambivalence in the Victorian story itself.

1. See above, p. 17. 2. See above, p. 349.

BIBLIOGRAPHICAL NOTE

This bibliographical note is highly selective; it is designed primarily for the assistance of the reader who wishes further to pursue the subjects of the separate chapters. Several of the books have appeared since *Victorian Cities* was written.

I. INTRODUCTION

There is a valuable bibliography of books and articles about social aspects of British cities, with a stimulating introduction by Ruth Glass, in *Urban Sociology in Great Britain; A Trend Report* (Unesco, *Current Sociology* No. 4, 1955). See also W. H. Chaloner, 'Writings on British Urban History, 1934–57' in *Vierteljahrschrift für Sozial und Wirtschaftgeschichte* (1958). More recent writings are covered in the *Urban History Newsletter*, edited from Leicester University by H. J. Dyos, and in an important article by Dyos, 'The Growth of Cities in the Nineteenth Century: A Review of Some Recent Writing' in *Victorian Studies* (1966).

Basic statistical information is set out in A. F. Weber, *The Growth of Cities in the Nineteenth Century* (1899; Cornell Reprints in Urban Studies, 1963); T. A. Welton, *England's Recent Progress* (1911); T. W. Freeman, *The Conurbations of Great Britain* (1949); and D. Friedlander and R. J. Roshier, 'A Study of Internal Migration, 1851–1951' in *Population Studies* (1966). For the geographical background, see S. J. Low, 'The Rise of the Suburbs' in the *Contemporary Review* (1891); A. E. Smailes, 'The Urban Hierarchy in England and Wales' in *Geography* (1944); 'The Site, Growth and Changing Face of London' in R. Clayton (ed.), *The Geography of Greater London* (1964), and *The Geography of Towns* (5th edn 1966); R. E. Dickinson, *City and Region* (1964); H. M. Mayer and C. F. Kohn (eds.), *Readings in Urban Geography* (1959).

The development of local government is examined in S. and B. Webb, *The Manor and the Borough*, 2 vols. (1908); H. J. Laski, W. I. Jennings and W. A. Robson (eds.), *A Century of Municipal Progress, 1835–1935* (1935); E. S. Griffith, *The Modern Development of City Government*, 2 vols. (1907); more briefly in K. B. Smellie, *A Short History of Local Government* (1954); and in more depth in a number of articles, including G. B. A. Finlayson, 'The Municipal Corporation Commission and Report' in the *Bulletin of the Institute of Historical Research* (1963) and 'The Politics of Municipal

Reform' in the *English Historical Review* (1966); and R. Lambert, 'Central and Local Relations in Mid-Victorian England' in *Victorian Studies* (1962).

For public health and related problems, see M. W. Flinn (ed.), *The Sanitary Condition of the Labouring Population of Great Britain* (1965); Sir John Simon's classic study *English Sanitary Institutions* (1890), along with R. Lambert's monograph, *Sir John Simon and English Social Administration* (1963); S. E. Finer, *The Life and Times of Sir Edwin Chadwick* (1952); R. A. Lewis, *Edwin Chadwick and the Public Health Movement* (1952); E. J. Syson, 'On the Comparative Mortality in Large Towns' in the *Transactions of the Manchester Statistical Society* (1871); and D. V. Glass, 'Some Indicators of Differences between Urban and Rural Mortality' in *Population Studies* (1964).

For transport and other services, see T. C. Barker and M. Robbins, *A History of London Transport*, Vol. I (1963); D. Ward, 'A Comparative Historical Geography of Street Car Suburbs in Boston, Mass. and Leeds, 1850–1920' in the *Annals of the Association of American Geographers* (1964); F. W. Robins, *The Story of Water Supply* (1949); H. Finer, *Municipal Trading* (1941); and G. F. Chadwick, *The Park and the Town* (1966).

For building and housing, see E. R. Dewsnup, *The Housing Problem in England* (1907); J. Parry Lewis, *Building Cycles and Britain's Growth* (1965); H. J. Dyos, *Victorian Suburb* (1961); N. Davey, *A History of Building Materials* (1961). For town planning, see W. Ashworth, *The Genesis of Modern Town Planning* (1954).

Leading questions about 'provincialism' are asked by S. G. Checkland in 'English Provincial Cities' in the *Economic History Review* (1953), and some of them are dealt with more fully in D. Read, *The English Provinces* (1964).

2. CITY AND SOCIETY: VICTORIAN ATTITUDES

The city as a centre of social and cultural study is examined in a number of interesting general books, notably E. W. Burgess and R. D. Mackenzie, *The City* (1925); P. Geddes, *Cities in Evolution* (1949 edn); L. Mumford, *The City in History* (1961); P. Hauser and L. Schnore (eds.), *The Study of Urbanization* (1965); G. Friedmann (ed.), *Villes et campagnes* (1953); R. E. Dickinson, *The West European City* (1950); C. Tunnard, *The City of Man* (1953); K. Lynch, *The Image of the City* (1954); H. Rosenau, *The Ideal City and its Architectural Evolution* (1959); and, invaluable for statistical information, Kingsley Davis and H. Herz, 'The World Distribution of

Urbanization' in the *Bulletin of the International Statistical Institute* (1951) and 'The Origin and Growth of Urbanization in the World' in the *American Journal of Sociology* (1955).

Early-nineteenth-century criticisms and defences of the city are set out in the following books, representative of a far larger number: C. T. Thackrah, *The Effects of the Principal Arts, Trades and Professions, and of Civic States and Habits of Living, on Health and Longevity* (1831); P. Gaskell, *The Manufacturing Population of Great Britain* (1833); T. Chalmers, *The Christian and Civic Economy of Large Towns*, 3 vols. (1821–6); F. von Raumer, *England in 1835*, 3 vols. (1836); E. Buret, *De La Misère des classes laborieuses en Angleterre et en France*, 2 vols. (1840); C. E. Lester, *The Glory and Shame of England*, 2 vols. (1841); W. Cooke Taylor, *Notes of a Tour in the Manufacturing Districts of Lancashire* (1842) and *Natural History of Society* (1844); A. de Tocqueville, *Journeys to England and Ireland*, edited by J. P. Mayer (1958); L. Faucher, *Études sur l'Angleterre*, 2 vols. (1845); F. Engels, *The Condition of the Working Class in England*, translated and edited by W. O. Henderson and W. H. Chaloner (1958); R. Vaughan, *The Age of Great Cities* (1843); H. Colman, *European Life and Morals*, 2 vols. (1849); J. S. Buckingham, *National Evils and Practical Remedies* (1849); W. O. Henderson (ed.), *J. C. Fischer and his Diary of Industrial England* (1966).

For the mid-Victorian period, the following contemporary works provide indispensable evidence: H. Gavin, *Sanitary Ramblings* (1848); G. Bell, *Day and Night in the Wynds of Edinburgh* (1849); J. Garwood, *The Million-Peopled City* (1853); G. Godwin, *Town Swamps and Social Bridges* (1859); H. Mayhew, *London Labour and the London Poor*, 4 vols. (1851–62), with parallel studies of provincial cities printed in the *Morning Chronicle*; J. Hollingshead, *Ragged London in 1861* (1861); H. D. Littlejohn, *Report on the Sanitary Condition of the City of Edinburgh* (1865); F. L. Olmsted, *Walks and Talks* (1857).

For late-Victorian England, see Sir B. W. Richardson, *Hygeia: A City of Health* (1876); W. R. Lethaby, *Of Beautiful Cities* (1897) and *Form in Civilisation* (1957 edn); E. Howard, *Tomorrow, A Peaceful Path to Real Reform* (1898). The social survey approach is best revealed in Charles Booth's massive *Life and Labour of the People of London, A Study of Town Life*, 17 vols. published between 1889 and 1903, and in B. S. Rowntree's *Poverty* (1901). See also Rev. A. Mearns, *The Bitter Cry of Outcast London* (1883). There are interesting general reflections in T. H. S. Escott, *England, Its People, Polity and Pursuits* (1879), and C. F. G. Masterman, *The Condition of England* (1908).

For contemporary American views, see *The Great Metropolis* (1892); the New York Association for Improving the Condition of the Poor, *First Report of a Committee on the Sanitary Condition of the Laboring Classes in the City of New York* (1853); E. H. Chapin, *Humanity in the City* (1854); A. Mayo, *The Symbols of the Capital* (1859); C. Nordhoff, 'The Mismanagement of New York' in the *North American Review* (1871); C. L. Brace, *The Dangerous Classes of New York* (1872); W. Glazier, *Peculiarities of American Cities* (1883); J. A. Riis, *How the Other Half Lives* (1890) and *The Battle With the Slum* (1902); *Hull House Maps and Papers* (1895); H. Fletcher, *The Drift of Population to Cities* (1891); W. H. Tolman, *Municipal Reform Movements in the United States* (1897); J. A. Fairlie, *Municipal Administration* (1901); D. F. Wilcox, *The American City, a Problem in Democracy* (1904) and *Great Cities in America* (1910); L. Steffens, *The Shame of the Cities* (1904) and *Autobiography* (1931); and F. C. Howe, *The City, the Hope of Democracy* (1905), *The British City* (1907) and *European Cities at Work* (1913).

Other useful international material can be found in M. du Camp, *Paris: ses organes, ses fonctions et sa vie*, 6 vols. (1875); P. Meuriot, *Des Agglomérations urbaines dans l'Europe contemporaine* (1898); P. Lavedan, *Histoire de l'urbanisme*, 3 vols. (1926–52); B. and J. M. Chapman, *The Life and Times of Baron Haussmann* (1957); D. H. Pinkney, *Napoleon III and the Rebuilding of Paris* (1958); L. Chevalier, *La Formation de la population parisienne au XIXe siècle* (1950) and *Classes laborieuses et classes dangereuses* (1958); R. R. Kuczynski, *Der Zug nach der Stadt* (1897); G. Simmel, *Die Grossstädte und das Geistesleben* (1903); E. Pfeil, *Grossstadtsforschung, Fragestellungen, Verfahrendweisen und Ergebnisse einer Wissenschaft die dem Neubau von Stadt und Land von Nutzen sein Könnte* (1960); A. M. Schlesinger, 'The City in American Civilisation' in *Paths to the Present* (1949), and *The Rise of the City* (1933); R. C. Wade, *The Urban Frontier* (1960); A. Strauss, *Images of the American City* (1961); M. and L. White, *The Intellectual versus the City* (1962); and B. McKelvey, *The Urbanization of America* (1967). The best general book on American background and attitudes is R. Hofstadter, *The Age of Reform* (1955), and there is a good bibliographical guide by C. N. Glaab in the general *Study of Urbanization* (1965), edited by Hauser and Schnore. There is also an anthology edited by Glaab called *The American City, A Documentary History* (1963).

For some aspects of religion and the city, see K. S. Inglis, *Churches and the Working Classes in Victorian England* (1963); Canon Wickham, *Church and People in an Industrial City* (1957); and A. I. Abell, *The Urban Impact on American Protestantism* (1943), the first and last of which have good bibliographies. Philanthropy and the cluster of motives associated with it are discussed in D. Owen, *English Philanthropy* (1965); B. Harrison, 'Philanthropy and the Victorians' in *Victorian Studies* (1966); M. Simey's fascinating monograph, *Charitable Effort in Liverpool in the Nineteenth Century* (1951); and J. F. C. Harrison, *Social Reform in Victorian Leeds, the Work of James Hole* (1954).

For the role of the historian, see the searching essay by W. Diamond, 'On the dangers of an Urban Interpretation of History' in E. Goldman (ed.), *Historiography and Urbanization* (1941); E. E. Lampard, 'American Historians and the Study of Urbanisation' in the *American Historical Review* (1961); E. Jutikkala, 'The Borderland: Urban History and Urban Sociology' in the *Scandinavian Economic History Review* (1958); and, above all, O. Handlin and J. Burchard (eds.), *The Historian and the City* (1963), which contains useful bibliographical information.

3. MANCHESTER, SYMBOL OF A NEW AGE

For the Manchester of the 1840s, as local contemporaries saw it, the guide books provide much the best introduction. See B. Lowe, *Manchester as it is* (1839; 2nd edn 1842). This guide may be compared with J. Ashton, *The Manchester Guide* (1804). Such accounts provide a necessary background for understanding the comments of visitors and foreign critics, like Faucher and Engels, whose work is mentioned in the bibliographical note to Chapter 2. A local study of basic importance, although it precedes Queen Victoria's accession, is J. P. Kay, *The Moral and Physical Condition of the Working Classes Employed in the Cotton Manufacture of Manchester* (1832). This should be set alongside Gaskell's work also mentioned in the note to Chapter 2. For later comments on the period covered in this book, see J. T. Slugg, *Reminiscences of Manchester Fifty Years Ago* (1881), and W. A. Shaw, *Manchester Old and New* (1894).

For Manchester's history as seen by Manchester men, see A. Prentice, *Historical Sketches and Personal Recollections of Manchester* (1851) and *The History of the Anti-Corn Law League* (1853); J. Wheeler, *Manchester, its Political, Social and Commercial History, Ancient and Modern* (1836); J. Reilly, *History of Manchester*, 2 vols. (1861); and W. E. Axon, *The Annals of Manchester* (1886). Another interesting book is H. Dunckley's *The Charter of the Nations* (1854). Illuminating later studies are by G. Saintsbury, *Manchester* (1887); G. B.

Hertz, *The Manchester Politician 1750–1912* (1912); and K. Chorley, *Manchester Made Them* (1951).

For the novelists, see L. Cazamian, *Le Roman social en Angleterre* (1935); K. Tillotson's study, *Novels of the Eighteen-Forties* (1954); Mrs E. H. Chadwick, *Mrs Gaskell, Homes, Haunts and Stories* (1913 edn); R. D. Waller (ed.), *Letters Addressed to Mrs Gaskell by Celebrated Contemporaries* (1935); A. Pollard, *Mrs Gaskell: Novelist and Biographer* (1965); E. Wright, *Mrs Gaskell: The Basis for Reassessment* (1965); M. Masefield, *Peacocks and Primroses: A Study of Disraeli's Novels* (1953); B. R. Jerman, *Young Disraeli* (1960); R. Blake, *Disraeli* (1966); and K. J. Fielding (ed.), *The Speeches of Charles Dickens* (1960).

The Anti-Corn Law League has been examined very fully in D. G. Barnes, *A History of the English Corn Laws* (1930) and N. McCord, *The Anti-Corn Law League* (1958). The history of the term 'Manchester School' is set out in T. S. Ashton's article on the subject in the *Manchester School* (1954). An early account of the School is given in Goldwin Smith's *Reminiscences* (1910). Professor Ashton's *Economic and Social Investigation in Manchester, 1833–1933* (1934), a history of the Manchester Statistical Society, is also extremely useful. A more recent discussion of the Manchester School is to be found in W. D. Grampp, *The Manchester School of Economics* (1960). See also A. Redford, *Manchester Merchants and Foreign Trade, 1794–1858* (1934), and the second volume covering the period from 1858 to 1939 by Redford and B. W. Clapp. Dr Clapp's *John Owens* (1966) is also useful, as is A. Silver, *Manchester Men and Indian Cotton* (1966).

The later history of the Liberal Party in Manchester has been examined by P. Whitaker in an unpublished University of Manchester thesis entitled 'The Growth of Liberal Organisation in Manchester from the 1860s to 1903' (1956). There is important and original material, highly relevant, on mid-Victorian politics in J. R. Vincent, *Formation of the Liberal Party, 1857–68* (1966), which includes an interesting discussion of Rochdale.

The history of local government in Manchester is well covered in A. Redford's *History of Local Government in Manchester*, 3 vols.(1939), and S. Simon, *A Century of City Government* (1938). See also W. E. A. Axon, *Cobden as a Citizen* (1907), and W. H. Brindley, *The Soul of Manchester* (1929).

Attempts have been made to 'place' Manchester in world social history by Ralph Turner, in 'The Cultural Significance of the Early English Industrial Town' in C. W. de Kiewiet (ed.), *Studies in British History* (1941) and 'The Industrial City: Center of Cultural Change' in C. F. Ware (ed.), *The Cultural Approach to History* (1940).

L. S. Marshall wrote an article in the latter volume on 'The Emergence of the First Industrial City, Manchester, 1785–1850' and a useful book, *The Development of Public Opinion in Manchester, 1780–1820* (1946).

For Manchester on the eve of its great industrial and demographic expansion, see W. H. Chaloner, 'Manchester in the Latter Half of the Eighteenth Century' in the *Bulletin of the John Rylands Library* (1959). cf. J. Aikin, *A Description of the Country from Thirty to Forty Miles Round Manchester* (1795). See also H. Baker, 'On the Growth of the Commercial Centre of Manchester' in the *Transactions of the Manchester Statistical Society* (1871–2); and E. Cannan, 'The Growth of Manchester and Liverpool' in the *Economic Journal* (1907).

4. LEEDS, A STUDY IN CIVIC PRIDE

Although much has been written about particular aspects of the history of Leeds in the nineteenth century there are no general introductions to the history of the city or major works of scholarly synthesis. For useful information, see *Leeds and its History*, reprinted from the Tercentenary Supplement of the *Yorkshire Post*, 8 July 1926, and *Leeds and Its Region* (1967), prepared for the visit of the British Association. The background chronicle of Yorkshire history is set out in John Mayhall's invaluable *Annals of Yorkshire*, 3 vols. (1878), and H. Schroeder's earlier and less full *Annals of Yorkshire* (1852). See also the four volumes, excellently illustrated, called *Yorkshire Past and Present* (1871). These were edited by T. Baines.

Aikin's account of late-eighteenth-century Manchester may be usefully compared with T. Housman's *Topographic Description of Yorkshire* (1800). Anon., *A Walk Through Leeds or a Stranger's Guide* (1806), carries the story further. A later guide book which has been freely used in this chapter is *An Historical Guide to Leeds and its Environs* (Leeds, 1858). This may be supplemented by J. Measom's *Official Illustrated Guide of the Great Northern Railway* (1861). For a modern study of value, see L. Cooper, *Yorkshire West Riding* (1950). A specialist article which is relevant to this study is D. Ward's 'The Building Cycle and the Growth of the Built-up Areas of Leeds' in the *Northern Universities Geographical Journal* (1960).

Biographies of Leeds men discussed in this chapter include W. G. Rimmer, *Marshall's of Leeds, Flax Spinners* (1960); *The Life of Edward Baines by his Son* (1881); T. Wemyss Reid, *A Memoir of John Deakin Heaton, M.D.* (1883), a fascinating study of provincial life; and W. R. W. Stephens, *The Life and Letters of Walter Farquhar*

Hook, 2 vols. (1878). See also G. G. Lang, *Church and Town for Fifty Years, 1841–91*, and for local politics J. S. Curtis, *The Story of the Marsden Mayoralty* (1875).

The work of Cuthbert Brodrick is examined in T. Butler Wilson, *Two Leeds Architects* (1937). The history of the musical festival has been briefly told by F. B. J. Hutchings in the Leeds Centenary Music Festival Souvenir Programme (1958). See also F. R. Spark, *Memoirs of My Life* (1913).

On Bradford there is a mass of badly co-ordinated information. A history of Bradford is even more urgently needed than a history of Leeds. The following books are necessary reading: J. James, *The History and Topography of Bradford* (1841) and *Contributions and Additions to the History of Bradford* (1886); J. Fawcett, *The Rise and Progress of the Town and Borough of Bradford* (1859); E. Collinson, *The History of the Worsted Trade and Historic Sketch of Bradford* (1854); W. Cudworth, a voluminous writer, *Notes on the Bradford Corporation* (1881), *Round About Bradford* (1876) and *Histories of Bolton and Bowling* (1891); W. Scruton, *Pen and Pencil Pictures of Old Bradford* (1889); J. Burnley, *Phases of Bradford Life* (1889); and E. Sigsworth, *Black Dyke Mills* (1958).

The *Memoirs of Sir Jacob Behrens* (1885) touch on the contrast between Bradford and Leeds. Another interesting biography written by a man who knew Leeds better than Bradford is T. Wemyss Reid's *Life of the Rt Hon. W. E. Forster* (1888). See also the autobiography of Fred Jowett, the Bradford pioneer of the Independent Labour Party, *Fred Jowett of Bradford* (1952), with a good introduction.

Ibbetson's *Directory of the Borough of Bradford* is a useful source book. I have used the 1845 edition in this chapter. See also F. Hooper, *Statistics Relating to the City of Bradford* (1898). For essential data about the two cities in the twentieth century, see R. E. Dickinson, 'The Regional Functions and Zones of Influence of Leeds and Bradford' in *Geography* (1930).

On Saltaire, see W. H. G. Armytage, *Heavens Below* (1961), and Ashworth, op. cit. Among earlier studies, see W. Cudworth, *Saltaire, Yorkshire, England* (1895); B. Allsop, *Sir Titus Salt* (1878); and T. Balgarnie, *Sir Titus Salt* (1878). There is a recent article on Saltaire by R. K. Dewhirst in the *Town Planning Review* (1960–61).

5. BIRMINGHAM: THE MAKING OF A CIVIC GOSPEL

The account given of Birmingham in this chapter rests on an extension and re-evaluation of the material which I used in my book

The History of Birmingham, Vol. II (1952). The first volume of this history by Conrad Gill, published in the same year, is a definitive account of fundamental importance. Some of the distinctive features of Birmingham's social and political structure are discussed in a number of articles I have written about the city, particularly 'Thomas Attwood and the Economic Background of the Birmingham Political Union' in the *Cambridge Historical Journal* (1948); 'The Background of the Parliamentary Reform Movement in Three English Cities', ibid. (1957); and 'Social Structure in Birmingham and Lyons' in the *British Journal of Sociology* (1950). See also C. Gill, 'Birmingham under the Street Commissioners, 1769–1851' in the *University of Birmingham Historical Journal* (1948) and the extremely important Vol. VII of the *Victoria County History of Warwick* (1964) with essays on most aspects of Birmingham.

Older books of value are J. A. Langford's *Century of Birmingham Life*, 2 vols. (2nd edn 1871), and his *Modern Birmingham and Its Institutions*, 2 vols. (1873); R. K. Dent, *Old and New Birmingham* (1879–80) and *The Making of Birmingham* (1894); J. H. Muirhead (ed.), *Birmingham Institutions* (1911); E. Edwards, *Birmingham Men* (1878); J. S. Jaffray, *Hints for a History of Birmingham* (MS. Birmingham Reference Library); T. Anderton, *Tale of One City* (1893); G. C. Allen, *Industrial Development of Birmingham and the Black Country* (1926); and the British Association, *Birmingham in its Regional Setting* (1950), a parallel volume to that on Leeds.

Dr T. R. Tholfsen, an American scholar, has written a number of most useful and stimulating articles on Victorian Birmingham. Among them are 'The Chartist Crisis in Birmingham' in the *International Review of Social History* (1959); 'The Artisan and the Culture of Early Victorian Birmingham' in the *Birmingham Historical Journal* (1954); 'The Origins of the Birmingham Caucus', ibid. (1959); and 'The Transition to Democracy in Victorian England' in the *International Review of Social History* (1961). Another valuable American article is F. H. Herrick's 'The Origins of the National Liberal Federation' in the *Journal of Modern History* (1945). This article notes the shortcomings of M. Ostrogorski's *Democracy and the Organisation of Political Parties* (1902), which is still treated by many historians as if it were the only source. Much the most valuable recent study of Birmingham's local government politics is E. P. Hennock's unpublished Cambridge doctoral thesis 'The Role of Religious Dissent in the Reform of Municipal Government in Birmingham' (1956). Many of its conclusions have been incorporated into my analysis.

For the individuals who made such an important contribution to the foundation of the civic gospel in Birmingham, see J. H. Muirhead, *Nine Famous Birmingham Men* (1913); N. M. Marris, *Joseph Chamberlain* (1900); J. L. Garvin, *The Life of Joseph Chamberlain*, Vol. I (1932); R. A. Armstrong, *Henry William Crosskey, His Life and Work* (1895); A. W. W. Dale, *The Life of R. W. Dale* (1899); W. Wilson, *The Life of George Dawson* (1905); and R. W. Dale, 'George Dawson: Politician, Lecturer, and Preacher' in the *Nineteenth Century* (1877). See also J. Buckley, *Joseph Parkes of Birmingham* (1926).

There is useful material about Birmingham's cultural history in R. E. Waterhouse's *The Birmingham and Midland Institute, 1854–1954* (1954).

6. MIDDLESBROUGH: THE GROWTH OF A NEW COMMUNITY

There is a most valuable nineteenth-century account of Middlesbrough in H. G. Reid (ed.), *Middlesbrough and its Jubilee* (1881). See also for early accounts *Middlesbrough, its History, Environs and Trade* (1899) and T. Bulmer's *History, Topography and Directory of North Yorkshire*, Part 1 (1890). Lady Bell's *At the Works: A Study of a Manufacturing Town* (1907) is a classic description of what late-nineteenth- and early-twentieth-century Middlesbrough was like. It should be compared with Ruth Glass's *The Social Background of a Plan, A Study of Middlesbrough* (1948).

In Middlesbrough Public Library there is a useful manuscript history of the town – the Tweddell manuscript. There is also a lively *Record of the Proceedings* at the opening of the Town Hall in 1889. The newspapers, however, provide the only account of most of the critical and interesting episodes in the life of the growing community.

The steel history and its economic vicissitudes are discussed in D. L. Burn, *An Economic History of Steelmaking* (1950).

Cowen, whose views on Middlesbrough and on Victorian cities in general have been quoted, is the subject of a book by E. M. Jones, *The Life and Speeches of Joseph Cowen, M.P.* (1885). Its motto is taken from Emerson – 'Eloquence is a Triumph of Pure Power'. Lowthian Bell's *Principles of the Manufacture of Iron and Steel* (1884) and his memorandum on 'The Iron Trade' which he offered to the Royal Commission on the Depression of Trade in 1886 are important documents.

Mr D. C. Hearn has collected much valuable material relating to Middlesbrough's iron masters and their social and political affiliations which he hopes to be able to put together in published form.

It is interesting to compare Barrow-in-Furness and Middlesbrough. See S. Pollard, 'Town Planning in the Nineteenth Century: The Beginnings of Modern Barrow-in-Furness' in the *Transactions of the Lancashire and Cheshire Antiquarian Society* (1952–3); J. D. Marshall, *Barrow-in-Furness* (1959); and F. Barnes, *Barrow-in-Furness and District* (1957). See also P. H. White, 'Some Aspects of Urban Development by Colliery Companies' in the *Manchester School* (1953).

7. MELBOURNE, A VICTORIAN COMMUNITY OVERSEAS

Much the best introduction to the study of Melbourne is the excellent anthology of comments about the city with valuable introductions by James Grant and Geoffrey Serle, *The Melbourne Scene, 1803–1956* (1957). It has a short but useful bibliography. Alan Birch and D. C. Macmillan have prepared a companion volume on Sydney, *The Sydney Scene, 1788–1960* (1962). See also the excellent anthology edited by A. Brissenden and C. Higham, *They Came to Australia* (1962).

English readers will find A. G. L. Shaw's *The Story of Australia* (1954), R. M. Crawford's *Australia* (1952), W. K. Hancock's *Australia* (1930) and Manning Clark's *A Short History of Australia* (1963) extremely useful introductions to the Australian background. So too in recent English perspectives is J. D. Pringle's *Australian Accent* (1958) which shows how different to most Australians the comparison between Melbourne and Sydney appears at the present time from what it did in the Victorian age. See also G. Greenwood (ed.), *Australia, A Social and Political History* (1955).

Russel Ward's brilliant monograph, *The Australian Legend* (1958), is controversial and extremely suggestive in the best sense. Behind it is Vance Palmer's *The Legend of the Nineties* (1954). Cyril Pearl's *Wild Men of Sydney* (1959) makes fascinating reading.

Two books on earlier periods are illuminating – George Nadel's *Australia's Colonial Culture* (1957), which has a good selective bibliography of titles, some of which are not listed elsewhere, and Douglas Pike's *Paradise of Dissent, South Australia, 1829–1857* (1957). See also C. Hadcraft, *Australian Literature* (1960); B. Smith, *Australian Painting* (1962); and R. Gollan, *Radical and Working Class Politics: A Study of Eastern Australia, 1850–1910* (1960). N. G. Butlin's informative *Private Capital Formation in Australia, Estimates*

1861–1900 (1955) is No. 5 of the Australian National University's Social Science Monographs, and more recently he has published *Investment in Australian Economic Development, 1861–1900* (1964). F. S. Greenhop's *History of Magazine Publishing in Australia* (1947) is useful for reference.

For recent trends in Australian historiography there is much of interest in Professor J. La Nauze's articles 'The Study of Australian History, 1929–59' in *Historical Studies* (1959) and Professor Manning Clark's inaugural lecture at Canberra University College, printed in *Signposts* (1959).

In writing this chapter, however, I have made as much use as possible of contemporary materials. F. W. L. Adam's searching *Australian Essays* (1886) and *The Australians, A Social Sketch* (1893) are excellent commentaries, particularly when checked and supplemented by the volumes of *The Vagabond Papers* by 'the Vagabond', Stanley James, who usually called himself Julian Thomas (1877). These books are far more penetrating than J. A. Froude's *Oceana* (1886); A. Trollope's *Australia and New Zealand* (1876); and C. W. Dilke's *Greater Britain* (1868 and later edns) and *Problems of Greater Britain* (1890), which are best read in their inverse order of appearance. H. Mortimer Franklyn's *A Glance at Australia* (1881) is a good introduction, written by the editor of the *Victorian Review*. James Allen's *History of Australia, 1787–1882* (1882) gives a clear picture of what were thought to be the essential 'facts' concerning Australia at the beginning of Melbourne's golden decade.

For Melbourne, see H. Perkins, *Melbourne Illustrated and Victoria Described* (1880); the *Argus* Exhibition Supplement (2 October 1880); W. Westgarth, *Personal Recollections of Early Melbourne and Victoria* (1888); R. E. N. Twopeny, *Town Life in Australia* (1883); Fergus Hume, *The Mystery of a Hansom Cab* (London, 1935; 1st edn Melbourne, 1886); 'Garryowen' (E. Finn), *The Chronicles of Early Melbourne*, 2 vols. (1888); J. Freeman, *Lights and Shades of Melbourne Life* (1888); T. W. H. Leavitt and W. D. Lilburn (eds.), *The Jubilee History of Victoria and Melbourne* (1888); A. Sutherland and others, *Victoria and Her Metropolis* (1888); D. A. Gresswell, *Report on the Sanitary Conditions and Sanitary Administration of Melbourne and Suburbs* (1890); H. C. J. Lingham, *Juvenal in Melbourne* (1892); H. G. Turner, *A History of the Colony of Victoria* (1904); W. H. Newnham, *Melbourne, The Biography of a City* (1956); G. Serle, *The Golden Age* (1963); and E. Graeme Robertson's beautifully illustrated *Victorian Heritage, Ornamental Cast Iron in Architecture* (1960). Margaret Kiddle's *Men of Yesterday* (1961) is particularly sensitive and illuminating.

There are two well-documented University of Melbourne Studies, one a B.A. dissertation by J. R. Parris, *The Melbourne Exhibition 1880–1* (1955), the other an M.A. thesis by R. J. Moore, *Marvellous Melbourne* (1958), which cover leading themes in Melbourne's life in this period. For novels, see F. Hardie's *Power Without Glory* (1930) and Henry Handel Richardson's *The Fortunes of Richard Mahoney* (1910).

8. LONDON, THE WORLD CITY

Despite the recognized importance of the subject, there is no good general history of nineteenth-century London. Much of the material in this chapter is culled from articles in newspapers and periodicals, notably the *Fortnightly*, the *Nineteenth Century* and the *Quarterly Review*. Perhaps the best general introductions to the study of London are the numerous anthologies about it which have appeared during the last century. Among them see R. Harling, *The London Miscellany, A Nineteenth-century Scrapbook* (1937), and D. M. Low, *London is London: The Unique City* (1937). F. Bedarida deals with the neglect of London as a topic among historians in his article 'L'Histoire social de Londres au XIXe siècle' in *Annales* (1960).

A brief Victorian account of London's growth and development during the period is provided by G. L. Gomme in his *London in the Reign of Victoria, 1837–97* (1898), one of the many books written for the Jubilee. See also the instructive and indispensable book by H. Jephson, *The Sanitary Evolution of London* (1907). The many books by Sir Walter Besant are mainly of antiquarian value, but there are points of interest in the symposium which he edited, *London in the Nineteenth Century* (1909), and in his *South London* (1899). I have also made use of C. Capper, *The Port and Trade of London* (1862), and W. J. Loftie, *A History of London* (1883). J. Grant's *The Great Metropolis*, 2 vols. (1836), sets the scene at the beginning of the reign, and C. Knight's *Cyclopaedia of London* (1851) is a good guide to limited aspects of mid-Victorian London.

Apart from books like those of Mayhew and Booth mentioned in an earlier note to Chapter 2, see also, on the growth of London, D. Lyson, *The Environs of London* (1795), which may be compared with Aikin on Manchester; R. Price Williams, 'The Population of London, 1801–81' in the *Journal of the Statistical Society* (1885); Sir John Summerson, *Georgian London* (1945); H. J. Dyos, *Victorian Suburb, A Study of the Growth of Camberwell* (1961), 'Railways and Housing in Victorian London' in the *Journal of Transport History*

(1955), 'Some Social Costs of Railway Building in London', ibid. (1957–8), and 'Workmen's Fares in South London', ibid. (1953–4). See also D. L. Olsen, *Town Planning in London in the Eighteenth and Nineteenth Centuries* (1964).

Relations between East End and West End are discussed in A. Morison, *Tales of Mean Streets* (1894); G. Lansbury, *My Life* (1928) and *Looking Backwards and Forwards* (1935); E. Sinclair, *East London* (1950); and M. Rose, *The East End of London* (1951). There is no shortage of local studies. See, for example, W. Robins, *Paddington, Past and Present* (1853); A. Montgomery Eyre, *Saint John's Wood* (1913); R. O. Sherington, *The Story of Hornsey* (1906); and S. Potter, *The Story of Willesden* (1926).

For London's government, see Sir Gwilym Gibbon and R. W. Bell's standard *History of the London County Council* (1939), although there is little detail about the Victorian period in this book. This may be supplemented by the Fabian Society's *Facts for Londoners* (1889) and *The London Programme* (1891); S. West, *The Reform of London Government* (1888); J. Lloyd, *History of a Great Reform* (1889); W. Saunders, *The History of the First London County Council* (1892); A. G. Gardiner, *John Benn and the Progressive Movement* (1925); B. Webb, *Our Partnership* (1926); and W. A. Robson, *The Government and Misgovernment of London* (1939). P. Thompson's *Socialists, Liberals and Labour in London, 1889–1914* (1967) is an extremely valuable recent study.

9. EPILOGUE: OLD CITIES AND NEW

An enormous amount has been written about Britain's older cities. Perhaps the best starting point for their further study, a Victorian starting point, is provided by the eleven volumes called *Historic Towns*, which were edited by Edward Freeman and by W. Hunt and first appeared in 1889. See also for the beginnings of the story H. A. Merewether and A. J. Stephens, *History of the Boroughs and Municipal Corporations of the United Kingdom* (1835), and J. Doran, *Memoirs of our Great Towns* (1878); E. A. Freeman, *English Towns and Districts* (1883).

For Bristol, see the recent general history by Bryan Little, *The City and County of Bristol* (1954), which includes a bibliography. The first history of Bristol by William Bassett appeared in 1789, a few years after W. Hutton's pioneer *History of Birmingham* (1781). J. F. Nicholls and J. Taylor's *Bristol Past and Present*, 3 vols. (1881–2) is a magnificent Victorian quarry. See also J. Latimer, *The Annals of Bristol in the Nineteenth Century* (1893).

Bibliographical Note

On Liverpool, see J. A. Picton, *Memories of Liverpool*, 2 vols. (1873), and G. Chandler's *Liverpool* (1957), which covers the whole period of Liverpool's development from its creation as a borough in 1207. A particularly valuable monograph, which makes the historian realize how useful such monographs would be for other cities, is B. D. White's *A History of the Corporation of Liverpool* (1951).

Leicester's history is well chronicled in R. W. Greaves, *The Corporation of Leicester* (1939), and A. Temple Patterson, *Radical Leicester* (1954). See also J. Thompson, *Short History of Leicester* (1879), and R. Read, *Modern Leicester* (1881), for Victorian portraits. J. T. Spencer's *Guide to Leicester* (1888) may be compared with the Manchester and Leeds guides. Compare also *Bemrose's Visitors' Guide and Handy Book to Derby* (1881). There is a good bibliography in a useful, unpublished Leeds M.A. thesis, *The Social, Economic and Political Development of Derby, 1835–1888* by J. A. Standen (1959). Nottingham's Victorian history is examined in great detail in R. A. Church, *Economic and Social Change in a Midland Town* (1966). See also J. D. Chambers, *The Vale of Trent*, a supplement to the *Economic History Review* (1956), and *Modern Nottingham in the Making* (1945); J. Orange, *History and Antiquities of Nottingham*, 2 vols. (1840); T. Bailey, *Annals of Nottinghamshire* (1853); *Pictorial Guide to Nottingham and its Environs* (1871); and W. H. Wylie, *History of Nottingham* (1893). Nottingham politics are discussed in A. L. Wood's 'Nottingham's Parliamentary Elections, 1869–1900' in the *Transactions of the Thoroton Society* (1950). For Coventry, see J. Prest, *The Industrial Revolution in Coventry* (1960). For York, see J. Bigland, *A Topographical and Historical Description of the County of York* (1819); J. J. Sheahan and T. Whellan, *The History and Topography of the City of York* (1855), and C. B. Knight, *A History of the City of York* (1944).

Exeter's problems are examined through the eyes of Thomas Latimer in R. S. Lambert's *The Cobbett of the West* (1939). James Cossins's *Reminiscences of Exeter Life Fifty Years Since* (1879) may be supplemented by the painstaking and authoritative reports of Dr Thomas Shapter, *The History of the Cholera in Exeter in 1832* (1849), *Remarks upon the Mortality of Exeter* (1844) and *Report on the Sanitary Conditions of Exeter* (1845). There is a full study by R. Newton, *Victorian Exeter* (1967). On the cholera generally, see H. H. Creighton, *History of Epidemics* (1893), and my article 'Cholera and Society in the Nineteenth Century' in *Past and Present* (1961).

For Norwich the main source used in this chapter is A. D. Bayne's *Royal Illustrated History of Eastern England*, 2 vols. (1880), and his *History of Norwich* (1875).

INDEX

VICTORIAN PEOPLE

Asa Briggs

'With this book Asa Briggs makes good his right to be regarded and respected as one of the leading historians of the Victorian Age' – G. M. Young, author of *Victorian England*

That 'Victorian' need no longer be considered a derogatory word is made very plain by Professor Briggs's reassessments of people, ideas, and events between the Great Exhibition of 1851 and the Second Reform Act of 1867.

A few of his chapter headings indicate the type of personality on whom the author has based a fresh viewpoint of the period: 'John Arthur Roebuck and the Crimean War', 'Samuel Smiles and the Gospel of Work', 'Thomas Hughes and the Public Schools', 'Robert Applegarth and the Trade Unions', 'John Bright and the Creed of Reform', 'Benjamin Disraeli and the Leap in the Dark'.

Recounted with unusual clarity and humour, the story of their achievements conjures up an enviable picture of progress and independence and adds substantially to the ordinary reader's knowledge of the last century.

'A warm and vivid book, as readable as it is well informed' – *New York Herald Tribune*

THE MAKING OF THE ENGLISH WORKING CLASS

E. P. Thompson

The Making of the English Working Class, now published as the thousandth Pelican, is probably the greatest and most imaginative post-war work of English social history. This account of artisan and working-class society in its formative years, 1780 to 1832, adds an important dimension to our understanding of the nineteenth century, for Edward Thompson sees the ordinary people of England not as statistical fodder, nor merely as passive victims of political repression and industrial alienation. He shows that the working class took part in its own making. In their religious movements, the political struggles and their growing community organizations, working people in very different walks of life gradually developed an identity of interests which was expressed in a vigorous and democratic popular culture.

Within the conventional framework of English history in the Industrial Revolution, Mr Thompson gives controversial assessments of the popular traditions of the eighteenth century, the cost-of-living controversy, the role of Methodism and the genesis of parliamentary reform. He also includes radically new interpretations of underground traditions usually ignored by historians, from clandestine Jacobin societies and millenarian movements to the Luddites.

But the most impressive feature of this exceptional book is its re-creation of the whole life-experience of people who suffered loss of status and freedom, who underwent degradation, and who yet created a culture and political consciousness of great vitality.

NOT FOR SALE IN THE U.S.A.